Hope for the Nations

Paul's Letter to the Romans

Tom Holland

Apiary Publishing

Copyright

Copyright © 2017 Tom Holland.

Apiary Publishing Ltd., 71-75 Shelton Street,

London WC2H 9JQ enquities@apiarypublishing.com

All rights reserved. No part of this book may be reproduced or transmitted in any form or by any means, electronic or mechanical, including photocopying, recording, or by any information storage and retrieval system, without permission in writing from the publisher.

The text and arguments herein are in part derived from the author's earlier work

Unless otherwise indicated, Scripture is from the ESV® Bible (The Holy Bible, English Standard Version®), copyright © 2001 by Crossway Bibles, a publishing ministry of Good News Publishers. Used by permission. All rights reserved.

Scripture quotations marked "NKJV" are taken from the New King James Version®. Copyright © 1982 by Thomas Nelson, Inc. Used by permission. All rights reserved.

Scripture quotations marked "NIV" are taken from THE HOLY BIBLE, NEW INTERNATIONAL VERSION®, NIV® Copyright © 1973, 1978, 1984, 2011 by Biblica, Inc.® Used by permission. All rights reserved worldwide.

ISBN: 9781912445004

Foreword

Dr Holland takes the reader deeper into the world of the Roman Church and the culture into which Paul wrote this magnificent epistle. Others have sought to do this without an appreciation for or a confessional commitment to the inerrancy and the infallibility of Romans being the very Word of God. Tom Holland's work stands out in that he believes that. The material, thus, comes forward as both scholarly and confessional.

I commended this well researched and well written book to the Church and believe that the reader will benefit from it as I have in my own reading. I trust and pray that the material will find a wide audience, for it is indeed most deserving of such attention. And it now takes its rightful place in that considerable library section on Romans but stands out through both confession of true faith and courageous scholarship.

Congratulations to Dr Tom Holland and the publisher for this valuable and timely contribution to studies on Romans.

Michael A. Milton, Ph.D. (University of Wales, Trinity-St. David's), Presbyterian (PCA) minister; Chancellor and CEO and the James M. Baird Jr. Chair of Pastoral Theology, Reformed Theological Seminary.

Preface by the Author

This book is a re-working of my Romans: The Divine Marriage which was published by Wipf and Stock in 2011. This book follows much of the same arguments as the original book but has been amended in order to make it more accessible to the less technical reader.

Although much material has been retained, many of the detailed academic arguments have been dropped or précised. The result, I hope, is a work which will address the wider audience of all those believers that love the Lord and are looking to engage with the gospel message that is Paul's legacy to us in this letter. For any who would want to engage with the technical details that led to the conclusions reached in this commentary, I suggest that they consult Romans: The Divine Marriage.

I want to take this opportunity to thank Colin Hamer and Mathew Bartlett for their kindness in providing their editorial and proof-reading skills that have improved the work.

Tom Holland, Bridgend, 2015

For details of all Tom's publications visit www.apiarypublishing.com

Dedication

To my daughters: Lois, Elisabeth & Abigail

Contents

Copyright	i
Foreword	iii
Preface by the Author	v
Dedication	vii
Contents	ix

Introduction: Getting into Romans — 1

Facing the Problems — 1

- Historical Reconstruction — 2
- Practical Implications — 3
- Key Questions — 3

Changes in Understanding — 4

- A Different Understanding — 5
- The Influence of Hellenism on Post Enlightenment New Testament Studies — 6

Redemptive History—The Key to the Mind-set of the Early Church — 8

- The Failure of the Son of Promise — 10
- The Promises of Restoration — 11
- Continuing Pain — 12
- The New Testament and the New Exodus — 13
- The Messiah and His Work — 14
- Common Themes — 15
- Paul and Isaiah — 16

The Reason for the Letter — 18

- Common Problems — 18
- Second Class Citizens — 20
- A Pastoral Letter — 20
- The Corporate Setting of the Letter — 21
- Community and Initiation — 23
- Community and Identity — 24

Covenant Fulfilment and the Theology of Romans — 26

The Extra-Canonical Writings — 27

Textual Certainties — 30

Conclusion — 31

Romans 1: The Messiah King and His Mission — 33

Introduction	33
Paul: Convert, Servant and Apostle	33
Jesus: The Messiah	35
A Descendant of David According to the Flesh	36
Declared to be the Son of God with Power	37
According to the Spirit of Holiness	40
The Messiah King and His People	41
The Messiah King and His People's Needs	43
The Messiah King and His Mission	46
To The Jew First, and also to the Gentile	48
The Righteousness of God	50
The Messiah King and the Rebellion of Man	51
An Eternal Exile	52
Suppressing the Truth	52
Further Study: Questions for Romans 1	58
Romans 2: Rebellious Subjects	**59**
Further Study: Questions for Romans 2	75
Romans 3: The Required Solution	**77**
Introduction	77
The Messiah King and His Work of Redemption	83
The Messiah King and His Mercy	90
Further Study: Questions for Romans 3	92
Romans 4: Committed Faith is not an Option	**93**
Justification in the Theology of Paul	93
Justification and the Reformers	93
The New Perspective View	93
Abraham Counted as Righteous	95
A Covenant of Grace	96
The Background to Genesis 15	97
Phinehas also Counted as Righteous	97

Introduction: Getting into Romans

The Bigger Picture	98
Paul's Use of Psalm 32	98
Galatians and Righteousness	99
Justification, Circumcision and Divine Marriage	101
Justification and the Passover	101
Justification and the Law	102
Justification as a Corporate Event	103
Justification and Covenantal Relationship	105
Conclusion of Introductory Considerations	106

Examining the Text 107

Further Study: Questions for Romans 4 128

Romans 5: The Family Story — 131

Introduction 131

The Messiah King and His Mission of Recovery 140

Further Study: Questions for Romans 5 150

Romans 6: The Messiah King and His People's Deliverance — 151

Introduction 151

Baptism in Romans 6	152
Baptism in 1 Corinthians 10	153
Baptism in Ephesians	155
Baptism in Galatians	156
Baptism in 1 Corinthians 12	156
Corporate Baptism of the Spirit	157

Examining the Text 158

Our 'Old Self'	164
The 'Body of Sin'	165
The Messiah King and His People's Obedience	170

Further Study: Questions for Romans 6 178

Romans 7: An Analysis of the Problem — 181

Introduction to Romans 7 181

Further Study: Questions for Romans 7 197

Romans 8: The Liberated People — 199

Introduction	199
The Messiah King and His Bride's Suffering	215
Further Study: Questions for Romans 8	237

Romans 9: When People Try to Justify Themselves — 239

Introduction	239
Adopted as Sons	245
The Presence of God	246
The Covenant Promises	246
The Law	247
The Temple	247
Election to Privilege and Service	255
Further Study: Questions for Romans 9	272

Romans 10: Painful Concern — 273

Introduction	273
Further Study: Questions for Romans 10	293

Romans 11: What Will Happen to Israel? — 295

Introduction	295
Further Study: Questions for Romans 11	322

Romans 12: What an Incredible Transformation! — 323

Introduction	323
Further Study: Questions for Romans 12	356

Romans 13: What Shall We Do with the Law? — 357

Introduction	357
Further Study: Questions for Romans 13	369

Romans 14: Caring for the Weak — 371

Introduction	371
Further Study: Questions for Romans 14	385

Introduction: Getting into Romans

Romans 15: When All is Going Well	**387**
Introduction	387
Further Study: Questions for Romans 15	408
Romans 16: Catching up on Friends	**409**
Introduction	409
Further Study: Questions for Romans 16	425
Bibliography	**427**
Index of Biblical References	**455**
Selected Topical Index	**475**
Other books by Tom Holland	**481**

Introduction: Getting into Romans

It is understandable if you are tempted to skip the introduction. You might not be interested in technical details about the letter but in what the letter says. Despite this, I hope you will read this section because it is important to help your understanding of what is going on in Paul's letter to the Romans.

In the introduction, I am not going to discuss topics usually found at the opening of commentaries such as the dating of the letter, where or to whom it was written, whether the last chapter was part of the original letter etc. There are plenty of commentaries which deal with such matters and I feel that I can add nothing to what has already been said. That is why in this commentary, I wish to keep to the message of the letter.

Facing the Problems

Reading any part of the New Testament presents us with certain challenges. Firstly, the New Testament writers were mostly Jews (Luke was probably an exception, but it might be shown that he had been heavily influenced by his Jewish companions). In writing their accounts of Jesus and his teaching, the history of the Jewish people was crucial to their plots. Yet there is an added complication, for much of the New Testament was written for Gentiles as well as Jews, and this might have considerably influenced the cultural settings against which they are to be understood. Was the setting Jewish or Greek; or did the writers slide between the two cultures in an unconscious way, just as Europeans slide between American culture and their own? The answer to this question will no doubt influence our understanding of how this collection of texts should be read.

A second problem arises from the fact that the New Testament documents were written almost two thousand years ago. We know of course that ideas and language can change from one generation to another. Today, it appears that the cultural gap between older and younger generations is widening faster than ever; and perhaps this is partly due to the rapid advances being made in technology and science. The meaning and significance of familiar words, symbols and stories have changed, and the older generation generally feels uncomfortable with this. But if such alterations can take place within one generation and within the same people group, how much greater are the changes that have happened over two thousand years? And how greater is the cultural gap between people of totally different societies? The western reader especially has huge cultural hurdles to overcome when reading the Bible and all of these things must be taken into account if we are to understand Paul's letter to the Romans correctly.

Historical Reconstruction

These obstacles to understanding the message of the New Testament are not new. Scholars have been aware for a long time that different variations of thought existed in the New Testament; and most modern scholars have assumed that the early church was willing to sacrifice its Jewish inheritance in order to communicate its message effectively to the Gentile world. Until recently, it was widely assumed the early church had been swamped by Greek thinking.

Most scholars claim this process of Hellenization (that is, the domination of Greco- Roman culture) can be understood in terms of a three-layer of tradition in the New Testament documents, especially the gospels. The first layer is thought to be Jewish, coming from the actual life and teachings of Jesus in Palestine. After the first Easter, when the church took its message to the Jews who were scattered throughout the Roman Empire (the Diaspora), the message was simplified for them because they lacked the background of Palestinian Judaism. To help them understand the teaching of Jesus, his message was rewritten. So, for example, imagery was dropped that would have been understood in Palestine but was meaningless in their cultures. In its place, imagery familiar to the Diaspora Jews was used. Hence, a second layer of tradition emerged.

The third layer of tradition is thought to have appeared when the church began to explain its message to the Gentiles. These knew even less of the Palestinian background of Jesus' life and teaching, and they lacked the knowledge of the Old Testament that the Diaspora Jews shared with the

Palestinian Jews. Indeed, many scholars believe the original Jewish message was all but abandoned by the church as it attempted to communicate its message in a Hellenistic context to the Gentiles. Imagery familiar to them was used to explain the message concerning Jesus. An example of imagery thought to have been adopted at this stage was slave purchase, which was likened to redemption. This kind of 'evolution' of the message about Christ is still assumed by many scholars to be the way in which the New Testament writings developed historically.

Practical Implications

If the above hypothesis is correct, then it has certain implication for the church of today. If the apostles changed their message to suit the culture in which they were preaching then whenever Christians take the gospel into a new culture, they are at liberty to follow the apostles' example and discard from their message anything offensive or obscure. Indeed, it would be our duty (just as it was for the early church) to rewrite the gospel using culturally acceptable symbols that would help the people we are seeking to evangelize. The legitimacy of this contextualization is so widely assumed that it is hardly commented upon.[1]

Key Questions

However, this idea raises two very important questions. The first is, 'How can we know the meaning of the New Testament documents if we do not know the culture against which they should be read?' The second question is, 'Should we preserve the details of these documents in their apostolic form or is it our responsibility to copy the early church's apparent example of reinterpreting their message in a way that speaks to people today?' If the

---

[1] The belief that Hellenization controlled the emergence of the New Testament documents is applied to most documents but not all. Those that are normally exempt are the letters of James, Jude and the epistle to the Hebrews. These are commonly seen to be written to Jewish Christian communities and so needed little contextualization.

answer to the latter question is affirmative, then the outcome would be the collapse of objective biblical truth, because truth would change according to the context in which it was read or heard. This approach is at the core of much modern thinking, leading many to abandon hope that there is such a thing as objective biblical truth.

The difficulty of preserving the meaning of a set of beliefs while taking them into another culture is not an obscure academic dilemma—it is relevant to the mission of the church today! The problem exists on all five continents as Christian evangelists take the gospel into new cultures. How should they fulfil their task? Do they follow the apostles' supposed model of contextualization, allowing, for example, the Indians of South America to adopt Christ and surround him with all the paraphernalia of their own cultural and religious understanding? This is the dilemma and heartache of many Christian missionaries as they see the gospel distorted and effectively abandoned when it absorbs alien traditions. Would not the same loss have happened in the early church if this process had been pursued by the apostles in their evangelism of the Gentiles?

Changes in Understanding

If the assumption is correct that Paul and the other apostles Hellenized the gospel, it follows there were significant Greek influences on the theological understanding of the early church. In other words, God had not finally revealed himself through the words and writings of the prophets of the Old Testament and Jesus. His final message came through philosophical debate, as well as intellectual and spiritual syncretism. From this perspective, it ought to be clear why liberal theology has been so devastating for the life and witness of the church. Its teaching has resulted in the Bible being abandoned in favour of human speculation.

But things are changing in scholarly understanding. The assumptions outlined above are at last being seriously challenged. The evidence suggests this process never happened when the New Testament was being written. The original teaching of Jesus and the apostles was not Hellenized, and the teaching of the church remained faithful to its Jewish origin. This Greek influence did not begin to pervade the thinking of the church until the second century A.D.—too late to have any influence on the early church.

The Hellenization of the church was due to two momentous events. The first was the division that took place between the Gentile church and the Jewish mother church in the latter part of the first century. The second was the rise of Gentile leadership within the emerging Gentile church. These Gentile leaders brought with them the baggage of their Hellenistic training and unwittingly read it into the Greek text of the Hebrew Scriptures and the New Testament writings. In other words, the Hellenization of the Christian gospel was later than scholars have assumed—it was not in the apostolic age but in the time of the church fathers. The outcome was that Gentile Christians lost touch with the Jewish roots of their scriptures.

The appreciation that the New Testament is essentially Jewish is partly the fruit of studies done on the Dead Sea Scrolls which were discovered in 1947. These pristine Jewish documents—entirely unaffected by Hellenistic influences—used much of the same language and imagery that had previously been assumed to be Hellenistic in origin. Formerly, the presence of this language in the New Testament was understood to be proof that its documents had absorbed Hellenistic teachings, but here was crucial evidence—in authentic Jewish writings—that language which had been supposed to be Hellenistic was not unique to Hellenism. In other words, the liberal argument which held that the Christian message and the church's understanding of the person of Christ evolved 'from Jewish prophet to Gentile God' crumbled; there was, after all, no evidence to support such a theory.

A Different Understanding

It is now being realized that there is a much better way to explain how the gospel of Jesus was communicated by the early church. Instead of the message being adapted to the culture of the people who were hearing it for the first time, they were taught something of the Jewish history and culture from which the gospel originated. The Jewish Scriptures (the Christian Old Testament) dominated this, of course. Converts were helped to understand the significance of the life and teaching of Jesus against his Jewish background. The responsibility of the Christian teachers was to apply the principles of this Jewish message to the life of the churches which were made up of both Jews and Gentiles.

This is the probable scenario. The first missionaries were Jews who went to the synagogues with their message. In the synagogues, Jews shared their culture with God-fearers. These were Gentiles who were disgusted with the corruption and teaching of their own religions and had turned to the God of the Jewish people; attracted by the moral standards of Judaism. Despite attending the synagogue services, few God-fearers became Jews because of the initiation ceremony of circumcision. Most Gentiles found this an immense obstacle to converting to Judaism.

The good news about Jesus was first taken to the Jews and God-fearing Gentiles in the synagogue. They had knowledge of the Old Testament and did not need to be taught Israel's history and culture. After a short period of instruction, they were able to understand the message of Jesus almost in its entirety. Furthermore, they were soon capable of teaching others who came to faith in the Messiah.

Often the apostles were driven out of the communities in which they had preached, leaving behind a handful of believers who were young in the faith (Acts 13:40—14:7), but who were able to grow because they had the Old Testament. These scriptures formed the cultural base of Judaism and taught the believers the mind and will of God. The scriptures gave them a framework to understand the past and find hope to face the future.

What sort of things guided a Jew in his thinking in the first century of Christianity? To understand this, we need to know something of the history of the Jewish people; especially how this history related to Jewish thinking at the time of Christ and the apostles—for this is the background against which the New Testament must be understood.

The Influence of Hellenism on Post Enlightenment New Testament Studies

For many decades, the New Testament has been interpreted by relying on Greek secular texts. They appeared to be the source of many New

Testament ideas. This reliance on Greek texts, and hence Greek culture, has been reinforced by the academic preparation for studying theology. Since the New Testament documents were written in the common Greek that pervaded every level of the Hellenistic world, it was understandable that a thorough grounding in the Greek classics was thought to be the most appropriate preparation for studying theology.

As a result, New Testament scholars of previous generations followed this well- trodden and little-questioned route into the discipline. Those who had this classical education were considered to be eminently suited to the task of New Testament exegesis. They were able make use of their classical training by applying it to the interpretation of New Testament documents. They had the advantage of their broad knowledge of the Hellenistic world with its culture, thought patterns and vocabulary. They were supremely equipped, it was thought, to interpret the texts.

Few saw the flaw in this method. While the vocabulary of the New Testament could be found throughout the Hellenistic world, it did not have the same meaning when used in a religious sense within the Jewish community. Here, the language had imbibed its own theological meaning as a result of translating the Hebrew Bible into Greek two hundred years or so before Christ. The Hebrew meaning had been poured into the text of the Greek translation to produce a language which had its own particular meaning. Yes, its alphabet and vocabulary were Greek, but its mind-set and essential meaning were Hebraic. This is the language Judaism bequeathed to the infant church as the message of the prophets was interpreted and proclaimed.

Seen from this perspective, the classical methodology of training for theological study was fundamentally flawed. The writers of the New Testament had drawn their ideas from Jerusalem, not Athens. Much of the theological literature that exists demonstrates this confusion. Even those who hold to the New Testament's dependence on the Old Testament invariably turn to the classics for help in unravelling ideas or words. It is not unusual to find them referring to Hellenistic culture and literature from which they suppose ideas in the text were drawn. Until this dependence on Hellenism was exposed there was little chance of identifying the Old

Testament origins of New Testament thought, and of appreciating the importance of the old exodus paradigm (a subject which will soon be discussed).

Thankfully, this misplaced dependency is increasingly being rectified, with more New Testament scholars seeing its documents as Jewish literature. However, even those who are attempting to rectify the previous error still fall into the trap which ensnared former generations and naturally turn to Greek sources to unravel exegetical problems. It is extremely difficult to change a default mental position and the practice of reading the New Testament as a collection of Greek texts still controls the minds of many scholars. Yet altering this practise is a process which is vital not only for scholars but also for the church and its teachers.

Redemptive History—The Key to the Mind-set of the Early Church

The Jewish people could boast of their unique history. Their great ancestor Abraham lived in Ur, the remains of which are located in modern Iraq. God called him to leave the security of his home and journey to a land that he was promised he would be given (Gen. 12:1–9). This is modern Israel. God made a promise to Abraham regarding his descendants. This promise, or covenant, is the basis of all that was to happen to Abraham's offspring (Gen. 15:1–21; 17:1–27).

After many trials and setbacks Abraham and his household eventually settled in the land of Canaan, and his descendants prospered. As with most families, there were difficult times. A major setback came almost two hundred years later when Abraham's descendants moved to Egypt to survive a famine that had ravaged Canaan. They settled in Goshen and enjoyed a time of plenty. As time went by the government of the land changed, and the new rulers took a hard line against them. The Hebrews became the object of ferocious persecution and were forced into slavery. Their situation worsened, and the Pharaoh commanded that their male babies be put to death at birth (Exod. 1:8–22).

At this point, another great Hebrew figure came on to the scene of history. As a baby, Moses' life was spared when an Egyptian princess found him (after his mother, to save his life, had hidden him amongst the reeds at the edge of the river), and adopted him into the royal family (Exod. 2:1–10). Eventually, as an adult, he transferred his allegiance to his own people, the Hebrews. He led them out of slavery in Egypt into the wilderness to begin a journey back to their Promised Land.

The events surrounding this exodus tell of how God protected his people when Pharaoh, the Egyptian ruler, did everything possible to stop them from leaving (Exod. 5:1—11:10). Moses warned the king that if he did not let the Hebrews go, his firstborn son would be struck dead, as would those of all the other Egyptian families. This warning was ignored. The Jews, however, obeyed God's instructions given through Moses, taking the blood of slain lambs and smearing it on the doorposts of their homes (Exod. 12:21–24). That night, as the LORD went through the land of Egypt, wherever he saw the blood, he passed over the dwelling. Where no blood was found, the LORD destroyed the firstborn male child. This was the night of the Passover. Still celebrated by the Jews to this day, it is the greatest event in Jewish history for it precipitated their exodus from Egypt.

The Jews eventually settled once more in the Promised Land and their subsequent history had its highs and lows. The nation became a monarchy, believing this would change its fortunes (albeit this entailed their rejection of God as their king). Their first anointed earthly king was Saul (1 Sam. 10:20–24), and he was succeeded by another important figure in Jewish history, King David.

The Bible records that David was a man of integrity who mostly strove to do God's will. Under his leadership the nation was made secure and prospered, but he was denied the one thing he wanted. David desired to build a Temple in which God could dwell. God would not allow him to do this because, as a military commander, he had shed much blood. He was pleased with David's desire, however, and pledged that rather than his building a house for God, God would build a house for him. The family of David would become the Jewish royal dynasty and David was promised that one of his descendants would always rule over the chosen people (2 Sam. 7:1– 17). This promise made by God to David is known as the Davidic covenant.

The Failure of the Son of Promise

Tragically, David's son Solomon was not the king the nation needed. Although known for his wisdom in dealing with Israel's problems, he could not apply this same wisdom to his own life. He demanded too much tax from the people to fund expensive building programs, and abandoned God's clear instruction not to marry foreign wives. This command was intended to prevent the gods of the other nations gaining a foothold in the affections of the nation. However, this is exactly what happened. Solomon's foreign wives brought their entourages with them, and soon not only were thousands of aliens living in Jerusalem as part of the extended royal family, but their gods were being worshipped also. The monotheism of Israel's ancestors was being abandoned and paganism, which they had suffered so much to overcome, was being practised.

With the worship of these foreign gods came the lifestyles of the surrounding nations. The Jewish people imitated them and by so doing broke the moral commands that God had given them. This act of flirting with the gods of the surrounding nations was described as 'adultery' (Ezek. 16:15ff. Hosea 3:1); for Israel's God was described as the husband, and Israel as his bride. When the Israelites left Egypt under Moses' leadership, they entered into a solemn agreement—a covenant (Exod. 24:8). They promised to be faithful to their God, and in return he promised that he would be faithful to them as a nation. Included in the covenant agreement was a strong warning that God would not tolerate Israel sharing her life with other gods. If she did, God would put Israel away (Deut. 30:17–19).

As her national life declined, God sent prophets to warn Israel of her sins and the consequences of not turning back to him. The nation eventually became divided under two kings (1 Kgs. 12:1ff.), both of which rejected the messages of the prophets so that the divided nation declined further into moral chaos. Ultimately, God acted against his people. The breakaway northern kingdom was invaded by the Assyrians in B.C. 721, resulting in deportation. Its cities were destroyed, and its people were taken into exile

(2 Kgs. 17:1–20). Later, the Babylonians came against Judah, who had stayed faithful to the house of David, and destroyed its towns and villages. They laid siege to Jerusalem, its capital, and eventually overthrew it in B.C. 586 (Jer. 39; 2 Kgs. 25:1ff.), destroying the entire city including the sacred Temple. Members of the royal family were either put to death or taken into captivity along with most of the population (2 Kgs. 25:1ff.). It was the beginning of one of the darkest periods of ancient Israel's history.

The Promises of Restoration

Understandably, the morale of the nation collapsed. The people never thought God would allow this to happen to them. They saw the exile as punishment for their sins and found great difficulty in thinking that there could be a new start. This, though, is the very thing the prophets had promised them. In spite of the collapse of the royal family, they predicted that a descendant of David would be raised up (Isa. 11:1; 55:3–4; Jer. 33:14–17) who would lead the people from their captivity back to the Promised Land (Isa. 11:11; 48:20–21; 52:1–12; Ezek. 36:24). He would be anointed with the Spirit of the Lord for this task (Isa. 61:1–2) and would lead the people through the wilderness (Hosea 2:14; 12:9). It would be like when the Hebrews left Egypt—it would be a second exodus.

The pilgrimage through this new desert would be under the protection of the Holy Spirit (Isa. 44:3; 59:21; 61:1–3; Ezek. 36:24–28; 37:1–4), just as the pilgrimage from Egypt had been. There would be miracles (Mic. 7:15) as there were when they came out of Egypt, and the desert would be transformed as nature shared in the re- creation of the nation (Isa. 55:13). The exiles would return, telling of the salvation of God (Isa. 52:7–10); and a new covenant would be established which would centre on the Davidic prince (Isa. 9:6–7; 11:1; 55:3–4; Jer. 33:14–17). Unlike the exodus from Egypt when the men were circumcised in their flesh, the hearts of the people would be circumcised (Jer. 31:31–34; Ezek. 36:26–27).

Once the people arrived back in Jerusalem, they would build a magnificent Temple which the descendant of David would dedicate (Ezek. 44–45). Into this Temple, all the nations would come to worship Israel's God (Isa. 2:1–5; 9:1–7; 19:23–25; 49:6–7; 49:22–23; 56:3; 60:3, 10). The Lord would come into his Temple (Mal. 3:1), and the marriage between God and his people would be celebrated with a great cosmic banquet (Isa. 54:1–8; 61:10; 62:4–5; Hosea 2:16, 19).

The promises contained in the three paragraphs above are so important for understanding the New Testament that they are worth committing to memory. These are the promises we find repeated throughout the New Testament, the claim of its writers being that Jesus has fulfilled—or will fulfil—them all (2 Cor. 1:20).

We find the history of the return of the Jews from exile in Babylon in the books of Ezra, Nehemiah and the Minor Prophets such as Haggai, Zechariah, and Malachi. What these books show is that while the people attempted to rebuild a Temple in Jerusalem (Ezra 3:7ff.; Neh. 4:1ff.), it did not compare with the one which had been destroyed by the Babylonians (Hag. 2:3–9). They constantly looked for the coming of the descendant of King David (Hag. 1:13–14; Zech. 3:8–9), but he did not appear. For four hundred years they groaned in their sense of failure, guilt, and disappointment.

Continuing Pain

The next four hundred years saw no significant change for the Jews. They were always under the control of another nation. Their exile seemed to continue, and they longed for its end. They had returned to their own land but were as far from God as they had ever been; for apart from a brief period during the days of the Maccabees they never had their own independence. For them, God had not yet fulfilled his promises. Not until they had complete freedom could they accept that their punishment was over. The literature of the Jews during this period—known as the Intertestamental or Second Temple period—shows the faith they continued to have. They clung to the hope that God would fulfil the promises he had made to them through the prophets. The Scriptures surveyed above became their light throughout the long dark years of shame under the domination of Rome. They longed for the promised deliverance from their helplessness, and the degradation of enslavement. These promises, though interpreted differently, seem to have been the source of hope for all Jewish groups.

This brief survey indicates the degree to which the expectation of a new exodus had saturated the nation at the time of John the Baptist's ministry. To ignore this expectation in any attempt to understand the development of the Christian message would be folly. What is abundantly clear is that the hope that these promises would one day be fulfilled did not die. In all the Jewish literature of the period, there is clear evidence that this hope is what sustained the nation. The people waited in hope, praying for the day when these promises would be fulfilled.

The New Testament and the New Exodus

God's response to this cry for deliverance resonates throughout the pages of the New Testament. Its message is that God has acted decisively in the death of Jesus, his own Son, to bring about salvation, not from physical or political bondage, but from spiritual slavery. Among the expectations commonly held in relation to the new exodus was a belief in the identity of the new Moses who would lead the Jews out of captivity. He was not to be of the tribe of Levi, like Moses, but of the tribe of Judah. He was to be none other than the promised descendant of David who God had declared would have an everlasting throne (Isa. 9:7). The identification of Jesus with the promises relating to the Davidic deliverer is crucial for appreciating how the early church understood the person and work of her Saviour. It is no coincidence that the evidence brought against Jesus, which secured his crucifixion, related to his claims to kingship. Nor is it coincidental that Jesus denied claims to an earthly kingdom while asserting his claim to a spiritual one.

The significance of these details would be clear to any Jewish believer when he heard that Jesus had died with the inscription above his head: 'THIS IS THE KING OF THE JEWS' (Luke 23:38). The king was establishing the kingdom in which his followers were to be subjects. If we bypass the eighth century prophets (Amos, Hosea, Isaiah, and Micah), and merely link the significance of Jesus' Davidic descent with the promise to David of an eternal throne, we miss the new exodus motif lurking beneath the surface of the title. Not only is this seen in the gospel narratives, where Jesus is continually honoured as the long-awaited descendant of David, but also in the preaching of the early church as recorded in Acts. The reference to the raising again of the tent of David (Acts 15:16–17) is particularly significant, since it demonstrates that the early church saw Jesus as the promised Davidic king through whom all the blessings of the Davidic covenant were to be fulfilled. The title 'Son of David' is coupled with the title 'Christ' (which means 'anointed one'), and is used regularly throughout the New Testament, carrying with it all the Messianic associations of the Son of David. In other words, the Davidic king is the Christ.

The New Testament emphasis on Jesus being the promised Son of David must not be missed. Its writers did not need to keep using the term Son of David because they could choose from a range of related titles which, to the first-century believer, meant exactly the same thing. Many scholars say that Matthew's gospel (recognized by most as written for the Jews) shows Jesus as the second Moses. But this misses the fact that Moses is only mentioned as a person twice in the gospel (Matt. 17:3–4)—all other references are to laws given by him—whereas Jesus is repeatedly called the 'Son of David' (Matt. 1:6, 17, 20; 9:27; 12:23; 15:22; 20:30– 31; 21:15; 22:42–45). So, whilst Matthew's gospel clearly has an exodus structure, it is not Moses who brings about this deliverance, but the Son of David, as the prophets had foretold. This fact will be very important for our exposition of the letter to the Romans.

The Messiah and His Work

For most readers, the name 'Jesus Christ' reads like a forename and a family name as is normal in the west. This is unfortunate, as the term 'Christ' should be understood as a title. In the Old Testament, there were many messiahs. Anyone who was 'anointed' was a messiah. So, the priests, kings, judges, and prophets were all messiahs. They were anointed with oil when they were set apart for the work God called them to do. The anointing was a symbol of the provision of the Holy Spirit for their task (1 Sam. 10:1; 16:13; Isa. 61:1–3). While there is nothing unusual in Old Testament terms about someone being called a messiah or Christ, the Jews came to expect that God would send a special one, the Messiah, the one anointed to deliver Israel from her captivity. So, for example, when Peter calls Jesus 'the Christ' in

Matthew 16:16, he is confessing his faith that Jesus is the king whom God had promised.

We could go through Romans and refer to Jesus as the Messiah or the King, but to reinforce Old Testament roots I have decided to use the term 'the Messiah King'. This is deliberately done with the hope that the reader will reflect on the roles that the Messiah would fulfil (roles which have been briefly noted in the above section 'The Promises of Restoration'). The entire letter is about the Messiah King, and how he has completed the work that God promised he would do for his people.

The centrality of the Messianic theme in the letter to the Romans has frequently been overlooked. This has largely been due to the fact that the letter has been read within a Hellenistic framework which has filtered out the significance of the term 'Christos' from its argument. More recent commentators have alerted their readers to its importance but, in my judgment, not sufficiently. While they have acknowledged the importance of the title, they have not driven its significance through the letter.

All four gospels begin with the theme of the kingship of Jesus, expressed in the terms kingdom/king/Messiah/Christos, indicating that it was a key theme for the early church. The importance of this theme is further reflected in the use of Christos in Romans, since Paul uses the title no less than sixty times. As the Roman church appears to have had a large Gentile membership, the saturation of the letter to the Romans with the term Christos has considerable significance: it emphasizes the importance of the theme of Jesus being seen as the fulfilment of the Old Testament Scriptures.

Common Themes

Other new exodus themes are widely dispersed throughout the New Testament. The New Testament writers continually showed that the Old Testament predictions of what would happen when the new exodus came to pass were fulfilled in the birth, life, death, resurrection, and ascension of Jesus of Nazareth. The infant church was not groping for understanding. She had inherited a theological framework from the Jewish 'mother' church which had been taught by her Saviour. They knew how to read these key texts. These Scriptures spoke of him, and this realization changed the hearts of people as they entered into the new creation. Once the ministry of Jesus, the true Son of David, was placed at the centre of these predictions, the meaning, and significance of his person and work broke out with such energy, power, and meaning that it drove the early church on to achieve remarkable things for her master.

This then is the background to the New Testament. Each gospel begins with John the Baptist announcing that he was the voice of one crying in the desert to prepare that the way of the Lord (Matt. 3:3; Mark 1:3; Luke 3:4; John 1:23). The importance of this text is clear in that it is one of the few events recorded in all four gospels. John was taking his words from the prophecy of Isaiah which announced the coming of the descendant of David who would fulfil God's promises. When the Lord Jesus stood up in the synagogue and said the Spirit of the Lord was upon him to preach the good news to the poor (Luke 4:18–19), he was claiming to be the one who had come to bring freedom from captivity. He was announcing that he was the Son of David.

Paul and Isaiah

The influence of Isaiah's prophecy on the thinking of Judaism inevitably meant that it also influenced the apostle Paul. Isaiah is not only quoted by Paul more than all the other prophets put together, but it appears that Paul may have used Isaiah's writings as the skeleton of his gospel. He arranged citations from Isaiah in such a way as to outline the history of salvation from the fall of Adam to the eventual establishment of the Messianic kingdom. Around these quotations, Paul built the arguments which frame the letter to the Romans. The full import of this fact is only appreciated when the quotations are listed in the order in which they appear in the letter and read in that same sequence. If we can imagine the original letter being laid out as a continuous papyrus with the citations being raised out of the text and suspended at their point of use, the texts summarize the history of salvation. Such a pattern is mathematically highly improbable, and their sequential use can be nothing but intentional.

Introduction: Getting into Romans

> 'For as it is written "The name of God is blasphemed among the Gentiles because of you"' (Rom. 2:24; Isa. 52:5 LXX). (LXX refers to the Septuagint, the translation of the Old Testament into Greek in about 300 B.C.)

> 'Their feet are swift to shed blood; in their paths are ruin and misery, and the way of peace they have not known' (Rom. 3:15–17; Isa. 59:7–8).

> 'Isaiah cries out concerning Israel: "Though the number of the sons of Israel be as the sand of the sea, only a remnant of them will be saved, for the Lord will carry out his sentence upon the earth fully and without delay"' (Rom. 9:27–28; Isa. 10:22–23; LXX).

> 'If the Lord of hosts had not left us offspring, we would have been like Sodom and become like Gomorrah' (Rom. 9:29; Isa. 1:9 LXX).

> 'As it is written, "Behold, I am laying in Zion a stone of stumbling, and a rock of offense"' (Rom. 9:33a; Isa. 8:14).

> 'Whoever believes in him will not be put to shame' (Rom. 9:33b; Isa. 28:16 LXX).

> 'For the Scripture says, "Everyone who believes in him will not be put to shame"' (Rom. 10:11; Isa. 28:16 LXX).

> 'As it is written, "How beautiful are the feet of those who preach the good news!"' (Rom. 10:15; Isa. 52:7).

> 'For Isaiah says, "Lord, who has believed what he has heard from us?"' (Rom. 10:16)

Paul foresaw the same response of unbelief to the gospel message as Isaiah did to his own (Rom. 10:16; Isa. 53:1); even so, the electing purposes of God would not be overturned by the sinfulness of humanity. What God purposes, he will achieve (Rom. 10:21; Isa. 65:2; Rom. 11:8; Isa. 29:10); his plan will be fulfilled and all Israel, as Paul defined her (Rom. 4:11–12), will be saved (Rom. 11:26–27; Isa. 27:9; 59:20– 21). All of this is beyond humanity's ability to conceive; the design is of God alone (Rom. 11:33–34; Isa. 40:13). The salvation promised through Abraham (in which the nations share in the covenantal blessings) will finally be fulfilled. Those who were never part of the people of God have come into the eschatological (end-time) community (Rom. 15:21; Isa. 52:15).

Paul's use of the prophecy of Isaiah was systematic, and it formed the framework of his worldview. His reasoning and exposition of the good news of Jesus were arranged around this structure because Jesus, the Son of

David, and deliverer of his people, is the fulfilment of all that the prophets had been saying. Paul does not merely use the texts; he is driven by their message. Indeed, it could be said they control him! Their meaning forms the foundation of Paul's argument throughout his letter to the Romans.

The Reason for the Letter

There are many possible reasons why Paul wrote to the Romans. It could be argued that he wanted to prepare for his trip to Spain (Rom. 15:23) and hoped that his letter would generate support to make this mission possible. While he may have hoped to get help from the church, it is difficult to think this would be the reason for his greatest work. A more personal letter would have been far more appropriate for such a task.

It is a fact that there were pastoral problems in Rome that needed to be addressed. These problems had their roots in theological confusion. Once they had been unravelled, the pastoral difficulties would begin to be resolved. But what were these problems? Is there evidence that Paul knew any existed? If he did, there is another question that needs to be asked. How did Paul become aware of these problems, if it was true that he had never visited this church?

While the themes of the letter have been carefully examined and traces of conflict searched for, discovering the pastoral and theological misunderstandings of the Roman church would be a matter of guesswork if we limited ourselves to this one New Testament letter. This speculation is part of the reason why so many views are offered. It would be sensible to consider letters to the wider church to see if any problems that are identifiable in different congregations match the remedies prescribed in the Roman letter.

Common Problems

The main problem experienced by Gentile Christianity emanated from the believing Jews. There were many sincere Jewish believers in Christ who could not accept the idea of Gentiles being admitted into the covenant unless they went through the initiation of circumcision. This affected virtually every church, mainly because Judaizers were roaming the empire in an effort to persuade Paul's converts to take the final step of circumcision so they could be brought into the full grace of the covenant.

The issue of circumcision was threatening to split the young church, separating the Gentile church from its 'Jewish Christian' mother. For Paul, this would have been disastrous as there was one body and one Lord who dealt with all people on the same grounds of grace. Not only do Paul's letters show him struggling to maintain the relationship between the two communities—a relationship that was costly in the extreme for Paul to advocate—but the writer of the Acts of the Apostles records the lengths he went to in order to keep the doors of communication and fellowship open. His two time-consuming visits to Jerusalem are evidence of how important he believed relationship to be (Acts 15:1–2; 21:17–26). His first visit was to allow the apostles to examine his ministry, and the second was to take a gift from the Gentile churches to the poor in the Jerusalem church. Some scholars see this substantial gift as Paul's attempt to remove Jewish Christian suspicion of the Gentile churches while others contend that he wanted to lead a gift-bearing Gentile team into Jerusalem as fulfilment of prophecy (Isa. 60:8–14).

Churches with no evidence of Judaizing subversion were nevertheless divided by other issues. A common problem concerned meat which was offered to idols and then sold in the street market (Rom. 14:14–17; 1 Cor. 8:4; 10:20, 25–32; Col. 2:16). For the converted Jews, eating such meat was not a problem. With their strong background of monotheism, they knew the idols did not exist (1 Cor. 8:4–7) but were merely the product of the darkened imaginations of men. When a Jewish person became a believer, he understood there were no other gods. This knowledge was not from some esoteric insight but gained directly from Old Testament teaching. But such indifference to the meat's origin was a real problem for those who had lived for many years in fear of the gods to which it had been sacrificed. While the Gentile converts knew that there was only one God, they could not forget the things that had so deeply affected them—they knew that behind all of these ceremonies was Satan who had exploited their ignorance and fear. For the Gentile converts, there was a real concern of being associated with anything that happened in the pagan temples.

When we bring these two problems (that is, circumcision and the eating of meat offered to idols) to the letter to the Romans, we find a remarkable fit with the theology and practice advocated by Paul. We shall see that its first eleven chapters are essentially about the way God has dealt with the Jews. Early in the letter, in chapters 2 and 4, Paul argues that they were uncircumcised when God accepted them in Abraham. In other words, the Gentiles were being brought into the covenant in exactly the same way as the Jews.

Second Class Citizens

Being treated as second-class citizens of the kingdom provoked the Gentile believers to respond to the Jews. Some goaded the Jews by saying they had displaced them, that God no longer had any purpose for his ancient people in his redemptive plans. The evidence in support of their argument was all around them. The increasing number of Gentiles coming into the church was shifting the balance of power within the congregations, with Gentile believers far outnumbering Jewish believers. Such tensions had to be resolved, not least because both Jewish and Gentile believers were members of one body and belonged to the same Lord.

In the midst of the theological debates over priority, the Gentiles were faced with a very practical problem. Before their conversion, they had worshipped in the temples of the local gods. Often these temples were centres of social activity, and the gods were seen as patrons of the various trade guilds. When a man was converted, he stopped attending the temple, and could no longer be involved in the guild under which his trade operated. Thus, his conversion threatened his livelihood.

A Pastoral Letter

These problems were common in the Jewish/Gentile churches. Indeed, because of the intense loyalty of the Jewish community to the Law of Moses, it was inevitable these problems would arise wherever the two communities coexisted. The letter to the Romans was not an attempt to guess at their problems, nor was it merely an opportunity for Paul to explain his gospel. The letter was an attempt to keep the two communities in Rome together so that they could bear a common witness of the Lord who had saved them. The letter demonstrates Paul's keen theological and pastoral awareness. He writes meaningfully, addressing the Jewish/Gentile relationship frankly. He is acutely aware of the pastoral problems caused by the integration of the two communities. The removal of the dividing wall of hostility (Eph. 2:14) was yet to be worked out in the life of the believing community in Rome. They might be one new man in Christ (Eph. 2:15; Col. 3:10), but the new man was at war within himself.

It was only from a united Roman church that Paul could effectively embark on his mission to Spain. He was aware that divisions in his supporting churches would distract him from the task of evangelism. The gospel was not about casting the Jews off in favour of the Gentiles, but about bringing both into the eschatological covenant community. The nations would take note of what God was doing in Christ only as they accepted each other and lived together as the 'new man'. The reconciliation of enemies to each other remains one of the most powerful witnesses to the saving ability of Christ. Their unity was vital to Paul's mission to Spain.

The Corporate Setting of the Letter

In attempting to explore Paul's Jewish mind-set, we need to ensure that he is not isolated from the corporate outlook of the Old Testament—one that has its focus on a community of people rather than the individual. It is easy to forget that Paul was a devout Jew before he responded to the claim of Jesus on his life. Even after his conversion he did not reject his heritage. One of the features of that heritage was the public reading of the Scriptures to congregations in their synagogues. These gatherings were an essential part of Paul's experience from the earliest years of childhood until (by reason of his house arrest) he was denied access to the synagogue in Rome (Acts 28:30).

The significance of the synagogue experience was that it controlled the way Paul heard the Jewish Scriptures. Hearing them corporately was not a distorting influence, for the messages of the prophets were delivered to the people of the covenant collectively, and rarely to individuals (Isa. 44:1; 48:1; Jer. 19:3; Ezek. 2:3– 5; Hosea 4:1; Amos 3:1). The gathered synagogue congregation was, therefore, the ideal setting in which another generation of the covenant people could hear the same word being delivered. The reference to the blessing of the readers of the book of Revelation (Rev. 1:3) is clear evidence of the role that corporate readings of texts had in the early church.

This principle of congregational reading is found in other churches that received letters from Paul. He expects believers to meet for this purpose and composed his letters with congregations in mind. In other words, the practice of interpreting the letters as though they were written to individuals is misguided. The letters are not about what God has done or is doing for a Christian, they are what God has done or is doing for his covenant people, the church. It is not permissible—despite widespread practice—to read the details as though they describe the experience of the individual believer. Such practice not only makes much of the individual, it makes little of the covenant community. The privilege of an individual owning his own copy of the Scriptures for private reading is a recent blessing.

If it is argued that this loses the perspective of the New Testament addressing individuals, the reply must be made 'what do you mean by that?' Western individualism is not the same as biblical individualism. That there is responsibility in both the Old Testament and the New Testament for individuals to apply the Word of God to their lives hardly needs stating (Lev. 19:3ff.; 18:6ff.; 20:3ff.; Job 19:11; 31:1–40; Ps. 31:1–5; Prov. 3:21–26; Matt. 5:21–48; 18:15–17; 19:16–22; Luke 3:10ff.; 8:12; John 14:15–21; Acts 2:40–41; 1 Cor. 10:6–14, etc.), but this is not the individualism of post-modern understanding. The biblical perspective is that every person is a member of a community, and that membership determines his identity. In the New Testament this community is the church. The Old Testament prophets primarily spoke to Israel reminding her of her unique relationship with God, calling her (and by implication each individual Jew) to live it out. So Paul in the New Testament constantly reminds the church of her calling (Rom. 1:7; 1 Cor. 10:3ff.; Eph. 1:13–14; 2:11–3:13; Col. 1:12–14; 1 Thess. 1:12–14), and appeals to her to live as the covenant community in the world (Rom. 12:1ff.; Eph. 5:1; Phil. 2:1ff.; Col. 3:2ff.).

At times, Paul applies his exhortations to specific groups of people (1 Cor. 7:25–28; Eph. 5:22–25; 6:1–9), spelling out the ramifications of what he has said for their daily lives. While very occasionally he addresses individuals (Rom. 16:1ff.; Phil. 4:2; Col. 4:17), the undoubted thrust of his letters is to the church. If this is lost sight of, his letters become texts that wrongfully endorse all manner of unbiblical individualistic behaviour and understanding.

By insisting that the letters are to the church, I am not saying anything new. Most commentators say the same thing. However, despite acknowledging the corporate dimension of the letters, they are not consistent in their corporate interpretation of them. Some commentators do identify sections of the letters to be about corporate experience but lapse into individualism when interpreting the remainder of the text. My intent is to keep this corporate perspective to the fore of my thinking as I interpret the letter to the Romans. I shall seek to interpret it as a corporate document unless there is clear evidence that Paul is directing his teaching to a particular individual or group of people within the church.

Community and Initiation

If my claim concerning the corporate nature of the letter is correct, it inevitably raises the question of initiation into the Christian life. This is unavoidable because passages which have been seen to refer to the individual's entrance into the covenant community will, with this refocusing, be seen to refer to the historical creation of the covenant with the covenant community. The question that must therefore be answered is this: where does the individual believer fit into this scheme of reading?

The question is an important one. There are those who view salvation as applying to the whole of mankind and who would accept the corporate reading with enthusiasm. Such euphoria is not well-founded. It will become clear that Paul insists there is a fundamental division in the human race. There are those who are in Adam (Rom. 5:12; 1 Cor. 15:22), and those who are in Christ (2 Cor. 5:17; Eph. 1:2; Phil. 1:1; Col. 1:2; 1 Thess. 1:1; 4:16). To ignore this fundamental premise of Pauline theology is to destroy the very basis of his argument. Regardless of the doctrine of salvation that one accepts, it does not correspond to the apostle's teaching if this fundamental division is ignored.

However, one thing is clear: the early church saw the need for personal repentance and faith (Matt. 3:1–6; Acts 2:38–41; 8:34–38; Rom. 10:9). While there is no suggestion that people automatically benefit from Christ's death, God calls all people everywhere to repent and believe (Rom. 10:9–15). Any argument arising from the corporate nature of the letters must respect this clear basic tenet of the early apostolic church's thought, expressed so clearly in her evangelistic ministry.

To suggest solutions to this problem of initiation into the Christian life at this stage is to anticipate the arguments that need to be made; the relevant texts need first to be considered and a case made for their corporate perspective.

Community and Identity

How does Paul view the congregation in Rome? It would be natural to say it is a local church. Strangely, however, there is an unexpected silence concerning this theme in the letter. Throughout the body of the letter to the Romans (Paul's magnum opus), he does not refer to 'the church'. It is not until we get to the end of the letter that the term 'church' appears, and it is not in a significant theological sense but in the context of the fellowship of believers. In Romans 16:1, Paul writes, 'I commend to you our sister Phoebe, a servant of the church in Cenchrea'. In Romans 16:3, 5a, he writes, 'Greet Priscilla and Aquila, my fellow workers in Christ Jesus...Greet also the church in their house'. Finally, in Romans 16:23a, Paul writes, 'Gaius, who is host to me and to the whole church, greets you'.

Clearly, none of these references to churches are in any sense theological; even in his private letter to Philemon, Paul begins by greeting the church that meets in his house (Phlm. 1:2). But it will be noticed in his letters to the Ephesians and to the Colossians that, despite not greeting the believers as churches, the theology of the church pulsates within their teaching. However, in Romans this does not happen. Indeed, when he greeted the Roman believers at the opening of his letter, he did not greet them as 'the

Introduction: Getting into Romans

church that is in Rome' as was occasionally his practice (1 Cor. 1:2; 1 Thess. 1:1; 2 Thess. 1:1).

The fact that the redeemed community is not referred to as 'the church' in the theological section of Romans (nor in any part of the letter to the Galatians) could be significant. Both are dealing with the identity of the Gentiles and their right to be included in the covenants of promise. The argument of both letters is highly dependent on Old Testament exegesis—far more than any other New Testament letter. It is possible that Paul's concern is to debate these issues in clear Old Testament imagery, emphasizing that the Gentiles are fully part of the promised new covenant community. They are not to be shunted off by the Jews into a second division called 'the church'. To do so might suggest that the church was a mere steppingstone toward final inclusion into the true people of God. The believing Gentiles are bona fide children of Abraham and not part of an entity that still waits for admission.

While it would be a fascinating study to see what determines the language Paul uses in his different letters, this is not the purpose of the present work. I am interested in seeing how Paul speaks of the Christian community in this pivotal letter and the reason for the language he selects.

In Romans 14:17, Paul writes, 'For the kingdom of God is not a matter of eating and drinking, but of righteousness and peace and joy in the Holy Spirit'. As this is the only reference to the kingdom in the entire letter, the kingdom of God is not a major theme.

What we do find is language and imagery which stress continuity with the Old Testament. The members of the believing community are those who are circumcised in the heart, not in the flesh (Rom. 2:28–29). They have been redeemed through the true Paschal sacrifice (Rom. 3:21–25) and are now on a pilgrimage (Rom. 5:3–5; 8:25–39). They belong to the community which has been grafted into the Abrahamic root with all of its promises. They are described as a priestly people (Rom. 12:1–2) who are responsible for completing Israel's failed mission (Rom. 11:11–24).

It would seem from the above that Paul wants to identify the believers in Rome with the pilgrim community which has been redeemed and showered 'with every spiritual blessing in Christ' (Eph. 1:3b). He is deliberately using language that makes this connection clear, and is reluctant to use any vocabulary that might, for whatever reason, obscure the extraordinary calling the church has as the Israel of God (Gal. 6:16).

Covenant Fulfilment and the Theology of Romans

It will be evident that the perspective I am taking presupposes a covenantal framework for Paul's thinking. It would be tempting to justify this framework at the beginning of the exposition, but we must delay this task (as we are doing with regard to how an individual is initiated into the Christian life), until there has been an examination of the text and the theological substructure upholding its arguments. Justification for using a covenantal framework for interpreting the letter will have to come from the evidence of the letter as a whole. What can be said is that if Paul is dependent on the new exodus model outlined earlier then the heart of his thinking is the fulfilment by God of his promises to Abraham and David. The new exodus theme is a very important subsection of the Old and New Testament themes of covenant and fulfilment.

The letter to the Romans begins by introducing Jesus as the Christ who was born of the seed of David according to the flesh (Rom. 1:3). The theme of salvation, promised by the prophets (Rom. 1:2), is heavily covenantal in that the promises were all part of the covenant. Clear echoes of the theme of righteousness as found in Isaiah come through in Romans 1:17. This righteousness, or saving response from God toward his people, was the hallmark of the prophet.

In chapter 2, there is discussion about the true Jew. Whilst circumcision was at the heart of the Old Testament covenant (Deut. 10:16; 30:6), and without it no one could truly claim to be a member of the covenant community, yet Paul insists that the true Jew must be circumcised in heart, and not the flesh only (Rom. 2:28–29).

Chapter 3 has distinct echoes of the Passover event (Rom. 3:21–25) which inaugurated Israel as the people of God under the Mosaic covenant.

Chapter 4 returns to covenant community membership. We will see that the passage has a significant corporate perspective, dealing with the status of Gentiles in relation to the law and its demands. Whatever position is taken, it is beyond dispute that the covenant is embedded in the argument to such an extent that the chapter cannot make sense without the recognition of its significance, purpose, and role.

The same is true of chapter 5. The argument for two communities—one in Adam, and one in Christ—can only be made in the light of federal headship and covenant.

We find covenantal themes in chapter 6 with the church being baptized into Christ's death and sharing his life through being raised with him. Some have recognized the exodus imagery which throbs behind the letter's teaching, and by keeping that imagery in mind, all the ideas of covenant flood into the passage.

Chapter 7, with its presentation of someone who is battling with the law, does not exclude the fact that the law for any Jew is covenant law. This is confirmed in the opening verses where the imagery speaks of being married to the law. Marriage is nothing if it is not covenantal.

Chapter 8 is about the community's experience of the Spirit, and again its reading requires a covenantal context. The Spirit's presence was one of the distinctive blessings promised to the new covenant community by the prophets (Isa. 44:3; Ezek. 39:29).

Chapters 9, 10, and 11 are so widely recognized as being about the issue of covenant membership that their reliance on covenant assumptions does not need to be defended.

This brief overview of the theological section of Paul's letter to the Romans suggests that it should be read in a covenantal framework. Its covenantal argument will be worked out in detail as we engage with its text.

The Extra-Canonical Writings

While the mistakes of previous generations of scholars are slowly being rectified, the present generation is falling into its own trap. The mushrooming of intertestamental studies as a result of the discoveries of the Dead Sea Scrolls at Qumran has produced another method for training theologians. The Jewish literature of the period immediately prior to, and contemporary with, the New Testament writings have become key texts for deciphering their message. It is argued that the literature provides a vital understanding of first century Jewish thought; the New Testament writers in particular. There is no doubt these documents give fascinating insight into this period of Judaism, but their relevance for the New Testament message must be questioned.

As we have seen, the mistake of the past was to assume the Greek of the New Testament was the same as that used in secular society. Many New Testament scholars today are making this same assumption but in another guise. They assume there is a strict equivalence in terminology and themes found in the intertestamental writings and in the New Testament. They use the intertestamental texts as the key for understanding the New Testament texts. This presupposes they share the same theological outlook, and that their meanings are transposable. However, this understanding is flawed.

There were, and still are, many theologies in Judaism. Those who specialize in the intertestamental literature are fond of saying, 'We cannot speak of Judaism but of Judaisms'. The documents represent various Jewish perspectives, many of which are distinctively different. They cannot be used safely until those distinctions are understood and their compatibility with the New Testament writings established. Unloading these texts mindlessly into footnotes or the main text of commentaries in order to give a sense of scholarly respectability achieves the very opposite. Some of the writings would never have been held to represent mainstream Judaism. To argue for a uniform Jewish intertestamental understanding is to disregard the important fact that there was not a single Jewish view, but rather a broad agreement as to which beliefs were essential for one to be considered as part of the Jewish fold.

Even if it was possible to demonstrate theological equivalence between the New Testament texts and those of the many Jewish religious writings of that time, what would that prove? How widely were the writings of Qumran known? How far had their message penetrated Judaism? How can we know that we have correctly identified a reference, or an echo, from the Jewish Pseudepigrapha or later rabbinic traditions? How many members of the early church had even heard of the Psalms of Solomon, let alone knew what the document contained? When claims are made that echoes of books like Maccabees are found in the New Testament, what evidence is there that they would have been recognized by the early church? This approach assumes these writings represent a common mind-set in intertestamental Judaism and, therefore, should determine how the New Testament documents are read. For example, the Qumran documents were far from representative of Judaism. Indeed, they were a protest against it, and are the product of a minority grouping. Many critical issues need to be addressed before they can be used to understand Judaism.

It is likely that these writers, while sharing a common source with the New Testament writers (that is the Old Testament) interpreted that source very differently. There are plenty of texts which demonstrate that different groups used the same Old Testament passage to make a case which supported their own viewpoints. Common ideas cannot be assumed because common terminology is found.

The following example illustrates the concern I am expressing. A student seeks to understand the meaning of baptism. He enquires at his local Anglican church, a Methodist church, and a Baptist church, and finds that despite common vocabulary, baptism means very different things to each denomination. However, he amalgamates all that he has learned into an essay explaining what Christians believe about baptism and returns to the churches for their approval of his work, asking the clergy to endorse his essay with their signatures. However, on reading his work, they find their own distinctive understanding has been lost in the quest for a common meaning with the result that none of the clergy are able to give approval to the proposed understanding of baptism.

This illustration reflects the conduct of much contemporary New Testament research. In the hands of scholars, the same terminology can often be used to convey different meanings.

Textual Certainties

But these observations are not meant to suggest that we must languish in ignorance concerning the mind-set of the early church. Our earlier discussion on Paul's use of the prophets has shown the dependence of the early church on their writings. Indeed, we know the whole of Judaism fed off these Scriptures, drinking from their streams of comfort, encouragement, and hope as they gathered to hear them read and taught, and using its Psalms to express their worship to God. These writings saturate the New Testament, and any understanding which fails to see them as the key for New Testament interpretation must be rejected as fundamentally flawed. The only allusions or echoes we can safely consider are those which reflect the Old Testament literature, for it was this set of writings alone that was nationally known. Indeed, it is the only set of writings that were known beyond the borders of Israel. To rely on texts which are the product of minority groups which opposed the Christian message is dangerous. In fact, this literature may not represent national thinking at all. We have no idea what was destroyed in the various national disasters following the birth of Christianity. We only have the Qumran documents because the members of the community had the foresight to store their treasures in the caves before the Romans arrived. Thus, to say that we know what Israel believed in the intertestamental period is not true, since most of the evidence has been destroyed and what remains may be massively misrepresentative.

However, what we do know is that the Old Testament Scriptures were influential, not only throughout every form of Judaism within the Promised Land, but in every synagogue throughout the Roman Empire. We also know we have accurate copies of this literature and that these texts were universally the basis of Israel's faith. Paul explicitly states it is these writings which are fulfilled in the person and work of Jesus, the Son of David (Rom. 1:3; 3:21ff.; 1 Cor. 15:3). It is true the different sects of Judaism read these Scriptures in different ways, but that serves only to strengthen the case that the way the Christians read the Old Testament was decisive for their understanding of its message. To introduce the reading of the Old Testament that other groups adopted—even if they could be recovered—would have little or no significance for the Christian church. If Baptists pay so little attention as to how Anglicans read New Testament texts today, how much less will the early church have been interested in the readings of communities such as the one at Qumran!

In the early church (as in that of the twenty-first century), there were many translations of the Hebrew Scriptures available for the Jews, and those who believed in Jesus, to study. Nevertheless, the overwhelming evidence is that there was one dominant translation in use, and this determined the theological mind-set both of Jews and the followers of Jesus. This was the Greek Septuagint version (LXX), which was used by the majority of Jews throughout the Roman Empire. This translation was destined to make an immense contribution to the early church's theological understanding. It served its members well as a commonly accepted translation for use in debate with Jews, and in the teaching of converts. The Septuagint translated the Hebrew Scriptures in such a way as to mostly preserve Hebrew ideas for future non-Hebrew speaking members of the community to access. This made the translation immensely important. Here was a Greek translation that was not tied to the classical meaning of the Greek world but carried the theological concepts of the Old Testament revelation of God to his people. Rather than intertestamental literature, the theological concepts poured into the vocabulary of the Greek Old Testament provide the authoritative key for interpreting the New Testament.

Conclusion

Paul was a Jew who lived in the full flow of Old Testament promises and expectations. In order to read him correctly, we have to immerse all his arguments back into the Old Testament, allowing its themes and patterns of thought to control how we read his writings. Only when we have exhausted the Old Testament's theology should we look at the possibility that the apostle was writing outside of the thought-patterns of his own upbringing. Of course, there are others who agree with this and have sought to follow such a principle. But this commentary goes further than merely recognizing Paul's dependence on the Old Testament. It is this author's conviction that Hellenistic models continue to be embedded in most New Testament exegesis, and that most commentators fail to appreciate the influence of these hermeneutic assumptions. The claim of this work is that the Old Testament, with its promises and expectations (particularly of a new exodus), provides all the material that we need to rightly understand Paul's, (and the New Testament church's) understanding of the divine marriage as the conclusion of the gospel's message; the heart of Israel's hope.

Romans 1: The Messiah King and His Mission

Introduction

Like any introduction, the opening of Paul's letter to the church in Rome is intended to help the reader understand what the letter is about and prepare them for its unfolding content. It is significant that this letter, written to a largely Gentile community, begins with a statement about a Jewish king—David—who had lived a thousand years or so before. Understanding the promise which God gave to David (and through him to Israel, the people over whom he ruled) will be crucial if we are to understand how and why there came to be Christian believers in Rome at all. For these promises, and how they were fulfilled, defined the faith of the community that was meeting in the name of Jesus. So, in these opening verses, Paul introduces Jesus as the Son of David, and explains the nature of the salvation he brought; showing why it was so desperately needed, and how it related to the lives and confession of the Roman Christians.

The opening section of the letter (the salutation) contains important theological information which provides Paul with an opportunity to establish the way in which he wants the letter's recipients to engage with its central message. As the letter unfolds, we shall observe how Paul develops the themes of his opening verses; for they show how the Son of God, who came through the line of David, fulfilled his Father's mission; bringing to completion the promises made throughout the Old Testament to Israel.

Paul: Convert, Servant and Apostle

1:1 Paul, a servant of Christ Jesus, called to be an apostle set apart for the gospel of God.

First of all, Paul must introduce himself to his readers; and the term he uses to describe himself is *doulos* ('servant'). This term has been the cause of a great deal of confusion. In classical Greek it meant 'slave' and many commentators have assumed that Paul intended to describe himself as one who, without any rights of his own, was owned by Christ. But when this word was used in the Greek Old Testament (the LXX) it was a translation of the Hebrew word ebed—a title which is applied to a wide variety of people in the Old Testament; not only to slaves, but also kings (Isa. 37:24), prophets (Isa. 20:3), the nation of Israel (Isa. 41:8–9), the Messiah (Isa. 42:1), and even ordinary Israelites (Isa. 65:13–15). Hence the word ebed was used to denote someone who was subordinate either to God or to man. Hence in the LXX (unless the context makes it clear that it was otherwise) *doulos* describes a relationship to God within the covenant that he had made with Israel.

This is also the case in the New Testament, where it is used to describe the relationship between the believer and God within the new covenant which God has established through Christ. In such a context, *doulos* does not denote someone who has no rights, but rather someone who is showered with honour and privilege as a result of being a servant of the living God.

Paul could not think of himself apart from his relationship to his Saviour, a relationship that had cost him dearly. At one time he had hated Jesus Christ, doing everything to silence all who claimed to be his followers. He had been a fanatical Pharisee, and in his attempt to guard the purity of Judaism he had travelled far beyond the borders of his country to bring the followers of Jesus before the Jewish court. He would not tolerate the suggestion that Israel's Messiah had been crucified, because the law said that anyone who hangs on a tree is cursed by God (Deut. 21:22–23).

However, as he was on the way to Damascus to arrest some of Jesus' disciples, Paul experienced a life-transforming encounter with Jesus, and could no longer deny that he had been raised from the dead. He became a member of the new community which he had formerly tried to destroy and—accepting that Jesus was the Son of God—became his servant.

Paul's life became dedicated to spreading far and wide the good news that Jesus Christ had fulfilled the Scriptures (v. 2). In writing his letter to the Romans, Paul is anxious that the church there might understand that this message of good news is for both Jews and Gentiles—for all who believe. The promises that the Gentiles would be brought into the covenant community as a result of the coming of the Messiah were now being fulfilled.

Paul's apostleship was 'by the will of God', and he describes his calling in terms which are reminiscent of the call of men in the Old Testament such as Abraham, Moses, David, Isaiah, and Ezekiel. He is 'a servant of Christ Jesus, called to be an apostle'. Furthermore, Paul says that he was *aphorismenos* ('set apart'). The word appears in the LXX in the context of the sacrificial ministry of the Temple. It spoke both of priestly service and of all Israel's service to God (cf. Num. 8:11; Lev. 20:24–26). Its use here suggests that Paul understands his ministry to be in some way priestly; indeed later in the letter he writes that he has 'the priestly duty of proclaiming the gospel of God' (Rom. 15:16)—yet he also extends the idea of priestly ministry to include all the believers in the church to whom he is writing (Rom. 12:1–2).

Paul was set apart for the 'gospel of God'. The term *euangelion* ('gospel') means good news. Paul here echoes the good news which Isaiah proclaimed; for as through Isaiah God promised to deliver Israel from their exile in Babylon (Isa. 52:7), so Paul's 'gospel' proclaimed deliverance of a different kind which would be brought about under the leadership of a descendant of David (Isa. 9:7; 11:1–5; 22:22; 55:3).

Jesus: The Messiah

Jesus of Nazareth was none other than the long-expected Messiah. The use of the term *Christos* ('Christ') is important as it translates the Hebrew *mašîah* ('Messiah'). David, the Jewish king mentioned earlier, was the leading Messiah figure of the Old Testament. In calling Jesus the Messiah, Paul is showing Jesus as David's successor; the one who would bring God's promises to completion.

It is Jesus who brings about deliverance for both Jews and Gentiles from the greatest exile—through Paul's proclamation of the gospel they are being called to leave their alienation from God and be reconciled to him. This is possible because Jesus, the Son of David, has dealt with the cause of separation and exile—the sin of humanity—a theme which Paul develops more fully in chapter three.

1:2 which he promised beforehand through his prophets in the holy Scriptures,

While it is legitimate to look for specific prophecies in the Old Testament to see how they may have been fulfilled in Christ, such a predictive promise-fulfilment approach is not at the forefront of Paul's thinking here. Rather, he sees the many prophecies about the ending of Israel's shame in exile, and her deliverance through the coming of the Son of David, to have been fulfilled in Jesus. As we continue to explore Romans, we shall see that Paul's understanding of the fulfilment of the scriptures is more at the level of typology. In this method of interpretation features of Old Testament events are identified in God's dealings with the New Testament church and it is from the resulting parallels that lessons are drawn (Rom. 15:4; 1 Cor. 10:1–13).

1:3 concerning his Son, who was descended from David according to the flesh

Many scholars believe vv. 3–4 to be a statement from an existing confession of faith—probably one that was used in the early church at baptisms. Paul was in the habit of quoting from confessions and hymns; possibly assuring the recipients of his letters that he was in agreement with the message embodied in those compositions—a message which the original apostles had received from Jesus (Phil. 2:5–8; Col. 1:13–20).

A Descendant of David According to the Flesh

Paul's statement that Jesus was 'descended from David according to the flesh' needs some careful unpacking. For the ancient Greeks, all flesh was evil, but all spiritual things were good; they believed that the spirit of man was imprisoned in his evil (physical) body. But this was not the Jewish understanding. The creation account in Genesis led a Jew to see all of God's creation as good, including the human body, the flesh. The Jewish people knew that the body was capable of great evil, but they did not for that reason believe that it was intrinsically evil. It is true that as a result of Adam's sin the whole of creation became fundamentally flawed, including the physical condition of humanity; but this 'spoiling' did not make human flesh sinful, it simply made it weak. As we will demonstrate, the term 'flesh' is used in a variety of ways in Romans, and it is therefore extremely important to read the word in context of the passage in which it appears in order to ascertain its particular meaning.

In this verse, Paul uses the term 'human nature' (or 'flesh') as a reference—not to sinfulness—but to this weakened human condition. The verse is simply saying that, according to natural descent, Jesus was of the line of King David. He was truly man and, apart from our sinful status, shared our human condition. Because of this he can be our faithful High Priest, understanding our needs, and sympathizing with us in our frailty (Heb. 2:17–18). One could argue that being born into the royal family brought Jesus privilege—but that would be to misread the plot. The Son of David was not destined to privilege but to suffer death. Isaiah had identified the Suffering Servant (Isa. 52:13–53:12) with the promised descendant of David (Isa. 55:3) whose sufferings would bring about Israel's release from exile. Paul clearly makes a similar connection.

If this crucial theme of Jesus being the promised descendent of David ('Messiah') is not permitted to control our exegesis at this point, then the result might be a serious misreading of the whole letter. What Paul is saying is that the good news he proclaims makes known how God has fulfilled his promises by sending his Son as the promised Davidic king (Rom. 3:21; 16:25–26; 2 Cor. 1:20). No Jew would have expected that the longed-for king was going to be the eternal Son of God; nor would he have anticipated what the Son of David would do once he had come. Jesus' choice to submit himself to death at the hands of the Roman overlords was unthinkable. The scandal of the cross (1 Cor. 1:23) was an insurmountable problem for any Jew who had not faced the reality of the resurrection and experienced the work of Christ's Spirit (1 Cor. 2:14; 2 Cor. 3:13–16).

Declared to be the Son of God with Power

1:4 and was declared to be the Son of God in power according to the Spirit of holiness by his resurrection from the dead, Jesus Christ our Lord,

That Paul understands Jesus to be 'his Son' (that is, the 'son of God') is clear from the text, and so what Paul means by this must be carefully explored.

The description 'son of God' has two layers of meaning; one which is familiar to both Jews and Christians, and another which is unique to Christian understanding. In the Old Testament judges (Ps. 82:6), kings (Ps. 2:7), angels (Job 1:6 NAS, RSV), and even the whole nation of Israel (Exod. 4:23; Hosea 11:1), were called sons of God. It is clear that this usage did not convey the idea of deity—even though these individuals and groups received a measure of the Spirit to fulfil their God given tasks.

When we come into the New Testament, we find that Christians are also called sons of God (Rom. 8:15–17). Their status means that they are heirs of all that God has (Rom. 8:17; Eph. 3:6), just as the kings of Israel were considered to be God's heirs in the Old Testament (Ps. 2:8). Their responsibility was to be ambassadors representing him to an unbelieving world (2 Cor. 5:20; Eph. 6:20) and, to enable them to do this, they have also been given the Holy Spirit (Rom. 8:9). Furthermore, the universal church—the Israel of God—is called 'the son of God' (Rom. 8:14, 19; 2 Cor. 6:18; Phil. 2:15). The church has been called to do the work that Israel failed to do in taking the good news of God's mercy to the nations (Phil. 1:27). Again, she has received the Holy Spirit to empower her for this work (Luke 24:48–49; John 15:26; 16:13; 1 Cor. 2:4; 12:7–13; 2 Cor. 3:18; Gal. 3:2; 4:6).

The term 'son of God' is not only used in the New Testament for Christians, or for the church, it is also used of Christ himself. Jesus is regularly called the 'son of God' (Matt. 16:16; 27:54). In the Old Testament sense, this title means nothing more than that Jesus is the promised king, the descendant of David (albeit with a ministry which excels that of other representatives of God). In other words, Jesus is the one the prophets had predicted would come to sit on the throne of his father David (2 Sam. 7:5–16; Jer. 33:15–16; Amos 9:11–12; Zech. 6:12–14). When the disciples used this term in the gospels, it is likely that they did so with this restricted Jewish understanding.

Following the resurrection, the disciples began to realize more clearly who Jesus was, and appreciate more fully the significance of the term 'son of God'. They came to see Jesus in a unique way. They already understood

Jesus to be the Son of David who would bring salvation to his people, as predicted by the prophets; and they— like many other Jews—had expected the resurrection of the righteous at the end of history. Yet when they witnessed that Jesus had already been raised from the dead, they began to realise that the end of history had in fact begun.

The apostles would have known that accompanying the prediction of the redemption of Israel from Babylon was the promise of the redemption of creation itself (Isa. 55:13). If Jesus had fulfilled the prophets' predictions, then the redemption of creation had—at least in principle—taken place. This may have led the apostles to deduce Jesus' identity in the light of what he had accomplished. For the prophets had predicted that God would redeem his people from exile (the new exodus) and restore creation to its state of perfection. Jesus, the 'son of God' had achieved the redemption of creation, something beyond the ability of any earthly king, no matter how exceptionally endowed he was with the Spirit. Hence the disciples would have realised that the Old Testament categories of 'son of God' were entirely inadequate to properly describe him.

This kind of evidence for the divinity of Jesus based on what he has accomplished may be termed 'functional Christology'; we can understand who Jesus is through what he has achieved. Paul will use this functional Christology argument in chapter eight, linking Jesus' redeeming death (Rom. 8:3) with the redemption of the entire created order (Rom. 8:19–25). Jesus' status as Son of David allowed him to gather all of the promises of redemption together so as to fulfil them; but the redemption of creation is something which only God could do. Therefore, since Christ's resurrection provided evidence that the work of redemption had been completed, it also—and as a consequence—attested Christ's divinity. Jesus was declared to be the Messiah by the disciples, the crowds, and most significantly by the Father at his baptism (Matt. 3:17); this testimony of his eternal Sonship was further established by his resurrection.

Such a Christological development came not as the result of wild speculation, but as the inevitable outcome of the resurrection. Growing confidence in the eternal Sonship of Jesus led the infant church to give expression to her increasing understanding that her Saviour was more than the promised descendant of David— he was himself God. The church chose to use the term 'son of God' in keeping with Jesus' own use of the term—in a way that suggested equality with God (Matt. 28:19; John 10:33–39). The early Christians, therefore, adopted this usage when they wanted to speak of Jesus' divinity.

In summary, the term 'son of God' has two levels of meaning in the understanding of the early church: the Jewish meaning which applies equally to Christ, the church, and her members; and the eternal (or ontological) meaning which uniquely applies to Jesus.

Moreover, in describing Jesus as 'declared to be the Son of God in power' Paul deliberately echoes God's saving activity in the Old Testament. Whenever God had acted in a saving or redemptive way in the past (e.g. in the deliverance from Egypt and then from Babylon) he had also demonstrated his power (Ps. 106:8–10; Exod. 9:16; 32:11; Deut. 4:37; Isa. 40:26; 66:1–2; Jer. 16:21). Moreover, when Israel was in exile, Ezekiel likened her return to the Promised Land to resurrection (Ezek. 37:1– 14; Hosea 13:14). While this was a symbolic resurrection, the typological fulfilment of Jesus—the descendant of David, the King of the Jews, and the true representative of his people—had been literal. What Paul is saying in this verse is that another major saving event has occurred in the death and resurrection of Jesus; an event so unique that it had achieved what no previous saving activity of God ever had. His real and historical resurrection was the exodus which brought deliverance from bondage and exile (1 Cor. 10:1–4).

According to the Spirit of Holiness

The term 'spirit of holiness' was used in the Old Testament to describe the perfection required for an animal sacrifice to be acceptable to God; in other words, the sacrifice which Jesus made was unique and perfect (Rom. 3:21ff.; 8:3). His death has been accepted by God as the means by which he could forgive his people and give them new life. But the term is not limited to being a reference to the sacrifice of Jesus. The prophet Isaiah spoke of Israel grieving God's Holy Spirit (Isa. 63:10), and David pleaded with God not to take his Holy Spirit from him (Ps. 51:11). So, the term also relates to the Holy

Spirit. This should not surprise us as Jesus was only able to make his sacrifice because of the Holy Spirit empowering him (Heb. 9:8–28).

The Messiah King and His People

1:5 through whom we have received grace and apostleship to bring about the obedience of faith for the sake of his name among all the nations,

Paul is saying that, because of Jesus' resurrection, it was possible to call Gentiles into the covenant that God made with his people. The prophets had said that the Gentiles would be allowed to come into the covenant with God on an equal footing with the Jews (Isa. 19:19–25; 42:6–7; 56:6–7). They declared that this would be possible after the new exodus, an event which they saw as Israel's resurrection, but which the apostles identified as being the New Israel (the church) being brought out of exile by the resurrection of her Saviour (Gal. 1:4; Col. 1:13–14).

Paul's former companions in Judaism were horrified; for he now argued that, on the basis of this new covenant, Gentiles were accepted by God without circumcision. Paul thus became regarded as a betrayer of Israel's law, and as a consequence they planned the apostle's death on several occasions.

The Gentiles are not only called to faith but to the 'obedience that comes from faith'. The New Testament knows nothing of a faith that does not obey. The Apostle James said that 'faith without works is dead' (Jas. 2:26), and another apostle, John, said that if we see our brother or sister in need and refuse to help him, our claim that the love of God dwells in us is meaningless (1 John 3:16–24). For Paul, obedience meant taking up the challenge of reaching the Gentiles with the message of salvation so that they could bring glory to God for his mercy toward them.

1:6–7 including you who are called to belong to Jesus Christ. To all those in Rome who are loved by God and called to be saints: Grace to you and peace from God our Father and the Lord Jesus Christ.

It is little short of miraculous that Paul could write these words to a congregation that was mainly made up of Gentile believers. He describes the Gentiles as God's beloved people ('loved by God'). This change of status was only possible because all God's blessings had been made available to them through the resurrection of Jesus from the dead. The Old Testament promises had all been fulfilled in Jesus (2 Cor. 1:20), including the promise of acceptance for believing Gentiles among the people of God. This fact was not easy for the believing Jews of Paul's day to accept. Because the apostle saw the full implication of the Gentiles being accepted by God, he strenuously defended them from the attempts of zealous Jews to bring them into Judaism via circumcision. Paul could not countenance this for one moment, as he saw that it would ultimately betray the essential message of the gospel; and it was perhaps this desire to shield the Gentiles from the requirements of Jewish initiation ceremonies that caused Paul to be despised by many of his fellow Jews.

When Paul says that his readers are 'loved by God and called to be saints' he is using distinctive Old Testament vocabulary which was used to describe Israel's relationship with God (2 Chr. 6:42; Ps. 37:28; Dan. 7:18). Once again, Paul expresses his conviction that the church has inherited the calling and mission of Israel. This is a view that he expresses regularly in his letters, giving evidence that the church is the fulfilment of the covenant promises (Gal. 2:2–5; Eph. 2:18–22). This does not imply that God is no longer concerned for the Jews but that, in terms of the gospel, they have no priority over Gentile believers. Together, all believers (both Jew and Gentile) form the new community of God's people (Gal. 3:26–29).

Paul uses the greetings charis ('grace') and *eirene* ('peace')—words which echo the Hebrew *hesed* and *šalôm* and which are saturated with Old Testament meaning (Num. 6:26; Judg. 6:23; Ps. 85:8; Zech. 12:10). These greetings feature extensively in Paul's letters (e.g. 1 Cor. 1:3; 2 Cor. 1:2; Gal. 1:3; Eph. 1:2; Phil. 1:2; Col. 1:2). Paul's readers in Rome would have no doubt heard these salutations regularly, for they were often attributed to the emperor in their public gatherings. Yet whilst the citizens of Rome looked to their emperor to show them grace and kindness, the believing community looked to God the Father instead, and to the Lord Jesus Christ for their salvation and peace.

Romans 1: The Messiah King and His Mission

The Messiah King and His People's Needs

1:8–10 First, I thank my God through Jesus Christ for all of you, because your faith is proclaimed in all the world. For God is my witness, whom I serve with my spirit in the gospel of his Son, that without ceasing I mention you always in my prayers, asking that somehow by God's will I may now at last succeed in coming to you.

Paul next informs the Roman believers of his prayers for them. He encourages them with the good reports that he has heard concerning their faith and assures them that he shares their faith and concern for the lost as his whole life is spent in preaching the same gospel that had brought them peace with God.

The term *latreuō* ('serve') refers to temple activity; in fact, when the term has a divine being as its object (as it does here) it often means 'worship'. As we have noted Paul speaks of his proclamation of the gospel as being priestly (Rom. 15:16) and urges the believers to fulfil their priestly ministry (Rom. 12:1). No doubt he saw his prayers for the Romans as part of his priestly ministry too.

Paul does not give any details of his prayers, but we can get an idea of what they might have been by reading the prayers in his letters to other churches (1 Cor. 1:4– 6; Eph. 1:15–23; 2:14–21; Phil. 1:3–11; Col. 1:3–14; Phlm. 1:4–7). From these prayers we can see that Paul's chief concern was not for happiness or comfort in the lives of his congregations but for the kingdom of God to be advanced through them. Even though he knew this might bring suffering, Paul prayed for faithfulness and spiritual growth in the lives of the believers.

He states that he prays constantly for the Roman believers (thought, by most, to be people he had never actually met). Clearly, he had a sense of oneness with God's people as he could not think of them without finding that he prayed for them. They shared the same task of making Christ known to a world that was under condemnation and in need of the salvation which God had secured through the death of his Son. Moreover, the Roman believers were in a crucial geographical location at the heart of the empire and would have a strategic role to play in fulfilling God's purposes.

It is not that Paul put them above other believers, as it is clear from his prayers in other letters that he valued equally all believers and their witness to Christ. Even so he longed to visit the church in Rome and prays that this will come about if it is God's will (Rom. 15:32). He distinguishes between what he wants to do—even though it is for God's glory—and what God might allow him to do (Acts 18:21). Paul is acknowledging in all he does that God is sovereign, and that his plans can only be achieved if God promotes them.

1:11–12 For I long to see you, that I may impart to you some spiritual gift to strengthen you—that is, that we may be mutually encouraged by each other's faith, both yours and mine.

Paul knew how important fellowship and mutual encouragement were (Acts 20:2; 2 Cor. 7:13; Eph. 6:22; Col. 4:8). While he had no sense of superiority over other believers, he knew that his God-given task was to encourage the church in Rome. However, Paul opens his heart to reveal that he needs encouragement and support too, and how he longs for the Roman believers to refresh his weary spirit. He looked forward during his planned visit not only to give as much blessing as he could give, but also to receive as much blessing in return. Such a valuable ministry of encouragement is open to us all; for even exceptional leaders, and therefore all believers, need this kind of support and love.

1:13–14 I do not want you to be unaware, brothers, that I have often intended to come to you (but thus far have been prevented), in order that I may reap some harvest among you as well as among the rest of the Gentiles. I am under obligation both to Greeks and to barbarians, both to the wise and to the foolish. So I am eager to preach the gospel to you also who are in Rome.

There appears to have been some misunderstanding about Paul's desire to visit the church in Rome. Perhaps he had made known his intention to visit at some earlier date, and his plans had not materialized. The pressures on him must have been considerable and demands on his time from many quarters would have meant that his responses would have to be prioritized. Sometimes he felt that a church was about to succumb to the seductions of skilful infiltrators who were teaching things that destroyed the Christian gospel (Acts 15:1–2, 20:26–35; 2 Cor. 11:13–15; Gal. 1:6–9). In the face of threats, Paul may have abandoned prior engagements in order to rescue believers from confusion. He knew that heresy would lead to the collapse of the testimony which he had sacrificed himself to establish. The book of the Acts of the Apostles and the letters Paul wrote give us some insight into the ongoing pressures upon him.

To assure the Romans that he had not deliberately ignored them, Paul emphasizes that he had no other desire than to reach all men with the gospel. By saying that he was obligated 'both to the Greeks and non-Greeks, both to the wise and the foolish', he encompasses all people. For Paul, there was no niche market for his message. He did not select a particular social class or religious grouping for his evangelism. His understanding of the gospel would have been quite incompatible with modern sophisticated marketing techniques which target some while ignoring others.

When such techniques are applied to evangelism, what sort of church is produced? Does it reflect the church that Christ has died to create (Col. 3:10–14), where there are no distinctions of age, race or social class? While specialized ministries may be necessary, they must not obscure the responsibility that churches have to ensure that all people in their local communities hear the gospel. If the message being preached does not make demands on those who believe to take up this task of evangelizing all people, it can be nothing other than a distortion of the gospel of Jesus. In describing the gospel's relevance as being for the Greeks and non-Greeks, both to the 'wise and the foolish', Paul spells out its limitless relevance for everyone. Clearly, Paul has complete assurance in the power of the Good News to transform people of every background. He has total confidence in its origin. It is the gospel of God, and he is eager to continue his ministry by preaching it in Rome.

1:15 So I am eager to preach the gospel to you also who are in Rome.

Why should Paul, a Jew, have such concern for Gentiles? I believe that in the first place it was based on his understanding of the Old Testament Scriptures. Even before his conversion he knew that the climax of the purposes of God was that the Gentiles would be brought into the covenant community. They were to be inheritors of the promise God had made to Abraham that the nations would be blessed through the seed of Isaac, and of the later promises he had made through the prophets that the nations would turn to Israel's God and worship him (Gen. 22:17ff.; Isa. 2:1–5; 19:23–25; 42:5–7; 56:3–8). This is one factor which motivated Paul's missionary work. The promises of God had to be fulfilled. Thus, what spurred him on was not only his concern for the lost but also his awareness that, unless the gospel went to the furthest parts of the world, the promise of God would not be completed. Not until that happened could the great celebration of the salvation of God take place. Indeed, not until then could God be justified before all humankind, as only then would it be seen that God had kept his covenant. In other words, Paul was motivated by his passion for the glory of God.

The Messiah King and His Mission

1:16–17 For I am not ashamed of the gospel, for it is the power of God for salvation to everyone who believes, to the Jew first and also to the Greek. For in it the righteousness of God is revealed from faith for faith, as it is written, "The righteous shall live by faith."

Why was Paul not ashamed of the gospel? When he says he is not reluctant to preach it because it is 'the power of God for salvation to everyone who believes' he is not speaking from an academic or theoretical position; the gospel had transformed his own life, and he was confident that it would do the same for others. Paul believed the gospel to be authoritative, being in accord with the Law and the Prophets (Rom. 3:21) and authenticated by the resurrection of Jesus from the dead (Rom. 1:4).

Paul's comments here seem to be rooted in Isaiah, as the term 'not being ashamed' resonates with echoes of Isaiah 28:16, which states that those who put their trust in the one who is 'the stone' will never be put to shame. This 'stone' passage is in fact the most quoted Old Testament passage in the New Testament (Matt. 21:44; Mark 12:10; Luke 20:17; Acts 4:11; 1 Pet. 2:6–8), so it is possible that the Roman believers may immediately have associated Paul's statement of 'not being ashamed' with faith in the promised Messiah. In fact, Paul quotes from this passage again himself in Romans 9:33. The one who is called 'the stone' is the promised Son of David, and in the book of Isaiah—as elsewhere in the prophetic writings—he is the one promised who would bring the Jews out of exile, and lead them back to Jerusalem (Isa. 11:1; 48:20–21; 52:1–12).

The term 'gospel' was used by Isaiah to denote the message that God was acting to deliver his people (Isa. 52:7), and Paul was 'not ashamed' of the message that God had indeed acted in Jesus to bring about this deliverance. Since, in Isaiah, Israel and the nations were to be ashamed for refusing to obey God (Isa. 1:29; 23:4; 24:23; 29:22; 33:9), Paul's claim to never be ashamed of the gospel reveals that he sees obedience to that gospel as obedience to God.

Moreover, Paul's use of the phrase 'power of God for salvation'—which will be the key to his description of the resurrection in chapter six—also comes from the Old Testament. As noted earlier, biblical scholars widely acknowledge that there were two major occasions when the power of God was displayed in the Old Testament: the first, when he brought the Jews out of bondage from Egypt, and the second, when he brought them back again from exile in Babylon. Both these deliverances are repeatedly spoken of as God's saving his people by his powerful action and are denoted by the technical term 'salvation' (in Hebrew, *yĕšû'â*, in Greek, *sōtēria*—see Exod. 14:13; 15:2; Isa. 49:6; 52:10; 56:1).

Yet it is not simply the case that Paul embraces the technical vocabulary of Isaiah; rather, he is using the historical situation of the Jews in exile as a model through which he can explain the gospel message. Paul sees the whole of humankind as being in bondage, alienated from its Creator through acts of disobedience, and under the control of Satan (Eph. 2:1–3; 11–13). Since humankind is held captive by sin in the kingdom of darkness (Acts 26:17–18; Col. 1:13–14), and can discover no way out, the situation is dire. The judgment that will come upon Satan will also come upon the human family, for it has foolishly accepted his lies and so become part of his rebellion.

To The Jew First, and also to the Gentile

While the Jews were the elect people of the Old Testament, Paul—one of their most fanatical members before his conversion—now insists that the gospel announces salvation for all who will believe; it is for both Jews and Gentiles. The calling of the Gentiles became so fundamentally important for Paul that he not only devoted himself to their evangelization, but constantly risked his life because many Jews thought he was compromising the integrity of Judaism (Acts 9:23; 23:12; Gal. 5:11).

Even so, it is not strictly correct to say that Paul's Jewish opponents objected to him engaging in Gentile evangelism. Some kind of universal mission had been anticipated by the Old Testament (Gen. 12:3; Jonah 3:10; Ps. 98:1–6; 100:1–5), and if Paul had led these Gentiles to become Jewish converts who submitted to the law, his opponents might have been content. But Paul simply could not do this; for it was not by the law that God had brought salvation to the Jews. The law was good and holy, being given by God as an expression of the covenant he had graciously established between himself and Israel—but it was never intended to provide a means of salvation.

In fact, it seems that Judaism was divided over the significance of the law at this time; for while some saw law-keeping as a way of pleasing God and attaining salvation, others saw the law as evidence that they had nothing else to receive from God. Its very possession was evidence that the Lord had accepted them, and as far as they were concerned, anyone who wanted to be accepted by God had to come under the yoke of this sacred gift. This was the point that Paul, the disciple of Jesus, could no longer accept. While he had previously rejoiced in the law (Phil. 3:1–6), he now realized that he had made it a substitute for Christ (Phil. 3:7–11). For many devout Jews, there was nothing beyond the law. The Torah itself (the first five books of the Bible) was the vital evidence that they had been accepted by God.

Without doubt, the giving of the law was certainly intended to bless the covenant community, but Paul's experience on the Damascus road caused him to review his understanding of salvation history. He came to see how his ancestors had broken the covenant at Sinai by committing spiritual adultery (abandoning God and going after other gods—see Exodus 32:1–8).

Romans 1: The Messiah King and His Mission

This happened on Israel's wedding night (the prophets' description of the Sinai event—Hosea 2:14–23), after her 'marriage' to her God. Israel broke the marriage covenant when she worshipped the golden calf, and so came under the covenantal curses. The law was intended to bring life, but because of her disobedience and unfaithfulness it became a ministry of death to Israel (see 2 Cor. 3:9). Paul came to see that his adulterous nation needed the same salvation promised to the Gentiles—a salvation that was entirely of grace.

The good news which Paul proclaimed was that the salvation promised by the prophets had now arrived. God had acted through his Son's life, death, and resurrection to bring salvation to Israel and all nations; a salvation based on God's free grace. Whilst Jews were by no means excluded from this salvation, they were not given any favours which were denied to the Gentiles. What had previously been the differing status of Jews and Gentiles counted for nothing under the new covenant (Col. 3:10–11).

Sadly, this universal bestowal of God's blessing was perceived by some to mean a loss of privilege for Israel; a matter which caused the Jewish community huge distress. The Jews were happy for Gentiles to be brought into Judaism on terms which they could accept—but the idea of free grace shown to the heathen was seen by many as a denial of the standards of God's law. In particular, the Jews could not accept that salvation would come via the death of their own Messiah. For most Jews, the cross was a scandal with which they could not come to terms (1 Cor. 1:23). They found immense difficulty in accepting a Messiah who had been defeated and put to death by their arch-enemies, the Romans. Furthermore, it was these same Gentiles who were now, according to Paul, freely invited into the covenant community.

Despite Paul's insistence on the equality of believing Jews and believing Gentiles, he still recognized the priority of the Jews in hearing the gospel, for it was through them that the message was to spread across the entire world. For this reason, the gospel is for the Jew first. In giving the Jews the first opportunity to hear, God fulfilled his promise to Abraham that he would respond to their cry for help, allowing them to fulfil their calling to be a light to the nations (Gen. 15:13–14; Isa. 49:6).

The Righteousness of God

1:17 For in it the righteousness of God is revealed from faith for faith, as it is written, "The righteous shall live by faith."

Paul's use of Habakkuk 2:4—*'The righteous shall live by faith'*—suggests that he is thinking again of the promised new exodus. In the original context the statement was addressed to those—about to go into exile—who were being tempted to reject the warnings of the prophets not to fight their captors. The way of faith entailed submission both to the judgment and the promise of God. The righteous do not seek to achieve their own freedom or deliverance but recognize the justice of the judgment that they are under whilst waiting for God to fulfil his word by bringing them salvation (Ezek. 34:1–16).

The word 'righteousness' is another key term borrowed from Isaiah, the prophets, and the Psalms. It is the term used to describe God's acts of doing right (of keeping his promises). In the prophecy of Isaiah, God acted to save his people from their exile. He had promised that he would not abandon them, even though they deserved rejection. God's righteousness (covenant faithfulness worked out in his saving activity) included his restoration of the Jews to be the people they should have been. They saw that for such a restoration to happen, and for God to accept their worship once more in the Temple in Jerusalem, forgiveness would have to be provided for their sins.

However, Paul is saying that it is not from Babylon that believers have been rescued, but from the kingdom of darkness. It is not in the earthly Jerusalem that they will worship, but in heaven itself. Of course, we are able to worship God now, as the Spirit enables us (John 4:23–24; Phil. 3:3); but any worship that we offer here is only a taste of what it will be like in heaven when we are totally free from sin (1 Cor. 2:9). Paul says that this astonishing salvation is not something we earn by impressing God with our sincerity or zeal—it is given to us simply because we put our faith (our total confidence) in the God who never fails to keep his promises.

The statement 'by faith from first to last' has been much analysed. The most natural meaning is 'from God's faithfulness to human faithfulness', meaning that it is God's faithfulness to humanity which begets human faithfulness in return.

The Messiah King and the Rebellion of Man

1:18 For the wrath of God is revealed from heaven against all ungodliness and unrighteousness of men, who by their unrighteousness suppress the truth.

Paul says that humanity is under the sentence of God's wrath. That is not to say that God is angry in some kind of uncontrollable way, but rather that he cannot be indifferent to those who break his laws. In the same way, it would be utterly shameful for a judge to excuse a murder, or if society were indifferent to the activities of paedophiles. God cannot be both holy and at the same time indifferent to humanity's sin.

Humanity sins when it seeks to usurp the authority of God, excusing its actions and attitudes as mature, liberal, and enlightened. But for Paul, sin is quite simply rebellion, no matter how culturally acceptable and reasonable it may appear to be; and God can have only one attitude towards it—one of hostility. For God to be just and holy, he must judge sin.

Paul says, 'the wrath of God is being revealed'; it is present in reality and will come to its climax on the Day of Judgment when God will pass sentence on those who have rejected his rightful authority (Rom. 2:5, 16; 14:10). Once again Paul is being faithful to Old Testament teaching. The great act of judgment on Israel for her sin was God's handing the nation over to her enemies (first the Assyrians, and later the Babylonians) who took her into exile. Paul says that God has given rebellious humanity over to sin, and the resultant sentence brought upon it is its imprisonment in the kingdom of darkness—exiled from the God who created and loves humankind (Acts 26:18; Gal. 1:4; Col. 1:13–14).

The 'wrath of God' is seen by many as an outmoded way of speaking of God's reaction to sin. It has been argued that this description is inconsistent with the picture of a God of love which the New Testament presents. However, such an argument does not do justice to the biblical evidence, because the New Testament regularly proclaims the wrath of God (Matt. 3:7; John 3:36;

Eph. 2:3; 1 Thess. 2:16; 2 Thess. 1:5–10). To remove God's wrath from the description of his character would be to create a god in our own image—in effect an idol. How shocking is the thought that Christian worship can so easily become idolatrous!

An Eternal Exile

The wrath of God is being revealed 'against all godlessness and wickedness of men'. Our sin will find us out, and its consequence is not temporal separation from God as in the Old Testament, but eternal exile. This exile is based on the Old Testament model. In the Garden of Eden, Adam preferred the voice of the serpent to the voice of God and was consequently exiled. Israel, a nation created for God to be his people, rejected his rightful claims, and was eventually exiled. While the language of hell in the gospels is vivid and awful, we must not lose sight of the fact that this language was used in the Old Testament to speak of God's judgment on faithless Israel. Expressions about the soul being cast into a lake of fire (Isa. 4:4; 29:6; 66:15; Jer. 39:8), and the sinner being 'cut off' (Prov. 2:22; Isa. 53:8), must be kept in their Old Testament framework where they speak of the loss of all that is valued and important, and of separation from God and his covenant blessings

Suppressing the Truth

Paul says that God's wrath is coming on those who 'suppress the truth'. We live in an age when truth is seen as nothing more than a private opinion. It is claimed that what is true for one person may not be true for another. Modern thinking has been largely shaped by the idea that truth is not absolute; each person has their own version of truth which is as valid as any other version. Such an understanding (the fruit of post-modernism) has been promoted both in academic circles and in the media until it has permeated society to such an extent that it now determines both private and public morality.

Before we argue that Paul's opinion is worth no more than any other, we must remember from whom his message came. Paul's gospel was not the result of his imagination, but of an unmistakable encounter with the Son of

God who had been crucified and raised from the dead; it was not based on speculation but on revelation. The Christian gospel is not a record of man's searching after God, but a record of God's saving initiative to save humankind from their desperate situation.

1:19–20 For what can be known about God is plain to them, because God has shown it to them. For his invisible attributes, namely, his eternal power and divine nature, have been clearly perceived, ever since the creation of the world, in the things that have been made. So they are without excuse.

Paul was aware that people claim innocence because of ignorance, and so he challenges the validity of such a claim. Nature itself (the creative work of God) bears witness to God's existence. Theologians call this 'natural theology'; it is knowledge about God that can be deduced from creation. The vastness of the universe points not only to design but also to majesty and power. While nature does not give humanity knowledge of God which leads to salvation, it does testify to a Creator God who deserves worship. This can be the first step in the search for the God who reveals himself through his Son. However, despite this observable evidence, man suppresses the truth and argues that no case can be made for the claims of God upon his life.

1:21 For although they knew God, they did not honor him as God or give thanks to him, but they became futile in their thinking, and their foolish hearts were darkened.

At this point in his argument, Paul goes back to the creation narrative in the book of Genesis where the story of the fall is recorded. He describes the process of depravity that was its consequence. Adam was a crucial figure in the message of the early church as it described the human predicament of guilt, darkness, and fear as the result of sin. This will become clearer when we consider chapter five. However, it is helpful at this point to appreciate that the theme of many of the hymns quoted in the New Testament is of Jesus being the last Adam, saving his people from the tragedy of the disobedience of the first (Rom. 1:3–4; 3:21–26; Col. 1:13–12; Phil. 2:5–11; Heb. 1:1–14; 2:6–13; Rev. 1:4–8).

We know that Paul visits the account of the fall in this verse because he writes, 'although they knew God'. For Paul, as a Jew, there was only one man and one woman who had known God in the intimate way he describes. Adam and his wife had perfect fellowship with God. They had been created for this unique relationship; yet despite this extraordinary privilege, they rejected God's love and friendship by believing the lie which Satan presented. They believed that, if they asserted their independence, they would be as gods who knew the difference between good and evil (Gen. 3:5).

Adam and Eve's descendants assert their independence in the same way today; men and women often accuse God of imposing his law simply to deprive them of fulfilment and self-realization. In reality, the situation is reversed. It is God who delights in the development and growth of humankind, whilst Satan seeks to make men and women into mindless beings without any freedom, trapping them in the darkness of unbelief (2 Cor. 4:4; Eph. 4:18).

1:22 Claiming to be wise, they became fools,

Although his or her heart is in darkness, the unbeliever still claims to be wise—and as a consequence becomes a fool. The actions and values Paul challenges are endorsed by many powerful and educated people today—even those who express some nominal commitment to Christianity. Indeed, whenever a true follower of Christ challenges the accepted wisdom of the age, they are often accused of being fanatical. But, for the true believer, the approval of others is not important; their values are not those of the kingdom that controls humanity. What matters is the approval of the king who has saved them from darkness and death.

1:23 and exchanged the glory of the immortal God for images resembling mortal man and birds and animals and creeping things.

The darkness and ignorance of unbelieving people resulted in them creating their own gods. The picture of them exchanging the glory of God for images echoes Psalm 106:20, which is a reference to Israel's sin in making the golden calf. In other words, even though Israel experienced the mighty saving power of God in bringing her out of Egypt, she still behaved like the people from whom she had been rescued.

Although Paul's contemporary culture was that of the ancient Mediterranean, his description of humanity's decline into depravity is equally true of people in the twenty-first century. Humans have made gods that they think they can control. However, it is not long before these very gods take control of their 'creators', engendering fear by their merciless rule. Moreover, this is not just a psychological bondage; elsewhere Paul shows that behind every idol is Satan, the prince of darkness and ruler of this fallen world (1 Cor. 10:19–22).

1:24 Therefore God gave them up in the lusts of their hearts to impurity, to the dishonoring of their bodies among themselves,

In saying, 'God gave them up', Paul is alluding to Psalm 81:

> *There shall be no strange god among you; you shall not bow down to a foreign god. I am the LORD your God, who brought you up out of the land of Egypt. Open your mouth wide, and I will fill it. "But my people did not listen to my voice; Israel would not submit to me. So I gave them over to their stubborn hearts, to follow their own counsels. (Psalm 81:8–12)*

In alluding to this text (and to Psalm 106:20 in v. 23) Paul seems to be preparing for his debate with the Jewish community which he will open up in chapter two. By using these allusions to Israel's idolatry, Paul indicates that humanity's sinfulness is universal, encompassing even the covenant community.

An idolater is one who lives without considering his Maker, believing that his own gods control and sanction his behaviour. One feature of humanity's rejection of God is their rejection of sexual purity. It is no accident that this sin is often referred to as evidence of human depravity (Matt. 15:19–20; 1 Cor. 6:9–10; Gal. 5:19–21; Rev. 18:2–3). When people are left to the imaginations of their hearts with no conscience restraining them, they become like the animals. In so doing, people destroy their unique dignity; for humanity without God is a creation without purpose, meaning or morality.

Sexual immorality is never seen in the Bible as unforgivable, but it is a sin with an unforgettable effect. Millions live with the knowledge that AIDS is the silent guest in their bodies. Many victims suffer through no fault of their own. Many live with the insecurity of not knowing who their father is, and countless children live day by day in the turmoil of marriage breakdowns due to the unfaithfulness of a parent. Sex is vitally important and deeply beautiful, but the consequences of infidelity and promiscuity continue to damage individuals and society.

1:25 because they exchanged the truth about God for a lie and worshiped and served the creature rather than the Creator, who is blessed forever! Amen.

Paul underlines the basis of this behaviour. He repeats that people have devised a system of values which has no authority other than what their darkened hearts approve. This opens the door to every form of perversion and corruption, and because a person substitutes the truth of God for a lie, there is no sense of guilt.

There is instead an arrogant denial of evil, and no limit to what a person might do in order to assert their rights.

But humanity's rejection of God is far from the last word. Paul indicates this by saying, 'the Creator, who is blessed forever'. Paul uses this doxology as a way of distancing himself from worship that does not recognize that all blessings come from the Creator. In contrast people, the pinnacle of God's creation, have become nothing more than self-deceiving creatures upon whom the majestic, powerful Creator looks in pain.

1:26–27 For this reason God gave them up to dishonorable passions. For their women exchanged natural relations for those that are contrary to nature; and the men likewise gave up natural relations with women and were consumed with passion for one another, men committing shameless acts with men and receiving in themselves the due penalty for their error.

Because people have excluded God from their thinking, they have been given over to the consequences of their self-created darkness. This results in the practice of every sexual perversion. Whilst Paul's argument in these verses may run contrary to modern popular opinion in the Western world, the fact remains that all forms of sexual immorality, including homosexual practice, are clearly condemned in Scripture. If one accepts the common modern argument concerning sexual expression is that 'God has made me like I am, and so he accepts me as I am. Hence I am free to have the sexual expression I want' then one has missed Paul's vital point—that humanity is no longer how it was created. Sin has radically changed its very being. There may indeed be a genetic orientation towards same sex relationships in some; but if one accepts the teaching of the Word of God on the subject, then even this cannot excuse behaviour which is contrary to God's commands. For God does not accept any of us as we are in our fallen state; he calls us to repent of all sin (including sexual sin). Without this repentance we will remain alienated from him forever.

The consequence of abandoning the commandments of God is that people 'receive in themselves the due penalty for their perversion'. The present tense is used, suggesting that Paul sees the process of judgment as having already begun. In exchanging the truth of God for a lie, the human race has devalued itself and is no longer the noble creation that God intended it to be. Instead, humanity has become a prisoner of sin.

1:28–32 And since they did not see fit to acknowledge God, God gave them up to a debased mind to do what ought not to be done. They were filled with all manner of unrighteousness, evil, covetousness, malice. They are full of envy, murder, strife, deceit, maliciousness. They are gossips, slanderers, haters of God, insolent, haughty, boastful, inventors of evil, disobedient to parents, foolish, faithless, heartless, ruthless. Though they know God's righteous decree that those who practice such things deserve to die, they not only do them but give approval to those who practice them.

Paul continues his analysis of the condition of humanity. Again, he asserts that God has 'given them up', this time to a depraved mind. There is one other place in the Bible where the phrase 'given up' occurs. Numbers 21:29 says, 'Woe to you, O Moab! You are undone, O people of Chemosh! He has made his sons fugitives, and his daughters captives, to an Amorite king, Sihon'. Moab's children have been given over to the enemy who will 'undo' them. If this reference is behind Paul's usage (and there are other parallels where God gives up his people to the enemy) then the meaning could be that God, no longer defends sinful humanity from Satan's attacks. This is the consequence of rejecting him.

It could be argued that Paul has been excessive in describing humankind in such horrific terms, since few sink to the depths of depravity depicted here. However, such a response misses the point that Paul is describing humanity in corporate terms.

Humankind as a whole is in a frightening dilemma. Instead of being the pinnacle of God's creation, it has become its destroyer. Instead of living in moral, intellectual, and spiritual purity, it lives in darkness and defilement. It was promised that it would become like God; but it has become the very opposite and is under condemnation. In its condition of exile, humanity needs a Saviour. Paul is going to explain how God, who still loves the human race, despite his love being rejected, has provided such a Saviour.

Further Study: Questions for Romans 1

1. From what you learned in the introduction, why is it important that Jesus is linked with King David?

2. What does Paul regard as the focus of his ministry?

3. What things does Paul thank God for in relation to the Roman church?

4. Why is Paul not ashamed of the gospel? How does his explanation fit into his Jewish background and its expectations?

5. Why is the wrath of God on people who have not received his righteousness?

Romans 2: Rebellious Subjects

Having illustrated the condition of humanity in the preceding chapter, Paul next focuses on the Jewish people and their claims to special privilege. To get his point across, Paul creates a situation in which he debates with an imaginary representative of the chosen people. We will find exegetical problems in the text that have caused commentators various difficulties, because Paul appears to contradict the understanding of justification which he teaches later in the letter. If the apparent contradiction is so obvious to twenty-first century readers, it will have been no less obvious to those first hearing the letter. What is going on in this passage on this crucially vital subject?

I will suggest that like many other points of confusion, the difficulties were neither in Paul's mind nor the minds of the original recipients of his letter. This was for one simple reason—they would have read or heard the argument in its corporate (community) setting without even having to try to adjust their understanding, because it was their natural way of thinking. Read in this corporate way the argument sounds quite different.

2:1 Therefore you have no excuse, O man, every one of you who judges. For in passing judgment on another you condemn yourself, because you, the judge, practice the very same things.

Paul has already made his argument regarding the depravity of humanity in general—he now applies his analysis to ordinary people. Paul stands in the line of Old Testament prophets who were condemned for their pessimism, but whom history proved right. Indeed, Paul's discovery of the perversity of his own heart gave him an understanding of the darkness and hopelessness of others. He came to understand the painful truth that all people live in active rebellion against the God who has made them. There is, therefore, no place for self-righteous judgment on others when they fail. Indeed, such condemning judgment rebounds on the one making it. Paul is not cautioning against exercising discernment against people, who may harm others, nor is he appealing for naivety; rather he is dealing with those who cruelly scrutinize other people's lives.

2:2 We know that the judgment of God rightly falls on those who practice such things.

Human beings pass judgment on other people continually; at best our judgment is flawed, and at worst it is malicious. This is not so with God, for his judgment is based on truth. He is omniscient, knowing all things, and so has no need to rely on the testimony of others; he sees all that we do, and knows all that is in our hearts (Gen. 16:13; Ps. 33:13–15).

2:3 Do you suppose, O man—you who judge those who practice such things and yet do them yourself—that you will escape the judgment of God?

Paul continues to warn the Jewish believers in Rome against self-righteousness. He asks them whether they think they are beyond God's judgment. The fact is they are not, and the longer they continue to behave in the way they do, the greater will be the number of offences brought to judgment on the day of reckoning.

2:4 Or do you presume on the riches of his kindness and forbearance and patience, not knowing that God's kindness is meant to lead you to repentance?

Paul challenges the Roman believers by asking them if they hold God in contempt because he is delaying judgment. This has been the history of humanity's relationship with God throughout the ages. Scripture is full of examples of nations and individuals who thought that God's delay in exacting judgment indicated his inability or unwillingness to act (2 Pet. 2:4–18; 3:3–5). They viewed him as a parent who had lost control of his children but was too sentimental to discipline them. Such a view of God totally misunderstands the Bible's teaching, for it is out of love that God holds back his anger—giving us opportunity to repent before visiting judgment on those who have despised his grace and kindness (Acts 17:30–31; Rom. 2:8; 1 Thess. 2:14–16; 2 Thess. 1:5–10; Rev. 6:16).

Romans 2: Rebellious Subjects

2:5 But because of your hard and impenitent heart you are storing up wrath for yourself on the day of wrath when God's righteous judgment will be revealed.

Moses might have addressed this statement to Pharaoh (Exod. 9:29–35) for it would have been appropriate. Indeed, there is a clear reference to Pharaoh and the hardening of his heart later in the letter (Rom. 9:17), although in that passage Paul takes what was said of Pharaoh and applies it to the Jews. It would seem that Pharaoh could be taken as a type of all those who choose to reject God and resist his will.

2:6 He will render to each one according to his works:

Although Paul is reasoning at the corporate level, he cannot avoid making this categorical statement about the responsibility of the individual before God. The Jews of Jeremiah's day had tried to argue that they could not be held responsible for the things that their fathers had done; for which they were being threatened with punishment. Their favourite excuse was to recite the proverb, 'the fathers have eaten sour grapes and the children's teeth have, as a result, been set on edge' (Ezek. 18:2). Jeremiah corrected this view, telling the people that they were not being punished for the sins of others but for their own sins (Jer. 31:29). In the same way, Paul is not prepared to allow anyone in Rome to think that he or she could avoid their responsibility by appealing to circumstance or heritage. Individuals will not be punished for the sins of others—but they will be held accountable for their own.

2:7 to those who by patience in well-doing seek for glory and honor and immortality, he will give eternal life;

This statement may seem to imply that a person is able to achieve acceptance with God through good works. The key to understanding this verse is to appreciate what is being sought. These people are seeking God's glory and honour. They are seeking the God who alone grants immortality (1 Tim. 6:16; Titus 2:11–14). Of course, such works can never save, but they can be evidence that a person is sincerely seeking and should not be despised (Luke 7:1–10; John 3:1–2; Acts 10:17–23; 16:14–15).

Paul's use of 'eternal life' in this verse is often interpreted in the light of John's use (e.g. John 3:16, 36; 5:24; 6:40; 10:28; 17:3). However, it seems that Paul and John use the term slightly differently. John views eternal life as a gift that is enjoyed here and now. For John, eternal life is very much about being in the kingdom of God (John 3:1–8)—he merges the present and future inheritance of the believer into the one expression.

When the rich young ruler asked, 'what must I do to inherit eternal life?' (Luke 18:18), it is most likely he was referring to the everlasting life in the kingdom to come (as in Daniel 12), rather than the eternal life John speaks of. Jews expected— or hoped—to receive eternal life, but this was not the 'eternal life' of the New Testament, for ideas about the 'kingdom' in the Old and New Testaments were very different, with the kingdom being a future prospect in the Old Testament but a present reality in the New.

We can see the distinctively Pauline use of kingdom language in Acts 14:22 where he encourages the believers in Antioch to remain true to the faith. He tells them that they 'must go through many hardships to enter the kingdom of God'—so here he seems to be referring to the kingdom yet to come. Elsewhere (e.g. Eph. 5:5; 1 Cor. 15:24–25) he suggests that even though believers are already members of the kingdom of Christ, they will suffer as they make their pilgrimage to the heavenly Zion. They will enter the kingdom of God at 'the end' when Christ delivers the kingdom to God the Father.

This Old Testament understanding (that of being on a pilgrimage) is the setting for Paul's statement in this verse. This becomes clear when it is appreciated that Paul is explaining to his Jewish readers that God has always left the door open for those who strive to enter the Messianic kingdom. His use of Old Testament language would have resonated immediately in every Jewish mind.

John does not seem to know of such a progression. Yet there is no fundamental difference between the understanding of John and Paul. John's use of 'kingdom' language reflects 'realized eschatology' where the future is already present.

Romans 2: Rebellious Subjects

If the question is asked as to whether Paul's readers could be expected to differentiate between these two meanings of 'eternal life', the answer must be an unreserved 'Yes!' You will remember that Paul uses the term 'Son of God' with its Old Testament echo of the descendant of David and with its distinctively ontological Christian meaning. This provides evidence that the New Testament church had no difficulty in discerning various shades of word-meaning. In doing this, they were not displaying exceptional ability but merely the universal characteristic of the human mind to process information.

2:8 but for those who are self-seeking and do not obey the truth, but obey unrighteousness, there will be wrath and fury.

The term Paul uses here is adikia which means 'unrighteousness' or 'wickedness'. This is the same word he used in Romans 1:18 in contrast with God's righteousness. Rejection of God's truth exhibits itself in eritheia ('self-seeking'), that is, selfishness or selfish ambition. Paul explained in Romans 1:18ff. that such behaviour leads to wrath and anger. Regardless of how cultural, religious, humane, or noble someone may be, if they are without God they are in darkness and prisoners of sin. Obviously, such an evaluation is bound to be offensive. In social terms, Paul would be supportive of a system which acknowledges and promotes stability and well-being (Rom. 13:1–7). However, he says—as does the rest of Scripture—that these qualities will have a different significance on the Day of Judgment if they have been used as arguments for rejecting the saving activity of God. For this reason, Paul raises this issue in the section of his letter which describes the condition of the Jews. It might be thought that religious people are excluded from the description of those who 'reject the truth and follow evil', but it is not so; evil can have many attractive faces—even one of religious devotion.

2:9 There will be tribulation and distress for every human being who does evil, the Jew first and also the Greek,

Thlipsis ('tribulation') means 'pressure to the point of breaking'. The term is used to describe the force put on grapes when they are pressed and can be used to denote acute suffering. Similarly, the term *stenochōria* ('distress') conveys the idea of being cramped for space, and so may be used as an expression of extreme affliction. Together, the two terms emphasize the anguish that will fall upon the ungodly.

Paul stresses that this judgment is not only for the Gentiles but also for those Jews who reject God's salvation. This was very difficult for Jews to come to terms with. They saw themselves as different from the Gentiles who (as they thought) deserved God's judgment for their obvious sins. A Jew was religious and devout, with a religious tradition that went all the way back to Abraham, to whom God had given several unique promises. The Jew could point back to the exodus and say, 'this is when God saved us'. As a result, the Jews saw themselves as being in a right relationship with God.

However, Paul insists that such is not the case. Wrath, fury, trouble, and distress will be experienced by all who reject God's salvation; the Jews will be the first to be brought to judgment, then the Gentiles. Because the Jews had religious privileges above the Gentiles, they could have no excuse before God for their disobedience. This had been made clear in the Old Testament, 'you only have I known of all the peoples of the earth, therefore I will punish you' (Amos 3:2). The Jews were appointed to be the first who heard (Rom. 1:17); and so now they are appointed as the first to be judged.

2:10 but glory and honour and peace for everyone who does good, the Jew first and also the Greek.

For those who seek God, the end is so very different than for those who reject him. For the true seeker, there is glory, honour, and peace. When Paul speaks of glory, he is not speaking of the glory of success. Man had been created for the glory (praise) of God, having been bestowed with a dignity that made him unique. However, this glory was lost when Adam sinned (Rom. 3:23). He was deprived of his position, as one might be stripped of rank in the army and put out of service. From then on man ceased to rule on God's behalf and ruled with his own interests to the fore. Paul's reference to 'honour' reflects this background and refers to the status that was lost through the fall; a status which is now being restored through God's saving action in Jesus.

2:11 For God shows no partiality.

This statement stands at the heart of the Mosaic Law. The judges of Israel were not allowed to show partiality or accept bribes (Exod. 23:1–9) because they represented God in their solemn work. To pervert the course of justice was to implicate God in unrighteousness and corruption.

The Jews perceived that they were objects of God's favour, but Paul insisted that this favour was not meant to be exclusive. The Jews were indeed a privileged people—called and blessed by God (Rom. 9:1–5), but God's intention was that Israel should become the means by which the same grace which they had tasted might be made known to the Gentile nations also.

The Old Testament theme of God's impartiality finds resonance throughout the New Testament. Jesus warned, for example, of the danger of being over-impressed with the rich and the powerful (Luke 6:24–26), and his message was repeated regularly to warn of the danger of respecting status (Jas. 2:1–7; 1 John 3:17). A Christian church should not be a place where the wealthy and successful are adulated, or where people are elevated to positions of responsibility because of their natural abilities. The church's values should cause her to identify the grace of God at work in the lives of all people; and to be concerned equally for those who have not succeeded materially as well as those who have. Christian leadership in our churches should reflect this, and not be a monopoly of the successful and wealthy. Christian leadership qualifications are about maturity, godliness, and spiritual gifting—not material success in this world.

2:12 For all who have sinned without the law will also perish without the law, and all who have sinned under the law will be judged by the law.

Paul now turns to consider the condition of the Gentiles. They have not had the same privileges as the Jews, so they will be judged by a different standard; because they have not had the law, the law will not be the standard by which they are judged. Yet because of the light they have received in Creation, they shall perish, nevertheless. By way of contrast, all who have sinned under the law, that is, the Jews, will be judged by the law. Even so, the result of this judgment will be the same as for the Gentiles. In stating this, Paul repeats his argument of v. 10, thereby closing off any way of escape for those who think they can avoid the issue of guilt. The statement, in so far as it refers to those not under the law, was not unique to Paul. The judgment he refers to is the Day of Judgment, when all Jews and Gentiles, Christian and non-Christians, will be judged. In the case of the Christians who have put their trust in the redemption that Christ has secured, and have accepted his lordship, the sentence has already been carried out as far as their eternal destiny is concerned (Rom. 3:21–26; Gal. 3:13; 2 Cor. 5:21). However, they will be judged on their work as believers (1 Cor. 3:8; 2 Cor. 5:10).

2:13 For it is not the hearers of the law who are righteous before God, but the doers of the law who will be justified.

Paul expounds the issue of the Jews' culpability; possibly because he is acutely aware of the way he had excused himself before becoming a follower of Christ. He had been comfortably satisfied with his religious achievements (Phil. 3:4–6), even though he knew that he had not kept the whole law. While he was aware of God's holiness, and his perfect standards, he saw himself as belonging to a nation that had been especially and graciously chosen by God. Perhaps Paul's attitude of self- confidence was something he had in common with many other Jews, for he here attacks the idea that any Jew should rest their confidence on the fact that God had given them (not the Gentiles) the law. It is not those who know the law who are saved, but those who obey it. This obedience means keeping all of the law's demands. Elsewhere in the letter, Paul states that breaking one commandment brought spiritual death (Rom. 5:12ff.; cf. Jas. 2:10). This is not dismissing the fact that it is better to keep nine of the Ten Commandments than break all ten, but—in terms of God's ultimate dealings with humanity—the purposeful breaking of one part of the law results in the same guilt as belongs to those who openly defy the whole law. It is, therefore, only those who obey the whole law who will be declared righteous.

Moreover, Paul is making something more than a 'throw-away comment' when he uses the phrase, 'the hearers of the law', reminding us of the corporate nature of Israel's religion. The Jews' knowledge of the law depended on hearing it read. Few private copies of the Scriptures were available in Paul's day, and so worshippers would gather regularly to hear the Torah being read. This comment reminds us that the New Testament writings would have been read to believing communities when they gathered for worship. The apostles, aware of this obvious fact, directed their messages to the communities that heard them rather than to individuals. This realization ought to direct us to read them as texts written to communities about their experiences of the grace of God. In other words, the long-held practice of reading the Roman letter as a description of the salvation of the individual believer is, I would argue, not in harmony with either the letter's historical setting or its theological perspective.

Paul's statement here that it is the 'doers of the law who will be justified' appears to conflict with what he says elsewhere about justification being by grace through faith; but at this point Paul is focused on the Jewish understanding of being right with God, and this is not the same argument as the one he constructs in the following chapters. Here he is dealing exclusively with Jewish claims. He allows them to glory in the law, but he eventually turns it back on them, by pointing out that this law will ultimately condemn them.

When he turns to the subject of Gentiles and the law later in the letter, his concern is whether the church, dominated by Jewish believers, should require Gentiles to be circumcised before they are accepted into full covenantal membership, to stand in the line of Abraham with all of the Old Testament promises that come to his offspring.

2:14–15 For when Gentiles, who do not have the law, by nature do what the law requires, they are a law to themselves, even though they do not have the law. They show that the work of the law is written on their hearts, while their conscience also bears witness, and their conflicting thoughts accuse or even excuse them.

Paul is acutely aware there were many Gentiles who were more righteous in their lives than his fellow Jews, showing that there is another law in operation which produces this behaviour. This is why he writes, 'they are a law to themselves'. This does not mean the Gentiles are lawless; rather, as Paul explains, there is a law 'written on their hearts' which nullifies any claim of innocence on the grounds of ignorance. Paul has already argued in chapter one that nature bears witness to the glory of its Creator, and that this is apparent to all who do not harden their hearts. Cornelius (Acts 10:22), Lydia (Acts 16:14), and many other Gentiles became God- fearers in this way.

In referring to this 'law', Paul does not seem to be referring to human conscience, for he goes on to say that this law, written on the heart, is acknowledged by the conscience. He goes even further, saying that 'their…thoughts' accuse and even defend them. So, it would appear that Paul divides human self-consciousness into various parts: conscience, heart, and thought. But this is not the actual thrust of his argument; he is merely describing human spirituality, and moral existence, in terms which would have been familiar to the people of his day. What he is talking about is the human conscience bearing witness to an internal law, written on the hearts of people by virtue of their being made in the image of God; a law that the Gentiles know they have not kept.

Part of the difficulty of interpreting Paul in cases like this is the uncertainty of knowing whether he is describing humanity in terms of Jewish or Greek understanding. The perspective favoured will inevitably affect the way Paul's argument is understood. In this commentary, I have taken the position that Paul stays within his Jewish heritage, and that his readers are Jews and Gentiles who have sought God within a Jewish/Christian community where they have learned the Old Testament perspective of the make-up of humanity. In this context, Paul would not think of a person as existing in three separate parts—body, soul, and spirit— but as one physical and spiritual being, described as body and soul. Many would point to 1 Thessalonians 5:23 to show that Paul did think like a Greek in this matter, but this statement is constructed in corporate terms which are typical of the Old Testament. In other words, the prayer is for them as a believing community.

2:16 on that day when, according to my gospel, God judges the secrets of men by Christ Jesus.

Paul says that the final judgment of all people will be through Jesus Christ. He declared the same message to the people of Athens, when he said, 'he has set a day when he will judge the world with justice by the man he has appointed' (Acts 17:31), and because Jesus 'has been tempted in every way, just as we are—yet without sin' (Heb. 4:15b) no mitigating excuses can be brought to the judgment seat of God. Paul makes the frightening statement that God's judgment will not be based on conformation to a set of rules but on the deep, hidden motives of the heart. A person may live up to acceptable standards of behaviour, and yet harbour wrong attitudes such as pride, selfishness or jealousy. Reality can be so very different in the sight of God (Ps. 33:12–15), and he is a God who will expose and judge men's secrets on the Day of Judgment.

2:17 But if you call yourself a Jew and rely on the law and boast in God

Paul has been dealing with the condition of the religiously self-righteous. As he builds his case against the bankrupt religion of such people, he begins to address an imaginary fellow Jew, treating him as a representative of the Jewish people. He starts in what appears to be a confrontational manner, 'But if you call yourself a Jew'. By this stinging address, Paul attempts to shake his Jewish readers out of complacency. He wants them to realize that true Jews are Jews inwardly, with hearts that are circumcised (Rom. 2:28–29), and that unless they are so circumcised their bragging about God and his law is without foundation. It is unacceptable for them to be proud of their supposed status as God's covenant people, qualified to judge others, if they themselves continue to do the same sinful things (Rom. 2:1– 3).

2:18–19 and know his will and approve what is excellent, because you are instructed from the law; and if you are sure that you yourself are a guide to the blind, a light to those who are in darkness,

Paul had prefaced his statements to this representative Jew with the conjunction 'if'. He knows what some Jews in Rome would have been boasting about, for he had in the past made the same boastful claims! But now it was time for evaluation. The irony is palpable. He challenges his beloved kinsmen where they are most sensitive—their relationship with God, and their possession of the law. He goads their imaginary representative, who believes, with his vast knowledge of the law, that he should be listened to as a guide, and a light, to unfortunate Gentiles who are in darkness.

2:20 an instructor of the foolish, a teacher of children, having in the law the embodiment of knowledge and truth

It is probable that Paul is here continuing the point he has just made, employing the same irony to describe the Jews as 'instructors' and 'teachers', and the Gentiles as foolish and infantile. But the reference to being an 'instructor of the foolish' could also imply Jewish dedication to helping God's people lead upright lives that are worthy of the covenant, and not their teaching of Gentiles. Moreover, the reference to the teaching of infants may be exactly that, as teaching children is a noble task in Judaism; preparing them to become upright, God-fearing citizens of the covenant community when they come of age. Whichever interpretation is correct— and I would favour the former—Paul is not against instruction and teaching. Before becoming a follower of Christ, he was probably involved in such activities himself when, in his zeal to please God, he strove to be blameless by the standards of the law (Phil. 3:4–6).

Despite his inveighing against hypocrisy, the statement, 'having in the law the embodiment of knowledge and truth' indicates the esteem in which Paul held the law. We know from rabbinical records that the Jews saw the purpose of creation to be enjoyment of the law. The Torah was seen as having an eternal existence. It was the manifestation of God's wisdom, and devout Jews meditated on it, finding joy and delight in its teachings (Ps. 119:16, 151–52, 158–60, 162, 167), and in doing this they have set a good example for Christians to follow.

2:21 you then who teach others, do you not teach yourself? While you preach against stealing, do you steal?

These questions which Paul asks the Jews in Rome do not so much concern their social morality as their spiritual reality. Paul asks them to face up to the fact that they are not living out the demands of the law. How can they teach it to others, guiding, instructing, and explaining all matters contained within, if their ears are closed to their own teaching, and their own spiritual needs are not met?

2:22 You who say that one must not commit adultery, do you commit adultery? You who abhor idols, do you rob temples?

Paul asks if his imaginary representative Jew has committed adultery—and in so doing delivers a wounding blow. The Jews had been teaching from the law that adultery is condemned; yet, as a nation they had committed adultery against God by going after other gods. They had failed to fulfil their God-given role to take the good news about him to the Gentile nations who—as a result—continued to live in the darkness of alienation from him. God longs for the salvation of the lost— Gentiles as well as Jews—but like the elder son in the parable of the prodigal son, Israel does not. The elder son despised his father's joy in his brother's return from the far country. Likewise, the Jews despised the heart of God for his willingness to welcome Gentile sinners into the covenant (Gal. 2:15).

What does Paul mean by 'do you rob temples?' There is not one recorded example in history of Jews robbing heathen temples. As a minority community in Rome, they would have put themselves in serious danger by attempting any such thing. To take his question literally is to have him construct an argument with no power. This was not how Jews behaved. His opponents would no doubt respond that he was out of touch with reality and not worth hearing.

But Scripture teaches that the church is the Temple of the living God. To evangelize people is to claim them for Christ's rule. Paul urged people to leave the control of Satan and come under Christ's headship. Paul in effect 'robbed Satan'—the very thing the Jews should have been doing themselves. This explanation is a possible solution to why Paul posed the question; robbing (heathen) temples of converts is something they should have been doing!

Another explanation is that Paul was actually accusing the Jews of robbing their own Temple. 'To rob a temple' can be translated 'to desecrate a temple'. By turning the Court of the Gentiles in the Temple over to trade (as is depicted in John 2:13– 15), the Jewish priests had effectively prevented Gentiles from seeking God. As a result, Israel had become a nation of Temple desecrators.

2:23–24 You who boast in the law dishonor God by breaking the law. For, as it is written, "The name of God is blasphemed among the Gentiles because of you."

Paul's question does not probe their fulfilment of Orthodox Judaism but of the obligation which the law laid upon them as God's appointed vehicle of revelation. Their rejection of this mission is the most serious form of law-breaking; for they not only disobeyed the command they were given but left the Gentiles in ignorance of God's character. The Gentiles could understandably conclude that God had no interest in them, causing them to blaspheme his name.

The quotation is from Isaiah 52:5 where the prophet says that Israel's suffering in exile caused the name of God to be blasphemed among the Gentiles. Paul changes the focus of the statement to say that it is Israel's condition (her spiritual exile) which has caused God's name to be shamed. This is not abusing the text, as Israel's Babylonian exile and consequent suffering were a direct consequence of her behaviour.

2:25 For circumcision indeed is of value if you obey the law, but if you break the law, your circumcision becomes uncircumcision.

For Paul, physical circumcision did not count for anything if the law was not observed. This important principle, that obedience (one's heart attitude) was the important thing was not, however, unique to Paul's thought. Jeremiah had told the Jews about the importance of having a circumcised heart (Jer. 4:4), and the same sense is found in the earlier writings of Deuteronomy, 'Circumcise your hearts, therefore, and do not be stiff-necked any longer' (Deut. 10:16). In Paul's day, the Jews of the Diaspora stressed that this was indeed more important than physical circumcision, and so Paul uses this understanding to challenge his Jewish readers in Rome; for the guilt of those who sin while circumcised renders them as though they had not been circumcised, and bestows on them the same status as the Gentiles whom they despised so much.

2:26 So, if a man who is uncircumcised keeps the precepts of the law, will not his uncircumcision be regarded as circumcision?

In a similar way, Paul argues that Gentiles who keep the law ought to be regarded as though they had been circumcised. Ritual or ceremony does not make someone right with God; what is important is the truth behind the ritual. But who are these uncircumcised who keep the law?

Scripture recognizes there are people outside of the covenant community who do good, but Paul does not seem to be referring to socially responsible unbelievers because such are still excluded from the redeemed community. The fact that Paul says they will be treated as circumcised suggests he is not speaking about moral people but genuinely spiritual people—those who though not physically circumcised are seeking Israel's God. Such people—who demonstrate by the lives they live that they are earnest about seeking God—conform to Israel's law. Although they may be ignorant of the fullness of the revelation that has come in Christ, nevertheless they trust in God's mercy to deal adequately with their sin and are treated as circumcised. It is the sense of need that distinguishes them from merely moral people.

2:27 Then he who is physically uncircumcised but keeps the law will condemn you who have the written code and circumcision but break the law.

Paul goes even further. He argues that Gentiles who live according to the light they have received will actually judge the Jews for failing to conform to the law's commands. Such a statement was an astounding challenge to opinionated Jews. If Paul is challenging his countrymen for failing to live up to their privileged position, he is doing the same thing that Jesus did in many of his parables. Jesus constantly warned that the kingdom (represented as a vineyard in Matthew 21:33–46 and a wedding banquet in Matthew 22:1–14) was about to be taken from those who had rejected it that it might be given to others.

2:28 For no one is a Jew who is merely one outwardly, nor is circumcision outward and physical.

In making this statement, Paul is encroaching on one of the most important beliefs of Judaism. While it was acknowledged that circumcision did not make a man right with God, it was seen, nevertheless, as the indispensable evidence that he sought to live within the requirements of the covenant. Paul was raising an issue that was going to bring him into unavoidable conflict with many of the believers in Rome. Being Jews, or Gentiles who had embraced Judaism, they could not conceive of the covenant without circumcision—to reject circumcision was to reject the law itself. A rejection of the law meant a rejection of the covenant and of the relationship it had established between God and his people.

2:29 But a Jew is one inwardly, and circumcision is a matter of the heart, by the Spirit, not by the letter. His praise is not from man but from God.

But Paul lays down the principle of true righteousness. It is not outward, no matter how pure the religious pedigree. What matters is that the outward rite is matched by an inward reality. The absence of physical circumcision does not render the inward reality void, but the absence of the inward reality makes the outward symbol valueless.

Circumcision was intended to remind the Jews of their special relationship with God; but while continuing to observe this religious ritual, they had turned from the commandments that he gave them to follow the ways of their pagan neighbours. A circumcised heart meant a change of heart resulting in a change of life—and this was meant to be the true fulfilment of circumcision. Without this, the prophets warned that God would judge such Jews for their sins.

Circumcision was the means of entry into the covenant community. While non- circumcised people were allowed to live with the Jews on condition that they accepted their law (Lev. 19:33–34), they were not allowed to eat the Passover meal, which celebrated God's redemption of his people (Num. 9:13–14). It is of great significance that whenever the New Testament mentions the death of Jesus, there are normally strong echoes of the Passover and almost always a reference to the importance of the circumcision of the heart, and not the flesh.[2]

---

[2] See Rom. 2:28, 29 (cf. Rom. 3:21–26); Gal. 3:13–14 (cf. Gal. 5:16); Eph. 1:7, 2:13, 5:25–27 (cf. Eph. 2:11); Col. 1:13 (cf. Col. 2:11); Phil. 3:10–11 (cf. Phil. 3:3).

Romans 2: Rebellious Subjects

As we will see, the Passover is crucial to Paul's understanding of what the death of Jesus achieved. I will later argue that in the letter to the Romans, Jesus' death is seen as the fulfilment of the Passover. If this is so, then in order for an individual to benefit from Jesus' death and be delivered from the kingdom of darkness, there has to be a 'circumcision'. The corporate circumcision of believers took place when Jesus underwent physical 'circumcision'; that is to say, the tearing away of his flesh in his death by crucifixion (Col. 2:11). Despite this awesome, corporate, and historic reality, the heart of each seeking person has to be spiritually 'circumcised', so that he may receive the benefit of this glorious salvation.

This reflects the situation for each Jew, who though baptized into Moses in the exodus, nevertheless entered into the covenant community as an individual through his own circumcision.

We are going to see how the themes of circumcision and Passover are united in Paul's explanation of the death of Jesus. Only those who have been circumcised in their hearts can receive the benefits of Christ's death and share in his Passover sacrifice. This means that the covenant people enter this freedom as a result of Jesus' death, and continually benefit from the achievements of his sacrifice as they feed on the living Passover (1 Cor. 5:7–8; John 6:32–70).

Further Study: Questions for Romans 2

1. What evidence in the chapter is there to suggest that Paul is focusing on either Jewish readers or Gentile readers?

2. What is the danger of passing judgment on the behaviour of other people?

3. What is the significance of Paul's use of the term 'eternal life' in this passage?

4. What will the end be for those who do good?

5. What will the end be for those who do evil?

6. In what ways might this passage be applied to Christians?

7. What is the danger of being 'religious'?

Romans 3: The Required Solution

Introduction

In this passage Paul continues to answer his opponents' claim that the Jews had a special status and were therefore exempt from God's judgment. In a subtle move, Paul quotes in 3:4 from David's psalm of penitence (Ps. 51:3–6). Even David, the chosen of the Lord, and the one with whom the everlasting covenant was made, had come under God's judgment. Paul then drives home his argument about the righteousness of God, and the guilt of humanity, by citing a series of texts from the Psalms, along with a passage from Isaiah.

The sting for the Jews is how Paul uses these texts. He does not apply them to Israel's oppressors but to those in the nation who are uncircumcised in heart. The ones who thought of themselves as examples of righteousness were in fact godless. They opposed the work of God, and thus kept the true people of the covenant from their inheritance. Paul will argue this more directly in chapter ten.

3:1 Then what advantage has the Jew? Or what is the value of circumcision?

Paul is aware that the argument he has given could be misunderstood. He does not want his readers to conclude that he sees no value in the law for the Jewish people. While the law did not bestow salvation, it had a vitally important role in preparing for it. The importance of the Old Testament as preparation for the coming of the gospel is a notable theme throughout Paul's writings, particularly his letter to the Romans. The fact that the Old Testament is regularly quoted in letters that were written to essentially Gentile congregations in Rome, Corinth, and Galatia is evidence that the Gentile church needed to know its teaching in order to understand the message of the gospel. Without the teaching of the Old Testament, the gospel's foundation would be like sand. Alas, all too many Christians tend to disregard the Old Testament, seeing it as a collection of writings which the church has outgrown. Such an understanding is perilous; for to ignore the Old Testament is to fail to put in place a firm foundation which is indispensable for a healthy and vital faith.

3:2 Much in every way. To begin with, the Jews were entrusted with the oracles of God.

Paul is decisive in answering the question of v. 1, 'what advantage has the Jew?' The Old Testament had prepared God's people for the coming of the Messiah, so Paul replies, 'Much in every way! To begin with, the Jews were entrusted with the oracles of God'. The Jews' privilege is that they were given the gift of God's revelation ('the very words of God').

The importance of the Old Testament for the early church cannot be over-emphasized. Since the New Testament documents did not exist as a collection of writings during the early years of the church, it is obvious that its Scriptures would have been the Jewish Bible—the Old Testament. The apostles saw it as the key to understanding what had happened in the life, death, and resurrection of their Lord.

The Old Testament not only helped them understand things about Jesus but also the experiences and responsibilities of the Christian community. The Spirit compelled the church to face important issues like the evangelization of the Gentiles (Acts 11:11–18) and confirmed the sense of God's guidance (Acts 15:12– 18). But in order to understand these and many other issues, the early Christians went back to the Old Testament (e.g. Acts 15:15–21 where James quotes from Amos). They understood that God had spoken through the prophets about the days in which they were now living (2 Tim. 3:14–17).

3:3–4 What if some were unfaithful? Does their faithlessness nullify the faithfulness of God? By no means! Let God be true though everyone were a liar, as it is written," That you may be justified in your words, and prevail when you are judged."

Paul denies that humanity's lack of faith will nullify God's faithfulness; for ultimately God will be seen to be true, and every man will be shown to be a liar. In support, he quotes Psalm 51:3–6. By quoting David's penitential

Romans 3: The Required Solution

Psalm, Paul gives an example of a Jew who had been elected and who stood in a covenant relationship with God. By doing this, he was able to show that there is no exception. Even the one in whom God had delighted, and on whom his love was set, came under the divine sentence of righteous judgment when he sinned. If David had not escaped the judgment of God, what hope did the rest of Israel have?

3:5–6 But if our unrighteousness serves to show the righteousness of God, what shall we say? That God is unrighteous to inflict wrath on us? (I speak in a human way.) By no means! For then how could God judge the world?

Paul raises an objection that might be in the believers' minds: if human sinfulness magnifies the righteousness of God, then it is unjust to condemn people for their sins. Paul responds emphatically that God is not unjust. He argues that if God compromised himself by treating sin lightly in order to magnify his grace, the inevitable outcome would be that he could not judge at all—his own righteousness would be tarnished.

3:7 But if through my lie God's truth abounds to his glory, why am I still being condemned as a sinner?

A comparison to this question might be seen if a convicted criminal were to claim that he should be compensated for giving the police an opportunity to practice the technique of arrest! Paul would not hear of any such defence, arguing that God is true, and never responsible for the sin of humanity. This is not to say that God does not cause the sinfulness of people to serve him (Ps. 76:10), but nevertheless, he is not the author of evil (Jas. 1:13–18).

3:8 And why not do evil that good may come? —as some people slanderously charge us with saying. Their condemnation is just.

Paul states that the inevitable outcome of the perverted logic he has been arguing against will be anarchy, with people saying, 'And why not do evil that good may come?' Paul is aware that he has been accused of saying such things himself. He is deeply alarmed that he and his colleagues have been spoken of in this way. Such a rumour could do untold damage to the gospel's progress in Europe. His Spanish mission was one of the reasons for Paul writing to the Romans as he hoped that they would make that mission possible (Rom. 15:23–24).

Romans 3:8 should challenge our use of the tongue, and our response to damaging slander. Paul did not ignore the accusation or seek to bear it meekly. He chose to raise it publicly in his letter. He knew that if his response reached the ears of those who had wronged him, further accusation would follow in an attempt to justify what had already been said. Despite this possibility, he felt that bringing it into the open was a risk worth taking. His defence is not about protecting his reputation. He would be content in the knowledge that in time, there would be a judgment for slanderers (Lev. 19:16). From Paul's distressing experience of being falsely accused, the believers in Rome could learn that confrontation is sometimes necessary when the gospel is at stake.

3:9 What then? Are we Jews any better off? No, not at all. For we have already charged that all, both Jews and Greeks, are under sin,

The argument which began in Romans 3:1 was concerned with the advantages that the Jews have over the Gentiles. Paul now asks the rhetorical question, 'Are we Jews any better off?' His answer is 'Not at all!' because both Jews and Gentiles are 'under sin'. This description of being 'under sin' is a key expression for Paul, and its full significance will be explained as his letter unfolds. Furthermore, he is saying that both Jews and Gentiles are 'under sin'. Such an expression is surprising. To have said they were under the condemnation of the law would seem to make better sense, and indeed, this is the way that the expression is normally understood. As Paul develops his argument in chapters five and six, we will see that when he speaks of sin, he is actually alluding to Satanic bondage. The statement in Romans 3:9 is saying that all people—Jews and Gentiles—are in bondage to Satan. This is the result of the cosmic conquest which Paul will describe in chapter five, when Adam was taken as Satan's willing prisoner, and all the members of the human family (of which Adam is the head) were taken prisoner with him. Of course, saying that people are 'under sin' (or bound by Satan) does not deny they are under the sentence of the law, and so will be judged.

3:10–12 as it is written: "None is righteous, no, not one; no one understands; no one seeks for God. All have turned aside; together they have become worthless; no one does good, not even one."

Paul here begins a long series of quotations from the Hebrew Scriptures in order to demonstrate the sinful state of humanity. Each text is related to the condition that led Israel into exile, and the sufferings which she subsequently experienced. The quotations in vv. 10–12 are taken from either Psalm 14:1–3 or Psalm 53:1–3. Both Psalms are attributed to David.

The fact that Paul says no one is righteous would anger and offend the religious Jew, who would accept this as a valid description of the Gentiles but not of his own race. However, Paul is not saying anything that has not already been said in the Old Testament. When Isaiah spoke of God's distress at the condition of the nation and her inevitable exile, he said that God looked for a righteous representative saying, 'I looked, but there was no one to help, I was appalled that no one gave support' (Isa. 63:5). Paul describes the nation as 'worthless'—those who had been the apple of God's eye, his inheritance—could not be described in a more stark way.

3:13–18 Their throat is an open grave; they use their tongues to deceive." "The venom of asps is under their lips." "Their mouth is full of curses and bitterness." "Their feet are swift to shed blood; in their paths are ruin and misery, and the way of peace they have not known." "There is no fear of God before their eyes." Now we know that whatever the law says it speaks to those who are under the law, so that every mouth may be stopped, and the whole world may be held accountable to God. For by works of the law no human being will be justified in his sight, since through the law comes knowledge of sin.

Paul, quoting from several Old Testament passages (Ps. 5:9; 10:7; 36:1; Isa. 59:7–8), paints the picture of Israel's depravity more strikingly by taking texts which speak of the sin of the Gentiles and applying them to Israel. Such descriptions do not typify her whole history, but they do match the sort of evil which the eighth-century prophets preached against when they predicted the nation's exile if she did not repent and seek God's forgiveness.

Paul touches on her rejection of God's word (vv. 10–11), her search for worthless pleasure (v. 12), and her evil speaking and vilification of others (vv. 13–14). He says that 'their feet are swift to shed blood'. Searching for the opportunity for violence towards those they hate, pursuing it with excitement and pleasure. Instead of being characterized by the peace of God, such was absent from Israel; instead of living in the fear of God, like the Gentiles (Rom. 1:29–31), the Jews too had lost their capacity to be ashamed.

3:19 Now we know that whatever the law says it speaks to those who are under the law, so that every mouth may be stopped, and the whole world may be held accountable to God.

Paul has spoken previously about being 'under sin' (v. 9), but here he speaks about being 'under the law'. Such an understanding is unexpected of one who valued the law as the holy gift of God to his people. Recent New Testament studies have focused on this positive attitude of the Jews of the New Testament period towards the law—and indeed we know Paul himself spoke of the law as 'holy' (Rom. 7:12).

The law was certainly intended as a blessing, but Israel had disobeyed the law given to her through Moses, and so was sent into exile. She came to be 'under the law', serving the sentence the law passed on her as a result of sinful disobedience.

If I am right in saying that 'sin' is to be read as equivalent to 'Satan' in Paul's writings (see v. 9 above), then being 'under sin' also means being under the authority of Satan. Being 'under the law' on the other hand refers to being under its sentence, which is alienation from God. Such a view of the law does not mean that Paul sees it as sinful (he deals with that objection in chapter seven) but as the instrument for upholding righteousness by judging sin.

Paul's view of humanity's condition is that all people outside of Christ are, because of sin, in bondage to Satan and held captive in the kingdom of darkness (Acts 26:17–18; Gal. 1:4; Col. 1:13–14). In other words, Israel's historical exile was a picture (or type) of humankind's alienation in sin. It is because Israel had been promised a Davidic deliverer who would lead her out of bondage in Babylon (just as Moses had led her earlier deliverance out of Egypt) that Paul is able to relocate the promises made to Israel; he applies them to the deliverance of humanity from bondage to Satan by the true Son of David. In transposing these promises, he keeps true to their original context, using them to show how Israel's history had been typological of humanity's condition and the response of God (1 Cor. 10:1–6; Rom. 15:4).

Paul has reached a climatic conclusion to his argument when he says that, because all of humankind is in spiritual exile from God, 'every mouth may be stopped, and the whole world may be held accountable to God'. This is the inevitable outcome of humanity being in Adam, a theme which he will develop in chapter five.

3:20 For by works of the law no human being will be justified in his sight, since through the law comes knowledge of sin.

In stating that no one will be justified in God's sight by observing the law, Paul cuts right across the path of Jewish expectation. Whether he refers to the legal fulfilment of the moral code or the acceptance of the boundary markers that identify Jews, the result is still the same; fulfilling the law's requirements does not lead to salvation.

This statement is all inclusive; the preceding argument makes it clear that it applies to all Jews and Gentiles. It cuts into the very heart of the Jewish sense of privilege which went beyond the intended purpose of the giving of the law. The nation claimed something that had never been her right (Rom. 9:4; 10:1–4; 1 Cor. 4:6). Indeed, the concluding statement makes it clear that the role of the law was never intended to achieve salvation but to alert people to their need of it, for the law brings consciousness of sin.

The Messiah King and His Work of Redemption

God's righteousness is more than moral perfection and being righteous before him is more than being declared morally innocent. Both interpretations are certainly part of biblical understanding, but they are not the full picture. The term also describes God's mercy toward his people (Ps. 71:15; 85:13; 98:2) and speaks of his saving activity in redeeming them (Isa. 45:13; 56:1). Righteousness is a key Old Testament concept with links to Israel's return from exile. Isaiah said that Israel was made righteous as a result of her return from exile (Isa. 54:14; 62:1–2). The prophet's view of righteousness was not only one of forgiveness but also of the nation's restoration to her inheritance (Isa. 51:5–11; 61:3).

This Old Testament background has increasingly led scholars to appreciate that Paul's concept of the 'righteousness of God' is rooted in the understanding of the eighth century B.C. prophets, and the Psalms; it has to do with Israel's restoration to a right relationship with God. Cut off from the Temple and exiled in Babylon (where the brokenness of her relationship with God was displayed to the nations), Israel needed to experience God's saving righteousness. She had experienced the judgment of his righteousness which he had threatened to enact the covenantal curses (Deut. 32:1–35). After many appeals from the prophets, and following their rejection, the ruthless destruction of her capital city and supporting network of communities, the nation had been swept away into exile. But after many years, the righteousness of God was to be experienced again as he delivered his people and restored them to their inheritance.

We have seen that Paul's use of the Old Testament is not arbitrary but is guided by clear theological principles. He sees the promises of the prophets as being fulfilled in Jesus; the prediction that the Jews would be released from bondage in Babylon was now fulfilled in Christ. Thus, Paul continues to use the term 'righteousness' in this Old Testament way. This is made clear when he says that the righteousness of God, as revealed in the saving death of Jesus, has been testified to in the Law and the Prophets (3:21). It is unwise to go outside of the Scriptures to find Paul's meaning of 'righteousness'. Traditionally many commentators used the Roman legal model to define the meaning of this key term, but by so doing limited their understanding to an exclusively forensic and moral one. Paul's constant appeal to Old Testament texts strongly suggests that his source of understanding for this vital concept is not the Roman legal system but the Old Testament covenants. Indeed, we will find as our exegesis develops that for Paul there is a crucial context for much of his justification language in the themes of the new exodus and the divine marriage.

In chapter one Paul introduced Jesus as the Son of David, the Messiah King. His death was the act of 'propitiation' (v. 25) that will redeem his people and

Romans 3: The Required Solution

atone for their sins. Most of the Roman believers were Gentiles; even so, they would know there were two great annual religious celebrations spoken of in the Old Testament. Both centred on animal sacrifice. These were the Day of Atonement (Leviticus 16), and the Passover (Exodus 12). Traditionally, Romans 3:21–25 has been seen to compare Jesus' death to the sacrifice on the Day of Atonement—a sacrifice that brought forgiveness and acceptance by God. This is an understandable conclusion, because Paul (v. 25) uses the word hilastērion, which is translated by some as 'sacrifice of atonement' (a payment for sin), 'expiation' (covering or cleansing) or by others 'propitiation' (making atonement or appeasing). 'Propitiation' is recognized by most scholars to be the meaning of the term hilastērion, and that it was the purpose of the sacrifice on the Day of Atonement.

However, since the middle of the twentieth century, scholars have been uncertain whether this feast was the setting in Paul's mind. This is because although the term hilastērion has clear links with the Day of Atonement, the rest of the imagery in this passage points away from it. The reference to *protithēmi*, the *'public display'* of the sacrifice (v. 25), stands in stark contrast to the complete solitude of the Most Holy Place. On the Day of Atonement, the sacrificial blood was presented to God in this inner room of the Tabernacle/Temple (Leviticus 16). Indeed, the act itself was even hidden from the high priest as the cover above the testimony (mercy seat lid), where the atonement was made, lay hidden in a cloud of smoke from the burning incense (Lev. 16:13–14).

The only religious event in the entire Old Testament (and in Jewish literature in general) in which redemption (deliverance) is celebrated is the Passover. Moreover, it is the one Jewish religious festival where a sacrifice was offered away from the Temple. More importantly, this is the only feast Jesus himself used to interpret his death (e.g. Luke 22:15–16)—and it was the one festival about which those Jews and God-fearers who were Paul's contemporaries would have had detailed knowledge, since it was celebrated in homes across the Roman Empire.

It was the prophet Ezekiel who foreshadowed a merging of these two great festivals. In Ezekiel 45:21–25 he tells how, having built the eschatological temple (that is the final 'temple'—the church), the Davidic prince (Messiah) will offer an abundance of sin offerings for the sins of the people. What is significant is that these sacrifices are not made on the Day of Atonement as would be expected. Indeed, Ezekiel never mentions the Day of Atonement in the context of the eschatological temple. What he does say is that these sacrifices will be offered to celebrate the Passover. Ezekiel—a priest who preached against the sin of tampering with the laws of God—does the unthinkable by changing the instructions of the Torah relating to the sacrificial system. He can be doing only one thing—he is emphasizing the importance of the Passover for dealing with the sins of the people as it had been in the original Passover. It is surely significant that Ezekiel had the Davidic prince making these Paschal-atoning sacrifices, and that Paul has introduced Jesus as the Davidic descendant in the opening of the letter (Rom. 1:3). Now, in this passage that we are about to consider, we will see that he describes King Jesus' death in terms of being a Passover offering.

Further evidence that this is how the early church followed the narrative is that it matches what Jesus taught his disciples (indeed, the gospels mention no other sacrificial feast). Jesus had instructed them on the purpose of his death, making it clear that it was to atone for their sins in order to renew their relationship with God (*'This cup is the new covenant in my blood'* Luke 22:20). It is equally clear that the timing of his death was deeply significant for himself and the early church. Jesus is probably drawing on Ezekiel as he interprets his death, deliberately bringing about his betrayal and death at Passover.[3] Thus, the Paschal tradition and its reinterpretation did not need to wait for the emergence of a thinker of Paul's calibre—it was in place well before his conversion.

The presence of this Passover model is supported by the reference to paresis—he 'passed over' sins previously committed (Rom. 3:25). Here, there is a clear echo of the LORD passing over the Jewish homes on the night of the Passover, whilst at the same time visiting Egyptian homes in order to strike the firstborn sons in judgment as representatives of their families. On

---

[3] John seems to have used the imagery of Ezekiel 40-55 as a background for Jesus' statement that he would build the Temple in three days (John 2:19).

the night of the eschatological Passover (1 Cor. 5:7), God 'passed over' the family of humankind but visited Calvary, where he struck his beloved Son—his firstborn, and our elder brother (Rom. 8:17, 29).[4]

3:21 But now the righteousness of God has been manifested apart from the law, although the Law and the Prophets bear witness to it—

The righteousness that has been secured through the death of Jesus is apart from the law. It cannot annul the law as though it did not matter, because God could not accept any arrangement that was unjust. This righteousness, though apart from the law, had to satisfy the justice that the law demanded. This is not a scheme that has been devised as a last-minute attempt to solve the problem of sin—it is one to which *'the Law and the Prophets bear witness'*.

3:22 the righteousness of God through faith in Jesus Christ for all who believe. For there is no distinction:

The ESV (like many other translations) says that this righteousness comes through faith in Jesus Christ, and in so doing has sidestepped the conclusions of much recent scholarly work. Many scholars accept that the expression should be translated, 'by the faithfulness of Jesus Christ'. This rendering, apart from its linguistic merits, has the great advantage in removing salvation from dependency on a person's faith. The sensitive soul will always ask the question, 'Do I have enough or the right kind of faith?' Paul's statement speaks of Christ's faithfulness (revealed in his act of propitiation) as the grounds of salvation. Of course, this does not remove the need for faith, as the rest of the New Testament makes clear, but it lays a much firmer foundation. We are saved by God because of the faithfulness of his Son, who achieved—through obedience and death—the great work of salvation.

3:23 for all have sinned and fall short of the glory of God,

---

[4] For further material on the New Testament use of themes from Ezekiel and the Paschal motif in the Bible, see Tom Holland, Romans: The Divine Marriage (Eugene: Pickwick, 2011), pp. 84–96

When the Jews in Rome heard this statement, they would have known it reflected part of their painful history. Not only did it refer to the head of the human family sinning, bringing all of his offspring into a state of rebellion against God, but it also alluded to Israel's time in exile. God had said to the nation, 'I have created you for my glory' (Isa. 43:7); but in exile, she was a picture of shame and sinfulness. Paul's kinsmen could acknowledge these ancestral sins but could not accept that they were in a state of exile too. This exile was far worse than being in Egypt or Babylon, for like the Gentiles they were dwelling in the kingdom of darkness (Acts 7:51–58).

3:24 and are justified by his grace as a gift, through the redemption that is in Christ Jesus,

This final act of justification is not the result of the community being punished for her sin, but of her representative taking the guilt of his fellows. Paul says this justification has been achieved by Christ Jesus. By deliberately putting 'Christ' first in the title 'Christ Jesus', Paul emphasizes that Jesus is the Messiah—the promised one who would deliver his people from bondage (see earlier comments on Rom. 1:3).

Paul states that the church was justified freely by God's grace 'through the redemption that is in Christ Jesus'. The Jews had claimed to be the people of God— a claim that seemed ridiculous in light of their condition (Psalm 80). Yet it was an entirely valid claim, which God validated when he delivered them from exile. Later in the letter, Paul writes that Jesus was 'delivered up for our trespasses, and raised for our justification' (Rom. 4:25), meaning that through God's delivering up and raising of his Son, he validated the claim of those who believe in him to be God's people—in this sense they are 'justified'. So, Paul here links justification and redemption; which is unusual because justification has nothing to do with redemption in Old Testament terms unless we appreciate the merger noted earlier, when Ezekiel brought the Day of Atonement sacrifices into the orb of the Passover—the feast which the prophet saw as a great act of redemption.

3:25a whom God put forward as a propitiation by his blood, to be received by faith.

Romans 3: The Required Solution

The word *protithēmi* ('put forward') means 'publicly displayed' or 'set forth'. Here, we have another hint that Paul is describing Jesus as the Passover victim. Of all the sacrifices the Levitical law legislated for, only the Passover sacrifices were displayed for all to see. While the Passover lambs' blood was daubed on the doorposts and lintels of Hebrew houses, the blood of all other sacrifices was offered to God within the Temple.

The term *hilastērion* ('propitiation') or turning away the anger of God has already been examined. The ESV has correctly retained this traditional translation. This meaning has been largely rejected by other modern translations because the passage does not support a Day of Atonement setting in which propitiation was considered to belong. In the minds of the majority of scholars, there was no propitiatory value in the blood of the Passover lamb (the theme of this feast being the redemption of the firstborn of Israel)—and therefore, it was not given the consideration it deserved. However, once it is appreciated there are good reasons to say that the early church, through the influence of Ezekiel 45:25, saw that a future Passover would be offered by the Son of David (the prince) as a sacrifice of propitiation, the natural setting for the passage becomes obvious. Jesus, the Son of David (1:3) has made the atonement through his death during the feast of the Passover. So, Paul elsewhere says, 'Christ our Passover has been sacrificed for us' (1 Cor. 5:7).

The NIVTM has 'God presented him as a sacrifice of atonement, through faith in his blood'. Again, the ESV has the better translation with 'by his blood, to be received by faith'; the relationship is restored not through faith but through the shedding of blood.

3:25b This was to show God's righteousness, because in his divine forbearance he had passed over former sins.

Paul says that God had 'passed over former sins'. The term paresis, which means 'passing over', is only found in Romans 3:25, so we are dependent on its context to understand its meaning. Once again, we find a distinct echo of the Passover in the passage, for on that night, the LORD 'passed over' the sins of the Jewish people, leaving them unpunished (Exod. 12:27). So, Jesus by his death on the cross, brought together the redemption of the Paschal lamb with the propitiation of the Day of Atonement, a thematic union alluded to in Ezekiel 45.

3.26 It was to show his righteousness at the present time, so that he might be just and the justifier of the one who has faith in Jesus.

By giving up Jesus to death, God is just and the one who justifies those who have faith in Jesus. When God justified Israel, she was in exile in Babylon, and he rescued her. In doing this, he was justifying her claim to be his covenant people. She was shown to be the people of the covenant-keeping God to the whole world.

Paul is saying that God has now justified his people, those who have faith in Jesus. As we have seen previously, the word 'justified' in the Old Testament is used to speak of deliverance from exile. The thrust of Paul's argument (which comes to a climax in Rom. 5:12ff.) is that God has delivered his people from the exile into which the first Adam took them.

The Messiah King and His Mercy

3:27 Then what becomes of our boasting? It is excluded. By what kind of law? By a law of works? No, but by the law of faith.

In commenting on boasting (cf. Rom. 2:17; 2:23), Paul echoes the warning of Jeremiah, 'let him who boasts boast about this: that he understands and knows me, that I am the LORD' (Jer. 9:24). Paul urges the believers in Rome not to even think of boasting, for they would be bragging about their own accomplishments and understanding of the law. Their salvation was not on the basis of the works of the law but on the basis of faith in God's intervention on their behalf.

3:28 For we hold that one is justified by faith apart from works of the law.

Paul repeats himself, for the issue is too important for there to be any confusion. Deliverance from sin's domain is not a human achievement but the result of God's saving activity. Again, he uses the term 'justified' with its prophetic/covenantal meaning, rather than the forensic meaning with which it is so often credited. The framework of this Old Testament setting does not exclude the features of the forensic model (where God is seen acquitting his people as in a court of law) but goes beyond its restricted horizon. The Old Testament provides the framework for us to understand God's deliverance, which here in Romans 3:28 is the deliverance of the people of God from Satan's control. This is made clear by the term's association with redemption in v. 24. We shall consider this further when we reach Romans 4:3.

3:29–30 Or is God the God of Jews only? Is he not the God of Gentiles also? Yes, of Gentiles also, since God is one—who will justify the circumcised by faith and the uncircumcised through faith.

Paul has returned to his earlier theme of God dealing with all people through faith (Rom. 2:25–29). In asking if God is the God of the Jews alone, he answers his question by appealing to the Law and the Prophets, which said that God was concerned for the Gentiles as well as the Jews.

The covenant with Abraham (Gen. 17:4–5; 22:18; 26:4) promised that all the nations of the earth would be blessed through his offspring, and the prophets repeatedly pointed to the time when the Gentiles would be accepted on an equal footing with the Jews (Isa. 19:23–25; Hosea 1:10). Both needed to know the salvation of God and be rescued from exile in sin. To deny that God was the God of the Gentiles was to deny monotheism itself, and such a denial would sound the death knell of Israel's faith.

3:31 Do we then overthrow the law by this faith? By no means! On the contrary, we uphold the law.

Paul was aware that the ultimate test for the Jewish believers in Rome was whether the matter discussed was according to the law. If he could not demonstrate this, he had no chance of convincing them that the gospel he was preaching was from God. In saying that the gospel upholds the law, Paul is stressing that the law looked forward to God sending a deliverer who would bring salvation, and the final revelation of himself. The law also looked to the time when Israel's bondage to sin would be over. The gospel, therefore, fulfils the law. The law was nothing less than a chaperone to bring both believing Jews and Gentiles to Christ.

Further Study: Questions for Romans 3

1. Does knowledge of the Scriptures have any significance for salvation?

2. In what way is God vindicated regardless of how humanity behaves?

3. What function does the law have in God's purposes?

4. What is the righteousness of God, and how is it received?

5. What hints are there in vv. 21–26 that Paul sees Jesus' death to be the fulfilment of the Passover sacrifice?

6. What is the nature of the boasting that Paul warns against in the closing verses of the chapter?

Romans 4: Committed Faith is not an Option

Justification in the Theology of Paul

Prior to our verse-by-verse examination of Romans 4 it will be helpful to explore several key issues surrounding the use of justification in Scripture, including its language and meanings, its place in salvation history, covenant making, Paul's writings, circumcision, and the law. We will also explore justification as a corporate event and as the foundation of covenantal relationship. We shall see that to one degree, or another each issue has played a part in the origin of the justification doctrine, as well as its evolution to the present-day application (or misapplication as the case may be).

Justification and the Reformers

The Protestant Reformers of the sixteenth century believed that acquittal and imputation (terms drawn from the legal and accounting world) were two key concepts framing Paul's understanding of justification. They understood that when Paul spoke of Christ's death and resurrection 'justifying' men and women, he was saying that God was acquitting them of their sin, not counting them guilty; God had imputed (credited) the righteousness of Christ to their accounts, so making them right before him. This concept was seen to be the key to interpreting Paul, especially in Romans 4.

The New Perspective View

In recent years the work of Oxford scholar E. P. Sanders,[5] and the subsequent debate, has challenged this widely held Protestant understanding of justification. As we have already mentioned (see

---

[5] Especially E. P. Sanders, Paul and Palestinian Judaism (London: Fortress, 1977).

comments above on Romans 3:19) rather than the Jews fearing the law, as the Reformers believed, there is evidence to suggest that first century Judaism took a positive delight in it; seeing it as Israel's greatest privilege and blessing. Sanders contended that the law was not Israel's accuser and enemy, as the Reformers had thought, but her friend and guide. This has given rise to a stream of thought known as the New Perspective—a phrase which actually embraces a number of diverse opinions, most of which have some common threads. Chief among them is a view that justification had more to do with Jewish-Gentile issues than with questions of an individual's status before God.

A key question that has arisen is, if the Jews delighted in the law, why would they think it condemned them? And if it did not condemn them—why did they need to be 'acquitted'? Had Paul misunderstood the law? Or had the Reformers misunderstood Paul? Many New Perspective theologians think the latter, for it appears that since the Reformers were engaged in a heated debate with the Roman Catholic Church about how sins were to be forgiven, they assumed that Paul was engaged in a similar debate within Judaism.

A source of confusion has been over the expression 'the works of the law'. I will argue that when Paul talked about the 'works of the law', he meant not only Jewish initiation ceremonies, including and especially circumcision (as the advocates of the New Perspective argue) but also the understanding that the Reformers had reached when they saw the 'works of the law' as embracing all the law's demands.

What the Reformers missed was that within the early church there arose a group of 'Judaizers' who were saying the Gentiles could not be 'one of us' (in the new community of believers in Jesus) without circumcision, and that this was the issue which Paul found the need to confront in many of his letters. The issue at stake was how one was accepted as a covenant member—not about how sins were to be forgiven. It is quite possible that many Jews believed they had no need to be forgiven in order to come within the covenant; they were already in it—they had, after all, been circumcised as a sign that they were God's people.

In contrast Paul argues in his letter to the Romans that circumcision did not grant anybody access to covenant membership—whether they were Jew or Gentile. So, at one level Paul's debate with the Judaizers was about whether the believing Gentiles had to be circumcised to be accepted by God, but he also argued that no one (not even Jews) could earn salvation by keeping the moral law.

It was this latter aspect that the Reformers focused on and built their view of justification thinking that all references to being justified by the works of the law could be taken as evidence that Paul was countering attempts to gain justification through obeying the law's moral precepts. But sometimes this is not the case; Paul is rather arguing that the Gentiles do not need to add circumcision to what Christ had done through his death to be accepted by God.

Thus, the Reformers were right in saying that people cannot earn their salvation— God's justification was a gift of grace made possible by the acquittal of sin and involved the imputation of righteousness provided through Christ and not by works. Nevertheless, the Reformers were wrong to press the concepts of acquittal and imputation into 'justification' every time the word was used by Paul. It seems that biblical justification is an even more glorious truth than even the Reformers grasped. Their understanding is therefore just a part (though a very important part) of the great salvation Christ has secured for those who love him.

Abraham Counted as Righteous

The declaration 'counted to him as righteousness' follows immediately after Abraham heard and believed God would give him a son. The patriarch believed God's promise—and that belief was taken as his acceptance of God's covenant blessing. There is no mention of sin or forgiveness; God simply told Abraham he would give him the land. In answer to Abraham's question, 'how am I to know that I shall possess it?' (Gen. 15:8) God formally inaugurated the covenant which had implicitly existed since Abraham heeded God's call to leave the land of his fathers (Gen. 12:1–9). Through it all, God took responsibility for the covenant into which he had called Abraham. Scripture brings out clearly in the inaugural ceremony that God was unconditionally bearing responsibility for the covenant he instituted with Abraham (Genesis 15:6–18).

There are two important points to notice in this account of the covenant ceremony. First, the covenant is essentially about the promise to deliver Abraham's descendants from bondage and exile. This is at the heart of the covenant and should be considered a possible meaning of 'counted as righteousness'. As we shall discuss in more detail, the Jews saw God's deliverance of Israel from her exile in Babylon to be her justification; that is, justifying her claim to be in a covenant relationship with God.

The second point to notice is the absence of Abraham's active involvement in the covenant making ceremony. The laying out of the pieces of the animals was part of the ancient contractual process. Normally, the two parties making a contract would walk together between the pieces, effectively saying to one another, 'If I fail to keep my part of the agreement, let me be like these animals which we pass between'. Here, however, in the covenant made with Abraham (Gen. 15:6–18), God does not call on him to take responsibility; it is something Abraham is unable to bear. God walks alone, taking full responsibility for maintaining the covenant. If it is broken, God will be the one to receive its curse.

A Covenant of Grace

In this way, the entire covenantal relationship established between God and Abraham was of grace. Abraham contributed only his assent; that is, his faith. In saying 'he believed God', the writer of Genesis effectively says Abraham's faith was his agreement to be the beneficiary of this extraordinary grace. Of course, the bigger and more glorious picture is that God remained committed to his people, even when they broke the terms of the covenant. He took sole responsibility for this, bearing the curse through the death of his Son. He did this so that the true seed of Abraham (that is all believers in Jesus) could be redeemed (Gal. 3:13) and brought out of the kingdom of darkness to be partakers of the heavenly kingdom (Col. 1:12–13).

Romans 4: Committed Faith is not an Option

The Background to Genesis 15

The immediate background to all this is found in Genesis 14, where Abraham risked his life to save his nephew Lot—who had been taken captive by a raiding party— and the subsequent exchanges with the King of Sodom, and with Melchizedek (King of Salem). There is nothing in this narrative to suggest that Abraham had done anything wrong for which he needed forgiveness. Yet these were the events leading to the vision and discourse with God in Genesis 15; especially the justification statement in v. 6.

It seems then that neither the writer of Genesis nor Paul (if he is following the meaning of the original text) saw the primary concern of Abraham's being counted righteous as forgiveness and acceptance by God. Rather, it was God's commitment to Abraham in covenant to make him the father of a great nation that, in turn, would bless other nations (Gen. 18:18).

Phinehas also Counted as Righteous

Abraham is not the only Old Testament character to be 'counted as righteous'. Psalm 106 tells of Phinehas the priest, who took action against his fellow countrymen for indulging in sexual immorality. As Psalm 106:31 states, 'And that was counted to him as righteousness from generation to generation forever'. The original account in Numbers 25:10–13 provides us with the context:

> *And the LORD said to Moses "Phinehas the son of Eleazar, son of Aaron the priest, has turned back my wrath from the people of Israel, in that he was jealous with my jealousy among them, so that I did not consume the people of Israel in my jealousy. Therefore say, 'Behold, I give to him my covenant of peace, and it shall be to him and to his descendants after him the covenant of a perpetual priesthood, because he was jealous for his God and made atonement for the people of Israel.'" (Numbers 25:10– 13)*

The meaning of 'counted to him as righteousness' in this context could not be clearer: Phinehas was brought into a covenant relationship with God. Thus, the justification language in Psalm 106:31 and Genesis 15:6 is actually covenant making language; and while the covenants are made with individuals, they both have corporate implications for their descendants.

Genesis 15:18 says, 'On that day the LORD made a covenant with Abram, saying, "To your offspring I give this land, from the river of Egypt to the great river, the river Euphrates,"' and Numbers 25:13 says, 'and it shall be to him [Phinehas] and to his descendants after him the covenant of a perpetual priesthood'. Comparison between the two incidents reveals common important features: both speak of the making of a covenant, and of changing the status of the men involved. Hence for Abraham and Phinehas, their 'being counted as righteous' meant the beginning of a new relationship with God.

The Bigger Picture

God foretold his plan of salvation in Genesis 3:15, when he said he would place enmity between Satan and the seed of the woman. He moved that plan forward in Genesis 15:4–6 with the promise of a son for Abraham, and that from this son would come many descendants. This puts the patriarch's justification at the heart of salvation history. However, it was not Abraham, but God's people—the offspring of the child of promise—who were the focal point of the promise. This understanding becomes clearer in Genesis 17:1–8 when God—committing to deliver Abraham and his seed from slavery and oppression—widens his promise to include all who will believe from the entire human race. It is, therefore, a covenantal promise of a collective nature which shows that God justifies those whom he will make his own people.

We will note later how this corporate understanding of justification is also at the heart of New Testament teaching. For example, Paul uses the full import of a corporate covenantal meaning of justification when he reasons that the seed who was to bless the whole world was, in fact, Christ (Gal. 3:16). He is 'the seed to whom the promise referred' in Galatians 3:19; and it is he who brings justification to God's people as he saves them from their sins.

Paul's Use of Psalm 32

Having said all of that, in Romans 4:6 Paul links Psalm 32:2 (which is about the acquittal of sin) with Genesis 15:6 in order to make a second and telling point which destroys the argument of the Judaizers. Abraham had been brought into the covenant without works, and without circumcision; so now Paul will show that continuing in that covenant does not depend on works or circumcision either. From Psalm 32 he expounds that even the great King David needed forgiveness—he needed to be restored to a right relationship with God. His circumcision did not protect him from God's anger concerning his acts of adultery and murder. In other words, like David, all Jews need to receive God's forgiveness offered through the death of Jesus.[6] They need to be justified even though they are in the Old Testament covenant community.

Thus, in the Old Testament there are two levels of justification: one of being a member of the covenant community, and then a second of being made right with God after sin had marred that relationship. Paul also argues for these two levels of relationship in his writings, although this time they are bound up with the gospel of Jesus. Everyone needs to be part of the new covenant community, and this is only possible because God has made a new covenant with human beings, by which people enter through forgiveness and acquittal to become God's people.

Galatians and Righteousness

In Galatians 3:6 Paul says, 'Abraham believed God, and it was counted to him as righteousness'. This passage concerns the Galatians who, much to Paul's astonishment, were leaving the true gospel. Paul insists that the Galatian believers must not yield to the pressure of Judaizers who argue that circumcision is a requirement for full covenantal membership. He reminds them that justification is by faith in Jesus Christ, not by observation of the law in matters such as circumcision (Gal. 2:15–16). Moreover, he takes the opportunity to raise the matter of how the law had uncovered their sinfulness. So here Paul shows his new 'Christian' understanding of the law,

---

[6] A fact which convinces many that the traditional view of justification remains perfectly valid.

although meant as blessing and received that way by many Jews, it now condemned them.

Paul in the next chapter asks the believers if they came into the covenant through works or by faith. What is surprising is he does not ask if they received God's forgiveness by keeping the moral law. Why not? Because that was not a perspective they held. Instead, and significantly, he asks if they had received the Spirit (the prophesied blessing of the new covenant in Ezekiel 36:27) by observing the law or by faith (Gal. 3:1–5).

Then Paul introduces Genesis 15:6 again, 'just as Abraham "believed God, and it was counted to him as righteousness"'. Those who are of faith are sons of Abraham (see Gal. 3:6–7), and the evidence that they have been accepted into the covenant is that God has given them his Spirit. In Galatians 3:14, Paul says, 'so that in Christ Jesus the blessing of Abraham might come to the Gentiles, so that we might receive the promised Spirit through faith'. One of the promised blessings of the Abrahamic covenant is the birth of a community which has been given the Spirit; its members are the true children of Abraham—the very point raised by Peter at the Council of Jerusalem in Acts 15:6–11.

It is clear that the Lukan Peter's concern is identical with that of Paul as discussed in his letter to the Galatians. The evidence that God had accepted the Gentiles was that he had given them his Spirit; a fact which is linked with their hearts being purified by faith. It is also clear that the focus of the debate in the Council of Jerusalem was not the acceptance of an individual Gentile, but of believing Gentiles as an entirety. In other words, we are hearing the same corporate argument being made at the Jerusalem synod which was made by Paul throughout Romans. It did not originate with Paul—he simply expounded the Law and the Prophets concerning the justification (acceptance into the covenant) of the Gentiles. Indeed, the events Peter witnessed seem to have forced this position on the early church. It is wrong, therefore, to see justification (as some have) as being a doctrine created by Paul. The gift of the Spirit did not signify that the Gentiles had been brought into the Jewish community, but into the new covenant community. It is into this community that Jews themselves must also enter, and in this community, they have no advantage over the Gentiles.

Justification, Circumcision and Divine Marriage

The themes of circumcision, covenant membership, and divine marriage run through the writings of the prophets (e.g. Jer. 4:4; 31:31–34; Ezek. 16:59–60; Hosea 11:9–11). Among these themes was the promise of the eschatological marriage— the new people of God being made fit to marry the divine husband because their hearts were circumcised. They would be able to share the eschatological Passover— God's promised redemption of his people. This Passover was to inaugurate the (eschatological) divine marriage as had been intended at Sinai.

These themes are very much part of Paul's thinking too. He teaches that Gentiles, along with Jewish believers, are now able to partake of Christ (that is be justified by him) because Christ underwent circumcision on their behalf (his flesh being torn on Calvary). When Paul writes to the Colossians (Col. 2:11–13a) he also links circumcision with baptism; that is the corporate act of baptism, the great ontological event that makes the people of God acceptable to their Creator, allowing the new covenant community to become the bride of the divine groom.

A similar framework may be observed in Ephesians: circumcision, Passover, and marriage. Christ has redeemed his people (Eph. 1:7); the Gentiles have undergone spiritual circumcision (Eph. 2:11–13) to form one new covenant community with Jewish believers (Eph. 2:14–22); it is this community which Christ takes as his bride (Eph. 5:25–27), a truth that Paul describes as a 'profound mystery' (Eph. 5:32).

In Galatians, there are distinct echoes of the same themes. The believers are redeemed (Gal. 1:4; 3:13), share in the new heart which circumcision symbolizes (Gal. 5:6; 6:14–15), and are part of the community that will be the bride of the divine marriage (Gal. 3:26–29; 4:21–31).

Justification and the Passover

The Passover theme is clearly linked with justification and circumcision in Pauline thought. This link is further found in Colossians where, just as in the paschal passage in Romans 3:21–26, Paul speaks of the public spectacle of Christ's death, 'having forgiven us all our trespasses, by cancelling the record of debt that stood against us with its legal demands. This he set aside, nailing it to the cross. He disarmed the rulers and authorities, and put them to open shame, by triumphing over them in him' (Col. 2:13b–15). This is a clear echo of the public daubing of blood on the Hebrews' doorframes on the night of Israel's Passover (Exod. 12:7). They also have experienced circumcision, through the circumcision of Christ (Col. 2:11). The statement that Christ 'is the head of the body, the church' (Col. 1:18) also carries marriage imagery.

Justification and the Law

Another issue needs clarification in order to follow Paul's argument on justification. As we have seen, leading New Perspective theologians have challenged the Reformed understanding of justification and the law. They say intertestamental literature shows the Jews did not fear the law but lived under it with joy and gratitude. This picture is in stark contrast to the Lutheran understanding of the law as that which 'hunts man down' as a sinner in order to drive him to Christ.

It is clear Paul delighted in the law before his conversion. He seems to have been like many in Judaism who saw and experienced the law in a very positive way (Phil. 3:3–6). When did Paul's perspective change? I do not intend to appeal to Romans seven, as do others; for I believe that chapter, like the whole of Romans, is meant to be interpreted within a corporate perspective. Consequently, it is difficult to identify with any certainty at what point Paul's own story enters the narrative. Even so, Romans seven makes it clear the law was high-jacked and made to serve the purposes of sin (Rom. 7:10).

In Romans 4:15, Paul says, 'for the law brings wrath', and in Galatians 3:19, he says, 'What then was the purpose of the law? It was added because of transgressions until the Seed to whom the promise referred had come'. Further, he says, 'the Scripture declared that the whole world is a prisoner of sin' (Gal. 3:22). The inclusive terms, 'whole world' and 'all have' make it clear that Paul understands the law to condemn Jews as well as Gentiles; that Jews are included in this state of condemnation (Rom. 3:23). Indeed, his preaching at Antioch in Pisidia confirms this (see Acts 13:38–41).

A similar point could be made from Romans 5, Galatians 3 and 2 Corinthians 3. So why had Paul changed his mind? I suggest that before his transforming encounter with Christ, like the rest of Israel, he perceived himself as blameless according to the law, excelling in righteousness above his peers (Phil. 3:3–6). However, following his conversion, Paul was forced to reflect on the purpose of the law. He then realized that, while the law had been given to bless Israel, this intention had never been achieved. Indeed, even on the night God gave the law to Moses (the occasion Jews were later to see as the marriage of God to Israel), the very people who had experienced God's salvation from Egypt turned to the idols of their captivity (Exod. 32:1–6). This fact could mean only one thing. On the night of her marriage, Israel played the harlot.

Clearly, this understanding does not reflect that of Second Temple Judaism (the period of time between the return of the Jews from Babylon, and the destruction of the Temple in A.D. 70), when Israel basked in the law as though her unfaithfulness had never happened. Admittedly, she had been spared judgment by Moses' intercession, and a covenant making ceremony followed (Exod. 33:12–17; 34:1–10); but despite being given time Israel never repented and never returned to God.

It is this reality Paul discovered in his post-conversion days when he worked through the implications of what Israel had done to her Messiah. He abandoned the position he once held and acknowledged that the Jews too were in Adam and so under the same judgment as the Gentiles. The Jews lived thinking their sin at Sinai had never mattered, and that the law showered the covenant blessing on them as intended. In reality, the law now played a very different role. It condemned Israel to death— eternal separation from God. Their exile in Babylon many centuries later was a type of a far greater separation (in which Israel shares) that the whole of humankind experiences in the kingdom of darkness.

Justification as a Corporate Event

As we have seen, justification language was used to describe God's rescue of Israel from judgment in exile (see Isa. 45:25; 54:14; 58:8; 62:1). In each case the Hebrew expression tsādek is the equivalent of 'justify'. In other words, when God acted in righteousness towards Israel, he justified her.

In Romans five, the emphasis is on Christ. He is called the last Adam, who undoes the work of the first Adam by restoring his people to God. Justification language is repeatedly used; in fact, it is used more times in Romans five than in any other section of Scripture. So, the argument of Romans five is a thoroughly corporate one. It is about Christ recovering a people for himself; paralleling the saving event of the Jewish people when God recovered them from exile in Babylon and restored them to their inheritance and fellowship with himself. Thus, the exile of Israel from the Promised Land is a micro-version of the spiritual exile of humanity from their Creator's presence which was the fruit of the fall.

When Israel came out of exile, it was the community as a whole which God justified. So, the moment of Christ's death occasioned the collective act of justification for the church (Rom. 5:18–19; 6:7; 7:4). Paul works through a corporate application of this truth in Romans in order to show the covenantal status of the Gentile believers. He holds they do not have to submit to circumcision to have acceptance—it is the same issue he deals with in Galatians.

This argument does not deny that individuals must be justified but suggests each individual will become part of the justified community only when, by the Spirit's work, they believe. At conversion, the individual catches up experientially with what Christ has already done for all of his people (see chapter six for a discussion on the significance of baptism into Christ.) Each individual Gentile has to respond in faith to share in this salvation (Luke 3:7–8; 9:62; 12:21; John 3:16; Acts 2:40–41; 8:34–38; 17:34; Rom. 10:12–18) as faith and repentance are required before anyone can inherit the covenant's blessings. These blessings include forgiveness, reconciliation, inheritance, and all the other riches which are part of the good news of Jesus Christ. However, as we read the text of Romans (and other letters of Paul), we must keep this important element to the fore, that justification language is often, but not exclusively, corporate. This demands that we pay careful attention to the context of each use of the term in Scripture.

Justification and Covenantal Relationship

I have argued that Genesis 15:6 is about the creation of a covenant, and that this must govern how we understand the passage. Thus, as we have seen, the phrase 'counted to him as righteousness' in this particular context has nothing to do with acquittal of Abraham's sin.

Israel's release from exile meant she was acquitted (God declared her righteous) because she had no outstanding matter for which to account before his law. In acquitting her, God had not overlooked Israel's sins. She had paid the price for breaking the conditions of the covenant throughout her time in exile. He could justify her now, upholding her claim to be his covenant people. God did this by leading the remnant back to the Promised Land to retake possession of their inheritance, particularly the city of Jerusalem.

Additionally, Israel's justification was an act of corporate salvation in the sight of the nations. This was the proof to the nations she was the covenant people of God. Importantly, in bringing her back to Jerusalem, God was also justified. He justified himself before the nations that he really was the Creator God who had revealed himself to Abraham and kept covenant with his people. Paul echoes this double meaning in Romans 3:26, 'to demonstrate his justice at the present time, so as to be just and the one who justifies those who have faith in Jesus'.

At the heart of this second exodus was a new covenant, a new relationship. It was a covenant-making event when Israel was to be justified, counted righteous, given covenantal status, and made right with the God she had offended. This is significant, as it means Israel's justification was not only about her being declared to be in the covenant. It was primarily about her being brought into the new covenant.

The same truth applies to believing Gentiles—the 'many nations' Paul references in Romans 4:17—whom God has brought from darkness into this same new covenant and declared righteous as part of the new exodus in Christ. Like the Jewish believers, they too are acquitted from sin through the blood of the Paschal sacrifice; their transgressions forgiven, their sin covered, never to be counted against them (Rom. 4:7–8).

Conclusion of Introductory Considerations

I have suggested that the legal and accounting aspects of justification taught by the Reformers can be located in more appropriate texts than Genesis 15. Paul's application of Psalm 32:2 in Romans 4:6–8 is an example of this. It shows Israel in need of receiving both forgiveness (acquittal) for her 'lawless deeds' (Rom. 4:7), and 'righteousness apart from works' (imputation, Rom. 4:6). Hence the meanings at the heart of the Protestant doctrine of justification remain valid; yet if we are to avoid imposing a singular meaning of justification as a blanket over every instance where Scripture speaks of justification, then it becomes necessary to distinguish when the discussion relates to God dealing with sin, and when the discussion relates to God creating covenant relationships.

Many meanings fall under justification's semantic domain. At times it is about acquittal and imputation as taught by the Reformers, such as in Paul's use of Psalm 32:2 regarding David's sin. But we have also seen within justification the theme of salvation, God delivering his people from captivity as in the first exodus when Moses led Israel out of Egypt. It was the corporate community that came into a new relationship with God. While there is a very important place for individual justification, and no one can be 'saved' without this experience, we have seen how this is only accomplished through the individual's participation in the corporate righteousness which has come to God's entire community of the faithful—the descendants who share the faith of Abraham, whose number is as the stars in the sky (Gen. 15:5). Apart from 'salvation' or 'deliverance', there are two other uses of the Hebrew term tsādek ('justify')—and these were the focus of the Reformers. When something is deposited in a person's account, such as a bank account, he is 'credited' or 'justified' with the deposit. Also, when a person was found not guilty in a court of the charge brought against them, they were acquitted or justified. These are additional meanings of the term. God treats us as innocent people (crediting to us something that isn't ours, that is Christ's righteousness), and he dismisses all charges that are brought against us because of what the death of his Son has achieved.

Finally, there is justification in relation to God's act of creating a covenant with his people. This is the basis of his dealings with Abraham in Genesis 15 when the patriarch was justified—counted as righteous—and promised descendants beyond his imagining solely because of his faith. We found that Genesis 15:6—so central to the Reformers' doctrine of justification, and generally understood in relation to God's acquittal of sin—is not at all about sin, but rather about God making a covenant; initiating a new relationship by his sovereign choice which is entirely his to uphold. In similar manner Psalm 106:31 speaks of God justifying—counting as righteous—Phinehas and his descendants by bringing them into a covenant because of his reaction to Israel's sin; it was not simply about the acquittal of Phinehas's own sin. Covenant making is also at the heart of Paul's use of Genesis 15:6 in Romans 4 and elsewhere when he speaks of those—Jew and Gentile alike— who are brought by God into a covenantal relationship with him and declared members of his covenant community in Christ.

All of these things live within the doctrine of justification, with each meaning or theme having its own part to play, at times on its own, and at times in partnership with one or the other. Running throughout from start to finish, like a thread binding them all together, is the God who makes a covenant in order to reconcile 'the world to himself' (2 Cor. 5:19); restoring that which was broken in the fall of Adam. Justification as an all-encompassing doctrine cannot singularly be about any one of these meanings; but working together, each complements or enriches the other depending upon the context in which each is used.

Examining the Text

4:1 What then shall we say was gained by Abraham, our forefather according to the flesh?

Paul continues to anticipate the difficulties of the Jewish members of the Roman church as they listen to his letter. If he can demonstrate that the law was not instrumental in Abraham's acceptance, they might come to see that being justified by God does not depend on law-keeping. If Paul can establish this truth, he will have delivered a decisive blow to their objections to his all-inclusive gospel. It is necessary, therefore, to explain Abraham's relationship to the law so that his Jewish brothers and sisters may be convinced that the gospel of Christ, which welcomed both Jews and Gentiles, was not a challenge to God's covenant with Abraham, but rather its fulfilment.

All Jews held Abraham in the highest regard. Since they considered his words decisive in matters of faith, it was vital for them to know of any judgment which he had made. Abraham was not only their national ancestor and father but also a friend of God (Jas. 2:23), and the one with whom God had made the sacred covenant (Gen. 15:1–20). They all would have known the story of his life of faith from their earliest years (Genesis chapters 12–25), particularly his remarkable act of obedience on Mount Moriah, when he was prepared to slay his promised son in response to God's command. Paul, therefore, asks the question, 'what then shall we say was gained by Abraham, our forefather according to the flesh?'

4:2 For if Abraham was justified by works, he has something to boast about, but not before God.

Paul begins to answer the question he has just posed by considering Abraham's justification. Initially, he teases his Jewish readers by leading them in the direction of their own argument. However, at the point where they would have endorsed his words, Paul turns the argument around by adding, 'but not before God'. The point that he seeks to make is that even if Abraham had kept the law of conscience (there being no law in Sinai-terms at this point), and so deserved the praise and admiration of men, God knew the truth of his heart. Jews should have known this, as the narrative in Genesis does not gloss over Abraham's weaknesses and failings. It presents him as a flawed man who rose to be a great example of faith. God did not justify Abraham because he kept the law, but rather conferred on him a new status because of grace.

If we examine the Genesis passage, which speaks of the justification of Abraham (Genesis 15), we find it does not suggest, or even infer, that Abraham's sin was the issue. The declaration of justification (of being counted righteous) was in response to his belief that God would give him a son.

Romans 4: Committed Faith is not an Option

So, the question has to be 'what has the belief God would give Abraham a son to do with his justification?' If we believe justification refers solely to acquittal from sin (the normal understanding of Protestant theology), the answer has to be 'very little'; however, if justification is to do with God delivering his people from a condition that they cannot change, then it has to be 'very much'.

Promising the birth of this child was the beginning of the outworking of God's plan of salvation. This promise included God's commitment to deliver not only Abraham and his seed from slavery and oppression but the entire human race (Gen. 15:13– 14). Paul sees the full import of this when he reasons that the seed who was to bless the whole world is, in fact, Christ himself (Gal. 3:16). Abraham is the one from whom 'the offspring should come to whom the promise had been made' (Gal. 3:19). It was to be one of his descendants who would bring justification to God's people because he saves them from their sins; sins which had separated them from God.

4:3 For what does the Scripture say? "Abraham believed God, and it was counted to him as righteousness."

As noted, we must ensure we understand the use of being 'counted righteous' (justified) in the story of Abraham. We have considered above the different meanings of the term, where we noted Abraham's justification in Genesis 15:6 meant his being brought into the covenant inaugurated by God. While Reformed teaching interprets the act of being declared righteous as the acquittal of sin, we saw that—although a valid meaning elsewhere—it did not apply to Genesis 15:6; nor does it apply to all texts employing justification language. We also noted those who accused the Reformers of error have themselves misunderstood Paul. Too often they have focused on one meaning of the term (a declaration that an individual, or a people, is in the covenant) and have imposed it on texts containing justification terminology irrespective of context.

4:4 Now to the one who works, his wages are not counted as a gift but as his due.

Paul tries to explain the significance of the statement that Abraham's faith was counted as righteousness. To use a modern example, most people earn money as a result of their employment—their employers being obliged to pay—it is not counted as a gift. The covenant God made with Abraham (where God gifted him with righteousness) made no demands on the patriarch other than the demand of faith. Since Paul insists that faith is the gift of God (Eph. 2:8), we can see that the justification of Abraham was all of grace.

4:5 And to the one who does not work but believes in him who justifies the ungodly, his faith is counted as righteousness,

If we adopt the traditional legal meaning for 'justifies' in this verse, we have Paul saying God does the very thing he has said he will not do—acquit the guilty (Exod. 23:7).

The only way the conflict in this verse can be resolved is by appreciating that here Paul used the term 'ungodly' in a particular covenantal context. Those outside the covenant were called 'ungodly'. If we are to avoid imposing 'acquits' on 'justifies' for fear of having God doing what he prohibits, then we must choose the alternative meaning for the word that comes from the Psalms and the Prophets. There, the term speaks of God rescuing his ungodly people from their condition in exile and restoring them to their inheritance (Isa. 32:1; 54:14; 62:1–2).

In spiritual terms, Paul is saying that unconverted person is outside of any relationship with God because of their condition in Adam. He or she is ungodly, and therefore unable to meet the perfect demands of God (Rom. 3:23); his or her acceptance is possible solely because God delivers those who have faith in Jesus.

When someone is gifted with faith that God is trustworthy and has made a covenant into which he has been called, God responds by counting that person as righteous. In other words, God brings them into a covenant relationship. They are accepted as though they had kept the whole law and had done nothing to offend. They are removed from the kingdom of darkness and made to share in all the promises of God's mercy and grace.

The statement is worthy of repetition: being counted righteous in response to faith is much greater than just being treated as innocent. It speaks about

Romans 4: Committed Faith is not an Option

being the recipient of covenant promises and blessings. Also, it must be remembered that, while the discussion is rooted in how God justified Abraham, Paul's argument is not about individual salvation but the salvation of the Gentiles. It is about how they have come into the covenant with God. In other words, Paul's is a corporate argument; albeit that it is clear individuals must respond in faith, like Abraham, to be brought into the covenant.

It could easily go unnoticed that the description asebēs ('ungodly') applies to Abraham as well as to the Gentiles. Abraham, according to Genesis 17:43, was not circumcised until he was ninety-nine years old. But his encounter with God was several years before (when he was less than eighty-five). In other words, God justified him when he was a Gentile—when Abraham was 'ungodly'!

4:6 just as David also speaks of the blessing of the one to whom God counts righteousness apart from works:

Paul now turns to the justification of David, referencing David's thoughts in Psalm 32:2. Along with Abraham, he was a key figure in Jewish history and, as with Abraham, God made a covenant with him (2 Sam. 7:11–17)—a covenant the Jews still expect to be fulfilled. In introducing both Abraham and David, Paul plays a masterstroke. He can now put a case before his Jewish hearers that they will not be able to answer.

Abraham and David are the two giants of the Old Testament; they are regarded by Jews as great examples of men who pleased God. If these great men needed to be counted as righteous by God, there is no way an 'ordinary' Jew could be exempt from this necessity. Paul focuses on the extraordinary joy which floods into a forgiven person when he says David 'speaks of the blessing'; the word used is makarismon which has the same root as the word 'blessed' used by Jesus in the Beatitudes.

The danger we face when reading the text is to think that Abraham's need was identical to David's. However, whilst the problem for Israel's king was his sin, there is no suggestion that such was the case with Abraham. It is a presumption to assume a forensic meaning for 'being justified' in both cases. Another difference between Abraham and David is that, while

Abraham was brought into a covenant relationship with God, David was already sharing in that relationship as part of the covenant community.

The Reformed understanding of Psalm 32:2 is that it speaks of sinful David's justification, or acceptance, by God; an interpretation which is then used to support the need of justification for a sinner. This has a problem, however. It misses the fact that—in Old Testament terms—David already had that relationship with God. In New Testament terms, David is not seeking initial acceptance (which is what the doctrine of justification traditionally expounds) but is longing for the return of the fellowship which has been spoiled by sin.

What is identical between Abraham and David is that they are both men in need of the saving activity of God: Abraham as a Gentile, David as a fallen Jew. We need to remember that Paul is addressing Jewish objections to the gospel, and we would be failing in our exegetical task if we assumed the argument is identical for both Jews and Gentiles. To take that step of application without reflecting more carefully on the subject of the original statement, and David's status concerning the covenant, will cause us to lose the thrust of the argument. We must understand the meaning of the statements in their original settings before we look for legitimate extensions of their application. In other words, Paul is demonstrating the necessity of God's grace for those within the Old Testament covenant as much as for those being brought into it. God's grace maintains the covenant just as God's grace initially creates the covenant.

Thus, in Psalm 32:1–2 LXX, David speaks of the blessedness of the man 'whose transgression is forgiven, whose sin is covered'. Many would have observed David and said God blessed him because of his immense power and prestige. Having been born into a humble home, he progressed from shepherd boy to great military leader, and then became the King of Israel. This progression was not the result of burning ambition, but the result of God fulfilling his promise to him. This is clear in the way he exercised mercy toward Saul (1 Sam. 26:9–11). Most would have seen David's elevation to kingship as the pinnacle of blessing and happiness—but not David. For him, the blessed person was the one who had certainty about being right with

God, not because he had slavishly obeyed religious regulations, but because he knew the experience of God's forgiveness in his life.

The story of his fall is astonishing and painful. He descended from nobility to lust, then to adultery, and finally to murder (2 Sam. 11:1–27). Through a series of attempts at self-preservation David sank deeper and deeper into sin and guilt. His whole world, with its achievements and prestige, collapsed in ruins around his feet because he had thought himself to be exempt from the law of God. It is in this setting that we need to understand the relief that flooded David's heart when he wrote of the blessedness of those whose sins are forgiven. It was out of his personal experience that he wrote. What is also noteworthy is the absence of any clear reference to sacrificial ritual in the Psalm.

4:7–8 "Blessed are those whose lawless deeds are forgiven, and whose sins are covered; blessed is the man against whom the Lord will not count his sin."

Paul quotes this psalm of David for two reasons: firstly, it describes the stark contrast between guilt and forgiveness, contrasting men who are guilty before God with those who, having experienced forgiveness, have a new start in life where guilt and sin do not count against them. In this way Paul is able to drive home the seriousness and enormity of humanity's sinful condition.

Secondly, Paul quotes the psalm because King David composed it, lending weight to his argument. Jews saw David, as well as Abraham, as having a unique relationship with God; and as was the case with Abraham, so God had made a covenant with David. These two figures are not only important for Jews but for Christians as well; the New Testament writers continually stressing how the respective covenants made with these men have been fulfilled in Jesus. They are perfect examples of how God deals with Jews by maintaining the covenant with David (the circumcised), and with Gentiles by bringing Abraham (the uncircumcised) into the covenant. Contrary to much popular and scholarly opinion, Moses has little significance in the New Testament. While the covenant made with Israel at Sinai was important, it was only temporary (Gal. 3:24); moreover, it was not made personally with Moses, he simply acted as a mediator between God and Israel.

By placing Abraham and David before his readers, Paul delivers a blow to all in Rome who dared think they were special, having all they needed within their own religion. He seeks to use the example of these men to show the absolute necessity for everyone to be made right with God. God dealt with Abraham from outside of the covenant, and David from within. If such pillars of Israel needed to be counted righteous, it would be presumptuous in the extreme for anyone in Rome to deny their own need of justification.

4:9 Is this blessing then only for the circumcised, or also for the uncircumcised? For we say that faith was counted to Abraham as righteousness.

The danger remained however that some of Paul's fellow Jews in Rome—while agreeing Abraham and David were made right with God through faith in his promises—still thought these men were Jews. They could reason, therefore, that any who would know God's mercy must also become a Jew.

Paul was extremely anxious that the Roman church should resist this line of argument, for if Gentiles thought they had to become Jews to be made right with God, the gospel was at risk. It would mean that people did not become right with God through faith in the work of Christ but through a form of religious initiation. For Gentiles, circumcision would mean adding to the completed salvation God had given them through Jesus' death and resurrection (Rom. 4:25). If God had acquitted them of their guilt, what more could they do? Trying to add anything to this was tantamount to saying that Christ's saving act was insufficient.

4:10 How then was it counted to him? Was it before or after he had been circumcised? It was not after, but before he was circumcised.

To ward off the line of thinking that the Gentiles had to be circumcised, Paul puts before his readers the circumstances of Abraham's circumcision. He presses his readers to appreciate that, when God declared Abraham righteous, he was not circumcised. As noted earlier, he was not a Jew but a

Gentile! Furthermore, he continued to be uncircumcised for many years while in covenant relationship and fellowship with God.

4:11 He received the sign of circumcision as a seal of the righteousness that he had by faith while he was still uncircumcised. The purpose was to make him the father of all who believe without being circumcised, so that righteousness would be counted to them as well,

Paul's argument must have struck at the hearts of those Jews in Rome who had not appreciated that the Gentiles had equal status with them before God. Their belief in the uniqueness and privilege of Israel had preserved them and their ancestors throughout the nation's long history of suffering. This conviction of privilege was now being stripped away by one who had formerly been its champion.

It is difficult for Gentiles to understand what this argument must have meant to Jews who hold to the doctrine of the election of Israel as God's special people. True, Israel were elected, but their election was not intended to result in the exclusion of other nations; rather it was an expression of God's purpose that through Israel's witness the nations of the earth would also seek God and become his people (Gen. 12:3; Isa. 19:19–25; 42:1–4). Abraham was as much the father of the believing Gentiles as he was of the believing Jews. Indeed, the point Paul is subtly (yet powerfully) making is that when God made his covenant with Abraham, he was making it with a man who was a Gentile; with one who was not circumcised.

In this text, Paul speaks of circumcision as a seal of the righteousness Abraham had by faith. Some have sought to say this is grounds for linking baptism with circumcision, because the early church fathers spoke of baptism as being a seal. This association, however, although widely held, overlooks an important fact. Paul says the New Testament fulfilment of the symbol of the circumcised body is the circumcised heart (Col. 2:11–23). If we miss this typological fulfilment—whatever our view of baptism—we miss a vitally important part of the evidence of initiation theology. Because this heart circumcision is the work of God's Spirit, it is not of the will of man but of God (John 1:13).

4:12 and to make him the father of the circumcised who are not merely circumcised but who also walk in the footsteps of the faith that our father Abraham had before he was circumcised.

The new covenant, established in Christ, does not exclude Jews. Paul's argument is that it includes all who share the faith of Abraham. What Paul cannot accept is the idea of his countrymen claiming they had advantages over the Gentiles and trying to exempt themselves from God's salvation through the death of his Son. Paul is more than willing to concede the Jews had immense privileges (Rom. 9:1–5), but these were given in order that they may be prepared for the coming of the Messiah. Indeed, these privileges made them more responsible and in greater danger of judgment than the Gentiles (Amos 3:2). The Jews were given the law and could not claim ignorance of what God required. Paul, of course, has already countered any possibility of the Gentiles claiming ignorance of the law, writing that they had the law of their own consciences as had Abraham—a law they failed to follow (Rom. 2:14–16).

4:13 For the promise to Abraham and his offspring that he would be heir of the world did not come through the law but through the righteousness of faith.

The Jews believed their future inheritance was the consequence of having the covenant, and this in turn was the consequence of their being circumcised. However, this sequence of events reversed the progression of the Old Testament, where the promise of the land was given to Abraham before he was circumcised (Gen. 12:7; 17:11), as was his justification (Gen. 15:6). The Reformers understood the phrase, 'through the righteousness of faith' to mean a legal standing of innocence, and there are passages where it certainly does mean this (e.g. Rom. 5:17–19; Acts 13:38–52) but, in this verse, Paul is correctly following the meaning of Genesis 15:6 with its emphasis on covenant-making; just as he did in Romans 4:2 where he argued that being credited with righteousness was about God making a covenant with Abraham. If he echoes the same meaning here, then Paul is speaking of a relationship created solely because of God's mercy.

Romans 4: Committed Faith is not an Option

Thus, the gift of righteousness and the promise of the inheritance of the land of Canaan were independent of Abraham's circumcision; which God instituted as a sign that he had sworn an oath to him (Gen. 17:1–14). This oath had been made many years earlier, when Abraham was promised he would be the father of a mighty nation. The Jews, however, made a subtle but devastating change when applying this order of events to themselves. They came to believe that they had the covenant and had inherited the promises because of their circumcision, and for no other reason.

However, Paul understands the original promise of inheriting the land of Canaan (Gen. 17:8) as a promise to inherit the 'world'. This understanding had been slowly emerging in the Old Testament, as seen in the promise to the Davidic royal family at their coronation, 'Ask of me, and I will make the nations your heritage, and the ends of the earth your possession' (Ps. 2:8). Eventually, it was understood that, because God was the God of the whole earth (Neh. 9:6; Ps. 24:1–2; 96:1–5), his people's inheritance extended way beyond the original promise of Canaan to Abraham. Perhaps Paul is deliberately adopting this latter understanding because it served his purpose well. For Paul, the good news is for all the peoples of the earth; Abraham's children of faith are being found throughout the nations. They are the inheritance of Jesus, the Son of David; they will inherit the earth, and reign with Christ (Matt. 5:5; 1 Cor. 6:2).

4:14–15 For if it is the adherents of the law who are to be the heirs, faith is null and the promise is void. For the law brings wrath, but where there is no law there is no transgression.

Paul continues his argument by making two important points. Firstly, if the Jews believe the keeping of the law exempts them from the requirement of faith, their understanding of its purpose is erroneous. We have seen that scholarship has clarified how the unconverted Paul, along with most Jews, did not see the law as a constant threat. Most saw it as the instrument God had given to maintain the covenant into which he had brought them through his free grace. In the Jewish mind, the law (with its associated rituals) was about maintaining salvation, not about obtaining it.

It had been true that the law maintained Israel's unique relationship with God throughout the Old Testament, but now Paul is saying its task is completed. The promise has been fulfilled, for what the law pointed to has now arrived (Gal. 3:24). The promised new covenant, which would welcome Gentiles on an equal basis with Jews, had been established. Now, if the Jews insisted on maintaining a covenant that had served its purpose, they were rejecting God's ongoing plan for their lives. Paul challenges them to face the consequences of their understanding of the law's purpose. The Judaizers sought to turn the law into a means of salvation—something it was never intended to be. They had developed arguments about the need to keep it in order to control the Gentile believers. By insisting on circumcision, the Judaizers thought that they could determine who was admitted into the covenant.

They had no problem in Gentiles converting to Judaism and becoming people of the covenant, but what horrified them was the thought that this admission could occur apart from circumcision—that is outside of Judaism. Paul points out that, if they want the law to play this role, they are removing themselves from the grace of the covenant made with Abraham because their illustrious ancestor had not come into a covenant relationship with God through circumcision, but through grace. Now, if this was so, they had put themselves outside of the covenant and, to their horror, into the same condition as the Gentiles.

There are a number of logical consequences to this legalistic understanding of the law. The Jews are not only reconstructing its purpose, but also reinterpreting the covenant made with Abraham. If law-keeping is the condition of entrance, then the Abrahamic covenant is of no value (something no orthodox Jew could contemplate); hence faith has no value, and the promise is void. In other words, Paul is saying the Jewish understanding of Israel as the elect nation is a misguided illusion because it makes Abraham's faith worthless, the covenant wrongly administered, and Israel outside of it. And why is this so? It is because Abraham was counted righteous when he was not circumcised!

Romans 4: Committed Faith is not an Option

The ultimate outcome of Israel's nationalistic self-righteousness will be to bring down God's wrath. By removing herself from the principle of faith, she invites judgment by the law, which she knows brings wrath.

Secondly, Paul raises another consequence of their argument by saying, 'where there is no law there is no transgression'. Responding to the Jewish claim that the Gentiles were not under the law, he will show in the next section (from a line of argument familiar to Jewish thought) that guilt is only attributable when there is full knowledge of the law (Rom. 5:13). Paul in effect says, 'you are putting the Gentile believers outside of the law. Well, if you are going to be consistent, you are declaring them guiltless!'

The logic is devastating. Their argument against the universality of the gospel caused the Jews to put themselves outside of the grace they claimed was the essence of the covenant with Abraham while, at the same time, assigning the Gentiles, whom they were seeking to control, to the place where they could be heirs of the Abrahamic blessings. This was because Abraham was without the Jewish law when he was declared righteous, as it had not yet been given.

4:16 That is why it depends on faith, in order that the promise may rest on grace and be guaranteed to all his offspring—not only to the adherent of the law but also to the one who shares the faith of Abraham, who is the father of us all,

Having demonstrated the fault in their logic, that salvation is through the keeping of the law, Paul reminds the Jews that the promise depends on faith. This need not threaten them, as the promise embraces the Jews as well as the Gentiles. However, it does demand that they stop seeing themselves as the only race that God loves and accept that the love of God extends to members of all races; these too can be brought into the covenant on the same condition of faith as Abraham.

Paul's closing statement, 'Abraham, who is the father of us all', would have been bitter medicine for the converted Jews in Rome to take, but take it they must. If Jews wanted to continue to insist God was only their father and deny the Old Testament message (Isa. 2:1–5), they cannot enter into the salvation the prophets had long predicted. They must remain outside of the covenant, for at its heart was the blessing of the nations (Gen. 12:2–3).

4:17 as it is written, "I have made you the father of many nations"—in the presence of the God in whom he believed, who gives life to the dead and calls into existence the things that do not exist.

Paul seals his argument by quoting the very Scriptures the Jews professed to be defending. He quotes from Genesis 17:5, showing there is nothing in his argument about the inclusion of the Gentiles which is contrary to the law. Indeed, the law demands their acceptance. In pointing out that Abraham was made the father of many nations by God, Paul tactfully hints it is not what the Jews make of Abraham that matters, but what God made of him. For God declared in Genesis 17:5, 'No longer shall your name be called Abram, but your name shall be Abraham, for I have made you the father of a multitude of nations'.

4:18 In hope he believed against hope, that he should become the father of many nations, as he had been told, "So shall your offspring be."

The patriarch accepted that God would do what he had promised in giving him an heir (Gen. 15:2–4). He also accepted that he would have countless descendants, 'he brought him outside and said, "Look toward heaven, and number the stars, if you are able to number them." Then he said to him, "So shall your offspring be"' (Gen. 15:5). Abraham's quiet acceptance of this amazing news suggests blind, simple faith (Gen. 15:6). At this point the text records no reaction to this announcement, other than his believing God. We know that he was not stunned into silence, because he swiftly articulated his anxiety to know how he would gain possession of the land God had promised him (Gen. 15:8).

Why did Abraham 'in hope' believe so readily that God would give him a son when his ageing wife had a long history of barrenness? Perhaps the answer lies in the next chapter, where Scripture reveals Abraham was not averse to taking another wife (Gen. 16:1–4a). Perhaps he could accept that God would give him a son if he embraced the convention of the day and took an unmarried woman to bear his children, so building a family for Sarah through her. It is clear Abraham did not expect Sarah would be the mother of the promised son from his reaction to the news in Genesis 17, "'I will bless her, and moreover, I will give you a son by her. I will bless her, and she shall become nations; kings of peoples shall come from her." Then Abraham fell on his face and laughed and said to himself, "Shall a child be born to a man who is a hundred years old? Shall Sarah, who is ninety years old, bear a child?"' (Gen. 17:16–18).

Paul's statement that Abraham would become 'the father of many nations' was part of the prophetic promise God gave Abraham in Genesis 17, describing him twice in this way (Gen. 17:4–5). God gave Abraham this promise when he instituted circumcision and announced that Sarah was to be the mother of the promised son, and of many nations (Gen. 17:4–5, 16).

4:19–20 He did not weaken in faith when he considered his own body, which was as good as dead (since he was about a hundred years old), or when he considered the barrenness of Sarah's womb. No unbelief made him waver concerning the promise of God, but he grew strong in his faith as he gave glory to God,

The reference to Abraham's steadfast faith is clearly linked to the statement about the frailty of his body, and the barrenness of Sarah's womb. It is understandable why this verse has traditionally been identified with Isaac's conception, but we need to ask if this is what Paul had in mind. Could there be another event when the reference to the condition of their bodies and steadfastness of Abraham's faith would be equally, if not more, appropriate?

Indeed, such an alternative would be helpful, for it is not easy to defend the claim that Abraham's faith did not waver through unbelief at the time of his son's conception. He had laughed, after all (as had Sarah), at the promise of a child being born to them because of their advanced years, and her barrenness (Gen. 17:17). Furthermore, immediately after receiving the promise of Isaac's birth, Abraham acted in an astonishing way.

In his hundredth year there was famine in the land, and Abraham again moved his household down into the region of the Negev where he had travelled some twenty-five years earlier when he first came to the Promised Land. Now, upon entering Egypt, he feared for his life because of the beauty of his wife. She agreed to say that she was his sister (a half-truth—she was the daughter of his father Terah), with the result that she was taken into the palace to be Pharaoh's wife (causing him, in ignorance, to commit adultery). The truth of her marital state was eventually exposed, and Abraham and his household were expelled from Egypt (Gen. 12:10– 20).

Tragically, he repeats this scenario. The now justified and circumcised Abraham, having received the promise of the birth of Isaac, travelled to Gerar, and settled there. He told King Abimelech that Sarah was his sister as, once more, he feared for his life should the king desire her. Again, Sarah was taken as the king's new wife, and the plan of salvation was in jeopardy. As happened in Egypt, the truth of Abraham's deceit came to light, and he was reprimanded by a distraught king who restored Sarah to her husband (Genesis 20). As we have seen, this was not a failure of the moment, for Abraham had done this on other occasions as well, such as on entering the Promised Land he said to Sarah, 'This is how you can show your love to me: Everywhere we go, say of me, "He is my brother"'(Gen. 20:13).

It is to this narrative, at the time when Isaac was conceived, that traditional understanding applies Romans 4:19–20, which testifies that Abraham's faith did not weaken, and that his belief that did not waver from the promise he and Sarah would conceive a son in their old age. However, Abraham's behaviour in surrendering Sarah to Abimelech at the time of Isaac's conception challenges this judgment. I am not challenging the fact that Abraham was emerging as a man of faith. He believed the promise regarding the birth of Isaac. Hebrews 11:11 states Isaac's birth was the fulfilment of this promise. But Abraham's faith here is faithfulness to God in the midst of the trials of life, not the special capacity to believe in such a way that allows the miraculous to happen. At this point in his story, Abraham's faith cannot be described as steadfast and unwavering.

However, there is an event when Abraham did exercise such faith, and in a way that can only be described as remarkable. That event was the offering of his son Isaac on Mount Moriah. How many years after the birth of Isaac this event took place, we cannot be certain? The boy Isaac had been weaned and was old enough to carry wood upon his back and articulate his concern for the animal to be sacrificed (Gen. 22:6–8). Perhaps Abraham was about one hundred and five years old. Paul describes him as being 'about one hundred years old'. He cannot be definite as the Genesis text only hints at Abraham's age at the time of this event, despite being specific at other key events in his life. These include setting out from Haran (seventy-five), the birth of Ishmael (eighty-six), circumcision (ninety-nine), the birth of Isaac (one hundred), the death of Sarah (one hundred and thirty-seven), the marriage of Isaac (one hundred and forty), and his own death (one hundred and seventy-five). However, the physical condition of Abraham and Sarah at the time of Isaac's sacrifice would have matched Paul's description of their physical weakness mentioned in Romans 4:19–20. While the description would have applied at the time of Isaac's conception as well, it would apply even more so at the later time of Abraham's testing.

This test was a challenge that demanded an amazingly strong and unwavering faith. Having been given Isaac, his heir, Abraham was asked to sacrifice him as a burnt offering (Gen. 22:1–2). All the promises of the covenant God had made with Abraham rested in Isaac's fathering of a family. Nevertheless, Abraham set about obeying the command immediately, and left Beersheba for Moriah in the early hours of the following day (Gen. 22:3).

Such unquestioning obedience could only be displayed by a man of living faith—a man who believed God could bring life from the dead, something both he and Sarah had experienced first-hand with the conception of Isaac. It is in this context, after Isaac's conception, that Paul's description of Abraham's faith as unwavering is entirely appropriate. Having seen God bring life to his and Sarah's 'dead' bodies, Abraham had to believe that, when God asked for the life of Isaac—the heir of the promise—he would raise him from the dead to fulfil his covenant promises (Gen. 22:5). Hence Paul's glowing description of Abraham as 'having not weakened in his faith' cannot be about the time of Isaac's conception; but such a statement is entirely appropriate for him when he was about to offer his son to God.

Is Paul reflecting upon this incident in Romans 4:19–20? Is he reminding his Jewish opponents of Abraham's amazing act of faith and obedience? The sacrifice of Isaac shows him to have become the man of faith that Paul presents him to be. All the failures that marred his earlier life have paled into insignificance. He has become the God-fearing man he aspired to be in his younger years—doing what God asked of him, regardless of the cost.

He began this journey of faith when he obeyed God's call to leave Ur. He exercised faith when he believed God would give him an heir and countless descendants; a faith that resulted in the birth of Isaac. However, one could argue Abraham's acts of faith, while praiseworthy, had less than pure motives. With each exercise of faith there was gain for Abraham, and obedience was a 'sensible' choice. Moriah, on the other hand, was different. Abraham soared to the highest heights of faith when he took the knife to slay Isaac. He believed God would give life to the dead. Nothing can be attributed to the patriarch to cast a shadow of doubt over his motives. He was putting himself to death in the sacrifice of his son. In this act of faith and obedience, Abraham showed he believed God in a way he had never shown before.

This is the occasion of Paul's description of Abraham's faith. When God challenged Abraham to make a sacrifice of Isaac, he unflinchingly obeyed. Indeed, the rabbinic teachers pointed to this event when they wanted to demonstrate Abraham's faith. In their earliest texts, they were reluctant to speak of the sacrificial nature of Abraham's actions, stressing instead the obedience of Isaac. However, probably due to pressure from the early church's preaching of the liberating death of Jesus for those who believed, they moved their emphasis from the obedience of Isaac to the faith of Abraham. In this way, they were able to show that the Jews also had a sacrifice, their own beloved firstborn son, who had 'died' for Israel.

That the offering of Isaac is the focus of Romans 4:19–20 is further supported by the verses in Hebrews which reflect Second Temple Jewish understanding of Abraham's faith:

> *By faith Abraham, when he was tested, offered up Isaac, and he who had received the promises was in the act of offering up his only son, of whom it was said, "Through Isaac shall your offspring be named." He considered that God was able even to raise him from the dead, from which, figuratively speaking, he did receive him back. (Hebrews 11:17–19)*

Abraham's response to the command to sacrifice his son was to believe that since God had promised that Isaac was going to be heir then God would raise him from the dead. This step of faith flies higher than that required for a seemingly impossible birth to an elderly couple. It is the act of faith the Jewish Rabbis emphasize when they discuss the righteousness, and the consequent merits, of Abraham.

There are other reasons for following this reading of Romans 4:19–20. Throughout this chapter, Paul has presented Abraham as the father of those who have faith (Rom. 4:16). In his obedient departure from Ur, and later Haran, he was certainly an example to follow; just as the new exodus community followed her deliverer, the Son of David, out of the realm of darkness. In what way then is Abraham's faith in Isaac's conception also an example? One could argue he sets an example of waiting patiently for God to fulfil his promise; but the reality is, as we have seen, that he did not do this. Abraham wavered, except on Moriah, where we see him obeying in faith by preparing to sacrifice the son of promise. It is this event, and the faith exhibited within it, that Paul urges his readers to follow, for it is an amazing example to his seed, and the pinnacle of his faith.

But can the text support this reading? I believe it can in two ways. First, Paul's argument is moving towards its concluding statement, which is the glorious affirmation, 'But the words "it was counted to him" were not written for his sake alone, but for ours also. It will be counted to us who believe in him who raised from the dead Jesus our Lord' (Rom. 4:23–24).

In believing the Lord Jesus Christ has been raised from the dead, the Roman believers and Paul are true sons of Abraham because they share with him the same faith in a resurrecting God. Secondly, scholars who support this reading see the following statement, 'who was delivered up for our trespasses and raised for our justification' (Rom. 4:25) as an echo of the sacrifice of Isaac. This event is called the Aqedah—the binding of Isaac—when Isaac was given up as a sacrifice. In Paul's later statement in Romans 8:32, 'He who did not spare his own Son but gave him up for us all, how will he not also with him graciously give us all things?' If the scholars who make these suggestions are right, they lend evidence to Paul's focus on the sacrifice of Isaac.

It is clear that Abraham's faith grew from its wavering beginnings in Genesis 12 to its climax in Genesis 22, about which Paul could write that Abraham 'gave glory to God'. What is Paul referring to in this statement? Perhaps he is implying that Abraham had a right understanding of God and was able to trust him implicitly. Abraham had not elected himself, for it was God's plan and initiative to call and covenant with him. God was responsible from beginning to end, and Abraham gave him glory by trusting him on this darkest of days. Alternatively, Paul may have believed Abraham gave God glory in the way he named the mount on which he sacrificed the ram in Isaac's place, 'So Abraham called the name of that place, "The LORD will provide"; as it is said to this day, "On the mount of the LORD it shall be provided"' (Gen. 22:14). This name, which persisted for centuries, speaks only of God and his faithfulness. It is on this mount that David sacrificed, and here that Solomon built the Temple (2 Chr. 3:1). Abraham made no mention of himself as part of the mountain's name, for it focuses on God's faithfulness alone. Perhaps it was because of this that Paul can say Abraham 'gave [undivided] glory to God'.

4:21 fully convinced that God was able to do what he had promised.

Abraham was fully convinced God would keep his promise because he was God; Creator, sustainer, and deliverer. While there is no suggestion that there was a shadow of doubt in Abraham's heart, it is not the quality of his faith which is being emphasized, but the power of God to do what he had promised. Abraham took God at his word and treated the accomplishment of the promises as a certainty. His confidence lay in his knowledge that God would not go back on a covenant he had promised to fulfil.

4:22 That is why his faith was "counted to him as righteousness."

The theme of people being made righteous in the sight of God is fundamental to Paul's understanding of the gospel of Jesus Christ. As we have seen, it has become clear that the idea of 'counting as righteous' in this chapter is not exclusively, or essentially, about God imparting or even imputing his righteousness to humans. It is about his saving activity, by which he honours his covenantal promise made to the patriarchs. This does not remove the important truth of a person being made acceptable by God,

Romans 4: Committed Faith is not an Option

but it places that acceptance in the much bigger framework of Old Testament covenantal theology.

4:23–24 But the words "it was counted to him" were not written for his sake alone, but for ours also. It will be counted to us who believe in him who raised from the dead Jesus our Lord,

The story of Abraham is the story of all who believe. The covenantal transaction between God and the patriarch is the same as that carried out between God and his new covenant people. They believe in the God who promised, and if they call on him, he will answer in saving grace (Acts 2:38–41; Rom. 10:12–13). The significance of faith in the covenant promises is the same for the believer in Christ as it was for Abraham. It has no meritorious value; it is simply a faith that accepts God as the redeemer who acts in righteousness to bring salvation to his people. The comparison is clear. The birth of Isaac and the promise to raise him from the dead (implied in the story of his offering) is the same as the story of the birth of the church with its Jewish and Gentile children. The Jews and the Gentiles are not two separate entities, but one body in Christ; once they were both dead in trespasses and sins but now, they are equally raised to life in and through Christ. Together they share the promise of partaking in the resurrection, as the people of God.

As noted in the comments on vv. 19–20, the focus of Abraham being 'counted as righteous' has moved from the covenant-making occasion of Genesis 15:6 (cited in Rom. 4:3) to the mount Moriah event. In recognizing this shift, we find Paul stands on the same ground regarding justification as does James (Jas. 2:21–23). Someone who is justified by faith is one who can do no other than obey the command of the one who has called him or her. The works Paul and James speak of in their understanding of the doctrine of justification are not the works of the law, but the works of the law of faith; works demonstrated by those who believe on him who raises the dead.

The remarkable way in which Paul follows the story of Abraham, and the stages of God's dealings with him, is a testament to his lifetime engagement with the Scriptures of his people. It is also a salutary lesson to those of us who specialize in New Testament studies, who assume the Old Testament text is only of limited value for our sphere of specialization.

4:25 who was delivered up for our trespasses and raised for our justification.

Many see the clear echo here of Abraham's willingness to obey God in offering Isaac as a sacrifice (Gen. 22:1–19). However, this is not the only echo in this text. Paul has already written about the sacrifice of Jesus in Romans 3:25ff., where we found indication that the death of Jesus should be seen as the eschatological Passover. While these ideas are not unrelated (that is the binding of Isaac, and the Passover) the most dominant model for Paul is that of Christ being our Passover (1 Cor. 5:7). The idea of justification expands in this new exodus setting. In the original Passover, the lambs' death spared the Hebrew firstborn from judgment. When the Hebrews were brought out of Egypt to begin their pilgrimage to the Promised Land, both God and the Hebrews were justified—God was justified by the public fulfilment of his promises to his people, and the people's faith in the God of their fathers was justified by their public exodus.

By his Passover, Christ protected his people from judgment and secured their redemption. When Jesus was brought out of the tomb, having been delivered from the bonds of death, both he and his people were justified. Christ was justified by the public fulfilment of his promises to his disciples, and they were justified by their exodus from the kingdom of darkness because they had been made one with him in his death (Rom. 6:1–4); moreover, they now shared his resurrection (Eph. 2:6), and his justification, therefore, became their justification as they followed in the train of his victory over the forces of evil. God is just, and the justifier of those who believe in Jesus (Rom. 3:26). It is significant that, as we move into chapter five, we discover clear allusions to the Passover and the death of Jesus (e.g. Rom. 5:9); allusions that continue into chapters 6–8.

Further Study: Questions for Romans 4

1. What is the significance of Paul using Abraham and David to explain what justification means and who needs it?

Romans 4: Committed Faith is not an Option

2. Why is Abraham's uncircumcised state when he was counted as righteous important to Paul's argument?

3. List the various shades of meaning contained in the Hebrew word which is translated 'counted to him as righteousness.'

4. Does the law have anything to do with being justified?

5. In what way is Abraham 'the father of us all'?

6. What significance has the story of Abraham offering Isaac for explaining what justification means?

Romans 5: The Family Story

Introduction

As we come into chapter five, we find the themes of chapter four being picked up and applied to the church—the true children of Abraham (Rom. 4:18). Like Abraham, the church is justified (Rom. 4:9; 5:1), and experiences God's glory (Rom. 4:20; 5:2). Moreover, like Abraham the church's deliverance came when she was totally weak (Rom. 4:19; 5:6), and like Abraham she lives in hope.

Pilgrimage is a thread running through the Old Testament into the New Testament (Gen. 42:13; Exod. 15:22; Josh. 1:2; 2 Kings 25:18–20; Ezra 2:1), and this theme unfolds in chapter five with the recounting of the story of Adam and his disobedience which led to his (and our) exile. The mission of redemption is about the reconciliation of people to God, and their pilgrimage back into God's presence in the new creation.

Just as the Jews journeyed back from exile in Egypt or Babylon, believers have a journey to endure before they arrive at the goal of their salvation. So, Paul sees the deliverance of believers to be the first step in their eschatological pilgrimage. The journey will inevitably involve suffering and discouragement, but this will not deter them, because the Spirit is with them, and the hope of God's glory lies before them. Both the giving of the Spirit (Isa. 42:1–4; 44:3; 59:21), and the promise of sharing in God's glory (Isa. 45:25; 58:8; 60:1–2, 13; Jer. 9:23–24; Ezek. 43:4), are new exodus expectations which this new pilgrim community now shares.

The first deliverance from Egypt centred on the death of the firstborn sons, with sacrificial lambs substituting for the Hebrew firstborn. The church's deliverance centres on Jesus, God's only Son, delivered up to death to bring about his people's salvation (Rom. 5:6–8). The new exodus theme continues in the statement, 'much more shall we be saved by him from the wrath of God' (Rom. 5:9).

Paul reflects on the reason why this salvation is necessary. He explains the solidarity of humankind, and how its representative head (Adam) brought it into a state of alienation towards God through disobedience. Representative (or federal) headship refers to one who represents a group bound by a common cause or agreement, such as those in a covenant or federation; not only as its spokesperson, but as one whose decisions are binding on the larger group by virtue of the individual's role as representative. In contrast to Adam, who as representative head of the human race brought alienation from God, Paul calls Jesus the 'last Adam', (1 Cor. 15:54) who as representative head of the new covenant community, reconciles his people to God through obedience and suffering.

As we have seen, we must take care not to impose our own understanding on Paul's use of justification language. If this happens, we will miss important points that Paul is making. We have noted his understanding comes from the Law and the Prophets rather than the Roman legal system. It is not only that believers have been declared innocent (although this is an important part of his understanding), but also that God has rescued them from a hopeless situation, fulfilling his covenant promises. God did this when he reversed Abraham's impossible situation by giving a son to Sarah in old age, when he forgave King David of his guilt, and when he rescued Israel from exile.

Justification is the outcome of Jesus' death and resurrection, for he 'was delivered up for our trespasses and raised for our justification' (Rom. 4:25). God has been faithful to his promise to Abraham in delivering his spiritual descendants from the realm of darkness and bondage (Gen. 15:13–14). The kingdom of darkness in the New Testament is equivalent to Egypt or Babylon in the Old Testament where Israel was held in captivity. It is the realm where Satan rules, and where humanity is cut off from fellowship with God. In the Old Testament, justification was especially to do with God delivering his people from their captivity (Isa. 50:9–10; 53:11), and Paul is keeping to this theological perspective as he develops his argument (see also Col. 1:13–15).

Paul says this justification results from the achievements of the Lord Jesus Christ, as explained in Romans 3:21ff. (especially v. 24), and Romans 4:25 (where the setting is the death of Jesus). He has described Jesus' death as

Romans 5: The Family Story

the Passover sacrifice that delivered the people of God from captivity to sin. Just as Israel's deliverance from Egypt was her justification, so Christ's redemptive work is his people's justification. God has put away all matters that kept him from accepting sinners into his presence, and he is now able to welcome them without any compromise of his holiness. Justification is as much about the declaration of God's innocence of complicity in the sin of humanity as it is about their deliverance from the guilt that condemns them (Rom. 3:23).

The ESV (like most translations) tells us the outcome of this justification, which is that 'we have peace' (Rom. 5:1). This translates the Greek echomen. There is a possibility Paul never used this word. There are many ancient texts of the letter that do not have echomen, but instead have echōmen ('let us have peace'). Scholars divide over this. The oldest texts support echōmen, and strictly speaking this should be followed. However, this would mean Paul is appealing to his readers to be active in establishing peace with God. But the argument of the preceding chapters is that it is Jesus who has made peace between God and humanity. Because of this, peace is an established reality that the people of God are to enjoy, so most translators follow echomen ('we have peace').

However, if Paul is following the exodus paradigm, it makes sense to stay with the older and better-attested echōmen ('let us have peace'). The Jews, delivered from their miserable condition of slavery in Egypt, must have found the unfolding experience of the pilgrimage daunting. Even though God had judged sin in the Passover sacrifice and redeemed the Jews from Egypt through the blood of the lambs, the knowledge that they had to journey to Sinai to appear before God must have caused grave misgivings. They had seen what he had done to the Egyptians and may have feared what he would do to them. One can almost hear the plea of Moses that they should put their confidence in their deliverer. We shall see Paul envisages a similar setting when he writes in Romans 5:9, 'since, therefore, we have now been justified by his blood, much more shall we be saved by him from the wrath of God'. It is clear Paul sensed a need to encourage the Roman believers to be confident that God, having redeemed them from captivity, was not going to abandon them on their pilgrimage.

This is similar to the setting of 1 Corinthians 10:1ff. where Paul warns the Corinthians of the danger of coming under God's chastening even though they are his covenant people. In this warning, he turns to the texts which I am suggesting should also guide us in the unravelling of Romans five. He explores the typology of the exodus and shows how the Jews fell in the wilderness because of hardened hearts. Having peace with God, therefore, is something Paul is anxious for the believers to actively embrace and enjoy, for it has been secured through the death of Jesus.

5:1 Therefore, since we have been justified by faith, we have peace with God through our Lord Jesus Christ.

Despite the dispute over the phrase 'we have peace with God', there is no question about what the death of Christ has achieved. The Roman believers have been brought into this grace in which they now stand as a result of Jesus' death and resurrection. Just as Israel could stand before Mount Sinai to worship God because of the Passover, so the Roman church can stand in the grace into which she has been brought as a result of the death of her Passover, Christ Jesus (Rom. 4:25).

5:2 Through him we have also obtained access by faith into this grace in which we stand, and we rejoice in hope of the glory of God.

The ESV translates kauchōmetha as 'rejoice', but it is much stronger than that. It has the strength of 'exult'. In the Genesis account the pinnacle of God's creative work in which he revealed his glory was the creation of man. Man lost the glory of God because of the fall, but this glory was revealed again when God established his covenant with Abraham (Gen. 15:18). It was revealed yet again when the Jewish people were delivered from slavery (Exod. 14:17–18), when the law was given at Sinai (Exod. 19:7–9), when the Temple was dedicated under Solomon (2 Chr. 5:11–14; 7:1–3), and when the exiles returned from Babylon (Isa. 40:1–5; 58:8; 59:19).

For the Christian community, the glory of God has been displayed in the death and resurrection of Jesus (John 12:23; Rom. 6:4), and in the outpouring of the Spirit on his church (Acts 2:1–4). The final revelation of God's glory will be when the church has completed her eschatological pilgrimage (1 Cor. 15:42–55; Rom. 8:9–11). Then, as the 'new man' (Eph.

2:15) she will be the pinnacle of the completed new creation, when God will dwell with her and his covenant promises towards her will have been completed. Paul describes this future experience as 'the hope of the glory of God'. As the people of God have suffered throughout the ages, they have been encouraged by the promise that they will see their Lord—the one whose death made their deliverance possible. No wonder Paul tells them to 'exult'!

The reference to 'standing in grace' is a reflection of how, at Sinai, the Israelites stood before Yahweh as a redeemed community. Then, as now, God is taking a people to be his bride. That first exodus deliverance is a shadow of the redemption God has now accomplished in Christ. The people of God have been delivered from eternal condemnation, and their subservience to sin and Satan has been brought to an end. There has been an exodus from the kingdom of darkness, because those who were once slaves to sin are now free and are children of the living God. What greater grace could they experience? The church is the new covenant community called out of the kingdom of darkness to be the bride of the living God. It could be that Paul's use of the term 'access' reflects the idea found in the Old Testament that the royal bride had 'access' to her husband (Esther 5:2). If this is so, then Paul intended the term to be about God redeeming a people to be his bride, further enriching the exodus imagery. If this is correct, it underscores that the text is meant to be read corporately—something few expositors do.

In Romans 1:3 we saw the importance of Jesus being the priestly Son of David. In the Old Testament the high priest was commanded to marry a virgin (Lev. 21:14). We shall see marriage imagery lies at the heart of Paul's gospel (see comments on Romans 6:7; 7:1–4). The letter to the Ephesians tells us that Christ died to wash his church from every blemish so he might present her to his Father in heaven as a spotless bride (Eph. 5:25–27). In addressing the church in Ephesus, Paul also makes use of strong priestly language and imagery (Eph. 2:18, 21), presenting Christ as the Son of David (Eph. 1:20), which most scholars recognize to be an echo of Psalm 110:1; he is the priest-king who marries a virgin (Eph. 5:25–27).

In Hebrews Jesus is described as a great high priest. What is more, he is not an ordinary high priest for he did not belong to the priestly tribe of Levi, but a priest 'after the order of Melchizedek' (Heb. 5:1–5). He offered a sacrifice that was unique—the perfect sacrifice of his sinless life—and in so doing has made his people clean in God's sight (Heb. 9:11–14). The letter to the Hebrews also tells us Jesus prays for his people as the Old Testament priests did (Heb. 5:7–10), going before them to bring them into their inheritance in the Promised Land (Heb. 12:1–17).

A similar high priestly picture appears in Romans also. Jesus is the Son of David (Rom. 1:3) who is the Melchizedek priest (Ps. 110:1–4). He has sacrificed his life to secure redemption for his people (Rom. 3:21–25; 8:3, 32), and is now leading them on their pilgrimage to the Promised Land into the very presence of God. Thus, for 'Melchizedek' in Hebrews, we can read 'Son of David' in Romans. Both figures lead their people and pray for them.

5:3–4 Not only that, but we rejoice in our sufferings, knowing that suffering produces endurance, and endurance produces character, and character produces hope

Although the pilgrim community of the new exodus experiences difficulties, these problems are not to be viewed negatively, as though they had no purpose. God's grace is to be learned in the discovery of human frailties (Psalm 131). Paul's appeal that 'we rejoice [or glory] in our sufferings' is not a Christian version of Stoicism. Sufferings serve God's purposes, making the Roman believers—and Paul—focus on their inheritance which is not of this world (Phil. 3:20–21). Suffering was also part of God's purpose for Jesus in order for him to become a faithful high priest who could sympathize with his people's needs (Heb. 2:17–18). Paul is not alone in this view; it is shared by other apostles and reflected the understanding of the early church (Matt. 5:10–12; Acts 4:23–31; 1 Pet. 1:6–7; Jas. 1:2–4).

We might have expected Paul to write that suffering merely produces hope without interjecting perseverance and character. Yet a hope that concentrates on the cessation of suffering can be very self-centred and can fail to see the bigger issues with which God is concerned. Paul highlights the process of coming to true Christian hope because it is different from the

Romans 5: The Family Story

'hope' many have of a better tomorrow. It is a hope for the vindication of God in his creation. Thus, the hope of the Christian is pure, and centred on the glory of God. Paul supports this understanding with his comments on the last Adam's recovery of the glory of God for his people in Romans 5:12–19.

5:5 and hope does not put us to shame, because God's love has been poured into our hearts through the Holy Spirit who has been given to us.

The Holy Spirit led and protected the Jewish community on its pilgrimage (Isa. 42:1– 13; 61:1–11; 63:11–19). Paul is saying God has given the same Holy Spirit to the church in all of his fullness. The Spirit's presence means the church continually experiences the love of God. The Greek can mean either God's love for us or our love for God. The ESV and NIVTM prefer the former, because God's love for his people is the major theme of vv. 6–10. In addition, it is better to see hope as grounded in truth about God rather than in ourselves. The Greek verb *ekcheō* ('pour out') is used in the Septuagint version of Joel 2:28–29, and in Acts 2:17–18, 33; 10:45, as well as in Titus 3:6, where it speaks of God giving the Holy Spirit to people. This suggests that the pouring out of the Holy Spirit is not an individualistic experience but God's gift of himself to the church at its inception. His pouring out fulfils the prophecy of Joel that, in the last days, God would pour out his Spirit on all flesh. Such an understanding supports the corporate reading of the text. This does not deny the indwelling of the Spirit in the individual believer, but it puts that indwelling into its proper context. It is as members of the covenantal Spirit-indwelt community that believers experience the Spirit in their lives, and his presence is the guarantee that they will be brought to glory.

The hope the Christian believers in Rome have is not a vague wish for something better. It is the certainty of knowing God will fulfil his purposes. He is the God in whom they have trusted, who keeps his promises, and who gave up his Son to death in order to save them. He is the God who raises the dead, and he is not going to leave his saving work in Rome incomplete.

5:6 For while we were still weak, at the right time Christ died for the ungodly.

In his letter to the Galatians, Paul refers to the first coming of Christ, and his subsequent death, as being 'at the right time', or, 'when the fullness of time had come' (Gal. 4:4–5). Some have argued it was the right time because the Roman Empire had created conditions vital for the spread of the gospel. This is hardly likely to be the reason, as the gospel has spread as fast at other times in history without the facilitation of social, political or transport infrastructures. It is more likely the 'right time' refers to the time when humanity's inability to keep God's law was fully displayed, having exhausted any efforts to keep it.

Paul reminds his readers their salvation was not the result of their attainments but the result of the free love of God in giving his Son. His concern is to emphasize that the Christian life, from its beginning to its end, is a work of the grace of God. Just as no one can claim he deserved forgiveness, no one will be able to claim that he accomplished his pilgrimage in his own strength. The Old Testament covenant communities in Egypt and Babylon were powerless until God intervened. Likewise, the New Testament covenant community was powerless in the kingdom of darkness, and in a condition which only the coming of Christ, the Son of David, could reverse. The deliverance from Egypt was at the right time (Exod. 2:23; Ps. 69:13; Isa. 42:13–14; 49:8), as was the deliverance from Babylon (Jer. 51:7). For at these times, the people acknowledged their need and their dependence on God. Now, writes Paul, the time was right, and God sent his own beloved Son.

5:7 For one will scarcely die for a righteous person—though perhaps for a good person one would dare even to die—

Paul encourages believers to reflect on the death of Christ. He reasons from human experience. He points out that for someone to be willing to die for another is a rare quality. He does not say it never happens but, when it does happen the motive is usually love or admiration. When Paul writes about God demonstrating his love, he is going to the very heart of the gospel. The gospel is not about a philosophy or a religion—it is about the saving activity of a loving God toward undeserving humankind in their need.

Romans 5: The Family Story

5:8 but God shows his love for us in that while we were still sinners, Christ died for us.

This is the unique characteristic of God's love. He loves his enemies and pays the ultimate sacrifice for their benefit and blessing. The corporate dimension of Paul's argument is clear, for he does not say, 'while you were still a sinner' but 'while we were still sinners'; Christ died for the community. Paul uses the present tense in the opening phrase of the verse, indicating the benefits of the death of Jesus are a present reality.

5:9 Since, therefore, we have now been justified by his blood, much more shall we be saved by him from the wrath of God.

Paul's reasoning is straightforward. If the death of Jesus has saved (that is justified) us—delivered and brought us into covenant with God through his blood—how much more will the life of Jesus save us! It is not that Paul is arguing that the life or example of Jesus has saving effect; for he has already made clear that Jesus had to die for the salvation of his people (Rom. 3:21ff.). Rather, the life Paul is referring to is Jesus' resurrection life in heaven where he serves as the mediator, or high priest of his people. He can represent believers in this way because he made the necessary sacrifice for his people's sins. Paul is reasoning that, because the death of Jesus turned away the wrath of God when we were his enemies, the presentation of the evidence of that death in heaven will turn God's wrath away from his people when they stumble and fall on their pilgrimage.

The image of Jesus, the high priest defending his people from God's wrath, echoes the imagery of the exodus narrative from Egypt. When camping at night the Levites, who had been substituted for the firstborn, were positioned in their tents between the tabernacle and the people, so that God's wrath did not fall on the other tribes (Num. 1:53). The Levites functioned as a living propitiation, protecting the people against the wrath of God.

5:10 For if while we were enemies we were reconciled to God by the death of his Son, much more, now that we are reconciled, shall we be saved by his life.

Paul repeats what he has been saying but in a slightly different way to emphasize his point. The repetition helps us to see how he uses his theological vocabulary; for Paul reconciled means justified and being saved means being saved by Jesus from the wrath of God. It is easy to imagine that Moses would have urged the Jews to appreciate they did not need to live in fear of God, as his love and concern were evident in that he had delivered them from Egypt.

They had no need to fear, therefore, that they would be consumed when the glory of God was revealed at Mount Sinai, because God had demonstrated his love in redeeming them from their captivity in Egypt. This is the point Paul is making, but with one exception—this redemption was not at the cost of the life of a lamb, but at the cost of the life of God's beloved Son. He supports the parallel with Moses by the mention of blood in v. 9. It is the first recurrence of the subject since it was mentioned in Romans 3:21ff. where it was clearly Passover blood that was being discussed.

5:11 More than that, we also rejoice in God through our Lord Jesus Christ, through whom we have now received reconciliation.

As the Roman believers fully appreciated what God has done for them through the death of his Son, they could not but be amazed and worship; not in cold recognition of God's greatness but in overwhelming appreciation of his personal love for each one of his people.

Paul does not write that he is hoping that the Roman believers will be made right with God on a future day, for their reconciliation is a present reality. God does not put new believers on probation to see how they get on as Christians before accepting them. He accepts all of his people as repentant sinners because his Son's death has satisfied his holiness.

The Messiah King and His Mission of Recovery

It might seem that in Romans 5:12–21 Paul is introducing a new subject without preparing his readers for it, but this is not so. As we have already seen, the typical Western mind approaches the letters of Paul from an individualistic perspective, interpreting all the descriptions about the work

Romans 5: The Family Story

of God in the light of individual Christian experience. This was not the way that the early church understood Paul's writings. The letters were to churches about the work of God for his people, and the arguments they contained were inevitably corporate. The change of perspective most of us detect once we get to v. 12 is not Paul's but ours—and it is false.

Having argued for the security of believers (or rather of the church) in Romans 5:1–11, Paul next considers what God has achieved by the death of Jesus. Paul uses an illustration with which Jews were familiar. Adam was the first man and is therefore the father of the human race. His status makes him unique in that he is the federal head of the entire human family. However, this has had dreadful consequences for, when Adam 'fell' in Eden, God's judgment fell upon him and all his descendants because of his decision to disobey God, and in effect join himself with Satan. We are familiar with the concept of federal headship in nation states. When a Prime Minister or President makes an international agreement, it is binding on all their people regardless of the lack of any individual participation in the decision making process. All citizens are part of such covenant communities. History is full of prominent individuals whose actions as a federal head have affected the lives of the peoples and nations they represent—Adolf Hitler being a prominent and ignominious example. As the country's representative head, when he declared war, he caught up every member of the German race in its awful consequences, drawing decent, family-loving, honest people into a state of alienation from other nations, whether or not it was their desire.

This is the argument Paul is now making. Adam represents the entire human race. He is the father of mankind with an all-embracing headship. When he sinned and broke off his relationship with God, he took all of his offspring with him into darkness. Not only was Adam cut off from God, but so too was every one of his descendants. In biblical terms, the doctrine of original sin has nothing to do with an inherited, inherently distorted nature; it is about being in a condition of enmity towards God because of the sin of our father Adam. To be born in sin is to be born into the rebellious human race. It is about being part of the kingdom of darkness that Adam's rejection of God has established. As children of Adam, all humankind shares in that same sin and rejection of God. The root of Paul's doctrine of the sin of all mankind is rooted in Adam's disobedience and the covenantal relationship with Satan (sin) that he, Adam, established. To be in sin is to be in Adam, and through him, to be in a covenant relationship with sin (Satan).

As we read this section, we must be careful not to read into the text something Paul has not written. He does not say that sins have entered into the world; he says that sin has entered into the world. This is not splitting hairs. When Paul speaks of sin in chapters 5–6, he refers not only simply to wrongdoing but also to Satan as the one responsible for all wrongdoing. We will see in chapter 6 Paul continually contrasts sin (and hence Satan) with God. They are opponents, and God calls humankind to obey him rather than Satan.

Paul is saying that, through the sin of Adam, something catastrophic took place. Not only did man lose the fellowship with God for which he was created, but also Satan stepped into the gap in that broken relationship. Indeed, he was the cause of the broken relationship in the first place, because he sought to separate man from his Creator. Having achieved this aim Satan entered the world and took control, leaving man a helpless victim. From then on, humanity's destiny was bound up with the purposes of Satan. This is a dramatic reversal of all God intended for man and makes sense of his subsequent history. Paul states that death itself is the consequence of sin coming into the world.

However, there is another side to the fall not generally recognized. In the writing of Hosea, God comments on Israel's unfaithfulness to him, saying, 'But like Adam they transgressed the covenant; there they dealt faithlessly with me…In the house of Israel I have seen a horrible thing; Ephraim's whoredom is there; Israel is defiled' (Hosea 6:7, 10). Israel's sin at Sinai, which involved the rejection of God in favour of other gods, was a repeat of the sin of Adam. The Israelites' behaviour in worshipping the golden calf is a repetition of what happened in the Garden of Eden.

This introduces another dimension into our understanding of the fall. When Adam disobeyed, he took another as his god. He deliberately put himself under the control of Satan. Satan took the place of God and became the husband. Thus, the fall was an act of spiritual adultery for which Adam was judged, being expelled from the Garden and the presence of God in the same way Israel was to suffer expulsion from the Promised Land and the presence of God. Both man and nation had turned their backs on their Creator, taking other gods in his place.

Without this covenantal perspective of the fall there are great difficulties in interpreting Paul's writings; many resort to changing his text in order to fit within an individualistic mind-set, and so make him appear to say what he did not write (for examples of this see comments on Romans 6:7 and 7:1–6). In contrast, the corporate covenantal approach taken here becomes a key that enables us to unlock Paul's intended meaning in the next two chapters. In saying all sinned in Adam, Paul is emphasizing people groups rather than individuals. He is cutting across any Jew who might have thought he was exempt from having to receive the same salvation as the Gentiles.

5:12 Therefore, just as sin came into the world through one man, and death through sin, and so death spread to all men because all sinned—

Rather than giving the opening of the verse as 'therefore', a better translation would be 'so it comes about'. Paul now describes the disintegration of the first family recorded in the Genesis account and the emergence of idolatry with all of its consequences. For the first time in the letter, Paul specifically introduces Adam, although we have seen his shadow since the opening chapter, where the decline of human morality was outlined (Rom. 1:18–32).

The story of Adam is important in Paul's theological system. Because of Adam's rebellion, his family (humankind) became truly dysfunctional, no longer loving or obeying its Creator. This ancestral rebellion, brought about by the representative head, is the basis of Paul's doctrine of sin as well as his explanation of the way Christ has brought about redemption. The story is found within key passages about the work of Christ (such as 1 Cor. 15:20–28; Phil. 2:4–11; Col. 1:12–21). Adamic Christology is also a crucial part of Paul's teaching concerning the identity and status of Jesus.

5:13 for sin indeed was in the world before the law was given, but sin is not counted where there is no law.

Paul reflects on the history of humanity as recorded in the book of Genesis. For a Jew, the law means the Mosaic Law, that is, the law given through Moses when Israel assembled at Mount Sinai after her release from Egypt (Exod. 19–20). In reality, God had given his law to Adam when he commanded him not to eat of the tree of the knowledge of good and evil (Gen. 2:16–17). The breaking of that law ruptured the relationship between God and man, allowing Satan's reign of terror over the human race.

Paul says that in the absence of law, sins (personal wrongdoing) are not held to account. He has already spoken about a law of the conscience by which God will judge the Gentiles (Rom. 2:12–16). This inward law obviously operated during the period from Adam to Moses, and for the Gentiles after Moses, but Paul seems willing to accept that this law does not have the same authority as the objective written Law of Moses. No Jew would want to concede that the law of conscience would stand comparison with the Mosaic Law for authority and privilege. This latter law was the sole property of the Jewish people and evidence of the covenant that bound her as a nation to God (Rom. 9:1–5).

Even though there was no Mosaic Law in that epoch, death was universal. As death is the consequence of sin there must have been 'sin'—but Paul has said God does not count sin in the absence of the law. Therefore, the sin that caused death before the giving of the law cannot refer to the sins of the descendants of Adam, but to the sin of Adam himself. His act of disobedience opened the door to the reign of Satan, bringing into existence the covenant relationship with Satan (sin) into which every human being has been born.

For Paul, Adam's sin is the sin of the entire human family. When Adam rebelled against God and accepted the prize with which Satan seduced him, his whole progeny was plunged into spiritual chaos and alienation. The evidence for this all- inclusive alienation is that humankind dies. An individual's guilt affects not only the individual but has consequences for the community to which he or she belongs. For this reason, the issue is not whether one is a good moral citizen, but whether one is in Adam or in Christ. In Adam, men and women remain in bondage to Satan by virtue of Adam's headship; in Christ, they belong to God by virtue of Christ's headship. For

Romans 5: The Family Story

Paul, this is the reality that all unbelievers need to be confronted with. They are members of the family of Satan from which there is no escape unless they call on the crucified and risen Lord.

5:14 Yet death reigned from Adam to Moses, even over those whose sinning was not like the transgression of Adam, who was a type of the one who was to come.

When Paul speaks of death having reigned, he means that it had absolute rule. For Paul, this is the conclusive evidence that all share in the sin of Adam. The absence of the Jewish law (not given until Sinai) meant individuals did not suffer death for the sins they had committed, and Paul has already conceded that sin is not reckoned when there is no law (v. 13). The sin that brought about the death of all who lived before Moses must therefore have been Adam's.

Naturally, many complain at being punished for the sin of Adam. But the solidarity that has brought judgment on all humankind is also the mechanism of salvation for everyone who would be freed from separation and judgment. Paul indicates this when he writes of Adam as 'a type of the one who was to come'. Because of humanity's solidarity with Adam, judgment has come on all; but the same principle of solidarity will become the means by which people can become righteous. This is because another representative head, the second (or better, final) Adam was waiting in the wings to come on to the stage of human conflict.

Even though many object to this corporate guilt, it cannot be denied to be at the heart of human existence. Those among the German people who were complicit with Hitler shared also in his guilt. The passengers on the Titanic shared the consequences of the flawed design that caused the vessel to sink. And the human race shares in the consequence of Adam's sin. It is at the heart of being human; and we are all bound to the guilt and failing of one another, and especially to Adam our family head.

5:15 But the free gift is not like the trespass. For if many died through one man's trespass, much more have the grace of God and the free gift by the grace of that one man Jesus Christ abounded for many.

Paul wants to show how Jesus reversed the catastrophic effects of Adam's sin. While Adam's sin brought death to all people, Jesus' obedience brought life to many. Despite the difference in their achievements, the same principle of federal headship applies. Jesus is head of a new humanity, doing for his people what they are unable to do for themselves, bringing about salvation from the curse of sin and death.

Paul describes the distribution of God's grace as *perisseuo* ('overflowing'), suggesting its immediate availability. Paul also emphasizes that the gift is the product of the 'grace of God' and 'the grace of that one man'. What happened on the cross was not a conflict between the Father and his beloved Son, but the perfect and gracious outworking of their loving concern for lost humankind. Indeed, as we shall see in chapter eight, this reversal of Adam's sin not only benefits humanity, but also the whole of the cursed creation (Gen. 3:14–19).

5:16 And the free gift is not like the result of that one man's sin. For the judgment following one trespass brought condemnation, but the free gift following many trespasses brought justification.

In this verse, Paul develops the difference between the sin of Adam and the obedience of Christ. Adam's one act of disobedience brought devastation on all humankind, but Jesus, the gift of God, reverses the guilt of all who call for mercy.

When Paul says the gift of Christ 'brought justification' he means more than acquittal from guilt. As seen in the discussion of Romans 4, the prophets spoke of Israel being justified when God released her from a condition of slavery and returned her to the Promised Land where she could enjoy her covenantal relationship with God. Paul has previously insisted the gospel is the fulfilment of the Law and the Prophets (Rom. 1:2; 3:21). As a corollary, he claims the death of Jesus rescues those who call on the name of the Lord, for they receive the same gift of mercy that rescued Israel from her condemnation. As with Israel, God brought the Roman believers out of an alien community into a new one whose head is the last Adam. What Jesus achieved is the recovery of what was lost through the fall, just as God recovered for Israel what she had lost in her exile. By his death, Christ has

Romans 5: The Family Story

rescued the elect from the kingdom of darkness and has brought them into the kingdom of light (Col. 1:13–14).

In writing that 'the free gift following many trespasses brought justification', Paul is saying that the gift of God brought righteousness. Justification and righteousness are the same, and refer to God's saving activity for his people, bringing them back into the relationship they had with him before the fall.

5:17 For if, because of one man's trespass, death reigned through that one man, much more will those who receive the abundance of grace and the free gift of righteousness reign in life through the one man Jesus Christ.

Paul cannot allow his readers to misunderstand the significance of Jesus' obedience and death. Once again—though in a slightly different way—he states the consequences of the good news of Jesus. Paul takes his readers systematically through the saving event in order to clarify the significance of the cross and the atonement which Christ has secured. He begins by writing that 'death reigned through one man'. In v. 12, he wrote about sin entering the world through one man's disobedience; in other words, sin took control.

When Paul speaks of 'the free gift of righteousness', he has two truths in mind. First, the state of innocence that people have before God when he forgives them because of Jesus' death. When God looks upon those he has saved through the death of his Son, he sees nothing but the perfect obedience of Jesus. In other words, God declares his people righteous, innocent, and sinless; with all traces of the effects of the fall eradicated. Second, while this truth of being made right with God is remarkable, it is possible Paul has even more in mind. For God not only delivered his people from sin's reign through the death of Jesus, but he also actively maintains that freedom. If God did not involve himself in protecting his people, then he would not be righteous—a suggestion the Scriptures could never countenance. This aspect of the righteousness of God is at the heart of the church's security. God is committed to saving and protecting those who have believed on his Son, who are his people.

This direct involvement of God in the salvation of his people is the result of 'the abundance of grace'. The point Paul is making is that God's people cannot enter into a situation where there is not sufficient grace to meet their need. The word charis ('grace') is more than agape ('love'). It speaks of love within a covenantal relationship. A courting couple may love each other, but within marriage the term 'love' is inadequate. There it is charis—covenant love, a love unreservedly committed, staying faithful until death to the one who is loved. God has covenantal love for his people because they belong to him through Christ. He loves his people in a way he does not love the world and because of his covenantal love, he makes demands on those who are its objects (e.g. Amos 3:2). God expects and demands the love of their hearts in glad response (Jas. 4:5; Heb. 10:29–31; 1 Pet. 4:17).

When Paul says, 'much more', he is referring to what has yet to happen. Believers are to 'reign in life through the one man Jesus Christ'. What does Paul mean by reigning in life? It is possible he intended it as a contrast to their condition in Adam when they were dead and ruled by sin and Satan. Now, in Christ, they reign! This is certainly the idea expressed in Ephesians 2:2–8, and forms part of the thinking behind the opening of Romans 6. It could also refer to the future kingdom, when believers will rule on Christ's behalf (1 Cor. 6:1–2); but it is not impossible that both meanings are included in the phrase.

5:18 Therefore, as one trespass led to condemnation for all men, so one act of righteousness leads to justification and life for all men.

Paul is anxious that his readers do not miss the scope of the redemption achieved through Christ. As all were condemned through the sin of Adam, so all will enter into life through the obedience of Jesus. This does not mean that all those who have been condemned now have life. Such a view is known as universalism, which holds that God will grant everyone life, even those who have never faced up to their guilt. Such an argument misses the comparison Paul is making. He is not arguing that all will be saved, but all who are of a certain status will be saved. In other words, God has made righteous and will save all those that although once under the representative headship of Adam, have now come under the representative headship of Jesus. To argue for any other position would be to ignore Paul's other letters and the Scriptures as a whole (e.g. Rom. 1:16–18; 1 Thess. 2:9–16; Eph. 2:3; Heb. 2:1–3; 9:24–27). Therefore, Paul is saying God will save all who belong to Christ, just as all who are in bondage to Satan because of the fall will be lost.

5:19 For as by the one man's disobedience the many were made sinners, so by the one man's obedience the many will be made righteous.

As we draw near the end of this section, we cannot escape the fact that Paul has continually repeated himself—albeit with slight changes of emphasis. The only sensible conclusion one can come to is that he was exceedingly anxious to be clearly understood on this matter; indeed, it is the crux of the Christian gospel. The failure to appreciate the truth of humanity's sin in Adam—and its undoing by Jesus—is at the heart of much misunderstanding in the Christian church. If the church does not get it right, what chance is there of the world properly understanding the gospel?

Paul is presenting a far bigger picture of Jesus than as humanity's sin-bearer. He is presenting Jesus as the last Adam. This image is the basis for much of how Paul understands the significance of Jesus and his death. The ancient hymns found scattered throughout the New Testament documents clearly show the importance of this imagery for the early church. They are based on the understanding of Jesus being the last Adam (Col. 1:3–21; Phil. 2:6–10; Heb. 1:1–6) and summarize the early church's doctrine in the same way modern hymns reflect the doctrine of the church today. Adamic Christology was foundational for the apostles' thinking. It stressed, among other things, that the exile from God, brought about through Adam's sin, has been ended by the obedience and suffering of the last Adam, Jesus Christ.

5:20 Now the law came in to increase the trespass, but where sin increased, grace abounded all the more,

The seriousness of humanity's condition demands that it be seen for what it is. Paul says that this was the purpose of the law given to the Jews at Mount Sinai. It acted as a mirror for the chosen people, enabling them to see their wretched condition and understand there had to be a sin offering to remove their guilt. Under the Law of Moses, an elaborate sacrificial system was established so the Jews could approach God and seek his forgiveness (Heb. 9:13). Ultimately, these sacrifices were never intended to remove Israel's sins (Heb. 9:9), but to teach her that a price had to be paid when the law was broken (Heb. 9:22). The law's purpose, with its sacrifices, was to point the way to a perfect representative or champion who could remove sin. It was God's intention to be the champion of his people—to remove their sin and guilt and restore them to innocence and unspeakable blessing. For this reason, Paul can say, 'where sin increased, grace abounded all the more'.

5:21 so that, as sin reigned in death, grace also might reign through righteousness leading to eternal life through Jesus Christ our Lord.

Paul writes that sin and death are the co-regents which rule over humanity, holding people in bondage. Unless humankind can escape from this situation brought about by its federal head Adam, there is no hope. But as one man's disobedience brought the reign of death, so through one man, Jesus Christ, we can be brought into a new eschatological community (Eph. 1:13–22; Col. 3:8–14; Rev. 1:5–6) where instead of death, eternal life reigns.

Further Study: Questions for Romans 5

1. What are the indicators that Paul has the exodus of the Jews from Egypt in mind as he writes the first eight verses?

2. List the features of the first eleven verses that suggest the argument is at the corporate level and therefore clearly linked with the latter part of the chapter, which is all about a community under its representative head.

3. What did Adam's disobedience result in?

4. What did Christ's obedience result in?

5. How does Paul explain the link between Christ's obedience and God's free salvation?

Romans 6: The Messiah King and His People's Deliverance

Introduction

Paul has been presenting a history of the human race, explaining the dire consequences of the fall and how the Jews are not exempt from the need of salvation despite having been chosen in Abraham and delivered from slavery through Moses. He has made clear in the preceding chapter that all people are either 'in Adam' or 'in Christ'. These two men are the key representatives of human history who determine the destinies of their members. It is clear how people came to be 'in Adam' for that is their natural condition as his descendants. But how do people come to be represented by Christ, and how did this new community come into existence? This is what Paul answers in Romans 6. He tells how the Spirit of God brought a new covenant community into existence through its participation in the death of Christ.

The background of Romans 6 is found in the previous chapter, where Paul discusses the existence of two communities: one in Adam and the other in Christ. The apostle describes how the members of these communities share in the transgression or obedience of their respective heads. I will argue that the expression 'the body of sin' (Rom. 6:6) is the unredeemed community which has Adam as its head. If this community argument is accepted, then the description of baptism in Romans 6:1– 4 lies between two corporate arguments. I therefore suggest that this baptism also has a corporate dimension rather than the commonly held individualistic one.

Baptism has divided the church for many centuries. To this day, opinions differ as to the significance of the ordinance. While the view that baptism was derived from the 'mystery' religions has declined in popularity, there is still no clear consensus as to the origin and significance of the rite. What is generally agreed is that baptism is closely associated with the death of

Christ, and that Paul used the exodus of the Jews from Egypt as a 'type' in his exposition of its significance (1 Cor. 10:1–4). There is also some agreement that there are texts where the emphasis is more on the inclusion of believers into Christ's baptism into suffering rather than baptism in water. In these texts, water is not the medium of baptism; all that is present is a historic recounting of what happened at Calvary.

Baptism in Romans 6

Interpretations of baptism in Romans 6:1–4 include: regeneration via baptism, water baptism as a symbol of regeneration, the Spirit's baptism of the believer into the body of Christ at conversion, and water baptism as a symbol of having died with Christ at his Passion. Those who hold the latter view are divided into two groups: the first see water baptism as the occasion when the Spirit is given and the benefits of Calvary are imparted to the believer, whereas the second group believes that the Spirit is given before baptism, with baptism being no more than the means of confession rather than the occasion of regeneration.

The problem with linking the baptism of Romans 6:1–4 with any interpretation involving water baptism is that it requires 'water' to be introduced into the text when there is no mention of it in the entire letter. Indeed most baptisms in the New Testament do not involve water; there is a baptism into or unto repentance (Matt. 3:6; Acts 2:38), baptism in the Holy Spirit (Luke 3:16; 1 Cor. 12:13), baptism into suffering (Luke 12:50; Mark 10:38), and baptism into Moses (1 Cor. 10:2). We do have a baptism in water in Acts 8:36, but clearly one needs to be careful to choose the right concept and not to automatically assume water baptism is the focus, until all other options have been considered to see if any make better sense of the passage.

What is common to virtually all the interpretations of Romans 6:1–4 is that the experience of baptism of the individual believer is read into the passage. But Paul in 1 Corinthians 10:1ff. speaks of Israel's baptism into Moses, a baptism in which the whole community shared at the same decisive moment, and I suggest that Paul is using the word in the same way here. He is referring to a major, redemptive event which happened long before the work of regeneration in the individual took place— and that event was Calvary. The baptism Paul speaks of in Romans 6 is the ground upon which the Spirit does his work in the church or in the individual believer; it is in this baptism that the saving work of the Spirit is centred.

Those who take the alternative individualistic approach to understanding the baptism in Romans 6 normally point to a passage like 1 Corinthians 12:13, where Paul writes about being baptized into one body (Christ) by the one Spirit at conversion. Those who hold this view, while agreeing that the reference to baptism in this passage has nothing to do with water baptism, still see it as a reference to an individual experience, one to which water baptism testifies.

Now, while this latter understanding has not imported water into the passage, it has still made a choice from the range of meanings of baptism. How can we be sure that the right meaning has been chosen? To make sure, we must look at the various options carefully. We must recognize that Old Testament theology is the foundation of all that Paul is saying. To work within this framework is to discover the treasures that false methodologies have hidden.

Baptism in 1 Corinthians 10

Paul's first letter to the Corinthians is crucial in helping us to understand the argument in Romans 6. There are several reasons for saying this. First, the two letters were written at approximately the same time. Second, the contents of the letters are similar. Both have a section on the church as the pilgrim community (Rom. 5:1–11; 8:35–39; 10:14–15; 1 Cor. 10:1–13), both refer to Jesus as the Passover offering (Rom. 3:21–26; 1 Cor. 5:7), and most importantly, both have a section dealing with baptism (Rom. 6:1ff.; 1 Cor. 6:11; 10:1–4; 12:13), which is closely linked to the idea of believers becoming sons of God (Rom. 8:15–17 and 1 Cor. 6:2 refer to the function of Messianic sonship). In 1 Corinthians 10:1–4 Paul writes about the church having been baptized into Christ. Paul speaks of the baptism of the Christian community into Christ as being foreshadowed by Israel's baptism into Moses. The baptism of Israel into Moses was a corporate event when the whole nation was united with him. It follows therefore, that the baptism which Paul refers to in 1 Corinthians 10:14 is that of the Christian community, who are baptised into a union with Christ. It is therefore a corporate baptism that has happened in the past.

The baptism into (or unto) Moses (the Greek carries both meanings) that Paul is referring to was nothing like the baptism that was practised by the early church, when the converts confessed their faith in the name of the Father, Son and Holy Spirit (Matt. 28:19). The baptism into Moses occurred as the people left Egypt. It was part of their exodus experience, even though the Israelites were unaware that it was happening. At that time, the Jewish people were brought into a covenantal relationship with Moses who became their representative before God. This was not water baptism; it was the creation of a community with Moses as its spokesman—or better, its divinely-appointed representative. God took Israel as his covenantal people and put them under the leadership, or headship, of Moses. All of God's dealings with Israel were now going to be conducted through Moses. Israel had been baptized into him, and it was a baptism that God accomplished for the purpose of uniting Moses and Israel. Through this baptism, Moses became the representative of the Jewish people.

We can get some idea of the Jewish understanding of this event when we read the account of the celebration of the Passover meal. The eldest son asks the father, 'What does this ceremony mean?' (Exod. 12:26). Each generation of fathers then teaches the family, saying, 'I do this because of what the Lord did for me when I came out of Egypt' (Exod. 13:8). In Jewish understanding, the entire nation was present as Israel came out of bondage, and not just the generation which had been enslaved in Egypt. All generations—past, present and future—shared in the exodus. This corporate participation is of course very much part of the argument about all mankind sinning in Adam (see comments on 5:12ff.).

Old Testament baptism was the collective entry into the covenant of the people of God: past, present and future. So, I suggest the baptism into Christ of Romans 6:1– 4 is the same (it is after all intrinsically linked with the corporate argument of chapter 5). And when did this baptism into Christ take place? It took place at the point of his death, for 'all of us who were baptized into Christ Jesus were baptized into his death' (Rom. 6:4). This collective concept is not only in 1 Corinthians 10:1–4, it is found elsewhere in Paul's letters.

Baptism in Ephesians

In Ephesians 5:25–26, Paul says, 'Husbands, love your wives, as Christ loved the church and gave himself up for her, that he might sanctify her, having cleansed her by the washing of water with the word'. Such cleansing is baptismal language, the picture being based on Ezekiel 16:1–14 where in recounting the history of Israel, the prophet reminds the nation that, before God chose her for himself, she had no hope or future. She did not exist as a nation. She was like a baby who had been born without anyone to care for her—thrown by the side of the road and still covered in the blood of birth. Ezekiel said that when God came by and saw her in her state of certain death, he had mercy on her. He took her to himself and washed her by giving his word to her.

This is the parallel that Paul draws in the letter to the Ephesians. The church is God's creation. There is nothing about which she can boast other than the grace of God, for she was dead in trespasses and sins (Eph. 2:1–10). In the letter, Paul tells how this transformation came about. Christ has cleansed his people from their defilement, reflecting the words of God to Israel, 'I bathed you with water and washed the blood from you' (Ezek. 16:9). As Christ died, the church was made clean.

This is what the death of Jesus has achieved for the people of God. They are made clean and pure so that they can become his bride. What ought to be clear is that Ezekiel and Paul are ultimately both talking about the same thing. Ezekiel is describing Israel being taken as the bride of God and Paul (in Ephesians) is describing the church being taken as the bride of Christ. The two washings are two baptisms, and both are corporate. This corporate baptism makes sense of Ephesians 4:4–6, where Paul says, 'There is one body and one Spirit—just as you were called to the one hope that belongs to your call—one Lord, one faith, one baptism, one God and Father of all, who is over all and through all and in all'. Baptism's place in this list of foundational realities should signal to us that something other than water baptism was in Paul's mind. In the light of our consideration of Ephesians

5:25–26, we can see that Paul is speaking of our baptism into Christ—that great ontological reality which is the basis of all God's saving activities.

Baptism in Galatians

Another famous baptism text of Paul is found in Galatians 3:26–29, where we read:

> For in Christ Jesus you are all sons of God, through faith. For as many of you as were baptized into Christ have put on Christ. There is neither Jew nor Greek, there is neither slave nor free, there is no male and female, for you are all one in Christ Jesus. And if you are Christ's, then you are Abraham's offspring, heirs according to promise.

The passage causes a problem for grammarians when they persist in thinking of water baptism. The Greek suggests that the baptism was one event. In other words, all believing Galatians—even those who were converted after Paul left Galatia— were immersed into the water at precisely the same time. But there is no mention of water in the entire letter. What we do find in the passage is a reference to the Christians being the children of Abraham—the true people of God. We also find echoes of the exodus in the letter (Gal. 1:3; 3:14; 4:1–7). In other words, it seems that this reference to the baptism of the Galatians is similar to that found in Ephesians and 1 Corinthians 10:2. It refers to the event when the Galatians were united with Christ in his death. Indeed, it was not only they who underwent this baptism, they were in fellowship with the whole church of God—past, present and future—just as the baptism into Moses had involved all generations of Israelites.

Baptism in 1 Corinthians 12

Another difficult passage for those who see baptism as the moment when the new believer is brought into the church, the body of Christ, is 1 Corinthians 12:13, 'For in one Spirit we were all baptized into one body— Jews or Greeks, slaves or free— and all were made to drink of one Spirit'. There are two points which suggest that the meaning is otherwise. The first is grammatical. The way that Paul constructs the sentence would normally mean that baptism was intended to achieve an end or goal. If this is accepted, then the correct translation would be 'we have all been baptized to form one body'. The problem with this individualistic approach is that it would mean that the church does not exist until all the baptisms are completed. Such imagery is at odds with the fact that the church not only exists now but existed in Paul's day (e.g. Acts 20:28; Rom. 16:5,16; 1 Cor. 1:2; 2 Cor. 8:1; Phil. 3:6; Col. 4:15). It is understandable why almost all translators opt for the less difficult rendering, 'into one body'.

Corporate Baptism of the Spirit

However, none of this is a problem if we see the baptisms of 1 Corinthians, Galatians and Ephesians as being one and the same event, a corporate baptism of the church. This baptism by the Spirit not only brought the church into existence, it was the baptism at which all members were present and in which they all shared (regardless of when, in their own individual experience, they were included in Christ through faith). Another advantage of this corporate understanding is that Paul has already used this imagery in his other reference to baptism in 1 Corinthians 10:2. In other words, 1 Corinthians 12:13 is a statement about the same event as found in 1 Corinthians 10:4; both are speaking about the creation of the Christian community which took place as a result of the baptism of its members into the death of Christ. Furthermore, this interpretation leaves Paul saying what he has actually said, that we have all been baptized 'to form one body'.

And so, we come to Romans 6. If there is consistency in the argument outlined, it suggests that Paul is not writing about individual baptism—either in water or by the Spirit—but about the great act of salvation that took place in the death of Christ. This was Jesus' exodus; in his dying and resurrection, he led his people (of all generations) out from the kingdom of darkness because they had all been baptised by the Spirit into union with him. What took place in Christ's death and resurrection was the transfer of the whole Christian community into the kingdom of light (Gal. 1:3; Col. 1:13).[7]

Examining the Text

6:1 What shall we say then? Are we to continue in sin that grace may abound?

Paul has been discussing the status of humanity. People are either in Adam or in Christ. Those in Adam are in the kingdom which his rebellion has created, and they share in the condemnation his disobedience brings. Those in Christ are in the kingdom which his obedience has inaugurated, and they are blessed with the riches that come from the relationship that he has re-established for his people with God.

In the last verse of chapter 5, Paul speaks of grace reigning through Christ. He is aware of how his ancestors abused the redemption that they had experienced when delivered from Egypt. They used it as a licence to live recklessly (1 Cor. 10:1– 10). Paul raises the question as to what receiving eternal life should mean for the believer (Rom. 5:20). He is aware that some might argue that, if they sinned, God would be given more opportunity to forgive. There is no evidence that Paul knew of this being argued in Rome, but it was the type of argument that had been used by his ancestors with terrible consequences (Amos 5:14–27). He raises the possibility of such an abuse of Christian freedom to ensure that such reasoning is robbed of its appeal.

If Paul had been alive in the days of Moses, he would have addressed the pilgrim community with a similar argument, 'You say that you have been redeemed from Egypt, then why are you living as though you were still there?' In other words, their lives should have been lived in the presence and for the glory of God who had delivered them from their misery.

---

[7] For a much wider treatment of this subject including the significance of baptism and sonship, and baptism and circumcision, see Holland, Romans: *The Divine Marriage*, p. 168–177.

Romans 6: The Messiah King and His People's Deliverance

There is no greater motive than love. It was God's love for the Roman believers that meant that he gave up his own Son to death (Rom. 5:8). It was God's love that had been poured into their hearts by the Holy Spirit (Rom. 5:5), and it was God's grace (flowing from his love) that had overflowed to the many (Rom. 5:15). To use John's words, 'We love because he first loved us' (1 John 4:19). If Paul is reflecting what the prophets have said about the coming new exodus, then the church has been redeemed from the bondage of sin to be the bride of Christ just as Israel had been in the Old Testament. The church is called to live as one who anticipates her marriage, anxious to be beautiful for her husband (Eph. 5:25ff.). Sin is to be shunned because it mars the very work of redemption that the death of Christ has brought about. This theological framework will clarify several problems not resolved by traditional interpretations of chapters 6–7.

The suggestion that Christians can deliberately sin so that God will be glorified is something that Paul could not countenance. They had not been redeemed for sin but from sin. They had been redeemed to be the bride of Christ, and his bride was to be without spot or blemish.

6:2 By no means! How can we who died to sin still live in it?

What does Paul mean by the phrase 'we who died to sin'? When the Jews left Egypt, they died to the way of life that had been dictated by Pharaoh. Because of the exodus, they were free to serve and worship God. While it can be argued that the Jews died to Egypt when they passed through the Red Sea, it was only a symbolic death. Neither the Jews—nor Egypt— actually died. This is not what Paul is arguing here. He says, emphatically, that the church has died to sin (and so to Satan's dominance). This is confirmed in the way that Paul continually links the experience of the church with the death of Jesus. What Paul is saying here is of vital importance, yet it is often missed.

Paul has already argued that, through the sin of Adam, humanity died to God and came under the control of Satan. The New Testament makes it clear that there are parallel relationships between the church and the world. Christians are children of God; unbelievers are children of the devil (John 8:44). Believers are citizens of the kingdom of light (Col. 1:14); unbelievers are citizens of the kingdom of darkness (Eph. 2:1–3). These texts suggest that the relationship the church has with Christ and God is the same in nature as the one that the world has with sin and Satan. The covenant that exists between God and his people would, therefore, be paralleled by a similar covenant between Satan and his community. This suggests that unredeemed humanity is in a covenantal relationship with sin (Satan). Both Adam and Christ represent their own people; they are representatives of human groupings and are bound to them. The inevitable logic of this comparison is that there is a covenantal relationship between Adam and his people which binds them to Satan, and this is the basis of humanity's sin. This is a reasonable conclusion because the basis of Christian righteousness is the covenantal relationship with God through Christ.

This desperate situation is one that no human being could reverse. Through union with Adam, all people are under this sentence of death. They are servants of sin and Satan, bound in a relationship of covenant solidarity. This ontological reality is of a different order of magnitude than people being sinners because they sin. The individual's personal accountability is but a tiny part of the whole picture of humanity's plight in Adam. Unless there is another who can die on his behalf, and through that representative death bring an end to this relationship, the entire human race is in an impossible situation.

This is the point that Paul is arguing. It might be claimed that images are being introduced that are not in the text. It is true that they are not in the immediate text, but as we shall see, Romans 7:2–4 is the summation of the argument of chapters 5–6, where Paul highlights the dilemma and drives home his argument with a reference to the Mosaic marriage law.

So, coming back to our verse, what Paul is saying is that the death of Christ is not 'just' about the propitiation of God's wrath towards the sinner; it is about the ending of the relationship with sin. This condition of humankind in Adam underlines the impossibility of people being able to make themselves acceptable before God. For God to accept them without the covenant-annulling death of Christ would implicate God in adultery! For this reason, Paul stresses that the Roman believers have shared in the death of Christ. This was not achieved through some act of will on their part. Indeed,

Romans 6: The Messiah King and His People's Deliverance

they had no knowledge of being involved in the event, for it happened in history—in the death of Jesus himself.

Thus, the relationship with sin is over—the death of Jesus has ended it! The death of the one for the many has had the reverse effect of the disobedience of the first Adam, whose sin brought his offspring into this terrible condition in the first place. When Paul says that we have died to sin, he is asserting that the previous relationship with Satan is terminated. Satan no longer has any legal rights, through covenant, to claim us. Our death in Christ has brought about this amazing reversal.

It is impossible for a believer to continue in his relationship to sin. It would be a return to the very relationship that Christ died to end. Paul's argument is clear, having died to that relationship, it is impossible to return to it. It would be the equivalent of re-establishing the covenant with sin that had been destroyed, and that in turn would mean the destruction of the new relationship that had been established through the death of Christ for his people. In other words, it is yet again a betrayal of the covenant love of God. This was something of deep concern to Paul. He had warned the Corinthians of this very danger, articulating it as clearly as he could. He warned that idolatry, sexual immorality, and speaking evil of God had been the cause of God's judgment on Israel in her wilderness wanderings (1 Cor. 10:1–10). Earlier, Paul had spelt out the consequences of such behaviour for individuals (1 Cor. 6:9–11) and for the church (1 Cor. 5:3–8).

6:3 Do you not know that all of us who have been baptized into Christ Jesus were baptized into his death?

Paul emphasizes the grounds on which the believers' relationship with sin has ended. He asks them, in a tone of incredulity, 'could it be possible that you don't know this?' This was at the heart of the early church's proclamation (1 Cor. 15:3). The possibility that it had not been part of the message that the Romans received is beyond Paul's ability to believe. That Christ has set his people free through his death was not on the periphery of the proclaimed message but at its heart; it is the gospel.

As we have seen above, when Paul says we were baptized into his death, he is not saying that we have shared in Jesus' death through water baptism. His argument does not relate to water baptism at all, but to the Spirit's inclusion into Christ of all of his people. As this took place in the moment of Jesus' death, it was a baptism into Christ's death. This sharing in the death of the last Adam makes deliverance from the kingdom of darkness possible, for death was the means by which Satan's authority was terminated and deliverance secured for those whom God foreknew.

This does not deny the importance of water baptism for the early church. It was the appointed way of making a personal confession of sin, of showing repentance, and faith in Christ; but it is not the subject of this passage.

6:4 We were buried therefore with him by baptism into death, in order that, just as Christ was raised from the dead by the glory of the Father, we too might walk in newness of life.

The verse can be paraphrased as follows, 'because we have been baptized into his death, we have been raised from the dead with Christ. This was done through the power of God that we should live a new life'. Because of our union with Christ, we have experienced all that happened to him. We have shared in his death as a result of the baptism (that is, the joining of Christ with his people by the Holy Spirit) which has taken place. However, this shared experience was not limited to his death. It continued beyond, for we were raised with Christ when the Father raised him from the dead (Eph. 2:4–10). This is firm evidence that the baptism spoken about here is neither individual nor confessional. If, as most concede, the reference to being raised with Christ signifies being part of the actual resurrection event and not to some later re-enactment, the union that the passage speaks about must have happened before Christ was raised from the dead in order for the church to have been included in the Easter resurrection. Thus, the baptizing (the means of inclusion into the experience of the death of Christ) must have preceded the resurrection. Paul has made this fact clear, for it was a baptism into Christ's death.

Paul is anxious to clarify that, in the case of Christ and the church, the union does not dissolve with death as other unions do (Rom. 14:9; 2 Cor. 5:14–15). This is probably the reason for the baptism being described as a baptism into his death. It is a union that is made in the process of death and one that death cannot break. All other unions are forged before death, and death severs them; the union of Christ with his people survives death, for unlike other relationships, that union is actually dependent on (his) death. His people have been united with the Lord of life who is the conqueror of death; they have been raised with him and are now seated with him in the heavenly places (Eph. 2:4–10). Thus, they share in his resurrection and exaltation. They are not physically raised and exalted, but their position in Christ is such that God deals with them as though they were. Just as God dealt with the Jewish nation as though everyone experienced the exodus, so God deals with every believer as though they have been raised and seated with the risen Christ. This acceptance can mean only one thing for believers—they are to live out the status that they now have in newness of life.

All that was achieved was 'by the glory of the Father'. This is another way of saying 'by God's power and might'. As we have seen in the Old Testament, the power of God was displayed supremely on two occasions—when he saved Israel from Egypt and when he saved her from Babylon (Exod. 14:31; Deut. 9:29; Isa. 40:5). In the New Testament, the power and the glory of God were supremely displayed in the death and resurrection of Jesus. Paul says that the Easter event is the fulfilment of the Old Testament type, the exodus. Indeed, as we have seen, he has linked baptism with Israel's coming out of Egypt under Moses in 1 Corinthians 10:4.

6:5 For if we have been united with him in a death like his, we shall certainly be united with him in a resurrection like his.

Paul writes in the plural, 'if we have…we shall', reminding us that he is not dealing with the experience of the individual but of the church—the community of people whom God has redeemed through the death of his Son. It not only suggests that dying with Christ is a corporate experience but that being raised with him is one also. While we talk of the resurrection of the individual believer, we must be aware that this is not the perspective of the Scriptures.

6:6 We know that our old self was crucified with him in order that the body of sin might be brought to nothing, so that we would no longer be enslaved to sin.

At first glance, it seems that Paul has reverted to considering the individual. But this apparent reversal cannot be maintained.

Our 'Old Self'

Anthrōpos ('our old self' in the A.V.) is rendered 'our old man' in the ESV, and normally it is assumed that the term speaks of the old life that was lived in Adam— the ungodly life that the Romans lived before their conversion. We must check to see if this is the correct understanding. The term is used elsewhere in a way which suggests that Paul did not have the individual in mind. In Ephesians 2:15, he speaks of God taking the Jews and Gentiles and making out of them one 'new man' (anthrōpos). This is a clear reference to the church being made up of Jews and Gentiles. The term is corporate, the church being called the 'new man'. In Colossians 3:9–12, Paul writes:

> *Do not lie to one another, seeing that you have put off the old self [anthrōpos] with its practices and have put on the new self [anthrōpos] which is being renewed in knowledge after the image of its Creator. Here there is not Greek and Jew, circumcised and uncircumcised, barbarian, Scythian, slave, free; but Christ is all, and in all. Put on then, as God's chosen ones, holy and beloved, compassionate hearts, kindness, humility, meekness, and patience.*

In this passage, it is clear that the new self (or new man) refers to a community, 'here [in this community] there is not Greek and Jew'. The only way this can be read is that the 'new man' is the church, as it is in Ephesians 2:15. It follows that the corresponding reality to the new man—the old man—is also corporate. This is the community that lives independently of God. It is the world of unredeemed humanity.

The old man to whom the Romans have died is their relationship with the world. They are no longer part of the Adamic community. They have been released as a result of the death of Christ and their own acceptance of him as their representative head. They are no longer in Adam and no longer part of the rebellion against God and his rule. They have died to the solidarity of sin and are now alive in a new solidarity which has Christ as its head. This new solidarity is one of righteousness.

The 'Body of Sin'

Paul also speaks in this verse of 'the body of sin' being done away with. Most expositors follow the individualistic interpretation and say that 'the body of sin' is the human body under the control of sin. The problem with this understanding is that it suggests that the body is in some way sinful. Also, it suggests that the only authentic Christian experience is one of total victory over sin, in other words moral perfection. Such claims can have devastating pastoral implications for sensitive souls who struggle with their failings. It casts them into darkness and turmoil—self- doubt and loathing brings them to question their faith and experience of Christ's salvation. Whether the term is held to be about the principle of sin that dwells in humankind, or the body under the rule of sin, both interpretations come perilously close to dualism. Almost all commentators are aware of such an implication, and arguments are mounted to avoid slipping into such an abyss. Even after these caveats have been given, the distinct impression remains that the body is in some way intrinsically sinful. But we know that Paul, as a Jew, could never accept anything that came close to a dualistic understanding.

The corporate interpretation, however, avoids this dilemma. The fact is that Paul's expression 'the body of sin' occurs nowhere else in the whole of Scripture. Because we find no help from outside of the passage, its meaning must be decided from within. All that we have to help us decipher its meaning is the flow of the argument that is being made.

Paul has been arguing about the plight of humanity in Adam and how this condition has been reversed for those who call on Christ to be their head. Elsewhere, Paul calls the community that is in Christ 'the body of Christ' (1 Cor. 12:12, 27; Eph. 2:16; 3:6; 5:23). Could not 'the body of sin' be the community that is in Adam? There has been much serious debate over the meaning of soma ('body') as used by Paul. A growing number of scholars see a Hebraic background to the way he uses the term. As would be expected, the Jews (with their strong sense of solidarity of family and nation) normally use the term soma ('body') when referring to a corporate reality.

This line of thinking certainly fits the covenantal setting which was argued for in the opening of the chapter. We have seen that the Old Testament background suggests that the death of Christ to sin has annulled a covenant (as will be argued in Romans 7:1–4). We are coming very close to the idea that the body of sin is the body that is in covenantal relationship with sin through Adam just as the body of Christ is the body that is in covenantal relationship with God through Christ.

One could argue that 'body of sin' is not an appropriate expression for such a corporate understanding. If the communities are parallel, the corresponding term to 'the body of Christ' ought to be 'the body of Adam', for sin parallels God in the argument that has been given and Adam parallels Christ. Is there a rationale for Paul avoiding 'the body of Adam' term? Certainly, the rabbis were familiar with it. They used it to speak of the human race. But for Paul, Adam's mediatory work was over. He had no further function to fulfil. Indeed, Satan could argue that he now owned the kingdoms of this world (Luke 4:5–6). There is no future event that will bring the work of Adam to completion. It has been completed. So, the community he has represented is no longer his body but sin's. Satan has control, and the significance of Adam as representative head has ended. In contrast to this, Christ's mediatorial work has not yet been completed. This will happen when he yields his kingdom (his people) up to the Father so that God becomes all in all (1 Cor. 15:25– 28). Because of this, the church is not called the 'body of God' or the 'body of righteousness'; it is still dependent on Christ and is therefore appropriately called the body of Christ. Adam's mediatorial work is completed, so Satan has taken possession of his inheritance, the body of sin.

6:7 For one who has died has been set free from sin.

This verse causes most commentators considerable difficulty because dikaioō actually means 'justified' and not 'set free'. Yet Paul's use of 'justified' is totally unexpected in this context because it seems to go against his doctrine of justification as it is traditionally understood. It is widely accepted by scholars that Paul uses 'justified' to speak of being accepted by God through Christ. Once this declaration of innocence has been made, the sinner (the emphasis being on the individual believer) begins to experience the blessings of God and the Christian life. However, what is clear is that if Paul meant to use 'justified', he has changed his theology. He would be saying, 'As a result of a man dying with Christ, he is justified'. In other words, Paul would have reversed the order of salvation, making Christian experience the source of justification. This difficulty has led scholars of almost every theological persuasion to believe that Paul's intention was to say that 'he who has died is freed from sin' (as most translations give).

'Freed' is used in this way so that it harmonizes with what is thought to be Paul's teaching on justification. However, no Greek manuscript of Romans supports this reading. Every other time Paul uses the verb dikaioō in this letter (Rom. 2:13; 3:4; 3:20; 3:24; 3:26; 3:28; 3:30; 4:2; 4:5; 5:1; 5:9; 8:30; 8:33), he means 'justified', and it is translated as such. What, then, could Paul have been intending to say if we allow him to mean what he says when he wrote, 'anyone that has died has been justified from sin'?

The most common explanation is that Paul is quoting a rabbinical maxim. The rabbis argued that there was no point in taking a man to court if he had died. Death had discharged him of all responsibilities and debts to the law. His death had released him from the legal system and the law was powerless to exact its punishment. It is argued, therefore, that Paul is saying there is no charge to be answered and the believer is free through sharing in the death of Christ.

One problem with this understanding is that it ignores the fact that the term hamartia ('sin') is a theological term. Men are not taken to court for sins but for crimes. If Paul had wanted to be understood in the way suggested, he would have used the term *aitios* ('criminal charge'). In other words, Paul would have said that death frees from *aitios* ('crime'). Another difficulty is that death does not discharge any man from the responsibility of his sins, and Paul clearly anticipated some sort of eschatological judgment (Rom. 14:11–12; 2 Cor. 5:10).

So, what is Paul saying by writing 'justified from sin'? If we follow the flow of the argument that has been made so far, its meaning becomes clear. We have noted the presence of exodus and Paschal language in the earlier part of the letter. It is, therefore, reasonable to suggest that Paul is dealing with the problem of how Christ can take a sinful people—even worse, a people who are under the rule of Satan— as his own bride.

But the elect from within the bride of Satan (the body of sin) have died with Christ, and the former relationship has been terminated. There is no adultery in the new marriage. There is no charge that can be laid at the feet of the parties in this new relationship. They are 'justified' before the civil law and the law of God. Paul is right to use the term 'justified' (or acquitted), and any who change this meaning are departing from what he intended to say.

6:8 Now if we have died with Christ, we believe that we will also live with him.

The new life of the believing community is bound up with its experience of death in her representative. There is no way into the covenant community other than through the covenant-annulling death of Christ. Having participated in this historically and then having appropriated its benefits by faith, the life of fellowship with Christ becomes a living reality. Paul is not concentrating on the life of the church in its earthly existence; he is raising the eyes of the Roman church to her final destiny, where she will one day reign with Christ (Rom. 8:13–25; 1 Cor. 6:1–3). This glorious fact ought to be to the fore of the Christian's values and hopes (Col. 3:1).

6:9 We know that Christ, being raised from the dead, will never die again; death no longer has dominion over him.

Paul stresses the finality of the victory of Christ's death in order to prepare for his appeal to the church that she lives her life for the glory of God. Paul has said in the previous verse that believers will live with Christ. Here, he says that Christ is the absolute victor over Satan. These two facts, coupled with the reality that the church has died with Christ, are the reason why the church is to live her life for him. The fact that he is the victor over Satan dispels any lingering fear that the former husband might catch up with his 'deceased wife' and renew his former authority and demands. While Satan may certainly do harm to the church in this life, he cannot overturn the new relationship and re-establish the old.

What greater turn-around could there be? The greatest victory Satan could have won was to put to death the Son of God, and yet God was turned the tables so that what seemed to be Christ's defeat became his absolute victory

Romans 6: The Messiah King and His People's Deliverance

and Satan's triumph became his utter ruin. The Jews had found it so difficult to accept the idea of the crucifixion of the Messiah—it was the great stumbling block that hindered faith (1 Cor. 1:23)—and yet when Paul met with the risen Christ he understood how Christ's resurrection transformed the meaning and significance of the cross; Jesus was not the victim but the victor!

6:10 For the death he died he died to sin, once for all, but the life he lives he lives to God.

The NIVTM translators have omitted the word 'for' at the beginning of this verse. But the word is rightly retained in the ESV as the passage continues to develop the argument. Paul underlines the finality of Jesus' death with 'once for all'. This finality is shared by other New Testament writers (Mark 10:45; John 10:11; Acts 4:10; Heb. 9:24–28; Rev. 1:18), and it was a truth that clearly made a great impression on the early church. Being Jewish, or saturated in Jewish theological thought, these believers understood that there was no finality about the Old Testament sacrificial system. Sin was never absolved in such a way that it no longer threatened the assurance of the one who had offered the sacrifice.

The impact of the truth that sin had been defeated is difficult for us to imagine in the twenty-first century. We have diluted the concept of sin to such a mediocrity that it does not press upon us with the seriousness that it ought. As the church assembled in Rome to hear Paul's letter, there would have been many who had known great fears, guilt, and anxiety over their sin, and they believed that these would come to fruition beyond the grave. As they listened to the letter, they heard what Christ had done in order to rescue them. His decisive victory over sin and death had brought them into the kingdom of Christ in all of its glorious, unspeakable fullness, and their fears for all that lay ahead were over.

When Paul writes that Christ lives to God, he means more than simply that Christ has been raised and is now seated in heaven; he means that God has accepted what Christ has done. This is another way of saying what Paul has already said in Romans 4:25, '[Jesus] was delivered up for our trespasses and raised for our justification'. The fact that Christ is in heaven is the seal of

God's acceptance. All who come through him to the Father are welcome! Moreover, it means that God will never deal with us as sinners. There, perpetually in heaven, is the evidence that our sin has been dealt with. Christ is fulfilling the office of the Jewish high priest who went into the presence of God in the Temple's Most Holy Place, the place where no other person could enter. He presented the evidence that the sacrifice for sin had been made (Heb. 9:1–7). Here, in Romans, we have the same idea. The theme of Jesus being the believers' high priest is not limited to the letter to the Hebrews as some think; it is present throughout the gospels and the rest of the New Testament.

The Messiah King and His People's Obedience

6:11 So you also must consider yourselves dead to sin and alive to God in Christ Jesus.

In making this statement, Paul is not inviting his readers to dream about an impossible situation. He adopts a term used in accounting, so that the phrase 'consider yourselves dead to sin' actually means 'credit to yourselves that you are dead' because Christ has died in the Roman believers' place. Because of this death, the old relationship with sin has been brought to an end and the church has been brought out of the domain of sin (the kingdom of darkness), and into the kingdom of light. The requirements have not been violated but fulfilled. There is no possibility of evidence being found that will show the new relationship is over and fellowship must terminate; theirs is an absolute right. The people of God are not in God's presence because of their achievements but because of what God has accomplished through the death of his Son.

6:12 Let not sin therefore reign in your mortal body, to make you obey its passions.

Paul appeals to the Roman church to exercise covenant loyalty. It would be easy to abuse the grace of God and use this freedom as an excuse for sin, as Israel had done. Since the same appeal is given to the Corinthian church in 1 Corinthians 10:1ff. it would be foolish not to investigate whether the letter to the Corinthians might help us to understand Paul's argument in his letter

Romans 6: The Messiah King and His People's Deliverance

to the Romans. The context of both passages is baptism (Rom. 6:1–4; 1 Cor. 10:1–4). In the original Old Testament type, Israel, after her baptism unto Moses, abused the covenant relationship and sinned against God. Paul appeals for loyalty—a loyalty that only a few in the Mosaic covenant community displayed.

In making this appeal, it is easy to think that Paul is calling each believer to live a holy life. He does this elsewhere (1 Thess. 4:3–8), but it is not the thrust of the argument here. His appeal is not to the believer to control his body, but to the church to maintain her purity. The term ('body') is corporate as the Greek shows: *hymōn* ('your') (pl.) sōma ('body') (sing.). So, the phrase 'your mortal body' is not a reference to the physical body of the believer but to the physical existence of the church in Rome. This verse is an appeal to the church to discipline its members who refuse to live the new life in Christ. Paul reflects on the failure of the Jews to deal with sin, for he is keenly aware of how it had spread through the community and damaged the whole nation.

6:13 Do not present your members to sin as instruments for unrighteousness, but present yourselves to God as those who have been brought from death to life, and your members to God as instruments for righteousness.

This exhortation could well have been given to the Jewish nation after being delivered from its captivity in Egypt. To Moses' horror, the Israelites turned away from the responsibilities of the covenant and sought the favour of the gods of the surrounding nations (Exod. 32:1). So again, this passage in Romans parallels a passage in Paul's first letter to the Corinthians (1 Cor. 10:1–14). It is not an appeal to individuals to control their bodies (an appeal which is normally taken to highlight sensual sins), but an appeal for purity in the life of the believing community in Rome. This broader corporate appeal identifies a wider range of sin that Paul was concerned with. For example, in the Corinthian situation, he was concerned with schism (1 Cor. 1:11–17; 3:1–9), fornication (1 Cor. 5–6), occult issues (1 Cor. 8:1–13, 10:14–33), and doctrinal unfaithfulness (1 Cor. 15:12–34). He urges the church not to tolerate or promote wrongdoing in believers who sin after the nature of the issues he raises in the letter.

He expressed this same concern in 1 Corinthians 5:6–8:

> *Your boasting is not good. Do you not know that a little leaven leavens the whole lump? Cleanse out the old leaven that you may be a new lump, as you really are unleavened. For Christ, our Passover lamb, has been sacrificed. Let us therefore celebrate the festival, not with the old leaven, the leaven of malice and evil, but with the unleavened bread of sincerity and truth.*

The ground for the appeal in Romans and in 1 Corinthians is the same. Christ, the Passover sacrifice, has died, and God's people have been included in his death. Just as Israel died to the rule of Pharaoh when she left Egypt, so the Christian community has died to the rule of sin. The church's responsibility is not to live as she had previously lived by fulfilling the whims of the old husband. She is to live a new life that pleases and honours the one who died for her and who is now her betrothed and Lord.

So, in this verse Paul addresses the church. This is not to deny that individuals must put the apostle's teaching into practice, but an exclusively individualistic focus misses the corporate context of his reasoning. If an individual Christian does not wholeheartedly obey Christ (v. 17), profound repercussions may be felt throughout the congregation of believers. Paul is saying to the congregation in Rome that although they tolerated godless living when they were part of the kingdom of darkness, their toleration must cease now that they are part of the body of Christ. The members of the church are members of one another, and Paul is appealing for corporate holiness. Not only is it the duty of the church to restrain evil, it is the duty of the church to promote righteousness among the believers. While the last thing Paul wants to encourage is a secret police mentality, he urges the church to face up to the reality of evil and recognize how a little leaven leavens the whole lump (1 Cor. 5:7–8).

6:14 For sin will have no dominion over you, since you are not under law but under grace.

Satan's exploitation of the law has been answered fully in the death of Jesus. By his death, Christ Jesus satisfied the law's demands, for its penalty has been paid. By his death, the covenant—by which sin demanded obedience and control—has been brought to an end for those who are now in Christ.

Romans 6: The Messiah King and His People's Deliverance

Under the new head (Christ), the law of sin and death (and hence the reign of Satan) is terminated, and sin's control of redeemed humanity has been brought to an end.

In saying that believers are 'not under law', Paul opens up an issue that has occupied the attention of scholars for centuries. What does he actually mean? Does the law have no relevance for the believer? Paul will discuss this in chapter 7. What we can say here is that the context is the fulfilment of God's promises, that is, the covenants which he made with Abraham and David. If Paul's understanding of law is removed from this covenantal context, there is no possibility of understanding his rationale. This corporate interpretation has significant pastoral implications. It shows that Paul is not urging some form of sinless perfection. Such teaching has crushed millions of Christians who have been tormented by their failures when urged to attain perfection. The passage makes no such demand. It tells the Roman believers that they are to live in the light of the greatest reality of history; Christ has rescued them from the kingdom of darkness and made them his people, his own special possession, his bride. It urges them to live out this glorious status and calling in the Empire's capital city.

6:15 What then? Are we to sin because we are not under law but under grace? By no means!

Once again, Paul challenges the suggestion that being under grace rather than law means that one can continue sinning without fear of consequence. Only after one sees the hatred that God has toward sin will the distress of such a suggestion be felt. Grace and sin cannot be mixed. To think that they can harmoniously coexist is to think that light can coexist with darkness, or that life can coexist with death. Paul responds to this much more strongly than the ESV suggests. His retort to the proposal is 'God forbid!' Paul is not responding to the question he posed in the opening of the chapter, when he wrote, 'Are we to continue in sin that grace may abound?' In this verse the argument is responding to is, 'Since we have been removed from the realm of sin, what we do now has no spiritual consequence'.

6:16 Do you not know that if you present yourselves to anyone as obedient slaves, you are slaves of the one whom you obey, either of sin, which leads to death, or of obedience, which leads to righteousness?

At this point, we encounter a difficulty with the word *doulos*, which is normally translated 'slave'. This is an understandable translation, as the word meant 'slave' in classical Greek. It was a word used to describe slaves who had no rights. Their masters owned them, and they were allowed to live only to fulfil the wishes of their owners. Often, such wretched people were the victims of war and subsequent deportation. It is thought by some that in this verse Paul is saying that the Roman believers, having once been slaves of sin, have now become Christ's 'slaves'.

Many sermons have been structured on the understanding that Christians are slaves of righteousness and hence have no rights. The believer is owned by Christ who has absolute claim upon him or her. Such a picture is powerful, inspiring many into sacrificial service. But is this what Paul is actually saying?

We have seen in Romans 1:1 that *doulos* has at least two meanings in the Old Testament. This fact needs to be remembered as we seek to understand what Paul is saying about being 'slaves to righteousness'. We found earlier that *doulos* can only be understood by giving attention to the context in which it is used. The context of the word has to be examined to see if it befits the appellation 'slave' or 'servant'. The latter will be expected to have terms associated with it that echo the Old Testament. In the Old Testament, the servant's role and his relationship with God are spoken alongside terms such as 'calling' and 'election'. This is exactly what we find in Paul's writings. Repeatedly, he uses *doulos* in contexts in which the Servant Songs of Isaiah are echoed or quoted (Acts 26:15–18; 2 Cor. 6:1–10).

The church is the servant of the Lord. Her members are the people called by God to do his will, serving him by taking the gospel to the nations as the Jews should have done. The status of 'servant' confers on the church and her members the highest honour as she and they are called to serve the living, saving God.

Paul's appeal to the Romans to turn from sin parallels Moses' appeal to the Jews to stay faithful to their God (see comments on v. 23). Again, a parallel

Romans 6: The Messiah King and His People's Deliverance

passage is found in 1 Corinthians 10:1–14, where Paul warns the Corinthians that sin leads to death. Earlier, he showed that a congregation which tolerates sin in the lives of its members comes under the sentence of judgment. Ultimately, that will mean temporary separation from the wider redeemed community and its God-given blessings. It also means being handed over to Satan (1 Cor. 5:3–5; Rev. 2:20–23), whose rage will be used by God to correct the wayward church or believer.

6:17 But thanks be to God, that you who were once slaves of sin have become obedient from the heart to the standard of teaching to which you were committed

What had kept the Roman believers from falling into the same condemnation as the Jews under Moses? Paul writes 'you...have become obedient from the heart to the standard of teaching to which you were committed'. The Jews of the exodus had refused to do this and had not submitted themselves to the authority of the law. They rejected the message that Moses proclaimed to them, even though they had experienced such a marvellous act of deliverance. Before Moses came down from his meeting with God on Mount Sinai where he was given the law, the people were worshipping a golden calf that Aaron, the priest, had made for them (Exod. 32:8). Despite all that the Lord had done for them, the people broke faith with God; turning to idols to lead them and worshipping them for the deliverance they had supposedly wrought (Exod. 32:1, 8b). For believers, the importance of the biblical message cannot be overstated. Their correct understanding of it and their obedience to it should keep them from being seduced back into the life they once lived before they were brought out of the kingdom of darkness.

6:18 and, having been set free from sin, have become slaves of righteousness.

Paul is confident that what he had heard of the Roman believers was true, so he encourages them that they have a true knowledge of God. They have changed their allegiance and are no longer part of the kingdom of darkness. When Paul says that they have been set free from 'sin', we should once again also read 'Satan'. The reality is that all the Roman believers will continue to be prone to sin and will fail to be the people they ought to be, but that is not the same as living under the rule of sin (Satan). Someone who takes out citizenship in a country other than his country of birth illustrates the point. Legally, he has a totally new identity and set of obligations. The old allegiance is over. Nevertheless, he is still the product of the first nation's culture and history. He must go through the long process of leaving that identity behind in his lifestyle, world-view, expectations and commitments, before he can become what his new citizenship signifies.

Again, we should translate 'slaves of righteousness' as 'servants of righteousness'. Paul sees Christians as servants of Christ, with all the privileges and dignity that this status bestows. Following the exodus type, Israel was Pharaoh's slave, but through her redemption she became God's servant. The relationships were totally different. The term 'righteousness' is a synonym for God (and has been used as such throughout the chapter), just as sin is a synonym for Satan. The Roman believers had been slaves of Satan, but now they are servants of God!

6:19 I am speaking in human terms, because of your natural limitations. For just as you once presented your members as slaves to impurity and to lawlessness leading to more lawlessness, so now present your members as slaves to righteousness leading to sanctification.

In what way does Paul want the Romans to understand him when he speaks of their 'natural limitations'—or 'weakness' (as in NASB and others)? It can hardly refer to physical limitations—even though this is a consequence of the fall and something from which the church waits to be delivered at the Parousia. It cannot mean intellectual limitation, for then there would be no point in Paul writing such a detailed letter which clearly presupposes intellectual capacity. The weakness must be spiritual. While Paul has asserted his confidence that they have obeyed from the heart the teaching delivered to them, they need to continually have the Word of God carefully explained and applied so that they can profit from it. The goal of this exhortation is that the church will live in holiness, reflecting the exhortation of God to Israel to be holy, as he is holy (Lev. 19:1 cf. 1 Pet. 1:15–16).

6:20 For when you were slaves of sin, you were free in regard to righteousness.

Paul is not saying that the Roman believers were free from responsibilities of personal righteousness before their conversion. Everyone is aware of the struggle between good and evil, whether they are believers or not. There are many non- Christians who live noble lives—striving to promote justice and righteousness in their communities—while there are those who call themselves Christians who have little concern for social issues. Paul would have been as aware of this fact in his day as we are in ours.

However, he is not talking at the level of personal morality or social justice. As has been argued throughout this exposition, Paul is evaluating the condition of the human race rather than individual people. He has divided humanity into two groups—those in Adam and those in Christ. Here, he speaks of the Roman church's deliverance from the kingdom of darkness, the realm where sin rules. Before their deliverance they were 'free in regard to righteousness' (God); instead they were covenanted to sin and were its willing servants.

6:21 But what fruit were you getting at that time from the things of which you are now ashamed? For the end of those things is death.

Paul reminds the believers of the futility and shame of their former lives. They had given themselves to the service of sin; but such service was rewarded with death. Satan was a ruthless master, with no care for those who served him—no matter how willingly. The only end that such service was going to bring was death. This would be physical (as Paul has argued in chapter 5) and spiritual (exile from the presence of God). The glory of the proclamation in this letter is that this exile is over for the people of God, and that death, the last enemy, has been conquered. This is the heart of the gospel (see 1 Cor. 15:37–58).

6:22 But now that you have been set free from sin and have become slaves of God, the fruit you get leads to sanctification and its end, eternal life.

The Jews were set free from Pharaoh's enslavement and became the servants of God. This was not merely a transfer of allegiance but a change of lifestyle. The nation's calling was to live out the will of God. She was his servant, and her call was not only to be holy (Lev. 20:7) but also to bring the knowledge of the God of Abraham to the Gentiles (Gen. 12:2–3), so that the other nations might worship him also.

This Israel singularly failed to do. She became obsessed with her own concerns, which distracted her from doing the will of God. The reality was that without the fulfilment of her missionary task, the most careful observance of the law was bound to degenerate into hollow religious activity that was nothing more than self- justification. At that stage, Israel not only failed to give the message of God's love to the nations, but she actually began to misrepresent him.

This is a salutary warning to the Christian church. Her calling is not to be comfortable and self-satisfied, but to be a servant who takes the message of the living God to those in darkness. Her calling is to be the servant of the Lord whose ministry brings light and life to the nations. For Paul, faith results in risk. It was this unwillingness to take risks that caused Jesus to warn Israel that what she had been given was about to be taken from her and given to another (Luke 19:11–27).

6:23 For the wages of sin is death, but the free gift of God is eternal life in Christ Jesus our Lord.

Moses and Joshua warned the Jews after they had come out of bondage that there were two ways ahead of them (Deut. 30:15–16; Josh. 23:1–16). One way rejected the law and led to death; the other way obeyed the will of God from the heart and led to life. Paul seems to be reflecting that same exhortation. This time, however, the appeal is directed to the church in Rome, urging her to be fully committed to loving and serving God. Again, we notice the personification of sin, this time as a master who pays a wage. The echoes of the appeal made by Moses further confirm the new exodus context of Paul's mind-set.

Further Study: Questions for Romans 6

1. What other passages in Paul's letters help us to understand what he means by being 'baptised into Christ'?

Romans 6: The Messiah King and His People's Deliverance

2. Why should our being baptised into Christ be thought of as a corporate event, and when did it take place?

3. What has happened as a result of our being baptised into Christ?

4. How does the idea of our being baptised into Christ provide the explanation for Paul's claim that we have 'died to sin'?

5. What is the meaning of 'sin' in the passage under consideration?

6. What is 'the body of sin'? What evidence is there for your answer in the passage?

Romans 7: An Analysis of the Problem

Introduction to Romans 7

We now come to a passage that has not only had a profound influence on the doctrine of sin but has also been at the centre of much theological debate in recent years. Some have claimed that Paul here describes his own Christian experience. Those who hold this view argue that the following chapter is about the victory of the Christian over sin and death. Amongst its advocates are those who teach some form of 'higher spiritual life', which emphasizes a post-conversion experience of the Holy Spirit, bringing the believer from defeat into victorious Christian living. Those who have supported this understanding include John Wesley; the holiness movements of the past two hundred years; and, especially, the original Keswick movement which popularized this view to hundreds of thousands of believers (the present-day Keswick movement has changed from its original position on this teaching). The other traditional view of this passage argues that Paul is not speaking of his past but his present experience as a believer. This position, which is held by most Reformed teachers, holds that sin is not eradicated until the believer is completely transformed at the coming of Christ.

In recent years, because scholars have come to appreciate the Hebraic (Jewish) nature of the passage, there has been a move away from seeing the passage as Paul recording his own experience, to one where Paul acts out the historical experience of a community, of which he is a representative member. This kind of approach is quite common in Hebraic literature. As to the identity of the community, there is lively debate. Some scholars say that Paul is playing out the experience of the whole human race—locked into its bondage to sin—while others understand the community to be Israel. This latter view focuses on her relationship with sin from which she thought she had been redeemed through the experience of the exodus from Egypt.

There are some good reasons for accepting these corporate perspectives of the passage, not least because it begins with an illustration based on marriage. The marriage analogy is never used in the Bible to speak of an individual's relationship with God; instead it is about the relationship of Israel with God in the Old Testament and the relationship of the church with Christ in the New Testament. Furthermore, Romans 7 follows the flow of Paul's reasoning from the previous chapters, and so it is logical to continue with his corporate perspective unless there is a clear indication that he changes tack.

His argument from chapter 5 has been that man is naturally in Adam and under the curse. He has shown in Romans 6:1–4 that the new solidarity with Christ, which the church enjoys, results from the Spirit's baptism of members who have been called from the body of sin into union with Christ. These members do not include all who are in the body of sin, but only those who God knew in his foreknowledge would call on the name of his Son for salvation. The Spirit's baptism formed 'one new body', and its members are those who have been brought out of darkness into light. The members of this new body have shared in the death of Christ (their new federal head), so the relationship to sin has ended. The community has been freed from its covenant bondage to sin, and Christ is able to take it as his bride. Because the death of Christ is a reality, the former covenant with sin (Satan) has been cancelled and Paul can say that those who have died are justified from sin (Rom. 6:7). In other words, Satan cannot lay at the door of either the church or Christ the accusation of adultery.

Paul then urges the local Roman church to live as the servant of God, just as Israel was urged to do after her redemption from Egypt. This redemption/marriage analogy is the very heart of Israel's own experience, for she had been redeemed from bondage in order to be the bride of God (Ezek. 16:8; Hosea 2:2). Thus, the passage is a perfect conclusion to the argument that Paul has been developing in the two preceding chapters. Indeed, it can be argued that it goes back to Romans 3:21–25, where the background was the event which inaugurated the exodus (the Passover).

Romans chapter 7 is not an apology for the law, nor is Paul digressing. He comments on the nature of the old relationship with sin and contrasts it with the new relationship with Christ. He has to explain how the old has passed away and how the new has come into being. To do this, he must show how the law had functioned and how it now functions. Thus, Romans 7:1–6a is the conclusion of chapters 5–6 and the introduction to Romans 7:7—8:34. This means the chapter might have been better started at Romans 7:7, 'What shall we say, then?'—having explained his argument, he asks his hearers for their response to what he has written.

Unfortunately, as Paul presses on with his argument, rather than clarifying his position, he introduces an idea which has confused the modern Christian. About what or about whom is Paul writing when he says, 'I was once alive apart from the law, but when the commandment came, sin came alive and I died' (v. 9)? Paul was born into a devout Jewish home and would have known something of the law from childhood. If it is argued Paul meant that, although the law existed objectively in his life, he had not experienced a personal sense of guilt that comes when the Spirit works through the law to produce repentance, then we have a position with a little more substance. But the problem with this interpretation is the notion that sin is dead without the law, which suggests there was no guilt until the law condemned. This is not a position that echoes the rest of scripture. Sin exists, even when there is no law. If sin does not exist without the law, it is better for people to be left in ignorance. Sin is not brought to life by the law; it is increased by it (Rom. 5:20).

But I will argue that Paul is not speaking of his own experience, but speaking as a representative—he speaks as Adam.[8] If taking an Old Testament story and moulding the experience of the apostle or church around it can be established as a literary technique, it would support the suggestion that chapter 7 is an example of intertextuality (the shaping of a text's meaning by other texts).

---

[8] This is not the only occasion he does this: in Phil. 1:18b–19 he seems to echo the experience of Job, expressing same confidence that God would eventually vindicate him.

Those who believe Paul was enacting out the experience of the Jewish people see the entrance of sin as coming after the covenant law was given at Sinai. The law that should have sealed her relationship with God did the very opposite—it condemned her and excluded her from her great calling; the commandment, 'You shall not covet' exposed Israel's failings and brought death. But the command, 'You shall not covet' actually came before the law—it was the very essence of the command to Adam, 'You must not eat from the tree of the knowledge of good and evil'. And the idea that the Mosaic Law could sentence Israel in this way was not part of Jewish understanding—as we have seen Jews generally had a positive view of the law.

The same phenomenon is found in Psalm 69. The psalm is a confession of David, but as it progresses, it is difficult to know whether he is speaking of his own experience or the nation's. As the psalm ends in vv. 34–36, the two ideas seem to merge with the focus being on the experience of the nation returning to Zion. Other Old Testament texts that use the personal pronoun to denote the nation of Israel include: Psalm 44:4–8, Micah 7:7–10, Jeremiah 10:19–22, and Lamentations 1:9–22; 2:20–22. It is worth noting the confessions in Ezra 9:7 and Nehemiah 9:2, 34, where the two reformers prayed and confessed as representatives of the nation. The features noted in Psalm 69 are present in these texts also.

If Paul was speaking as Adam, he was enacting the drama in the Garden of Eden where Adam indeed was alive without the law. But the very command not to eat of the tree of the knowledge of good and evil (Gen. 2:15–17) provoked the desire to have knowledge that was denied to him, and in his disobedience, he allowed Satan to establish his bridgehead and so man died to his relationship with God.

Paul starts with an illustration from marriage to show that the law of God, in binding humanity to her new 'husband' (Satan), has become the servant of Satan; he could appeal to the law for his exclusive rights to the obedience of man, and the law could do nothing but recognise them. Those rights, as we have seen, were ended by the death of Christ for his people.

Romans 7: An Analysis of the Problem

But some would argue that if the law had been used by sin, it was sinful itself! Part of Paul's following argument is to reject such a claim—a claim that would have been abhorrent to any Jew. However, his concern is not only to pacify the Jews but to make sure that Gentile believers do not become caught up in an anti-law movement. This would throw out the moral teachings of the law, leaving the believers in Rome exposed to the very corruption from which they had been redeemed.

7:1–2 Or do you not know, brothers—for I am speaking to those who know the law— that the law is binding on a person only as long as he lives? For a married woman is bound by law to her husband while he lives, but if her husband dies she is released from the law of marriage.

Paul uses an illustration that spans all cultures—marriage (Rom. 7:1–2). In biblical terms a marriage is intended to be permanent, ending only through the death of the husband or wife. No charge of unfaithfulness can be brought against a widow (or widower) who remarries. The authority of the husband ceases on his death. This is a vital point for Paul. Christ's death, on behalf of his people, ended the former relationship they had with sin. Through his representative death, in which his people have shared (6:1–8), those who were once prisoners in the body of sin have been freed. They now have a new status; having died with Christ, they are no longer bound to the law of the old husband—the law of sin and death.

At a corporate level, this illustration echoes the experience of Israel. In Egypt, she was bound up with the relationship that the Egyptians had with their gods. When she came out of Egypt at the exodus, she died not only to the reign of Pharaoh, but also to her involvement, through him, with his gods. Following this release, or redemption, she became the bride of God at Sinai. The trouble was that Israel betrayed the covenant love that God lavished upon her, and, in her heart, returned to her former lovers at the beginning of her marriage (Exod. 32:1, 4, 8). For this reason, Israel was repeatedly accused of playing the harlot (Ezek. 16:26–58; Hosea 4:15–5:7).

7:3 Accordingly, she will be called an adulteress if she lives with another man while her husband is alive. But if her husband dies, she is free from that law, and if she marries another man she is not an adulteress.

Many scholars find it difficult to determine which law the believer has died to. If the exegesis given so far is correct, it will be clear the argument is about the church and not the believer. Certainly, the individual believer in some way shares in the consequences of this death to law, but 'that law' is the law of the former husband. Or to use another description that Paul has already employed, it is the law of sin and death.

As we have noted previously, these terms are used as descriptions of Satan. He is the former husband. While it is true that Satan himself has not died, that is not a problem for a death has taken place—through Christ. By Christ's representative death—into which his people were baptized—the church has been set free. Her former husband has no legal power over her. She has died to his authority—his law—and is legally betrothed to another. Because she has died with Christ, she is justified from the law of her former husband. No legal charge can be upheld against her.

7:4 Likewise, my brothers, you also have died to the law through the body of Christ, so that you may belong to another, to him who has been raised from the dead, in order that we may bear fruit for God.

Paul brings this immediate argument to its conclusion. The purpose of Christ's death was to free his people from sin so that he could take them as his bride. This is possible because Christ not only died but was raised from the dead. His death is a historical fact, but its significance is a present reality. Through his death, the covenant his people once had with sin has ended and the risen Christ has taken the 'raised widow' for himself. Christ thus fulfils the role of the Old Testament redeemer, who married the childless widow of his near kinsman. We have seen that Christ is not called the redeemer in the New Testament, but his work is certainly described in terms which are modelled on the Old Testament redeemer figure. God promised to fulfil this role for the Jews in exile. He planned to redeem the nation so that she could become his bride (Isa. 49:20–21; 50:1–8; 62:4–5). Paul uses the same imagery of bride-purchase elsewhere (Acts 20:28; 1 Cor. 6:20; 2 Cor. 11:2; Eph. 5:25). These texts are evidence that the New Testament writers also saw marital imagery as describing the church's relationship to God (Matt. 22:1–4; 25:1–13; Luke 14:15–24; John 3:27–30; Rev. 19:9).

Romans 7: An Analysis of the Problem

The reference to bearing 'fruit for God' is a clear echo of the command to Adam to be fruitful and replenish the earth. Here, the statement is not about replenishing the natural order, but it is about the new creation. The church is called to enlarge the family of God, not through natural procreation, but through the proclamation of the life-giving gospel. The original context of the quotation from Genesis was marital. As the church lives under the law (or covenant authority) of her new husband she fulfils the command to be fruitful and replenish the earth. This fruitfulness is the natural consequence of the outflow of her love for her redeemer husband.

7:5 For while we were living in the flesh, our sinful passions, aroused by the law, were at work in our members to bear fruit for death.

The argument is that humanity is not in the covenant relationship for which it had been created, but instead is 'living in the flesh'—that is under the control of sin; exposing its individual members to all the guiles of the tempter. Humans sin because they are in solidarity with the community of sin (the body of sin—Rom. 6:6) which is alienated from God. What Paul is not saying is that the individual human body is sinful; it is not that which is driving and controlling the wicked passions.

If this corporate interpretation is accepted then Paul, representing either Adam or the Jewish nation, is speaking about the frailty of his 'members'. His members are individual people who have difficulty resisting the temptations that Satan lays before them, as did Adam in the garden.

Although the term 'members' is often seen as representing particular body parts (the eye, hand, foot, etc.) the word is melos, which has strong corporate associations in Paul's theology, lending support to the argument that Paul is speaking of individual people (1 Cor. 6:15–17).[9] If this is correct Paul is summarising the description of the human condition he has given in Romans 1:18–32.

---

[9] See Holland, *Contours of Pauline Theology* (Fearn, Scotland: Christian Focus, 2004), pp 125–127.

7:6 But now we are released from the law, having died to that which held us captive, so that we serve in the new way of the Spirit and not in the old way of the written code.

The corporate dimension of the argument continues with Paul saying 'we [not you singular] are released from the law'. He is not appealing to individual Roman believers to die. He is saying they, with all believers, have already died. He is focusing on the event that Romans 6:1–6 and 7:1–6 have spoken about; their death with Christ as a result of the union created with him by the Spirit.

7:7 What then shall we say? That the law is sin? By no means! Yet if it had not been for the law, I would not have known sin. For I would not have known what it is to covet if the law had not said, "You shall not covet."

Paul introduces the problem he knows must be tackled: the relationship of the law to sin. Does the fact that the law brings knowledge of sin make the law sinful? Paul could not tolerate such a thought but knows that he must defend his position lest weaker believers accept it.

He says that the law has made him (Adam, that is, humankind) know what sin is; the law has unlocked an understanding of sin. There is no suggestion the law itself stirs up desires for sin—rather it presents the very standard that sin opposes; that is God's standard. It is like light, and its introduction into darkness shows what was previously hidden. The problem is not the law; the problem is the 'heart' or condition of humanity. When Paul says, 'Yet if it had not been for the law, I would not have known sin'—'known' translates *ginōskō*; this normally means experiential knowledge rather than academic, intellectual knowledge. The law did not merely give a correct objective understanding of sin; it made humanity aware of its power and authority. The light of the law exposed the full horror of sin's true nature.

7:8 But sin, seizing an opportunity through the commandment, produced in me all kinds of covetousness. For apart from the law, sin lies dead.

Here we can see a shift from the concept of sin as breaking the law to sin as being a person who entices or seduces. The one who entices or tempts is Satan. So, we have the same pattern as we observed in chapter 6—Satan is

Romans 7: An Analysis of the Problem

spoken of as sin. It is possible that in v. 7, where Paul says he would not have known sin but for the commandment, he is not referring to sin as acts of violation of the law but to sin as a person. Indeed, in biblical terminology, to 'know' someone is a reference to the relationship of marriage. While there could be some debate as to the meaning of 'sin' in v. 7, there can be little doubt in v. 8. Here Paul brings sin into the open and speaks of it as the enemy that has gained a foothold in man's experience.

Paul says that apart from the law 'sin lies dead'. He has already said that the Christian community has died to sin (Rom. 6:6). In that passage, death terminated the covenant relationship that man had with sin (Satan). If the same imagery is applied in v. 8—and we recognize that when Paul says 'sin lies dead' he is speaking of Satan (as in chapter 6)—then he is saying that when Adam was in the garden, sin had no power over him. This changed when he violated the command not to eat from the tree of the knowledge of good and evil, for through disobedience the covenant with God was terminated. At this point, man entered into a relationship with sin (Satan), and the law was powerless to change it. Thus, in this covenantal/marriage paradigm, sin had no power before man disobeyed, for God was humankind's husband and the law was his will. Once Adam disobeyed, however, and acted like an adulterer by rejecting God's love and embracing Satan (sin), the law became powerless when it came to backing up God's covenantal claims. Through Adam's representative action, the covenant with God was severed and humankind became legally bound to another husband.

7:9 I was once alive apart from the law, but when the commandment came, sin came alive and I died.

Paul, as Adam, remembers the start of the story, before the tree of the knowledge of good and evil had been mentioned. As soon as the command was given, temptation presented itself and lured him to disobey the command of God. Sin came alive and took the opportunity to seduce Adam with false promises. This brought an end to fellowship with God and established humanity's bondage to sin. Satan assumed the place of the Creator and became humanity's master, and 'I [Adam] died'; humanity died to all that God had created them for.

7:10 The very commandment that promised life proved to be death to me.

At no point does Paul blame the law or God for sin, or for man's condition of being under condemnation. He knew the command was given for positive reasons, to bless and protect humanity. Adam's perversity in believing Satan's lie and in accusing God of malice was the problem.

7:11 For sin, seizing an opportunity through the commandment, deceived me and through it killed me.

Paul sees sin as a predator, waiting to attack and kill. Satan saw his opportunity in Eden when the command was given and realized that the law of God—given for humanity's blessing—could be used against Adam. By enticing him to disobey, he secured the decisive victory that he wanted. He turned man against God and put him into a position of guilt before the one who loved him. Adam fled from the pure love of God into the deceit and destruction of Satan. Satan had now, in effect, taken God's place, but without the truth, purity, holiness, and love that characterized the relationship he had destroyed. Adam's disobedience meant that sin would reign over man 'to death' (Rom. 5:17; cf. Rom. 7:2). Sin (Satan) achieved the death (or termination) of the covenant, which man was created to enjoy, and put Adam to death in terms of his relationship with God.

7:12 So the law is holy, and the commandment is holy and righteous and good.

This statement is at the heart of a crucial debate. Some think that Paul was speaking here of himself, either before or after his conversion. Those who think that this could not be Paul's pre-conversion experience argue that the unregenerate man has no pleasure in the word of God, so they believe the verse speaks of Paul's post- conversion experience, where he had been brought to love God and his word. The rest of the passage—the struggle with sin—is seen as Paul's Christian experience. The doctrine of sanctification then, is not about a naïve triumphalism but about continual conflict with the consequences of humanity's fallen condition. This view prevails amongst most Reformed scholars, and certainly matches the experience of countless believers.

The problem with this understanding is that, as we have previously noted, Judaism did not have this continual conflict with the law. The average Jew rejoiced in it as the gift of God and, far from seeing it as accusing him, saw it as protecting him and maintaining the covenant God had so graciously established between himself and his people (e.g. Psalm 19:7–14; 119:129–36). Paul testifies that he had this type of confidence in the law in his pre-Christian days (Phil. 3:4–6). So, the premise for such an interpretation is unreliable. Of course, this understanding envisages sin as indwelling but, as we have seen in chapter 6, Paul has a much bigger perspective of sin. Also, the traditional Reformed understanding, like most others, begins from an individualistic interpretation of the passage. I have suggested the evidence is not compatible with this. Rather, it points to the fact that Paul was speaking as a representative of a people. Scholars from a wide range of theological traditions share this conclusion. In making these comments about the passage, I am not denying that Paul struggled with sin or that individual believers continue to do so. I am saying that this existential reality should be interpreted from texts which deal with such issues of individual responsibility and conflict.

7:13 Did that which is good, then, bring death to me? By no means! It was sin, producing death in me through what is good, in order that sin might be shown to be sin, and through the commandment might become sinful beyond measure.

Paul reflects on the law and how it cornered him with guilt. He sees Adam questioning the purpose of the commandment that had been given and which he had broken. He hears Adam reasoning that it was because the commandment had been given that the fruit of the tree of the knowledge of good and evil was so appealing! 'It wasn't my fault,' he argued. 'It was the commandments. It had a negative effect by presenting me with temptation'. In other words, Adam was innocent; the commandment was to blame.

Such reasoning might sound reasonable to most twenty-first century readers, but it would be blasphemy for any first century Jew who gloried in the covenant God had made with his people! While the text suggests that Adam is the one who is making the case, Paul identifies with his argument. The apostle and his ancestor struggle with the effect of the law in exciting sin. They realize the law's negative effect is in stark contrast with its intrinsic goodness which reflects the character of God. The law has to be good because it is God's law. Paul reasons that it does what it does precisely because it is holy and true. The law, therefore, excites sin because it confronts it and accuses it (Jas. 1:23–25). It does not make man sinful; it exposes him to be so.

7:14 For we know that the law is spiritual, but I am of the flesh, sold under sin.

Israel's calling was to be the bride of God (Isa. 43:1; 44:22; 54:5; 62:5). This went disastrously wrong when his bride became the possession of other gods. She repeated Adam's error and sold herself to sin (Satan). Paul employs the same imagery he used earlier in chapter 6 and the beginning of chapter 7, saying that humanity is now found in a new marriage relationship 'of the flesh, sold under sin' for which they were not created. This is the consequence of rejecting the covenant and embracing the promise of Satan, who was a liar from the beginning. The adulterous relationship humanity has been seduced into is not the law's doing, but neither is it one the law can undo.

7:15 For I do not understand my own actions. For I do not do what I want, but I do the very thing I hate.

Members of fallen humanity are no longer in control of their lives. They might try to live according to their conscience but find that their conscience accuses them. This was not only the experience of Adam, but of Paul, and all who have begun to realize that they are not citizens of the kingdom of God. The promises that once gave an assurance of freedom, meaning, and fulfilment are discovered to be empty lies. The one who offered deity delivers nothing other than despair and hopelessness. The realization that we are powerless to change our condition is the first step towards receiving the grace of God.

7:16 Now if I do what I do not want, I agree with the law, that it is good.

This statement is the pivotal point of the chapter. In this statement, he has come to the point in his argument where he says the law is not at fault. This is demonstrated in his attempts to keep the law because he knows it to be right. Again, the drama can be observed at several levels, one being Adam's discovery that the law he had rejected was not meant to limit him, as Satan had claimed, but to protect his liberty. Having rejected the law and tasted Satan's false brand of 'freedom', Adam/Paul longs to keep the law in the way God intended. The experience is true for Adam, Israel, Paul, and all humankind.

7:17 So now it is no longer I who do it, but sin that dwells within me.

Whether Adam, Israel or Paul, this is the reality of every person's experience. There is something that overpowers humanity in its corporate, as well as individual, existence. It is the reality of sin. We have already seen that Paul's understanding of 'the body of sin' is mainly corporate. As a part of the body of sin, every person in Adam is under sin's control. No matter how strenuous and urgent the struggle to be free, humankind is under the power of Satan and helpless to change its condition.

Questions are often raised about the expression, 'sin that dwells within me'. In what way does sin dwell in Paul if he is speaking as Adam (humankind)? Some argue that the expression means that sin is 'biologically inherited'. I have argued this is a Hellenistic and dualistic intrusion into Paul's Hebraic mind-set and ought to have no place in biblical thinking.[10] The statement is about Adam seeing his offspring controlled by sin (Satan).

7:18 For I know that nothing good dwells in me, that is, in my flesh. For I have the desire to do what is right, but not the ability to carry it out.

The statement speaks of the utter despair of a person who realizes that all of the greatest achievements of humanity have ultimately been orchestrated by sin. There is no part of human experience—culture, education, music, art, politics, commerce, religion, psychology, ethics, etc.— that has not been defiled, corrupted, and flawed. People might long for the restoration of paradise, but they reject the affiliation that made it possible—

---

[10] See Holland, *Romans: The Divine Marriage*, pp. 203–225

the relationship between the creature and his Creator whom they were made to love and obey.

7:19 For I do not do the good I want, but the evil I do not want is what I keep on doing.

Satan's promise was that Adam would be as God, but it has become clear he became a stooge of the one who fooled him. He is now a slave of sin, with no claims to the blessings of his Creator, whom he abandoned.

7:20 Now if I do what I do not want, it is no longer I who do it, but sin that dwells within me.

Paul now establishes that there is something more evil than people—something that controls them which they cannot master. This does not take away his responsibility, but it does acknowledge an evil 'force' that is greater than himself. Whereas Paul's struggle to keep the law acknowledged its intrinsic goodness, his struggle with sin demonstrates sin's intrinsic evil. Paul is arguing for more than the weakness of humankind; he argues for the reality of evil, which is personified in Satan. It has deceived humanity, bringing it into a condition from which it cannot escape.

7:21 So I find it to be a law that when I want to do right, evil lies close at hand.

In referring to the law, Paul is not concerned with a particular commandment but with a principle or authority. He has already spoken of the woman who was under the law of her husband—this for humankind is the law of Satan, that is of sin and death, from which none can escape. Because it is legally binding, it effectively renders God helpless when it comes to rescuing humankind—their condition is the consequence of the relationship Adam willingly accepted. In this way, the offspring of Adam compared to a helpless woman who is married to an abusive husband. Although there were grounds for divorce in the Old Testament, it was only the husband who could free the wife by issuing the divorce certificate (Deut. 24). The only sure way for a wife to be able to take a new husband was on her husband's death—a situation that pertains in the Jewish community to this day.

Romans 7: An Analysis of the Problem

7:22 For I delight in the law of God, in my inner being,

Paul has a tortuous fascination with that which condemns. It ought to comfort him, but it terrifies him. Within his heart, there is a cry for the security the law once gave in protecting the relationship with God for which he had been created. But now, while Paul delights in acknowledging its perfection, at the same time he experiences dread in anticipating its condemnation. Some see that the following verses in this chapter and the opening verses of chapter 8 have been dislocated in the Greek copies of Paul's original letter. But a corporate view of Paul's argument means the verses make sense as they are.[11]

7:23 but I see in my members another law waging war against the law of my mind and making me captive to the law of sin that dwells in my members.

The other law Paul writes about functions in a different way. The Law of Moses had been given to rule the life of Israel. It was taught to every generation of Jews from infancy and it was intended to be a law that protected the people of God from Satan; but instead, because of her sin, it became a law that bound her to him. The essence of this law had been planted in the heart of the human family and so it operated as a safeguard to protect humanity from the father of lies. This law is holy and good, but now, because of the fall, it condemns! Its function in condemning makes it into 'another law' that wages war against the fallen will of man.

In a similar way, the civil law is intended to protect, but also condemns. With an individualistic perspective it is easy to read the statement 'in my members' as a reference to Paul's physical body and that his problem is one of sensual sins. If I am right to interpret the 'body of sin' (Rom. 6:6) as corporate and the exhortation not to yield members to unrighteousness as an appeal to the church to exercise discipline, then the expression 'my members' focuses on the experience of Adam and his offspring. Paul,

---

[11] For a discussion of this see *Holland, Romans: The Divine Marriage*, pp. 243–245

speaking as Adam, sees his progeny being taken over by sin, with murder, deceit, sexual impurity, etc. (Rom. 1:16–31) coming to fruition among them.

7:24 Wretched man that I am! Who will deliver me from this body of death?

Paul cries out the lament of death—he sees the condition of humanity as being hopeless. However, the cry is not for deliverance from his earthly body. It is much more than this. The argument continues to address the corporate aspects of sin. 'This body of death' is nothing less than the body of sin—the bride of Satan. So, Paul's cry is, 'who will deliver me from the kingdom of darkness?'

And who or what is the wretched man? If our reading has been correctly following Paul's corporate argument, then Israel is also in Adam along with the Gentiles; together they form the body of sin. In this exiled state there is a section of this community that is truly alarmed and desires to be freed from this desperate condition. This section of the body of sin is marked out in that it cries onto God for mercy and intervention. This strictly defined people are not only defined as members of the body of sin but also at another level as the wretched man, the self- loathing community that long for restoration of fellowship with God. They are the remnant whose cry God heard and responded to in Christ's saving death.

The rule of Satan has determined the developing argument since Romans 5:12 when the description of the human race in Adam was introduced. This is what Paul discovered through his encounter with Christ. His privileges as a Jew had counted for nothing, for he, like his fellow Jews, had been as much part of the kingdom of darkness as the Gentiles had been.

7:25 Thanks be to God through Jesus Christ our Lord! So then, I myself serve the law of God with my mind, but with my flesh I serve the law of sin.

Deliverance can come only through God sending his Son as a sin offering. Here, in his triumphant proclamation, Paul anticipates the next stage of his argument when he will continue to explain the process and significance of release from Satan's power and the provision that God has made for his people's subsequent pilgrimage.

Further Study: Questions for Romans 7

1. Why has chapter 7 been such a difficult passage to interpret?

2. What is it about the opening verses that suggest it is not about the experience of one person?

3. What does the term 'flesh' mean to a Jew, and how does this differ from the way a Greek person would use and understand the same term?

4. How does reading the passage as a piece of Jewish literature help to make sense of it?

5. Work through the passage and see if you can identify what 'law' Paul is referring to. Is it used consistently with the same meaning? If there is more than one meaning, list the possibilities.

6. What has Christ done to brings the outburst of praise and gratitude from Paul in v. 25?

Romans 8: The Liberated People

Introduction

An expression of relief marks the opening of the eighth chapter. Paul states that the longed-for salvation has been realized: not on the grounds of man's actions but of God's; not according to the flesh but according to the Spirit (Rom. 8:5–7); not through keeping the law but because of a perfect sacrifice for sin (Rom. 8:3).

It is Christ's death that liberates and brings the children of God out of bondage. By entering the realm of sin's domain, the Son challenged sin at the point where Satan's power was strongest. Subjecting himself to the full force of sin's attack, Jesus (in the realm of human likeness and weakness, but without sin) entered into conflict to deliver his own people (Rom. 8:3). This fulfilled the righteous requirements of the law. Indeed, it was to this event that the Law and the Prophets had pointed (Rom. 1:2; 3:21). Although the exodus under Moses was a national, geographical, and political deliverance, it failed to remove Israel from her spiritual bondage because she was still in Adam and under the same condemnation as the Gentiles. However, as a type (1 Cor. 10:1–6), the exodus under Moses pointed to this greater exodus, which Christ would bring about. When Paul speaks of living 'according the flesh' (Rom. 8:5), it could mean living in flagrant opposition to the law, or in such a way as to try and meet the law's demands in an attempt to achieve righteousness. Such righteousness rejects the divinely appointed way (Rom. 10:1– 4). The unbelieving Jew had put his confidence in Moses and the sacrifices of the Temple, not in God or in the sacrifice of his Son. But God had now set the Temple sacrifices aside, for it is Christ, the Passover sacrifice, who has wrought salvation from sin and death.

Paul insists there can be no neutral zone in man's relationship with God (Rom. 8:6), for to reject his purposes is to be at enmity with him. This does not necessarily mean a deliberate rejection of the law's requirements but of failing to grasp, and then live up to, its intent. This is where Paul and his fellow countrymen had stumbled so often. Rather than being guided by the law, they had made adhering to it their goal. It had become the barrier to doing the will of God, for they had made keeping it— something they gloried in—the grounds for the hope that they would participate in the eschatological salvation. The law had become an idol—their object of worship.

The difference between a man under law and one under grace is the possession of the Spirit. It was this gift that formed part of the promises to the community in exile (Isa. 44:3; 59:21; 61:1–3; Ezek. 36:24–28). The Jews were assured that because they could not achieve what God had purposed for them in their own strength, they would be empowered by the Spirit. He would not only guide, but sustain and comfort them in their pilgrimage, finally establishing them in their inheritance. To walk in the Spirit was to walk by faith and to receive the righteousness to which the law pointed. As with Abraham, it meant being a son of God through faith, leaving the natural dwelling place, and making a journey by faith to the Promised Land. It meant no longer keeping the Passover as Moses had done but acknowledging that Christ, the true Passover, was slain (Rom. 3:21–26; 1 Cor. 5:7). It meant abandoning all privilege and respectability as Moses had, and receiving the promise of mercy and forgiveness (Heb. 11:24–29).

To enter this righteousness was to enter into the eschatological community. While the church continues to live under the physical sentence of death, awaiting its final redemption, the gift of the Spirit (Rom. 8:11) guarantees what is to come. His presence not only transforms the believers' lifestyles in the present (Rom. 8:13) but will bring about a metamorphosis of the church's physical existence in the resurrection (Rom. 8:16–17).

Paul's theme of sonship has long been regarded as being modelled on Roman adoption law. However, this has been questioned because his reference to the gift of the Spirit, with Messianic associations of sonship, suggests that he continues to draw from the concepts of Old Testament redemptive history. The Messiah was the figure that God would raise up to accomplish his redemptive purposes for his people, and the giving of the Spirit was one of the essential provisions for accomplishing this task. The

Romans 8: The Liberated People

king, who was endowed with the Spirit, was the supreme model of the long-awaited Messiah, the Son of God. It is this Messianic imagery that Paul draws upon when he describes believers as 'children of God', who are destined to rule the world on his behalf. Jesus is described as the 'firstborn among many brothers' (Rom. 8:29). In the Passover narrative it was the firstborn son who was designated by God to represent the family—his life was threatened because of that. As the Old Testament unfolds, we see that it is the eldest brother (the firstborn) who shouldered the responsibility for being the 'redeemer' of the family and was considered to be responsible for the well-being of his brothers and sisters.

Jesus was Joseph and Mary's firstborn, but the fact that there is no mention in the gospels of his redemption according to the law (Exod. 13:14–16; 34:20) would be seen as a remarkable omission by any Jew—it in effect meant that Jesus was designated as God's firstborn. Psalm 89:27 declares, 'I will also appoint him my firstborn, the most exalted of the kings of the earth'—we have seen Jesus is continually proclaimed as such (Rom. 1:3).

So it is that Jesus was put to death, as the King of the Jews, when the Jewish Passover lambs were being slain. It is not that Jesus was the firstborn, but rather that he acted in such a capacity when he made a sacrifice for sin (Rom. 8:3); redeeming his people, and the 'whole creation' (Rom. 8:18–25; Col. 1:15). Because Jesus is the redeemer, the Christ, the Son of David, the Son of God, and the beloved firstborn Son, he is able to lead his people safely through their earthly pilgrimage, no matter what they face from the enemy of their souls (Rom. 8:30–39).

8:1 There is therefore now no condemnation for those who are in Christ Jesus.

Paul discussed the theme of condemnation in Romans 5:16 when he wrote, 'the judgment following one trespass brought condemnation, but the free gift following many trespasses brought justification'. In chapters 6–7, Paul explained the solidarity that man has with sin and death. The only way out of this condemnation was through the sacrifice of Christ. He was the last Adam, who acted for his people.

The opening of chapter 8 is a cry of glorious assurance. In Adam, there was nothing but condemnation and hopelessness; but in Christ, there is redemption, for he has brought his people out from under the rule and authority of sin. The end of this rule was not merely that their sins had been forgiven but that the covenant relationship, which had bound them into an existence with sin and death, had been terminated. The consequences of that relationship have been ended through the annulling of the covenant (Rom. 7:1–4).

There are distinct echoes of the original exodus in this verse. At the original Passover the Jews could assert that they were no longer living under condemnation; the power of Pharaoh to harm, or even destroy, was removed, and the fear of God's judgment was ended. Through the death of Christ, our Passover sacrifice (1 Cor. 5:7), God has provided the only adequate sin offering. He had to surrender his only Son to rescue his people from destruction. Like the deliverance of the Jews from Egypt, this deliverance was double edged. First, there was deliverance from Satan who determined to heap destruction on the people of God, seeking to control and silence the church's testimony. Second, there was deliverance from the judgment that God, the holy and righteous one, must pass on all who break his holy law.

This deliverance does not benefit everyone. It is only for those who are 'in Christ Jesus'. Those who, through unbelief, choose to remain members of the body of sin stay in the kingdom of darkness, remaining under condemnation and judgment put on Adam.

8:2 For the law of the Spirit of life has set you free in Christ Jesus from the law of sin and death.

By using the phrase 'set you free', Paul continues to act out the experience of man outlined in chapter 7. The opening verses of chapter 8 are the conclusion to chapter 7 and not the start of a new section. They describe the new man's liberation from bondage to sin and death. The section they introduce still deals with the process of redemption and describes the Spirit's involvement. The corporate reading of the text must continue.

Romans 8: The Liberated People

We have been set free from the law of sin and death; the covenant authority of Satan has now been cancelled through the representative, covenant-annulling death of Jesus, who is the last Adam. Those who have called on Christ are part of the church. This is his body, the eschatological bride who is under the law of her new husband.

There is now a state of transition as the church waits for the completion of her redemption and the consummation of her wedding to the lamb; the groom being represented by the Spirit who acts as the bride's custodian. It is the Spirit who is charged with leading the people of God to glory for the final revelation of Christ's love toward his people. Thus, the law of the Spirit is the law of Christ. This law is the authority the Spirit has as he guides, protects, teaches, and prepares the bride for her presentation before her groom, the Son of God. The paradigm is clearly that of the exodus—whether Egyptian or Babylonian—for the Spirit was active in both with the same goal of bringing the people of God to their inheritance and their final experience of God's love in the eschatological marriage (Hosea 2:14–16 speaks of God taking Israel as his bride during the Egyptian exodus and Isaiah 54:1–8 speaks of the divine marriage being the conclusion of the forthcoming exodus from Babylon). Jesus and the apostles clearly knew and used this imagery (see Matt. 22:1–14; 2 Cor. 11:2; Eph. 5:25–27; Rev. 19:7).

The Spirit's work is not independent—it is through Christ Jesus. In other words, it is only because Christ has died for his people that the Spirit can lead them as the sons of God (and soon to be bride of Christ). As the Spirit is obeyed, the old life is forsaken, and his ministry appropriates the deliverance that was the purpose of the Son's death (Rom. 7:4–6). The Spirit applies to the church what the Son achieved through his death. In this way, his ministry sets the church free from the law of sin and death. It is a constant reminder to the church of what Christ has done for his people, so the threatening accusations of Satan ('sin and death') can be seen for what they are. This assurance gives the church the freedom to enter the life to which Christ has called her.

8:3 For God has done what the law, weakened by the flesh, could not do. By sending his own Son in the likeness of sinful flesh and for sin, he condemned sin in the flesh

Paul's argument is about the condition of man rather than the sins he has committed—but this is not how many commentators and translators of Paul's letters see it. While most scholars acknowledge that, for Paul, sarx describes humanity in Adam (or in the kingdom of darkness) many commentators prefer an understanding of personal guilt. While Paul clearly had a doctrine of personal sin, to read Paul's letters (and the New Testament in general) from this Augustinian perspective is a mistake. Augustine's understanding of the biblical teaching about sin was tainted by his background in Greek philosophical schools, which he explored before his conversion. With this mind-set Paul's corporate view of sin is minimized and the power of his argument lost. In the context of Romans 8:3, Paul is not writing about a person's 'sinful nature' (as per NIVTM), but his fallen condition in Adam.

So, Paul is continuing the argument begun in Romans 5. The law was given as the covenant gift to protect Israel's relationship with God. But through that same law God was bound to condemn Israel for her actions—a new lover had taken the heart of his divine bride. The law was 'weakened by the flesh'—that is man's choice (in Adam) to have a relationship with sin. This new relationship was recognized under the law and so the wife was 'bound to her husband' (Rom. 7:2). The law was helpless to change man's new situation; in fact, it did the opposite—it held him in it.

However, what the law could not do, Christ has done. Through his death, he condemned sin in the flesh and brought to an end its dominance and authority. Christ's death terminated the previous marriage (Rom. 7:1–6). It was into this fallen condition that Christ came, experiencing the weakness and utter vulnerability of humanity. This was more than the weakness of being a creature—it was the weakness of the surrender of his glory (Heb. 2:5–18). Christ's experience was not identical with ours because he did not share our guilt, having never sinned (2 Cor. 5:21). For this reason, Paul qualifies his description of Christ's coming by saying that he came in the 'likeness of sinful flesh'. Such a statement is not suggesting that Christ was less than truly human.

We have seen that Paul views Christ's death as a Paschal offering, as do the other New Testament writers. We have seen earlier (see comments on

Romans 8: The Liberated People

Romans 3:21–26) that Ezekiel describes the Son of David as offering the sacrifices of the Day of Atonement at the eschatological Passover in order to deal with the covenant community's sin (Ezekiel 45:18–25). We have further seen that the original Passover took place so that God could take Israel as his bride. It is out of this type of the Paschal new exodus that Paul continues to argue. Christ's death is a sin offering; it is the Paschal offering that brings deliverance. It is the Messiah's death alone that is the foundation of the new age, for he established a new relationship with God for his people.

8:4 in order that the righteous requirement of the law might be fulfilled in us, who walk not according to the flesh but according to the Spirit.

Again, I would question the prevailing understanding of this verse, which sees that the penal demands of the law have been met. While this is part of the picture, it is probably the secondary meaning. Paul, I would claim, is saying that the death of Christ has brought to an end all former relationships for his people, and the law's demand regarding the establishment of a new relationship has been met. Paul is repeating what he has said in Romans 6:7, that those who have died with Christ are justified from sin.

There is no charge that can be made against the new relationship. It is not an adulterous one as the law's righteous requirements have been met in the representative covenant-annulling death of Christ. The argument continues to be a corporate one, describing the conditions of two communities.

Paul is saying that the requirements of the law have been met for those who live under the authority of the Spirit, the one who is the custodian of the bride. However, these requirements are not met for those who continue to be part of the body of sin. As fallen humanity, they reject the application of the covenant- annulling death of Jesus. Thus, living 'according to the flesh' is not primarily about gross sins but about continuing to live in Adam. This is the inevitable consequence of rejecting the lordship of Jesus, the last Adam.

8:5 For those who live according to the flesh set their minds on the things of the flesh, but those who live according to the Spirit set their minds on the things of the Spirit.

Paul is saying that those who are members of Adam (the body of sin) live governed by the headship of Satan. Those who have received the Spirit—who are part of the eschatological community—live under the authority of the Spirit. They desire to do what is asked of them because they are being prepared for their entrance into the presence of their redeemer God. The motivation for those who live according to the Spirit is God's love because this has been poured out, by his Spirit, into the hearts of his redeemed people (Rom. 5:5).

8:6 For to set the mind on the flesh is death, but to set the mind on the Spirit is life and peace.

'Flesh' means the value system of man in Adam, the carnal (or old) man. Living in this condition means eternal separation from God. Paul's statement to the believers in Rome (v. 6a) reflects the warning given to Adam in the Garden before the fall, 'for in the day that you eat of it you shall surely die' (Gen. 2:15–17), and the exhortation given to the Israelites before they crossed the Jordan into the Promised Land, 'I have set before you today life and good, death and evil. Therefore, choose life" (Deut. 30:15, 19). Thus, Paul is writing about the realm of human experience without God—the condition Adam chose in preference to loving obedience to his Creator. Paul is saying that all who choose this way will know death or eternal separation from the lover of their souls.

In contrast, the pilgrim people of God, led by the Spirit, are being taken to their inheritance. This will include the experience of dwelling forever with God, which is life and peace. The statement in Romans 8:6b is not about the believer experiencing peace at all times in this life, nor does it imply that when a believer is robbed of peace, his salvation should be doubted (Paul himself knew times of acute anxiety as 2 Corinthians 2:4, 13; 11:28–29 make clear). The statement is about the end of the pilgrimage, when the new covenant community—led by the Spirit—is brought safely into her inheritance, experiencing life and peace. Indeed, a characteristic of the new covenant was that it established peace (Isa. 52:7; 54:13; Ezek. 34:25; 37:26). The peace that the individual believer now has is based on the fact that God can be trusted to fulfil his promise and they are therefore safe, regardless of what happens to them.

Romans 8: The Liberated People

Paul, like Moses (Deut. 30:15–16), is telling the people there are two ways set before humanity: the way of life and the way of death. Just as Moses urged the Israelites to choose the way of life, Paul urges the Roman church to do the same and accept that believers have no abiding place on earth. They are part of the pilgrim community whose home is in heaven (Phil. 3:20). Pilgrimage language has been used in Romans 5:1–4 and we see it again in Romans 8:35–39. The parallel between Israel's pilgrimage and that of the church continues. The exegesis is essentially corporate and typological.

8:7 For the mind that is set on the flesh is hostile to God, for it does not submit to God's law; indeed, it cannot.

The 'mind that is set on the flesh' concerns the mind in its relationship in Adam rather than to its degree of sinfulness. This does not deny the fundamental reality of the sinfulness of each individual but does more justice to Paul's corporate perspective of humanity's state in sin through Adam. Such a mind leaves the true and only God out of its consideration and is concerned with man's immediate existence.

8:8 Those who are in the flesh cannot please God.

Paul sums up his preceding argument. He is concerned for the believers in Rome to appreciate that being in Adam (in the flesh) is to be incapable of pleasing God. It is for this reason that he is convinced of the necessity for all men to believe in Christ. From his experience, and from his knowledge of the Scriptures, Paul had come to understand that his sincerity in keeping the highest religious ideals and practices had not changed his state of 'being in Adam'. He had been at enmity towards God, and his religion had been an excuse for dismissing the claims of his Creator—the God of Abraham, David and Jesus.

8:9 You, however, are not in the flesh but in the Spirit, if in fact the Spirit of God dwells in you. Anyone who does not have the Spirit of Christ does not belong to him.

Because of Paul's use of the pronoun *hymeis* ('you'—plural) we know that he is addressing the church community in Rome. Having explained the condition of man in Adam (in the flesh), he wants to assure the believers there they have nothing to fear. He is persuaded they are no longer in Adam but in Christ, for they now have the 'Spirit of Christ'. In this realm, the church has the 'first-fruits' of all future blessings that will be enjoyed in heaven. In other words, on the basis of the work of Christ in his death, the Spirit is present with the believing community in Rome, leading her to the New Jerusalem.

The Roman Christians (along with all other believers) were united with Christ by the Spirit (Rom. 6:1–4). Here in Romans 8:9, Paul is writing about the Spirit who has been given to the Roman community to guide and protect her as she makes her eschatological pilgrimage to her inheritance. Along with all other believing communities she is making her pilgrimage to her heavenly home.

Most expositors apply statements concerning the Spirit directly to the experience of the individual believer, thus leading the reader away from the New Testament dimension of the Spirit and the church. It is a false methodology to individualize the pneumatology (the workings of the Holy Spirit) of a letter before it has been considered first as a statement of the Spirit's work in the community. Only then can its significance and meaning be extrapolated for the individual. This must be done with great care, however, as what is true for the church is not always true for the believer.

For example, while the Scriptures call the church 'the temple of the Holy Spirit', it is not true of the individual believer. It is true that the Spirit dwells in the individual (2 Tim. 1:14), but to say that a person is a temple is to say that God dwells in his fullness in each believer. The fact that God's Spirit will be poured out on all flesh in the last days (Joel 2:28), does not justify individualizing the promise. Paul is saying to the church in Rome that she is not under the dominance of sin and living in the flesh but is in Christ and living in fellowship with the Spirit who leads her. The church has already been described as the community on pilgrimage (Rom. 5:1–4), and Paul will soon echo those same themes of perseverance and triumph (Rom. 8:35–39). He kept in view the fact that he is dealing with the experience of the eschatological community on its earthly, heaven-bound pilgrimage.

In saying 'anyone who does not have the Spirit of Christ does not belong to him', Paul is not focusing on the individual but on the church. We saw in Romans 5:5 that the outpouring of the Spirit related to the birth of the church in Rome, the beginning of her existence. In the New Testament it was expected that every church established in an area that had not previously had the gospel was marked out by God through the gift of his Spirit. This was true on the Day of Pentecost (Acts 2:1– 36), when the apostles were sent down to see if the believers in Antioch had received the Spirit (Acts 8:14–17), and when the Gentiles turned to Christ (Acts 10:44–18); so it was the natural question for Paul to ask of the Ephesians who he thought were followers of Jesus, 'Did you receive the Holy Spirit when you believed?' (Acts 19:2)

8:10 But if Christ is in you, although the body is dead because of sin, the Spirit is life because of righteousness.

The text actually reads, 'But if Christ is in you (pl.), the body (sing.) is dead because of sin, yet the Spirit (sing.) is alive because of righteousness'. If Paul is writing about the experience of the individual believer, as many think, he would be saying that his physical body was still under the sentence of death, eventually yielding to the reality of its mortality. The problem with this interpretation is that it has departed from the corporate perspective of the letter. 'Christ in you' here is similar to the phrase in Colossians 1:27, 'Christ in you (pl.) the hope of glory'. Here, as in other passages, the emphasis is on Christ dwelling in the church, not in the individual.

So 'the body is dead because of sin', is better translated, 'The body being dead with respect to Satan'. The statement refers to the death to sin that Paul has explained in Romans 7:1–6. The people of God in Rome, with all other believers, are free to live in the Spirit and serve their new master. The church is, therefore, no longer under the power of death, sin or Satan. Paul will expound this tension of being in Christ yet still bound to the fallen earthly existence later in the chapter (8:21).

The NIVTM in our verse has 'your spirit' suggesting the individual believer, but the original Greek implies a reference to the Holy Spirit who dwells among the believers so ESV has gone correctly I believe with 'the Spirit'. This reading is supported by Paul's statement in the next verse (Rom. 8:11) which speaks about the Holy Spirit of God without introduction.

8:11 If the Spirit of him who raised Jesus from the dead dwells in you, he who raised Christ Jesus from the dead will also give life to your mortal bodies through his Spirit who dwells in you.

Elsewhere, Paul calls Jesus 'the first-fruits of those who have fallen asleep' (1 Cor. 15:20). In the Old Testament, the priest brought the first gathering of the wheat harvest, the first-fruits, into the Tabernacle or Temple to dedicate the coming harvest to the Lord (Lev. 23:9–11). The first-fruit offering was made three days after the Passover and explains the early church's insistence that Jesus rose on the third day (1 Cor. 15:3). His resurrection was seen as the fulfilment of the type found in the book of Leviticus; the Easter events being interpreted as the fulfilment of the Passover. Paul here encourages the believers that, because Jesus has been raised from the dead by the Spirit, they will, in turn, be raised in the same way.

Again, the framework of the argument is the community, not the individual. This is made explicit by the Greek. Paul says the Spirit 'dwells in you (pl.)'. However, the focus is about to change, as Paul writes that the Spirit will give life to 'your mortal bodies'. In other words, the focus is no longer the corporate experience of resurrection but that of each believer. Paul speaks of their common experience as members one of another and as members of Christ. This switch underlines that while we are seeking to follow the corporate thinking of the apostle, he never leaves the individual out of the frame of his thought. The church is made up of individuals and they will, with the rest of the church, be raised on the last day.

Thus, the concluding statement 'through his Spirit who dwells in you', can refer to the Spirit in them individually or collectively. If we accept that the arguments of letters written to churches are about God's saving action toward his people, the church, then the latter reading is natural. The former is not found in any of Paul's other letters to the churches, but it is found in the personally addressed letter to Timothy (2 Tim. 1:14). Thus, because the

Romans 8: The Liberated People

Spirit dwells in them collectively, as God's Temple, he will care for them and raise every individual member of that community on the last day.

8:12 So then, brothers, we are debtors, not to the flesh, to live according to the flesh.

Paul is arguing that, because the church is the redeemed community and her ultimate deliverance is certain, she has no reason to live as though she is a part of the body of sin, the kingdom of darkness. Her destiny is to be revealed as the spotless bride of the Messiah (Eph. 5:25–27). Her obligation, therefore, is to prepare for that momentous day and not live her life as though destined for judgment. Her destiny is glorious and secure because her redeemer, the firstborn, has died.

Christ has not only redeemed her through his death but will fulfil his redeemer role by marrying her (Rom. 7:1–4. See Deut. 25:5–10 and Ruth 3:12; 4:1–8 for the laws of levirate marriage). This marriage imagery is part of the second exodus motif (Isa. 49:20–21; 50:1–2; 54:1–8; 62:4–5). We have seen this imagery in Romans 7:1–6 and shall see it in themes developed later in the chapter, reinforcing the new exodus paradigm that is guiding our exegesis. Because the church is betrothed to Christ, she is obliged to live a life that pleases him.

8:13 For if you live according to the flesh you will die, but if by the Spirit you put to death the deeds of the body, you will live.

The statement echoes again Moses' warnings to the Jews in Deuteronomy 30:15– 16 (cf. Jer. 21:8). He set before the Israelites two ways: the way of life and the way of death. Moses urges them to choose life. The law was thought to have brought life; to reject it was to embrace death and judgment.

Paul is saying that, if the lives of the Roman believers are characterized by independence from God, they will die. This reference to death can be seen at several levels. It can refer to death as separation from God, but the problem with this reading is that it denies the eternal safety of the believers in Rome. However, if the corporate setting is taken seriously, this problem is removed. In this setting, the statement means that the church in Rome would die. She would come under judgment, and her 'lampstand' (witness) would be removed (Rev. 2:5). This is an experience that had fallen on some Christian communities. Indeed, some backslidden members of congregations might die, as happened in Corinth (1 Cor. 11:29–32). The importance of guarding a congregation from entering this realm cannot be over-emphasized. This is the reason for the appeal and warnings in Paul's first letter to the Corinthians (in 1 Corinthians chapters 5 to 6 and 10:1–22).

Paul has said that the Spirit will give life (Rom. 8:11); now he says that the same Spirit will help the believers die to their old existence in Adam. The 'deeds of the body' are not necessarily to do with physical sin, such as sexual immorality, but have more to do with the lifestyle of the body of sin, the life that characterizes those who are in Adam.

8:14 For all who are led by the Spirit of God are sons of God.

This statement has been characteristic of the people of God throughout the ages. It was true of Abraham as he obeyed the command to leave his father's family and country. It was true of Israel when she was led by the Spirit (seen in rabbinical writings to be symbolized by the pillar of cloud by day and the pillar of fire by night), and it was true of Israel when she returned from exile in Babylon (Isa. 44:3; 59:21; 61:1–3; Ezek. 36:24–28; 37:1–4).

In this verse, the new exodus theme is again the backdrop of Paul's thinking. He is saying that there can be no individualism, with believers separating themselves from the body of Christ's people. The leading of the Spirit is essentially a corporate experience, when the covenant community is guided on its pilgrimage to the New Jerusalem (Acts 15:28; 16:7–10). In arguing for a corporate setting for the passage, I am not denying that the Spirit can give specific guidance to individuals at crucial times in their lives (Acts 8:26; 13:1–3; 18:9). However, even in these texts, the guidance is about major steps that need to be taken to further the gospel's proclamation rather than about individual preoccupations.

8:15 For you did not receive the spirit of slavery to fall back into fear, but you have received the Spirit of adoption as sons, by whom we cry, "Abba! Father!"

Romans 8: The Liberated People

Paul exhorts the believers in Rome not to 'fall back into fear'. We can surely hear Moses saying such to the Jews as they panicked in the wilderness, wanting to return to the 'comfort' and 'security' of Egypt despite having had the Spirit present with them, guiding and protecting them, as did the church at Rome.

Paul urges them to continue living as the redeemed people of God. Such commitment brings difficulties—even hostility and persecution. He urges them not to be afraid but to recognize these have been the experience of the people of God throughout the centuries. Indeed, persecution is evidence of her calling. Without it there would be grounds for questioning her testimony (Acts 14:22; 2 Tim. 2:11–13).

The presence of the Spirit changes the circumstances of the people of God. It is not that they have learned to grin and bear their sufferings, but rather that their sufferings have been transformed and they can rejoice in them (Rom. 5:3; Jas. 1:2).

Paul speaks regularly about how the world is challenged by the way Christians suffer for their Lord (2 Cor. 12:7–10; Phil. 1:12–30; 1 Thess. 1:6–8). The Holy Spirit, as the Spirit of adoption, gives them joy. He reminds them their suffering is vital evidence that they are part of the eschatological community, and that they have left the acceptance and security of the world as they journey towards their inheritance (Rom. 5:1ff.).

The Aramaic term 'Abba' was deeply personal and carried huge respect. It is the type of greeting that a child might give to his father as he cries out 'Daddy, Daddy'. It speaks of belonging and confidence in a father's care. Using the term 'Abba' in a letter to people unfamiliar with Aramaic seems remarkable. But it is not so surprising if the passage preserves a liturgical formula that was used by the church's evangelists and teachers. If this is the case, its meaning would have been explained to the Gentile converts and retained in its original form as an expression of the church's heritage.

Alternatively, the church may have taught its converts the Lord's Prayer in Aramaic as this was also part of its heritage. In comments on chapter 12, it is noted that Romans 12:9–21 and Matthew's account of the Sermon on the Mount (Matt. 6:9–13) in which Jesus taught his disciples how to pray are similar. The idea has been propounded that the early churches possessed copies of Matthew's gospel. If that was so, the term 'Abba' at the opening of that prayer would be familiar to believers such as those in Rome.

So, the Spirit prompts the believing community to affirm God's Fatherhood. Israel was called God's son when she was brought out of Egypt (Exod. 4:22) and, at that time, she was given the gift of the Spirit as a down payment of the bridal gifts that were to be given at Sinai and on entering Canaan. Here, the same pattern is followed; for the church is not only redeemed and forgiven but given the Spirit to create the covenant/marriage relationship with Christ, her redeemer.

8.16 The Spirit himself bears witness with our spirit that we are children of God,

The Spirit has always been the undisputed evidence that God has accepted a people for himself. Peter was confident that the household of Cornelius had been accepted by God when he saw how the Spirit came upon them (Acts 15:6–9). Because of that, he dared not refuse them baptism—even though they were not circumcised. This acceptance was a shift of position for such a rigid Jew and shows how important the testimony of the Spirit was for the early church.

But the Spirit's work is not only historical. Paul uses the present tense when he says that the Spirit testifies with our spirit that we are God's children. His work is an ongoing work, in which he brings assurance and guidance to each generation of believers. The phrase 'with our spirit' suggests it is the church that is thus witnessed to, but it is individuals who are confirmed to be God's children. Just because God's dealings with Israel were at the corporate, covenantal, and historical level, they did not override the individual Jew's response to God, or his calling by him. The covenant community was the context in which the individual experienced all that God was to him. This same corporate experience of the people of God is found in this letter to the Romans. For Paul and the Roman believers, it would have been the most natural way of reading and understanding the letter.

The Messiah King and His Bride's Suffering

8:17 and if children, then heirs—heirs of God and fellow heirs with Christ, provided we suffer with him in order that we may also be glorified with him.

Here we begin to see more clearly the model Paul has used for sonship. There are scholars who would argue that he used the pattern of Roman adoption procedures to illustrate his argument, pointing out that a Roman could adopt a slave into his family, and the law would give the adopted slave the same status and rights of inheritance as the natural-born children. They argue that Paul is saying that, although the Gentiles were once slaves, God has chosen them. Now they have a status equal to those who are naturally of the Jewish family. They are co-heirs with Christ.

While this is an attractive picture of adoption, some things Paul says do not fit the scheme. The gift of the Spirit, and the necessity of suffering, form key parts of Paul's description of sonship; but these are not found in the Roman model. To make this position even less reliable, recent research has shown that this adoption procedure only happened in a very remote province of the Empire. It is most unlikely that Paul ever knew of this practice, or that the Roman Christians would have had sufficient familiarity with this adoption procedure to understand an argument based on it.

But these factors are not a problem for the Old Testament pattern of adoption. Indeed, they are essential parts of the picture. Israel was called God's son when she obeyed and followed Moses out of slavery ('Out of Egypt I called my son' – see Hosea 11:1). She was given the Spirit to guide and protect her, and her obedience brought conflict with the enemies of God so that her pilgrimage was characterized by suffering.

This picture of Israel being the son of God is supported by Romans 9. Paul writes that it is not the physical descendants of Abraham who are the sons of God but his spiritual descendants (Rom. 9:8). It is clear that being a son of Abraham is the same as being a son of God (Gal. 3:25–29). Another model of sonship in the Old Testament is found in Psalm 2:7, 'You are my Son; today I have begotten you'. The newly crowned king, like Israel, was called into a covenant relationship with God, and his task was to represent God to the nation. He was given the Spirit to equip him for his calling, and he knew continual conflict as he upheld the word of God by applying it to the nation's life.

It is possible that the idea of sonship in the New Testament could include this Old Testament picture of kingship and rule, in which case this is the likely meaning of 'that we may also be glorified with him' in this verse. This same theme of believers ruling with Christ is found in Revelation 5:10, 'you have made them a kingdom and priests to our God, and they shall reign on the earth'.

8:18 For I consider that the sufferings of this present time are not worth comparing with the glory that is to be revealed to us.

Paul takes up the same theme again in 1 Corinthians 2:9, where he quotes Isaiah 64:4, 'From of old no one has heard or perceived by the ear, no eye has seen a God besides you, who acts for those who wait for him'. In its original context, Isaiah's message was given to encourage the pilgrim community that the sufferings they experienced were of little consequence when compared to their future blessing. Paul is clearly using the same exhortation language to encourage the Roman church to persevere on its pilgrimage. While the believers must have often been tempted to be afraid of the authorities, Paul refuses to dwell on their earthly sufferings. He is not a pessimist. He says that no matter what sufferings he and the Roman believers endure, they are not worthy of comparison with the glory that is to be revealed in them.

8:19 For the creation waits with eager longing for the revealing of the sons of God.

One of the promises made by Isaiah was that when the people of God returned to their inheritance, a new creation would come into existence (Isa. 65:17; 66:22). The valleys would be raised up and the mountains made low (Isa. 40:3–5), the desert would spring forth and blossom, and the wolf would lie down with the lamb (Isa. 65:25). This was to be the response of creation to the saving activity of God.

Paul is saying that the final pilgrimage is now under way. It is the event that brings with it the completion of the eschatological hope—the renewal of creation. This renewal of creation—when God makes all things new (2 Cor. 5:17; Rev. 21:5)—will take place when the people of God enter into their inheritance. When the promised new creation is handed over to them, the people of God will be finally justified.

8:20 For the creation was subjected to futility, not willingly, but because of him who subjected it, in hope

Once again, we find the theme of the fall and the representative role of Adam embedded in the text. Indeed, it has never left the thinking of Paul—although it can slip from our own as we read the letter. All that Paul is saying about the liberation of humanity is against the backdrop of the Genesis story. He is clear that, although creation is a pointer to God's creative activity, it no longer reveals the perfection of its original order. It has suffered under the curse as well as from humanity's abuse and misuse. Yet, despite the spoiling of creation, it has been subjected in hope. It has not been cast off. God still values it and his plan is for its final transformation. Jesus is the one whose death has redeemed creation and who is, therefore, its firstborn (Col. 1:15). He is the firstborn of all creation—its redeemer.

The verse does, however, pose this question, who has subjected the world to bondage? The background of Genesis 3:1–3 is important for resolving this puzzle. From the Genesis text, it could be argued that it was Adam who subjected the world as a result of his disobedience. However, there is no direct statement to this effect in the account. Because of the lack of an explicit statement, most commentators see that it was God who subjected creation to bondage. Support for this comes from the fact that only God could subject 'in hope', which Paul explicitly states is the destiny of the cursed creation. Also, in the Genesis story it is God who curses, and therefore it is he who does the subjecting.

8:21 that the creation itself will be set free from its bondage to corruption and obtain the freedom of the glory of the children of God.

Redemption is not just about the liberation of people from the body of sin; it is the release of the whole created order that has languished in decay, pain, and chaos. Creation is seen as suffering and in need of redemption. As a result of Adam's disobedience, not only his descendants but also the whole of creation was plunged into turmoil as it came under the curse (Gen. 3:17–19). For this reason, the redeemer must restore creation, and to undo Adam's 'mess' he will need to be its firstborn—the 'firstborn of all creation' (Col. 1:13–20).

Isaiah had predicted that the forthcoming exodus would be accompanied by the removal of the curse (Isa. 65:23)—clear evidence that the reign of God had at last become a reality (Isa. 66:1–22). This theme is found throughout the Scriptures—the closing message of the last book of the New Testament trumpets the promise that God will be 'making all things new' (Rev. 21:5). In this new creation, the righteousness of God will not only be seen but it will permeate the whole created order. It will be heaven on earth! It will not be like the old creation which Adam, as its master, brought into a state of curse. It will be ruled by the redeemed people of God, who will be the opposite of the fallen Adamic community. The redeemed of the Lord will share in the glory of God. Through them, because of their Saviour's death, the created order will enjoy the status it had at the beginning of time.

8:22 For we know that the whole creation has been groaning together in the pains of childbirth until now.

The picture of childbirth was used by the prophets to speak of the sufferings that creation must go through before the coming of the Messiah. The imagery became known as the 'Messianic birth pangs' and pictured creation being brought forth into a new existence. This process of birth would be finalized with the coming of the Messiah (Isa. 26:16–18; Mic. 4:9–10). Paul envisages the whole of creation being in travail, waiting for the pain of the final contraction. Then, the cursed creation would emerge from its old order into a new life through the redemption secured by Christ. This redemption is of cosmic dimensions. Jesus is the Paschal sacrifice, the firstborn of all creation, who reconciles all things in heaven and earth to himself through his blood shed on the cross (Col. 1:20).

Even though Jesus' death has taken place, it has not brought an end to the suffering of the people of God. Like the Jews who had been delivered from Egypt, their sufferings will continue until they arrive at their inheritance. Although this suffering also precedes the birth of the Messianic kingdom,

Romans 8: The Liberated People

the comfort for the believer is that it indicates the consummation of all things is at hand. Paul's argument implies that creation is not to be destroyed but it is to undergo a new birth.

What will emerge will not be something totally different but something that is transformed through the redemption that is in Christ Jesus. As Abraham was promised the land as an inheritance, the true children of Abraham are promised a redeemed earth. Thus, the redemption of creation is implicit in the Abrahamic covenant.

8:23 And not only the creation, but we ourselves, who have the firstfruits of the Spirit, groan inwardly as we wait eagerly for adoption as sons, the redemption of our bodies.

Paul recognizes the tension for believers as they wait for the release from sin that has been promised. The anticipation of the completed work of redemption is highlighted by the presence of the Spirit. He not only gives the community a taste of what is to come but encourages them that their sufferings are part of God's purposes.

The unity of humanity with creation has been increasingly recognized as the ecology movement has made its message known. The Jewish-Christian scriptures have been speaking of this for thousands of years. But Paul is not unifying humanity and nature in some cosmic, mystical union. He understands from scripture that man is the crown of God's creation; while sharing in its weakness and vulnerability, he is still distinct from it. He is its master and not its slave. It is true, of course, that he has abused his authority. However, a theology of creation that does not understand God as Creator, man as his vice-regent, the fall as a reality, and the death of God's firstborn son as essential elements in achieving cosmic redemption, is an inadequate Christian theology.

Paul envisages that the redemption process will be complete when the people of God are transformed, becoming the people that God intended. The transformation of the 'body of Christ' is the final act of salvation. Paul, being a Jew, could not conceive of man's salvation without it also including his physical existence. This is what marked out the Christian gospel from all competing ideologies of the first century. The Greeks would have strongly opposed it; for them, salvation was not the restoration of the body but its destruction. It is here that we can see how faithful the early church was to the Jewish tradition of Jesus. She did not reinterpret its message to be culturally relevant as many have argued, but stayed faithful to the Old Testament Scriptures, proclaiming the resurrection of Jesus as the event that defined the Christian gospel.

The Old Testament gives various descriptions or titles for Israel. Two of the most important are that she was God's son and his bride. The Old Testament sees that, while Israel was God's bride on earth, the consummation of the marriage would happen in the future. In contrast, sonship is fully established on earth, with no future development or fulfilment of the imagery.

Despite the implication of the ESV translation, it is the church collectively that has the first-fruits of the Spirit and not the individual believer, Paul confirming this when he writes, 'we [believers]…wait for the redemption of our body (sing.)'; the singular noun clarifying that here is a reference to the church.

The 'first-fruits of the Spirit' probably refers to the beginning of the Spirit's work. What the church has already experienced is but a token of what she will experience on the day of Christ's coming. The lives of her members have been transformed by the presence of the Spirit but, when Christ returns, 'their body' (the church's life in its entirety—see notes on Romans 12:2) will be transformed. It will be the Spirit who will change her—raising her to immortality, just as he did when he raised the Lord Jesus (Rom. 8:11).

There have been times, such as revivals and other outpourings, when the Spirit's presence has been beyond the expected, and miraculous happenings have become the norm rather than the exception. Such events anticipate the eschatological goal when God will dwell among his people in all of his fullness. When outpourings occur, his presence affects not only the church's spiritual life but her physical well-being also.

8:24 For in this hope we were saved. Now hope that is seen is not hope. For who hopes for what he sees?

All that Paul has been describing lies in the future. He has already said that believers are groaning for the completion of their redemption. This is a future hope, but it is a hope that is grounded in the historical happening of the death and resurrection of Jesus. It is, therefore, not a vain hope. The hope of the Christian is not something akin to whistling in the wind; it is singing the songs of heaven, strengthened by the promises of the God who will never fail.

Paul acknowledges that this hope is not verifiable. It is the same as when Israel was in Babylon, waiting for her release. She knew the prophets had set a limit on her captivity and waited for that time to pass (Jer. 25:11). The Babylonians would have mocked any suggestion that her God was in control, demanding that she must face the facts of the situation. However, it was her Babylonian masters who were not facing the facts, for they did not acknowledge that Israel was the covenant community of God.

This is the present condition of the church. Many despise the faith of the people of God; others, at least, acknowledge that simple faith comforts Christians in their sorrows, and supports them in their need. But the fact is that such reasoning refuses to investigate the evidence. Jesus has been raised, and he is the first-fruits of those who sleep. All those who are dead in Christ are destined to share in his victory over death and to be transformed into the likeness of the Son of God.

8:25 But if we hope for what we do not see, we wait for it with patience.

Anxious to clarify what Christian hope is, Paul stresses that at the present time, it is not the fulfilment that the Roman believers enjoy but the promise. He argues in the following way, 'We will continue to suffer and be frustrated. But this certain hope, founded on the promises of God and the work of Christ, will one day be completed, and the fullness of our redemption will no longer be a hope, but a reality!'

8:26 Likewise the Spirit helps us in our weakness. For we do not know what to pray for as we ought, but the Spirit himself intercedes for us with groanings too deep for words.

Paul has been referring to the work of the Holy Spirit throughout his letter. In Romans 1:3, he spoke of the resurrection as being the work of the Spirit, and in this chapter, he says that the Spirit will raise the church (Rom. 8:11). The Spirit is bound up with the believers' adoption as sons, and in this verse, Paul tells us that the Spirit is the one who aids believers in their weakness by interceding for them.

These three ministries of the Spirit echo the experience of the Jewish people in their return from exile. It was the Spirit who raised them from the dead (Ezek. 37), it was he who conferred on them sonship (Isa. 51:1–3), and it was he who strengthened and supported them on their pilgrimage back to the Promised Land (Isa. 42:13–16; 48:16–18). This is the theme that Paul is developing here. Israel was the type; the church is the antitype. Recognizing the importance of typology for Paul's theology makes understanding his teaching much easier.

The people of God, once bound to Satan as members of the body of sin, have been released through the covenant-annulling death of Jesus, the last Adam. The Christian community has experienced the eschatological (end of time) new exodus the prophets had spoken about. This deliverance, as they had predicted, has been accomplished through the Son of David. It is the Spirit who has raised this community from spiritual death and given her life, and it is he who made her into the army of the living God. Having been freed from her bondage, the church is now led by the Spirit. He makes her members into sons and daughters of God who through him cry, 'Abba! Father!' It is he who assures, comforts, and strengthens them as they face all the opposition arrayed against them. It is he who triumphs over the forces of darkness which seek to stop the sons and daughters of God from arriving at their promised inheritance. This will become clearer towards the end of the chapter, where Paul writes about the impossibility of being separated from God's love (Rom. 8:31–39).

It is clear from this that the work of the Holy Spirit is vital for the life of the church (local and world-wide). He is responsible for her beginning, her continuation, her preservation, and her eventual triumph. Any Christian who does not understand the essential biblical teaching concerning the Holy Spirit is going to be confused and badly equipped for the Christian life.

Romans 8: The Liberated People

Although there are several dimensions of the Spirit's work and power, in this particular context, the Spirit is spoken of as the one who sustains the people of God when they are overwhelmed by opponents. Paul says that the Spirit helps us in our weakness.

It is often thought that endowment with some sort of exhilarating power is the defining characteristic of the Spirit's work in God's people. While there is certainly some truth in this, such a limited perspective can easily become a distorted understanding.

Both the Old Testament and New Testament affirm that before the Spirit's power can be displayed, the recipient must be brought to experience and acknowledge his total weakness (Zech. 4:6). At times the Spirit's ministry is like that of a lifesaver, who responds when the one in need comes to the end of his resources. The Spirit does not come to the church's aid to boost her strength; he comes to her aid when her strength is completely gone. While Paul's perspective is the church's experience, this experience is mirrored in the lives of millions of individual believers. He helps them in their weakness—at the point of their despair and anguish (cf. Rom. 5:6–8). Of course, the Spirit's work is not just about giving power, he imparts grace and gives gifts as well as empowering for witness.

Paul says that the Spirit intercedes with groanings that words cannot express. Some commentators see this to be a reference to the ecstatic utterances that the church knew and experienced; but these utterances (known as the gift of tongues) are not mentioned in the letter to the Romans. Indeed, they are only recorded in the Acts of the Apostles (Acts 2:4–8; 10:45–46; 19:6), and in 1 Corinthians (1 Cor. 12:10, 30; 14:4–28).

The context in Romans 8:26 does not suggest that Paul has this gift of the Spirit in mind. The experience he describes seems to go beyond the exercising of a spiritual gift. The groanings denote despair, which is only reversed because the Spirit comes to the church's aid. In the midst of such an experience, the God who came to the aid of the Jews in their desperate plight in Egypt comes again to the aid of his people in Rome. He not only gave the church his indwelling Spirit to intercede on her behalf, but also his Son, who intercedes for her at the right hand of God (Rom. 8:34).

8:27 And he who searches hearts knows what is the mind of the Spirit, because the Spirit intercedes for the saints according to the will of God.

Understanding this verse is problematic. It is difficult to know who it is that searches the hearts. Is it the Father or the Spirit? If it is the Father, then Paul is saying that the Father knows the mind of the Spirit and understands his groans. If it is the Spirit, then he is saying that the Spirit knows the mind, or desires, of the spirit of a person and, as a result, reliably represents those longings to the Father with groans that he can understand. Because of the previous verse where Paul wrote that the Spirit 'helps us in our weakness', it would be natural to expect that he continues to write about the Spirit's work. If this is the case, then Paul is saying that the Father knows the mind of the Spirit who intercedes for the believers as they attempt to pray. Because the Spirit is one with the Father, he prays for the believers according to the will of God.

We can understand this in one of two ways. First, Paul could be saying that the saints are the object of the Spirit's prayers. This is not suggested anywhere else in Scripture. What is taught is that Christ, as his people's high priest, prays for his people (1 Tim. 2:5; Heb. 4:14–16). The second possibility, and probably the correct one, is that the Spirit helps the believers pray and sustains them, so that in their weakness their prayers become effectual. Their prayers are not merely the prayers of men, but they are empowered by God, through the groans of the Spirit.

In the phrase 'according to the will of God' it is clear that prayer is not about changing the mind of God or about people achieving God's goals through his help. It could be about the human will conforming to the will and desires of God so that, when someone prays in the way that Paul speaks about, they pray according to God's will. Alternatively, it could be that God transforms believers' prayers so that they accord with his will, as there is no clear reference to a person's will being conformed to God's will in the text.

8:28 And we know that all things work together for good to those who love God, to those who are the called according to His purpose. (NKJVTM)

The phrase 'all things' is a reference not to the trials of life, but to the list of saving decisions and actions found in Romans 8:29–30, namely God's foreknowledge, our predestination, calling, conformation, justification, and glorification. These are all the glorious things that work together for good in the lives of all believers, regardless of their circumstances. They call from Paul the magnificent statement, 'If God is for us, who can be against us?' (Rom. 8:31). Of course, the trials of life can work for the maturing and character-building of people and this applies to believers and unbelievers, but I do not believe that is Paul's point here.

Such encouragement would prove essential to the church at Rome as the might, pride, and ruthlessness of the Roman Empire were unleashed against her with the intention of wiping the Christians from the face of the earth. The recollection of Paul's words from this part of his letter must have brought unspeakable comfort to many of the believers, when they were crushed and killed by the empire's barbaric and cruel onslaught. Ironically, despite the awful persecution, the Roman church grew while the decadent state went through its death throes.

The historical realities of suffering, and the seemingly meaningless triumph of evil over good, must make us wary of interpreting Paul's statements in too idealistic a way. Paul and the Roman believers knew how things would eventually turn out because they knew the one in charge had ultimate authority to achieve his will. Paul is not saying that God intervenes at every point of threat. History and our own human experience challenge such a claim as being totally unrealistic. Importantly, the Scriptures do too. We only have to read the Acts of the Apostles to see how Christians suffered poverty, famine, injustice, and untimely death. The early church would hardly interpret Paul's statement as being some sort of heavenly insurance from the ills of this life. Her experience could not allow such an interpretation, and it certainly did not fit Paul's own experience either (2 Cor. 11:23–29).

We must ask if Paul is making this statement about the individual or the Christian community. If we accept the proposed understanding, which is set in an eschatological context—that the ultimate goal of God is to work for the good of those who love him—then there is little difference between the two. The vindication of both community and member, and their ultimate blessedness, are not for this life but for the time when the believers enter into their inheritance.

However, the corporate concepts of the Old Testament persist in the thinking of Paul, for Israel had been called to fulfil the purposes of God (Gen. 12:3b). Tragically, she failed because she did not love the Lord her God and the covenantal purposes of her calling were transferred to the church (Eph. 1:3–14; Heb. 7:22). The church now has the high calling to represent God to the nations (Matt. 28:18). As she fulfils this calling, the believers are strengthened in the knowledge that God, who will justify, conform, and ultimately glorify them. Events in Rome may crush the Christians, but Paul has already comforted them by saying that their sufferings are not worth comparing to the glory that will be revealed in them (Rom. 8:18).

8:29 For those whom he foreknew he also predestined to be conformed to the image of his Son, in order that he might be the firstborn among many brothers.

The foreknowledge of God is not only about his omniscience. It is gloriously true that the God of creation, who knows all, saw from eternity those who would love him as they responded to the gospel. However, in saying that God 'foreknew' those who would be saved, Paul is not necessarily saying that they had been elected as individuals.

'Foreknowledge' has to do with God's covenantal relationship, and once the term has been put into its Old Testament setting it naturally conveys the idea of election—but it is an election of the nation. God said to Israel, 'I have loved you with an everlasting love; I have drawn you with loving-kindness' (Jer. 31:3). This same love is what Paul focuses on here as he tells the Romans of the certainty that God's purposes will be fulfilled. But what needs to be remembered is that if the proposed corporate reading of the letter is correct, this election is of a community like that in the Old Testament. Those who are in Christ are God's elect. This does not deny that there is a doctrine of personal election in the New Testament, but Scripture's focus is on corporate election.

There are two dimensions of what it means 'to be conformed to the image of his Son'—individual sanctification and, together with other believers, corporate transformation. First, the individual believer is sanctified or transformed by the work of the Spirit (1 Thess. 4:3–8). This change is a microcosm of a second, greater transformation which involves the church. It is this community, having been rescued from the kingdom of darkness, which is transformed into the likeness of Christ (Rom. 8:9; 2 Cor. 3:18; Phil. 2:5–11). It is the covenant community (not the individual) that is created in the image of the heavenly man. Being transformed is not essentially about physical appearance (although this will be part of the ultimate transformation), but about readiness to do the will of God (Rom. 12:1–2; cf. Heb. 1:8–9).

This was the supreme quality which characterized the life of Jesus. As the church delights to do God's will, she is being conformed to the image of his Son. The nation of Israel had been called to do God's will by taking the message of salvation to the nations (Isa. 49:3, 6; 52:7), but she failed in her task, as Jesus made clear (Luke 11:1– 14). So, the church was given the mantle of faithful servanthood, and her task remains to take the 'word of life' to the ends of the earth (Matt. 28:18–20; Rom. 10:14–15). To be so conformed is not some eschatological goal but the present reality of what God expects of his people. In his letter to the Philippians, Paul encourages the believers to have the same attitude as Christ, so that they would be 'blameless and innocent, children of God without blemish in the midst of a crooked and twisted generation...holding fast to the word of life' (Phil. 2:15–16). Transformation is costly. It will involve representing God in an evil, hostile, and indifferent world. The church should not take the option of keeping her head below the parapet with her mouth sealed in the hope of dwelling in peace. If she does, God may confer on her the name Lo-Ammi, 'not my people', as he did with Israel (Hosea 2:23).

The culmination of the church's transformation into the image of Jesus is when she completes her faithful witness to the nations and brings about the triumph of the kingdom of God. Only then will creation be transformed, for the redemption of all things, through the death of Jesus, will be completed. It is for this reason that Jesus is called 'the firstborn'. The firstborn was the redeemer in the Jewish economy. If one of the family members was forced to sell its inheritance through hardship, it was the firstborn's responsibility to redeem what was lost to the family and restore it as part of their inheritance. In this way, Jesus is the firstborn, or redeemer, of many brothers. Through his death, redemption has been secured. He has not only secured the salvation of his brothers but has recovered what they had lost as a result of humanity's sin. Through his death as the firstborn of all creation, he has redeemed the whole created order (Col. 1:13–21) which had come under the curse as a result of the sin of Adam. Now, through the last Adam, it is restored to its perfection, and returned to the new man (the church), who will once again rule over it as God's vice-regent (1 Cor. 6:2; Gal. 3:25–29; Heb. 2:5–9; Rev. 1:5–6).

8:30 And those whom he predestined he also called, and those whom he called he also justified, and those whom he justified he also glorified.

The language Paul uses is taken directly from the Old Testament Scriptures. He is saying that the privileges of Israel are now the possession of the church. The Old Testament speaks of the experience of Abraham, who was called to leave his homeland (Gen. 12:1–4), and of the nation of Israel, which was called out of Egypt (Exod. 3:10) and Babylon (Isa. 62:11–12).

The Old Testament repeatedly speaks of the pilgrim community journeying to Jerusalem to appear in the presence of God, so seeing his glory. In this way, the pilgrims were 'glorified'. This is the meaning of the word here, for it is also part of pilgrim imagery. Being 'glorified' is essentially being delivered from the damage inflicted by sin as well as its power and being restored to the perfection of Adam's pre-fallen condition in the presence of God.

8:31 What then shall we say to these things? If God is for us, who can be against us?

Some scholars think this statement preserves part of a primitive hymn. Israel's call to return home meant danger as she journeyed from the land of exile through the wilderness to the Promised Land. It was a journey beset with crises: wild beasts and bandits, internal strife within the oft-divided community, threats from surrounding nations, and physical discomfort. But God's presence was with them, and, with hindsight, the Israelites could respond to the fears that welled up in their hearts and cry, 'If God be for us, who can be against us?'

Romans 8: The Liberated People

Paul encourages the Roman believers that no opposition they encountered could overcome the purposes God has for them. No doubt, in future days, these words would be repeated time after time as believers watched the gates being opened in the Colosseum, and the crowds poured their vile scorn upon them. As lions ran to tear their bodies apart, the hope expressed in this verse would be a triumphant testimony to the faithfulness of God and their future glory.

8:32 He who did not spare his own Son but gave him up for us all, how will he not also with him graciously give us all things?

Again, the theme of pilgrimage is the background to this verse. As the Roman believers journeyed in their weakness, Paul reminds them that if God went to the lengths of giving up his Son, he will not rescind the purposes he has for them. God has given them his Spirit and now gives them 'all things'.

The pilgrimage in the Old Testament was no different, in that God provided for his people in order to bring about his purposes for the nation. The uncertainty of undertaking the journey without basic necessities must have created tremendous pressure on the Israelites. But the Old Testament records how God provided for those who responded in faith. The manna in the wilderness was evidence of his care (Exod. 16:13–16). The same imagery is found in John 6, suggesting its familiarity to the early church. Paul takes up the pilgrimage theme, assuring the pilgrim community in Rome that it can be confident that basic needs will be met.

The reason why he can be so positive is because of the logic of God's grace. Having given up his only Son to death to bring his people out of their captivity, he is not going to fail to bring them safely through their pilgrimage to the Promised Land. God did not achieve salvation for his people, and then expect them to battle through in their own strength and ingenuity. No! In Christ he provided all the resources his people would need. Success is assured, he will 'graciously give us all things'. Indeed, the church (and also the individual Christian) is called a co-heir with Christ (Rom. 8:17), sharing the same resources the Father provided for his Son so that he could fulfil his mission. Paul will develop the theme of the church's pilgrimage and her mission in Romans 10:14–15.

8:33 Who shall bring any charge against God's elect? It is God who justifies.

Paul has already dealt with the possibility of an accusation of guilt being brought against the church for entering into another marriage relationship (Rom. 6:7; 7:1– 4). Satan will accuse Christ and the church that their union is not lawful. Should the call go out, 'if anyone can show any just cause why they may not lawfully be joined together in matrimony, let him now declare it, or else hereafter for ever hold his peace', Satan is ready to cry out, 'She is mine! She is already married!' It is into this awful scene that Paul confidently declares, 'It is God who justifies!' The judge of the whole earth will not accept there is a charge to answer, and Paul states why this is so in the next verse.

This marital context for the charge against God's people is supported by those who identify vv. 33b, 34 as an echo of Isaiah 50:8. In this prophecy, the Servant asks, 'He who vindicates me is near. Who will contend with me?' If we examine this Isaianic text in its wider context, we find that the prophet has been explaining the marital status of Israel after God sent her into exile. Isaiah 50:1 asks, 'Where is your mother's certificate of divorce, with which I sent her away? Or which of my creditors is it to whom I have sold you?' The prophet is soon to say:

> *I will greatly rejoice in the LORD; my soul shall exult in my God, for he has clothed me with the garments of salvation; he has covered me with the robe of righteousness, as a bridegroom decks himself like a priest with a beautiful headdress, and as a bride adorns herself with her jewels. (Isa. 61:10).*

In Isaiah 62:5, he will say:

> *as a young man marries a young woman, so shall your sons marry you, and as the bridegroom rejoices over the bride, so shall your God rejoice over you.*

If Paul is consciously intertextualizing his sources (as he does elsewhere) then he is deliberately feeding off the divine marriage theme, and it is in this context that the significance of the charge should be read. There is no charge that can be brought that would nullify the relationship God is bringing his church into, that is the consummation of the divine marriage.

8:34 Who is to condemn? Christ Jesus is the one who died—more than that, who was raised—who is at the right hand of God, who indeed is interceding for us.

The accusation cannot stand. There is no illegal relationship. The death of the last Adam has brought to an end the reign of sin and death; the people of God have been released; and the pilgrimage, which will culminate in their marriage to the Lamb, has begun!

While on pilgrimage, the Jews had a high priest who constantly represented them before God (Heb. 5:1–4; 9:7–10). Throughout their journey, they faced spiritual and moral temptations as well as dangers from enemies who sought to prevent them from reaching their inheritance. Because of this, the ministry of the high priest was crucial. He offered sacrifices for the sins of his people and interceded for them. Yet this very high priest was under the same ultimate sentence of judgment and death as the ones he represented. However, this is not so for the high priest of the Christian church. He has a ministry which is based on the power of an endless life (Heb. 7:16), for he was raised to life. He does not have to sacrifice animals, for he has put away sin by offering himself (Rom. 3:21ff.; Heb. 9:11–15; Rev. 1:4–6). His priestly ministry is complete, for he has brought all his people out of the kingdom of darkness and made them fit for the kingdom of light. Jesus is able to do this because he is the Melchizedek priest who is the Son of David (Ps. 110:1–4; cf. Matt. 22:41–45; Heb. 5:1–10; Rev. 1:12–18). As the promised descendant of David (Rom. 1:3), he is the fulfilment of the Melchizedek priesthood in being both king and priest. It was Jesus who was raised up to bring salvation to his people, as the prophets had foretold (Luke 1:46–55, 67–79; 2:8–38).

The theme of Christ's intercession is found throughout the New Testament. His priesthood is not only in this passage but lies beneath the surface of much of the gospel material. It is found throughout the Pauline letters, in Peter, Revelation, and is particularly prominent in the Epistle to the Hebrews. Clearly, it was a theme from which the early Christians would have drawn comfort and assurance during the sufferings that engulfed them.

8:35 Who shall separate us from the love of Christ? Shall tribulation, or distress, or persecution, or famine, or nakedness, or danger, or sword?

Paul continues to paint the picture of the church's security in her Saviour. It began in v. 33 with, 'Who shall bring any charge against God's elect?' and continues in v. 34 with, 'Who is to condemn?' Now, in v. 35, Paul asks, 'Who shall separate us from the love of Christ?' Of course, the answer is 'No one!' The Roman Christians are absolutely safe. God's good purposes for them stand secure, and nothing—not even the extreme experiences of life in Rome—can affect their relationship with Christ, who intercedes for them at the Father's right hand.

While the list of hardships in v. 35 can find a natural home in Paul's life and ministry (2 Cor. 4:4–10; 6:4–10; 11:23b–28), they also reflect the extremes the Old Testament pilgrim community experienced as they travelled through the wilderness following their deliverances from Egypt and Babylon. We shall see, in chapter 10, that Paul deliberately adopts the pilgrimage language of Isaiah and applies it to the church, the New Testament pilgrim community. The description in this verse is not limited to physical hardships either. Many believers have suffered psychological persecution for being Christians, famine in their souls, nakedness in their spirits, and dangers at every level (2 Cor. 1:8–9a; 4:8; 6:8–10; 11:28–33).

8:36 As it is written, "For your sake we are being killed all the day long; we are regarded as sheep to be slaughtered."

The quotation used by Paul is from Psalm 44:22. Its context is the Babylonian exile, and the psalm speaks of how the covenant community was treated by its conquerors. They had no regard for the welfare of the people they had conquered— their lives were of little importance and they were seen as having no value (Ps. 44:13–16; cf. 2 Cor. 6:8–9). The exiles were put to death at the first sign of dissent (Ps. 44:10–11, 22), yet the Psalmist writes that their deaths were 'for your (God's) sake'. The fall of Jerusalem was only part of the conquering ambition of the Babylonians, and the deportation of most survivors into exile would ensure subordination. Among those deported were Jews who stayed true to God, despite the waywardness of the rest of Israel (Ps. 44:8–12). The Psalmist focused on the Lord's chastening of this remnant for, despite being faithful, these innocent Jews suffered with the guilty during their time in exile (Ps. 44:17–19).

Romans 8: The Liberated People

The remnant recalled the victories God secured for his people in the past, and they cried to him for help, asking that he would redeem them again (Ps. 44:23–24, 26). The outcome of such redemption would be the extolling of God's glorious name among the nations as they witnessed his righteous dealings with Israel (Ps. 44:24– 25). Such a clear display of his holiness would send out a warning to the nations that they must seek him while he could be found. Paul quotes from this psalm because it reflects the experience of the new covenant pilgrim community, the New Testament church; suffering in spite of their integrity and faithfulness to God.

8:37 No, in all these things we are more than conquerors through him who loved us.

The anticipation of suffering and death should not deter the members of the pilgrim community. If the phrase 'all of these things' refers to the list of tribulations in vv. 35–36, Paul is saying that, in all these experiences, he and the Roman Christians are more than conquerors because of Christ's love for them.

The alternate interpretation of the phrase, 'all these things' is that it is a recurrence of 'all things' in vv. 28, 32. In light of this reading, Paul is saying, 'No one can bring a charge against us! We have been called by God and our relationship with Christ is settled. No one can condemn us, as Christ has died to redeem us, and, what is more—having been raised—he now intercedes for us. He will never stop loving us. We are his bride whom he will never abandon. Even though the whole world is arrayed against us, we will remain conquerors because our election still stands, our calling still stands, our justification still stands, and our future glorification still stands. And how can we be so certain? We are sure of this because Christ, the lover of our souls and our betrothed, is forever faithful'.

Paul knows that believers have not been redeemed to be eventually forsaken. The history of the covenant people of the Old Testament demonstrates the faithfulness of God, and his commitment to his people. Not even judgment and exile could bring God's love for his people to an end. His covenant to Abraham was not abandoned but moved towards its fulfilment in the new covenant promised to those in exile. These new covenant promises (Jer. 31:31–34; 33:4–26; Ezek. 36:22–32) focused on the blessing of the Gentiles through the raising up of the descendant of David, who fulfilled the promise of the covenant made with Abraham (Isa. 11:1–10; 19:16–25; 42:1–9; 60:1–3). Thus, the new covenant brings to completion the promises God made to Abraham (Gen. 12:1–3) and to David (2 Sam. 7:4–17). The two possible interpretations of 'all these things' imply that believers were (or would be) victims of awful circumstances which they had not courted. But there is an alternative reading that could suggest otherwise.

The early church clearly understood that there would be a reward for suffering (Matt. 19:27–30; 1 Cor. 2:6–16; Phil. 1:19–30; Heb. 12:28). However, Paul does not focus on reward in this verse but goes to the very heart of the gospel. It is the love of Christ that has set believers free, and through him they conquer. This all- conquering love has driven thousands, including Paul, to take calculated risks for the sake of the gospel, putting themselves in the way of trouble, hardship, persecution, famine, and death.

Compared to the magnitude of God's self-giving in the person of Jesus, the magnitude of their self-giving is reckoned as very small indeed. Many, like Paul, count it joy to suffer as they 'go' to 'make disciples of all nations', because Christ said, 'I am with you always, to the end of the age' (Matt. 28:19–20).

Thus, in this context—which can be supported by what Paul will go on to say about the church's mandate to be the suffering servant who declares God's salvation (Rom. 10:5–15)—Paul refers to the sufferings of the church as the 'all things' that she conquers. Thus, the focus is much more honed—suffering is not about the consequences of being the people of God but is about the consequences of living as the people of God; fulfilling the master's mandate to make disciples of all nations. Sadly, the reason many Christians never experience suffering is because they fail to bear witness for Christ when the going gets tough.

8:38 For I am sure that neither death nor life, nor angels nor rulers, nor things present nor things to come, nor powers,

The strength of Paul's confidence in the faithfulness of God to keep his covenant promises enables him to use the strongest language to encourage

Romans 8: The Liberated People

the church as she faces the conflicts that will arise during her pilgrimage and service. This is no whistling in the dark with the hope that dangers may never materialize; for Paul has already faced most, if not all, of them. He was crushed and almost destroyed when fulfilling his calling (2 Cor. 11:16–33). He knew this suffering had not been an unfortunate accident; it was an inevitable part of the commission to preach the gospel to the nations (Acts 9:16; 2 Tim. 1:8–14; 2:8–13).

For the Jew—without the certainty of resurrection—there was the ever-threatening presence of death. Paul would remember the days when he feared that death would cause his separation from the covenant people and fellowship with God. This fear is evidenced throughout the Old Testament, especially in the Psalms (Ps. 30:8–12; 88:4–5, 10–12; 102:23–24; 116:3–4). Believers in the early church, however, knew that, as a result of the resurrection of Jesus Christ, life and immortality had been brought to light (2 Tim. 1:10). It is difficult for those who have known the Christian message from childhood to appreciate the darkness that many people live under as they face death. No unconverted person can have the confidence Paul speaks of in this verse; but, in contrast, the believer knows that his relationship with God will never be severed—not even by death. This is the wonder of the gospel!

However, it is not only death that threatens fellowship with God—it is life itself. Certain experiences can overwhelm people; they can find themselves swamped by dangers that threaten not only their lives but their confidence in God's love for them. Such experiences are well recorded in the Psalms (e.g. Psalms 22 and 88) where we find cries to God for help. However, the Psalms which express anguish repeatedly show that even though their composers may be distressed and feel abandoned, God had not left them or turned his face from them.

Paul writes to the believers about his conviction that neither angels nor demons could separate them from the love of God in Christ Jesus. The forces of darkness were no match for the power of God that was promised to his people as they made their journey back from exile in Babylon to their inheritance in the Promised Land. Travelling at night across the desert (a place where the forces of evil were understood to dwell) would have been a terrifying experience for the Jewish community. Even the heavenly bodies were thought to have deadly and lethal powers that could strike at night (Ps. 121:6).

As for the church in Rome, she is making her pilgrimage through a hostile world. Some of the hostility that greets her is nothing more than normal human conflict, which is an expression of a fallen world. However, some is of a different order, threatening her very existence and testimony. Such hostility comes from beyond those instruments of opposition—it comes from the forces of darkness; which Paul says believers must stand against (Eph. 6:10–18).

In saying the present and the future are not able to separate the believers in Rome from God's love, it is notable that Paul does not mention the past. For him the believers have nothing to fear from what has gone before. The death of Christ has dealt completely and finally with the guilt that lurks in their consciences—their pasts will never catch them up, at least not in terms of it being brought before God for judgment.

However, what could there be about the present or the future that would threaten the Roman believers as they seek to follow Christ? Perhaps they are afraid their faith might fail, their status might be lost, or their reputation discredited. They may fear the consequences of ill health, unemployment, bereavement, and any one of a host of social, spiritual, physical, and economic dangers. Paul knew these fears as well; he was no different from his fellow Christians. At one time he despaired of life itself (2 Cor. 4:7–18), but his testimony to them is that none of these things 'will be able to separate us from the love of God that is in Christ Jesus our Lord' (v. 39). The security of the Roman believers did not lie in their ability to negotiate the perils of life but in the certainty that God has promised to care, protect, and bring them safely home.

Paul leaves nothing outside of this tremendous declaration of confidence. Through these and the following phrases he gathers together everything that can possibly harm the believers in Rome, concluding with the affirmation that there is no power that can separate them from God's love in Christ Jesus.

8:39 nor height nor depth, nor anything else in all creation, will be able to separate us from the love of God in Christ Jesus our Lord.

Paul concludes his declaration of confidence by exposing every possible opposition, even considering those regions that are outside of the experience of humanity and says that there is no dimension that has the power to sever the believing community from the love of God.

'Nor height nor depth'—Paul uses the same word for 'height' when he spoke about the nature of his ministry and the warfare in which he is engaged (2 Cor. 10:5); the term 'depth' has roots in Old Testament thinking. In Ezekiel 32:24, the prophet spoke about Israel's enemies being consigned to the pit. We have seen how Ezekiel influenced Paul's theological understanding and this suggests that he might well be reflecting Ezekiel's meaning of the term. If true, it suggests Paul is saying that all the enemies that Christ has conquered—including death itself—can do no harm to his church.

In conclusion, absolutely nothing—not even events or powers that come from those areas that terrify man—can separate the people of God from the one who loves them. Hallelujah!

Further Study: Questions for Romans 8

1. Why is there no longer any condemnation for those who are in Christ Jesus?

2. Why was the law powerless to save humanity?

3. How has the death of Jesus changed the status of the church from being condemned to being blessed?

4. What story in the Old Testament is Paul using as he explains how the Christian community should live?

5. What does being 'in the flesh' mean?

6. What does being 'led by the Spirit' mean and who does it relate to?

7. What are the causes of the inner groaning and what do they signify?

Romans 9: When People Try to Justify Themselves

Introduction

Chapters 9–11 have been at the heart of attempts to grasp Paul's understanding of election. Many scholars have seen the section as an intrusion into the letter, disrupting the argument that was being made; but in recent decades it has been appreciated that these chapters are the purpose for Paul writing the letter. In fact, the continuity of the argument is evident in that Romans 9:4–23 has a number of close parallels with Romans 3:1–7.

Some Jewish believers were insisting that, in order to be true members of the covenant people, Gentile believers had to keep the law and submit to circumcision. While such demands may have come from sincere attempts to apply the law, it is likely they were motivated by unspoken political concerns. The believing Jews must have been intimidated by the ever-increasing number of Gentiles who were professing faith in Jesus as Messiah. At Paul's insistence, which was strengthened by the agreement he had won from the Jerusalem Council (Acts 15:12–35), the Gentiles were being admitted into the community of the Messiah on the same terms as the Jews. They were of little threat while their numbers remained relatively low. However, the blessings that accompanied their evangelization, their increasing numbers, and the growing resistance of the Jewish people to the message of the crucified Messiah, meant that the Gentiles were speedily taking the reins of power in local believing communities.

The problems produced by this growth were tearing the early church apart. A number of Jewish disciples came to believe that the only way to rein in the growing influence and power of the Gentile converts was to demand that they be circumcised. By controlling who was accorded full covenant membership, they could keep the upper hand. It was a simple, effective move, but one that Paul could not tolerate.

The danger with a divided community was that each faction would see the other as renegade. This was Paul's deepest fear, as it would damage the gospel message incalculably. On the other hand, believing Jews and Gentiles living in harmony with each other would be a great demonstration of the power of God to restore relationships, and overcome discord and alienation.

In the next section of his letter (chapters 9–11) Paul shows that believing Jews and believing Gentiles are part of God's salvation purposes, and that the rejection of one by the other is a denial of the gospel. He shows that it is God's intention, as expressed in the Law and the Prophets, for Gentiles to be converted, and that their successful evangelization might provoke unbelieving Jews to turn to the Messiah. Paul also wants the believing Gentiles to realize that they cannot exist, as far as God is concerned, without believing Jews—the remnant in Israel can neither be treated as having been cast off by God nor as being irrelevant.

However, Paul has to address another sensitive matter—the status of unbelieving Israel. In keeping with the corporate, covenantal framework he has been using throughout the letter, the text will be interpreted as a development of the new exodus theme. Paul is concerned to show that Israel is in danger of being left outside of the covenant, which has been brought to fulfilment in Christ. Ironically, this is the very covenant made with Abraham, the father of the Jewish nation. We have seen the developing new exodus theme in chapters 1–8.

The question Paul must now answer is, 'where do the Jewish people fit into the new exodus?' Are they automatically included on the basis of having been the people of the Egyptian exodus? Do they bypass the conditions that are imposed on Gentiles who wish to be part of this community? Do they have a privileged status within it? Can they cast a deciding vote over who is included?

Paul fears that this new community of Jew and Gentile—this 'new man'—is in danger of self-destruction, as Jews and Gentiles argue over their status before God. The Jews can, of course, appeal to their history and the promises given to their ancestor Abraham. The Gentiles, however, can claim that the experience of the Jewish people is no longer relevant, and that God

Romans 9: When People Try to Justify Themselves

has cast them aside in favour of believing Gentiles. Their growing numbers and increasing dominance in the church must have seemed like undeniable evidence of this.

In chapter 9 Paul begins his defence of Israel's status. Conscious of how crucial this issue is, he is concerned that the Gentile converts understand God's purpose for his ancient people, so that they can relate appropriately to them. However, behind Paul's argument is a further concern: if God can cast off his ancient people who were bound to him by covenant, what security can there be for the new covenant community? Can God's promises be taken seriously if he was able to abandon his people when they failed him? Is God's commitment to the New Israel as frail as his commitment to her predecessor? If he chooses to disengage himself from his covenant promises to Israel, will not his reputation and the confidence of his people be at stake? Paul reminds the Romans that the Jews have the birth-right. They had received blessings from which the Gentiles were excluded. They had been privileged beyond any other nation on earth (Rom. 9:1–5).

Paul goes on to show the principles of foreknowledge and election operating throughout salvation history. They were active when he called Jacob instead of Esau (Rom. 9:6–17), and when he dealt with Pharaoh. God is at liberty to show mercy or to judge as he wills—and none can argue. As the potter has freedom to mould clay however he wishes, so God has the right to express his will either by exercising justice in the form of judgment (which all deserve), or mercy and forgiveness (which none deserve) (Rom. 9:14–24).

It would be wrong to use these texts to support individual election. In line with the argument of the whole Epistle, they are dealing with representative heads of communities. The freedom that a person has to enter or reject membership is a different matter. As this material applies primarily to states of solidarity, there are hermeneutical issues that need to be faced before truths are removed from their intended context and applied to the salvation of the individual. There are important overlapping concepts and principles in corporate and individual models, and these must be worked through and clarified before using them without reference to their original context and purpose. In general, out of its great traditional concern for the salvation of the individual, Reformed theology has given insufficient emphasis to the corporate dimension of the argument being presented by Paul in this passage. However, while the corporate perspective must be kept to the fore—because Paul in this section is dealing with heads of communities—the current argument is presented in terms of individuals. This indicates that there must be an individual significance in what is being said, even though personal salvation is not the primary thrust of the passage.

What is most significant is that Paul uses Old Testament material that prophesies the Babylonian exile, bringing it into the developing new exodus theme. He says that the final manifestation of God's righteousness is displayed in the fulfilment of the promise he made long ago, to include the Gentile nations in the experience of the new exodus salvation. This new exodus is about bringing out the new covenant people of God from the domain of sin. It does not deny the earlier covenants made with Israel—faith has always been the principle of initiation for sharing in the righteousness of God. Israel 'after the flesh' was not being rejected but invited into the new covenant. Many would refuse, preferring to misuse the law in a hopeless attempt to secure righteousness. Nevertheless, a remnant in Israel would be saved. This was a constant principle in the old covenant. A remnant had always stood against the Jewish community's popular mind-set (2 Chr. 34:21; Isa. 10:20; 11:16; 37:32; Zeph. 3:13). They would share in the faith of the Messiah as the true people of God. This is in complete accord with the principle of election and is fundamental to all that the prophets had taught (Rom. 9:25–33).

The new exodus motif is further underlined as Paul considers Pharaoh. The hardening of his heart was prior to the exodus (Rom. 9:17–18), and amazingly Paul applies the same principle to his own unbelieving kinsmen (Rom. 11:25). By refusing to become part of the remnant, they have become the victims of the divine hardening, and as a result, have been excluded from the experience of the new exodus. In this attitude of disobedience, they have done everything they could to deter their fellow countrymen from joining the people of the Way. In other words, unbelieving Israel in the new exodus model reflects Pharaoh in the Egyptian exodus, for both resist God and both have hardened hearts.

Romans 9: When People Try to Justify Themselves

We have already noted the extensive use that Paul makes of Isaiah. Here, in chapter 9, there are quotations from Isaiah in vv. 15, 27, 29, and 33. Each of these has been carefully chosen by Paul to support his ongoing argument, without doing any injustice to their original contexts.

9:1 I am speaking the truth in Christ—I am not lying; my conscience bears me witness in the Holy Spirit—

Paul is concerned that he should not be perceived as rejecting his kinsfolk. He swears an oath, affirming that what he is about to say is a true reflection of his feelings for his kinsmen, and expresses grief over the state of unbelieving Israel. In the past, Paul's word had been doubted. Three years after his conversion, believing Jews in Jerusalem did not accept his story as true (Gal. 1:18–20), and Barnabas had to speak to the apostles on his behalf (Acts 9:26–27). It was fourteen years later that Paul's testimony was believed in Jerusalem; at that time, he was accepted by the 'pillars' of the church as an apostle to the Gentiles and given the right hand of fellowship (Gal. 2:1–10).

No wonder Paul had such strong feelings about telling the truth and defending his trustworthiness—a matter he touches on in a number of his letters. He warned of untruthfulness in his letter to the Colossians (Col. 3:9–10), where interestingly, he raised the issue in the context of church unity. When defending his ministry to the Corinthians, Paul wrote, 'The God and Father of the Lord Jesus, who is to be praised forever, knows that I am not lying' (2 Cor. 11:31).

Paul stressed that he is speaking the truth 'in Christ' and writes that his conscience supports his claim of truthfulness. The phrase 'in the Holy Spirit' could be a reference to Romans 8:26, where he acknowledged the help given by the Holy Spirit to all believers, aiding them in areas of weakness.

9:2 that I have great sorrow and unceasing anguish in my heart.

Paul's experience can only be understood by those who have been rejected by people they love. From his letters and the Acts of the Apostles, we learn of Paul's intense sufferings, including what he experienced at the hands of his fellow Jews. He was stoned in Lystra and left for dead (Acts 14:19), publicly misrepresented in Ephesus (Acts 19:9), beaten in Jerusalem (Acts 21:27–32), and lashed on five occasions (2 Cor. 11:24). In addition to physical sufferings, Paul writes these telling words in his letter to the Corinthians, 'Besides everything else, I face daily the pressure of my concern for all the churches. Who is weak, and I do not feel weak? Who is led into sin, and I do not inwardly burn?' (2 Cor. 11:28–29).

In recent scholarship there has been much attention to the supposed criticism by Paul of the Roman Empire. This I believe has been misplaced—during the New Testament period the Roman authorities were quite indifferent to the Christian church. When they had direct dealings with her, it was always because the unbelieving Jewish community had manipulated them for their own purposes and put them in a difficult situation by trying to silence the witness given to Jesus. That the Jews behaved in such a way caused Paul great distress.

Paul's frankness in these opening verses helps us to appreciate his personal qualities, for in addition to his immense concern for his kinsmen—and the memory of all he had suffered at their hands—he also carried a daily concern for all the churches. In spite of the ever repeating cycle of sorrow and anguish in his heart, Paul could not help but love his unbelieving kinsmen. He felt this way because he knew the privileges which they were rejecting, and the judgment that awaited them (Rom. 9:25–29) if they lived and died rejecting the Saviour whom God had sent (Rom. 11:26).

9:3 For I could wish that I myself were accursed and cut off from Christ for the sake of my brothers, my kinsmen according to the flesh.

The intensity of Paul's love and concern is such that he would be willing to exchange his own position of blessing for the awful state of condemnation, if that would secure the salvation of Israel. Scholars have noted the similarity between Paul's willingness to take the place of his people and the willingness of Moses to be cut off for the sake of the rebellious Israelites (Exod. 32:32). Some have argued that Paul saw himself to be a new Moses. This may be so (although disputed by some), because in 2 Corinthians 3:7–18 Paul seems to compare his ministry with that of Moses. The New Testament emphasis (contrary to most scholarly opinion) is not that Jesus is

Romans 9: When People Try to Justify Themselves

the new Moses, but that he is the promised Son of David, who would bring about the new exodus. This fact leaves it possible for Paul to see his own ministry as the antitype of that of Moses.

9:4 They are Israelites, and to them belong the adoption, the glory, the covenants, the giving of the law, the worship, and the promises.

In this verse Paul begins to list the remarkable privileges the Jews had as the covenant people of God.

They had been adopted as God's son (Exod. 4:22–23), had the Lord dwelling among them in his divine glory (Exod. 40:34), and had been the only nation with whom God had entered into covenants (Amos 3:2). Furthermore, they had received the law of God, which Paul sees as a privilege; even though he speaks elsewhere of it bringing condemnation. They also had the Temple in which the Creator God dwelt, and his promise of blessing when he sent his Messiah into the world.

The significance of these privileges is difficult for Gentiles to appreciate; they define the Jewish people and their relationship with God. How could a nation be more blessed? However, despite all of these privileges, Paul describes unbelieving Jews as fallen olive branches (Rom. 11:17–21), in desperate need of being grafted back into the tree.

So, Romans 9:4 is a reminder of the immense privileges afforded to Israel. It contains important information that will help us confirm the earlier claim that the letter should be read from an Old Testament perspective, carefully considering the legitimacy of importing into it Greco-Roman cultural thought.

Adopted as Sons

The first of the privileges was that the Jews had been adopted as sons. We have seen in Romans 8:17 that many scholars believe Paul's teaching on sonship to be modelled on the Roman practice of slave adoption, giving the adopted slave the same legal status as natural siblings. Here, the word *hyiothesia* ('adoption') is used again, but it is clear that this has nothing to do with Roman adoption patterns. The background is Israel's adoption as

God's son, the nation coming under God's covenantal care (e.g. Exod. 4:22; Deut. 14:1; 32:6; Jer. 31:9; Hosea 1:10; 11:1). This model pre-dates adoption in the Roman legal system. In the unfolding chapters, Paul explains how unredeemed Israel failed to fulfil this role. This is why the nation eventually lost the unmerited privileges that God graciously bestowed upon her when he elected Israel to be his servant.

Paul describes how the Gentiles are being grafted into the original stock as they take up the mantle of service. They draw nourishment from its root, as do the branches of the redeemed remnant of Israel. One assumes that, in Paul's mind, the stock is Abraham, and the believers have become his true seed. Together, redeemed Gentiles and redeemed Jews fulfil the purposes of the covenant, to the end that all the nations of the earth will be blessed.

The Presence of God

The second privilege was that the Jewish people knew the presence of God in a way that no other nation did. The divine glory was exhibited at the exodus when they were brought out of Egypt (Exod. 15:11), and in the second exodus when they were brought out from exile in Babylon (Isa. 40:5). The divine glory is the manifestation of God's presence and person. This is the glory that Moses longed to see; of which he was granted a glimpse (Exod. 33:18). The prophets looked forward to the day when, along with the nations, they would see the glory of God (Isa. 66:18).

The Covenant Promises

The third privilege was that, throughout Old Testament history, God made a series of covenants with the Jewish people. He promised Adam that he would protect him and send a redeemer from his family. He promised Noah that he would not flood the world again, and Abraham that he would establish him as the head of a nation that would represent him. Later he promised David that one of his sons would always rule over the house of Judah. While these are the key covenants of the Old Testament, God made many covenants of lesser significance with individuals for various reasons. In all of these covenants, God was committing himself to his people. These unique, privileged agreements were focused on the people of Israel, and were for their blessing.

The Law

The fourth privilege was that the Jewish people were blessed by the giving of the law. They esteemed it so highly that their teachers taught that the creation happened so that God could give his law to his people. The Psalms express the delight that devout Jews had in the law, for it instructed them in God's ways, and guided them in the paths of truth and righteousness. The commandments were not arid regulations that had to be observed, but expressions of God's love for his people; and because of this, they were joyfully observed (Ps. 1:2; 94:12; 119:29, 55– 92; Isa. 51:7). Of course, something went seriously wrong, for this same law became the means of Israel's condemnation.

The Temple

Israel's sixth privilege concerned the Temple, the importance of which cannot be exaggerated. It was there that God met with his people, and there that he dwelt among them. It was preceded for hundreds of years by the tabernacle. This tent was built when the Jews fled Egypt and was the place where the Ark of the Covenant was situated. It was eventually replaced by the Temple which Solomon built in Jerusalem (2 Chr. 1–7). However, Solomon's Temple was razed to the ground when Nebuchadnezzar invaded Judah and destroyed Jerusalem. Removing this privilege from Israel symbolized the end of her covenantal relationship with God; she was taken into exile in Babylon.

Seventy years later, a remnant returned to Jerusalem to rebuild the city, and their first priority was to rebuild the Temple. According to promise, this would be achieved by a descendant of David (Ezek. 40–48). However, no such leader emerged, and the community decided to restore the building itself. This building was eventually replaced by the Temple that King Herod built. By means of this gesture, the Gentile king hoped to endear himself to the Jewish people as their promised messiah (Cyrus, a pagan king, had been called God's messiah in Isa. 45:1); but his hope was in vain.

It was in this edifice that Jesus declared, 'destroy this Temple, and in three days I will raise it up' (John 2:19), confusing the Jews who did not realize that he was talking about his own body. As a result, the early church regarded Herod's Temple as redundant because the living Temple (the church), in which God dwelt by his Spirit, was raised to life in the death and resurrection of Jesus. The Jews, however, continued to see themselves as custodians of Temple worship. They believed that they alone had access to the living God and that he was delighted to receive their praise and worship, which could only be offered in the appointed place. Of course, such confidence was severely shaken as a result of the war in 70 A.D., when the Romans destroyed the Temple.

All these promises and privileges had been the unique property of the Jews. They were intended to bless the Jewish nation, and then they in turn were to bless the Gentiles, as they witnessed to them of the one true God.

9:5 To them belong the patriarchs, and from their race, according to the flesh, is the Christ, who is God over all, blessed forever. Amen.

Paul has a theological understanding of history, 'But when the fullness of time had come, God sent forth his Son, born of woman, born under the law, to redeem those who were under the law, so that we might receive adoption as sons' (Gal. 4:4–5). His understanding is like Matthew's (Matt. 1:1–17), and Luke's (Luke 3:23–38)— both gospel writers being anxious to show the lineage of Jesus, the promised seed. Paul asserts that there was nothing haphazard about Jesus' line, for it came about through the purposes of God. He was the one whom Jacob predicted would be raised up to secure his brothers' welfare (Gen. 49:10), the one about whom Nathan spoke (2 Sam. 7:11–16), and the one anticipated by the prophets (Isa. 9:2–7; Jer. 23:5; 30:9; 33:17; Ezek. 34:23; Rom. 1:3).

ESV has 'the Christ, who is God over all'. While such a reading is supported by the word order of the original Greek text, word order alone does not decide meaning. The translation could read, 'From them comes the Messiah according to the flesh, who is over all, God blessed for ever. Amen'. Nonetheless I consider the ESV (along with NIVTM, NET, NKJ) is an accurate translation of what Paul intended us to understand, especially in light of statements he has made elsewhere (Rom. 1:3–4; 1 Cor. 8:6; Phil. 2:5–11; Col. 1:15–20). This shows Paul ascribing divinity to Christ and is part of the cumulative evidence that the early Christian community acknowledged the divinity of Jesus. The early church came to this conviction from her understanding of the Old Testament Scriptures, as well as through her experience and growing understanding of the salvation Jesus had secured.

Some scholars are (understandably) hesitant to embrace the statement as an expression of high Christology, believing this came much later in the understanding of the church. Also, they reason that trinitarianism was framed when the church confronted several challenges stemming from Greek philosophy in the second and third centuries. But the statement should not be seen as a flight into speculation about ultimate realities. Its setting is that of salvation history. It asserts that Christ is the redeemer of his people, and of creation itself. As the Old Testament made abundantly clear, only God can redeem creation. Therefore, it must follow that if Jesus is the redeemer, he must also be God. Such a pathway to a high Christology is driven by the very doctrines of God, creation, and salvation; it is not dependent on any form of philosophical speculation or argument.

9:6 But it is not as though the word of God has failed. For not all who are descended from Israel belong to Israel,

In human terms it appeared that the word of God had failed. When, from his Christian perspective, Paul considered the condition of Israel's unredeemed majority, it looked as though the promises given to his people had failed. But, as the opening sentence in the verse states, this was not so! As the chapter unfolds, Paul quotes the prophet Isaiah, who stated that only a remnant of Israel would be saved, while the majority would be condemned (Isa. 10:27–28). He also quotes from the book of Hosea, in which God said of the Gentiles, 'I will call them my people who are not my people' (Hosea 2:23).

So, Paul is saying that, despite the pain Israel's condemnation brings to him, God's word is true; and he plays on the name 'Israel' to explain how this is so. There are a number of ways of interpreting this verse. Paul could be saying that not all of the physical descendants of Jacob (Israel) are members of the true Israel, without making any reference to the Gentiles. While he does not here state the fate of Israelites who do not belong to the true Israel, we know from previous verses that he mourns their rejection and the fact that they will be condemned should they fail to acknowledge Jesus as the Messiah.

On the other hand, Paul could be saying that the true Israel is the church—the body of redeemed people from all nations, made up of Gentiles and Jews. The implication of this is that the promises were not given to Abraham's natural descendants, but to his sons of promise, such as Jacob. It is interesting that when Isaac blessed Jacob (Gen. 28:3–4), he said, 'God Almighty bless you and make you fruitful and multiply you, that you may become a company of peoples' (Gen. 28:3); the blessing being confirmed to Jacob by God in a dream (Gen. 28:13–14). In Galatians 6:16 Paul says, 'Peace and mercy to all who follow this rule, even to the Israel of God'. It is clearly a reference to the church, the believing community.

At Pentecost, there was a tremendous wave of Jewish conversions (Acts 2:41; 4:4). To the disciples, it must have looked as if God was bringing the nation to her Messiah. Sadly, this promising start did not continue, for many of those who came into the church in those early days misunderstood the makeup of the new community. Their confusion is seen in the letter to the Hebrews, and in the closing chapters of the Acts of the Apostles, where divisions between the Jewish believers became obvious as some sought to impose the law on Gentile converts.

This major disagreement about the Gentiles and the law almost ripped the church apart. Many of the Jewish converts found it impossible to move on from the security the law had given them into total confidence in the completed work of redemption accomplished by Christ. They tried to straddle both camps, creating an ongoing problem for those who sought to welcome the uncircumcised Gentiles on an equal footing with the circumcised Jews.

So, in conclusion, it seemed that the promises of God to the patriarchs (including Abraham) had failed, as the number of Jewish converts was declining rather than increasing. However, Paul refused to accept this as the true picture. The physical descendants of Abraham—and therefore Jacob (Israel)—are not his true (spiritual) children. His true descendants are those who share the same faith as Abraham. It was not correct to count the number of Jews coming into the church as a measure of the fulfilment of scripture. The Gentile converts were just as much the children of promise and, in Paul's view, they must be taken into account when deciding whether the promises to the patriarch were being fulfilled.

9:7 and not all are children of Abraham because they are his offspring, but "Through Isaac shall your offspring be named."

Paul presses home the truth that being a physical descendant of Abraham does not mean automatic membership of the new covenant community. To show this, he points to the fact that the original promise was not given to all the physical descendants of Abraham. Neither Hagar's son Ishmael, nor the sons of his wife Keturah (Gen. 25:1–4), nor the children of his concubines (Gen. 25:6) were included.

At the time when Abraham was promised he would father a son (Gen. 15:2–6), he was not told the identity of the mother. So many years later, when his old and barren wife Sarah insisted that he should father a family for her through her handmaid, he agreed. His first child was born to Sarah's Egyptian handmaid, who came to be known as Hagar. When Hagar became pregnant, she was told by the angel of the LORD that her son Ishmael would father numerous offspring (Gen. 16:9–11). If Abraham had listened carefully to Hagar's account of the meeting, he would have realized that Ishmael was not to be the 'son of promise' because the LORD had warned Hagar that Ishmael would live in hostility towards all his brothers. In contrast, Abraham's descendants through his 'son of promise' would be a blessing to the nations. Despite Ishmael being his firstborn son (and being circumcised with the patriarch), Abraham's 'son of promise' had yet to be born. When Ishmael was fourteen years old, Sarah gave birth to Isaac. Paul confirms that he was the child of promise through whom Abraham's offspring would be reckoned.

In Galatians Paul goes even further, pointing out that the Scriptures say the nations would be blessed through Abraham's 'offspring' (singular)—not his 'offsprings' (plural) (Gal. 3:16). He argues that the promise is directed to a specific descendant, that is, Jesus Christ. In translating sperma 'seed' in Romans 9:7 as 'offspring' (as in Galatians), the ESV has obscured the fact that Paul is referring to Jesus as the true seed of Abraham. Paul uses 'seed' in this verse in the same way as he has used it in Galatians, referring to a particular descendant of Abraham's line. The term is not to be understood as encompassing all of Abraham's descendants.

9:8 This means that it is not the children of the flesh who are the children of God, but the children of the promise are counted as offspring.

What Paul is arguing would have been bewildering for Jews in Rome. They regarded the fact that they were the physical descendants of Abraham and of Jacob (Israel) as synonymous with being the children of the promise. Paul cuts right across this thinking—the same thinking he formerly shared. His claim that the Gentiles are equally, without reservation, children of Abraham through faith in Christ Jesus is the basis of his following argument. Indeed, their union with Christ, who is the true seed of Abraham, makes them not only the true seed, but also the remnant spoken of by the prophet Isaiah (Isa. 10:20–22; 11:11–16; 28:5; 37:4, 31–32. See also Jer. 23:3; 31:7; 42:2; 43:5; 44:7; 50:20).

9:9 For this is what the promise said, "About this time next year I will return, and Sarah shall have a son."

Paul quotes from Genesis 18, where the visit of the three men to Abraham is recorded, 'The LORD said, "I will surely return to you about this time next year, and Sarah your wife shall have a son." And Sarah was listening at the tent door behind him' (Gen. 18:10). It is of interest how—in Galatians 4—Paul saw God's involvement in the birth of Isaac. When considering Ishmael and Isaac, he writes, 'But just as at that time he who was born according to the flesh persecuted him who was born according to the Spirit, so also it is now' (Gal. 4:29). In other words, the birth of Isaac was the result of the divine promise, and not the result of extraordinary faith as discussed earlier (see comments Romans 4:19–20).

So, Paul's argument hangs on a correct understanding of the promise. The fact that Abraham and Sarah had to wait for the LORD's return in order for the promise to be fulfilled emphasizes that this birth was dependent on divine intervention. In human terms, God's appointed time for the couple was hardly their best time. They were both advanced in years (Abraham was one hundred and Sarah was ninety when Isaac was born), and the birth of a child, while joyous beyond measure, would usher in years of anxiety.

9:10–12 And not only so, but also when Rebekah had conceived children by one man, our forefather Isaac, though they were not yet born and had done nothing either good or bad—in order that God's purpose of election might continue, not because of works but because of him who calls— she was told, "The older will serve the younger."

Isaac's wife, Rebekah, experienced years of barrenness until God answered his prayer. His wife conceived and she bore non-identical twin boys. Paul makes the point that one was chosen, and the other was not. This choice was not made after they were reared, when their developing personalities and characters could be assessed, but in the womb, and before they were known to their parents.

The point Paul is emphasizing is that human choice is not necessarily God's choice. He is not swayed by personality, talent, or achievement; or bound by rights and privileges of any kind. God alone makes his choices. While they were still in the womb, God decreed that the firstborn would serve his younger brother. Paul is demonstrating that nothing can control the choices that God makes. The one chosen will not be able to claim that this privilege was his right by birth, or because of his works.

The phrase 'not because of works' recalls similar words in Ephesians 2:9, 'not a result of works, so that no one may boast'. This is the essence of the gospel Paul proclaimed—absolutely no one can boast in his or her status before God (1 Cor. 1:26–31). Nothing can be brought to God to convince him of human worth. Indeed, any such attempt to do so is grounds for rejection, as God will not share his glory with another (Eph. 2:9b). While it is valid to recall Ephesians 2:9, it must be realized that, in Romans 9:12, Paul is not dealing with how God chooses people for salvation, but how people are chosen for privilege and responsibility (this perspective continues into chapter ten). Indeed, when Ephesians 2:9 is examined, it is found to be saying a similar thing. Paul tells the Gentiles that they had been included in the covenant community solely because of God's grace and kindness. It is a corporate statement of the change of status afforded to all believing Gentiles—they have been included in the covenants of promise by God's grace, and not by law observance. In that covenant, they share God's saving grace. Since they are saved from the judgment that will come upon the godless, the covenant speaks ultimately of salvation. Indeed, even though Paul's argument is about being elected for service, it moves on to salvation from judgment (v. 27), that is the salvation of the believing community from the wrath it deserves. We shall see that Paul is insistent that this community is not exclusively Jewish or Gentile but made up of those from both groups who have faith in the redemptive purposes of God.

The detailed argument Paul has made prepares the believers in Rome for his claim that God has brought the Gentiles into the new community ahead of the Jews. He will go on to declare that God has set aside privilege, exalting those with none.

The term 'works' in the phrase 'not because of works' has been interpreted by those favouring the 'New Perspective on Paul' as referring to the law's requirements of rituals and practices. It is claimed that the term is not about keeping the moral or religious requirements of the law, but about issues such as circumcision, diet, and Sabbath-keeping. While Paul does make use of this meaning for 'works' in Romans 3:27 and 9:4, there are other times when it means much more than this. The meaning here encompasses the keeping of the law's commands as a set of moral precepts, as had been understood by the Reformers (Acts 13:38–39; Rom. 3:19–20; 5:13, 20). What Paul is saying is that Jacob, the heir, was not chosen because he had attained a greater righteousness than Esau through any devoted obedience to the law. Indeed, 'the works of the law' as understood in the New Perspective could not apply here, as there was of course no law until the exodus, which was many centuries later than the event Paul is describing.

9:13 As it is written, "Jacob I loved, but Esau I hated."

In saying that God hated Esau—the firstborn and natural inheritor of the promise— there is no intention to suggest there was malicious ill will towards him. The expression is a familiar Hebraism speaking of 'loving less'. It does not necessarily imply that Esau had been rejected by God in terms of his love; it simply means that he was not chosen to be the bearer of the promise made to Abraham. The same idiom is found when Jesus said that unless a man hates his father, mother, and wife, he could not be his disciple (Luke 14:26). Jesus was not calling for his followers to hate their families, but to love him more than them.

Election to Privilege and Service

What Paul is preparing to deal with is not individual salvation but how a people, who had been blessed above all others, could lose the privileges they once had. If this setting is not appreciated, alien issues will be imported into the case that Paul is making. While the benefits of the blessings are individually appropriated, they are corporately received.

The fact is that there is no theology of individual election to salvation or damnation in the Old Testament. The Old Testament understanding of salvation is about God saving people from physical and moral danger. This is not to deny that a development of the doctrine of personal election took place in the New Testament.

However, while I want to stand by the teaching that holds to God's electing grace toward the individual, I also want to assert that basing arguments for individual election on this particular passage confuses the discussion and misses some important issues that Paul is expounding.

This proposed election to privilege and honour does not deny that the theme of individual salvation is raised in chapter 10 (Rom. 10:9–11). However, introducing it into chapter 9 is contrary to the literary and theological controls of the passage, and cannot be justified. The proposed reading does not deny the doctrine of election to salvation; but it is on the evidence of other texts that it must be established. To see the thrust of Romans 9 as being about God electing individuals to damnation, rather than to salvation from the judgment that reprobate humankind deserves, goes beyond biblical evidence. Those who propose this argument appeal to texts such as Romans 8:32–34, Ephesians 1:4 and 1 Thessalonians 1:4. However,

I would also point out that these texts say nothing about election to damnation; they are about a corporate calling to be God's people.

We need to be careful that we do not allow long valued traditions of interpretation to control the message of this passage. Allowing the text to have its own voice is an essential part of the Reformed tradition. As we have seen in chapter 4, traditional readings have missed important pointers regarding the significance of Paul's argument about justification because details that were not present in his exposition have been unintentionally imported into the narrative. I want to suggest that the same mistake is being made by many here.

9:14 What shall we say then? Is there injustice on God's part? By no means!

Paul responds to a possible charge that, by reversing the natural order of priority, God is being unjust. His point is that because neither Jacob nor Esau deserved this honour, neither could claim merit. If they were to receive anything, it must be given by God out of his grace. The Old Testament narrative repeatedly demonstrates this in the twists and turns seen in the progressive succession of those who were selected to carry forth the covenantal promises given to Abraham. Scripture shows that God has regularly taken a surprising course, choosing the unexpected to be the bearer of the promises; yet all the while he is faithful to the covenant he made with Abraham.

9:15 For he says to Moses, "I will have mercy on whom I have mercy, and I will have compassion on whom I have compassion."

To drive home his claim that election to honour and service is not based on merit or status, Paul again appeals to the Scriptures. The use of Exodus 33:19 has particular relevance because of its context. Moses had asked God if he might see his glory and, in reply, he was told, 'I will make all my goodness pass before you and will proclaim before you my name "The LORD"'. God then made the statement, 'I will be gracious to whom I will be gracious and will show mercy on whom I will show mercy'.

The point is clear. God reveals himself to those who seek him, but not on the grounds of merit—his revelation is based solely on mercy. That God takes the initiative in salvation history has been demonstrated in the call of Abraham. The ancestor of the Jewish people was not chosen to be the conduit of God's blessings to all the families of the earth on the grounds of his merit, but on the grounds of God's free electing grace. The same applies to the true descendants of Abraham— the sovereign God elects those who are allowed to see his glory. Our election to service, and the privileges which it brings, are all of God's grace, prerogative, and initiative.

However, the case being argued is not for individual election, but for that of peoples. God elected the Jewish people in their ancestor, Abraham. Now the Gentiles are part of his elect people and included in the covenant. As such, they are chosen by God to serve his purposes in redemptive history; they are included in the servant community that is appointed to take the good news of God's grace to the nations.

9:16 So then it depends not on human will or exertion, but on God, who has mercy.

This is the only conclusion that can be reached from the texts considered. The scriptures Paul selects are not taken out of context but faithfully portray the nature of God's sovereign choice. We are chosen to serve God's purposes because of his mercy; hence our selection has nothing to do with our achievements or birth rights (John 1:12).

9:17 For the Scripture says to Pharaoh, "For this very purpose I have raised you up, that I might show my power in you, and that my name might be proclaimed in all the earth."

We can easily miss the argument that Paul is making. We need to remind ourselves that Paul is discussing the judgment that has come on Israel. To illustrate this judgment, he considers God's dealings with Pharaoh. Many understand this verse to imply that God created Pharaoh in order to destroy him, so showing himself to be greater than the Egyptian ruler. But was Paul saying this? The emphasis of the verse (and that of the exodus narrative) is God's mercy, and this message of how God's mercy triumphs over man's sinfulness will characterize Paul's conclusion to this entire section (Rom. 11:33–36). So, the text that Paul quotes must be considered in its original setting. Failure to contextualize the quotation, and so grasp its intended meaning, has frequently caused Paul's argument to be misunderstood. God was not going to destroy Pharaoh in order to display his power; he was, in fact, doing the very opposite. The power of God was demonstrated through his patience and kindness to a disobedient Pharaoh:

> *For by now I could have put out my hand and struck you and your people with pestilence, and you would have been cut off from the earth. But for this purpose I have raised you up, to show you my power, so that my name may be proclaimed in all the earth. (Exod. 9:15–16)*

Examining the Exodus passage in its context makes it clear that God's intention was not to glorify himself through the destruction of Pharaoh, but through his patient call to repentance. Indeed, although there is the warning of a future hardening, Pharaoh's heart had been hardened long before Moses addressed him. He had sought to kill the new-born sons of the Hebrew families, and it is impossible to argue that he could do that without hardening himself towards God's word. When Moses stood before him, Pharaoh was already a hardened man to whom God, in his mercy, continued to give the opportunity to repent. If Pharaoh had done so, he would have saved his people from the impending judgment.

Although God's show of power was demonstrated initially through his patience to Pharaoh, it became the grounds for God's judgment. In response to Pharaoh's wilfulness, God began the process of divine hardening; which is distinct from the hardening that Pharaoh's guilt had produced. The Lord had every reason to judge him, but he desisted in order that his power should be shown through his mercy. But because Pharaoh rejected his mercy, and continued to harden his heart, God sealed his fate with his divine hardening. God had no other option but to bring judgment upon him.

However, this was not the reason for raising Pharaoh up. The statement made to Pharaoh (quoted by Paul) has nothing to do with God's choosing him in order to harden his heart and display his power in judgment. Granted, the judgment did display his power—but that is not the context of the quoted verse. God wanted to change the heart of Pharaoh through patience and kindness. He was urging Pharaoh to receive mercy through repentance and obedience.

Romans 9: When People Try to Justify Themselves

Pharaoh had been chosen by God to rule, as had the Pharaoh who was ruling at the time of Joseph. In the closing chapters of Genesis, Joseph invites his father and his family to dwell in Egypt to escape famine. He could only do this with the consent of the Pharaoh ruling at that time; so, by granting Joseph's request, the Pharaoh acted as the Hebrews' benefactor, protecting them from danger. In the course of time, this benevolent relationship between Jacob's descendants and the office of Pharaoh changed. Rather than seeking to protect the Hebrews, a later Pharaoh sought to destroy them. He who had been appointed as a vessel of honour became a vessel fitted for destruction! This was a distressing development since he who had been given the privilege of acting as a redeemer figure to Jacob's descendants—a role that Cyrus would assume in the future—had not been elevated that he might be judged but that he might serve God's people. We will find that Paul echoes the role of Cyrus as he deals with the protest of the vessel which the potter has made. This juxtaposition of pagans in the text is crucial.

So, Exodus 9:15–16 (as above) is not about salvation, but about serving and honour. Paul is addressing the fact that Pharaoh's position had been given to him by God, but he had abused it. He was created for honour, but by steadfastly rejecting God's word and purpose, his heart was hardened and so, after exercising much patience, God judged him. Thus Pharaoh, who was chosen for honour, became a vessel prepared for destruction (v. 22). References to God telling Moses that he would harden Pharaoh's heart (Exod. 4:21–23; 7:2–4; 14:4ff.) clearly speak of what will happen when Pharaoh rejects Moses' message. Taking our hermeneutic from Paul's ongoing argument concerning men whom God raised up to bless and protect his people, Pharaoh is judged (hardened) because he refuses to be the servant he has been appointed to be. He failed to protect the promised seed.

We need to remind ourselves that Scripture has no difficulty in seeing pagan kings and leaders as 'servants of God'. God referred to Cyrus as his 'anointed...whose right hand I have grasped' (Isa. 45:1). Cyrus was a pagan king who served his own deities; nevertheless, God said of him, 'He is my shepherd, and he shall fulfil all my purpose' (Isa. 44:28). Cyrus did what Pharaoh refused to do—he served as a shepherd for the promised seed.

Not all of Pharaoh's court agreed with the position their master took. As the plagues fell, some of the Egyptians responded in fear to God's display of power (Exod. 8:19; 9:20). Many in the country thought highly of Moses and the Israelites (Exod. 11:3) and, by implication, respected their God. Were these the first Gentile converts— the first fruit from among the Gentiles? As many were familiar with the Hebrew people, did they hear about the coming plague on the firstborn? Did they avail themselves of the power of the blood of the Passover lamb?

Tragically and inevitably Pharaoh's hardening was now to reap its just reward, and he was to become a vessel of wrath. Judgment, so long held back, was to visit him and all of the Egyptian people who disregarded God's word. The principle that noble 'vessels of honour' can become 'vessels of wrath' not only applies to Gentile rulers and the people they represent, but it also applies to Israel herself; as Jeremiah implies:

> *O house of Israel, can I not do with you as this potter has done? declares the LORD. Behold, like the clay in the potter's hand, so are you in my hand, O house of Israel. If at any time I declare concerning a nation or a kingdom, that I will pluck up and break down and destroy it (Jer. 18:6–7).*

Clearly, individual leaders, and the nations they represent, are not necessarily vessels of honour forever. God responds and acts in mercy when a people repent and turn to him. Israel survived her exile; thus, God's judgment was about removing privilege from those who had enjoyed it previously. This observation supports the case being made that becoming a vessel of wrath, as used in Romans 9:22, is not about eternal damnation.

Paul's purpose here is to demonstrate how God elects the people who are to serve him, and to show that God can and does overturn privileges that he has given when the said communities misuse their privileges.

9:18 So then he has mercy on whomever he wills, and he hardens whomever he wills.

If the argument outlined above is correct, and Pharaoh was a vessel of honour until he rejected God's word, then it changes the reading of the text significantly. The emphasis is not that God has created people to be damned, but that he has created all people for dignity and service (to be vessels of honour).

In writing about salvation history and men who represent their respective nations, Paul focuses on communities, not individuals. By addressing God's dealings with Moses and Pharaoh as representative heads, he shows how God chooses people groups to fulfil his purposes. As Israel discovered, the fact that a people has been chosen by God does not mean that they were exempt from his judgment.

This divine principle of showing mercy to people groups can be seen throughout history. Nations and communities have experienced the mercy of God, with large numbers of their people turning to him in repentance. In Isaiah 34–35, the Gentile nations were warned of judgment, but promised restoration and redemption if they sought the Lord.

Blessing and salvation are never ends in themselves; nor is judgment. Any claim to having received God's blessing and mercy must be supported by evidence of service, exhibiting concern for others that they will become recipients of the same grace. For the Christian, the reality of blessing ultimately turns on a concern for people, which motivates us to reach out to others with the message of the gospel of peace (Isa. 42:1).

This principle also applies to local churches. All too often, when a time of revival recedes, the responsibility to witness to others wanes and energies become focused on divisive, peripheral issues. Believers within a church that has known blessing often become confused as non-essential features of its theology or cultural identity are seen as responsible for spawning the work of God. The congregation reasons that, in order to experience another visitation, their culture and value- system must be maintained.

When this stance is taken, the church unwittingly attempts to control God by exalting her own understanding. But God is never limited in this way. This was Israel's sin when she tried to impose non-essential practices on the Gentiles, idolizing her own status. When a church does this, her witness is often lost, her light goes out, and her candlestick is removed (Rev. 2:15). Even a church that has been richly blessed and used powerfully to advance the gospel can become arrogant, proud, and hardened. If she falls into this state and rejects the call of her Lord (as did Pharaoh and Israel), she will become a vessel of dishonour and destruction (1 Cor. 5:1–8; 10:1–13; Rev. 2:4–6, 14–16, 21–23; 3:1–3).

9:19–20 You will say to me then, "Why does he still find fault? For who can resist his will?" But who are you, O man, to answer back to God? Will what is moulded say to its moulder, "Why have you made me like this?"

Paul again anticipates an objection, 'If we are what we are because God has determined what we shall be, how can he judge us?' There is apparent substance to the complaint, but not when it is put into the context of God's sovereignty. Paul answers the anticipated objection by quoting what God said in response to a similar complaint made by Israel in Isaiah's prophecy.

The allegation of God's injustice is only possible because of the freedom he has given to the people he has made. The very fact that the creature can call the Creator to account is evidence that man has attempted to usurp God's authority. As the author of Lamentations wrote, 'Because of the LORD's great love we are not consumed, for his compassions never fail' (Lam. 3:22 NIVTM). Those who are embittered and who make a charge of injustice against God have been spared by his unfailing mercy, as God's justice without mercy requires that sentence be served forthwith. But they have been shown mercy, and the Day of Judgment is postponed.

The narrative about people being appointed to be vessels of honour continues in this passage. This time, however, Paul alludes to a passage that has in its background another world leader whom God raised up. Paul quotes from Isaiah 45, recalling Israel's response on hearing that Cyrus had been raised up to serve God's purposes. We cannot separate the quoted text in Romans from its original Old Testament context of Israel's complaint about decisions God had made. The theme of this passage in Romans 9 continues the argument about Pharaoh being raised up to display God's power. This is also the theme of Isaiah 45, from which Paul quotes the complaints that God anticipates Israel will make (Isa. 45:9b).

Romans 9: When People Try to Justify Themselves

Romans 9–11 is about God's sovereignty in choosing people to fulfil his purposes, and Paul gives biblical evidence to show that God reserves the right to include Gentiles among those whom he uses. Paul expands the theme in chapter 13:1–7, when he argues that the ruling authorities have been established by God to do the Roman believer's good, and that its servants are to be honoured and obeyed. In the past, his choices included Pharaoh and Cyrus; now they include Gentile believers and the Jewish remnant. God has now chosen these to serve him and, as in the past, the physical descendants of Abraham complain.

9:21 Has the potter no right over the clay, to make out of the same lump one vessel for honourable use and another for dishonourable use?

The imagery of the potter was well known to the Jews (Isa. 29:16; 30:14; 45:9; 64:8; Jer. 18:4–6). Here in v. 21, the potter takes clay and, pulling from it smaller pieces, he begins to work on each piece. He forms different types of pots, some beautiful— skilfully turned for eating and drinking—and some roughly made for common use. The potter made different pots in different ways and for different purposes. The clay had no choice as to how it would be worked, and it was the choice of the potter what each piece would become. There had to be vessels made for noble purposes and there had to be vessels made for lesser purposes.

This was also the case with the families of humanity. Some nations were elected for what appeared to be noble tasks, while others, in comparison, had less significant functions. Paul's argument is that just as clay has no right to argue with the decisions of the potter, so man has no right to argue with the decisions of God. It is not that such decisions are fixed—if a beautiful drinking vessel leaks and no longer serves its purpose, it is destroyed. As we have seen, vessels of honour can (and do) come under judgment when they turn away from God, and those that did not have honour can be promoted instead. As indicated in the earlier argument, this is how God has always dealt with humanity (Rom. 9:6–13; 9:25–26; Hosea 1:10).

In writing Romans 9:21, Paul may have had the Genesis creation story in mind. This narrative describes how man was made from the dust (or clay) of the earth. What God the potter decides regarding his creation is his own prerogative. In this argument, Paul is not saying that God is capricious, but that he does everything, at all times, according to truth and justice. He takes the fallen children of Adam (who, because of the hardening of their hearts through unbelief (Rom. 1:18–32) were under judgment) and bestows honour and blessing upon them. Who can complain about God's dealings?

9:22 What if God, desiring to show his wrath and to make known his power, has endured with much patience vessels of wrath prepared for destruction,

Paul is writing to the believers in Rome to say that they must understand they cannot question God's actions and decisions. He asks the question, 'What right do you have to challenge God if he chooses to show his wrath and display his power to rebellious people?' Paul reasons from what at first appears to be a hypothetical case. He focuses on the great patience of God, who keeps back his wrath from those who deserve judgment.

Paul's argument emphasizes that the only thing that is not fair or just is that God has acted in mercy. Humanity's attempt to usurp the position and authority of its Creator (an attempt that eventually resulted in the death of God's Son) should have left people under the sentence of separation from God and eternal judgment. When Paul writes 'prepared for destruction', he does not necessarily mean that people were created for destruction; rather, as a consequence of disobedience, they are being prepared for destruction.

Even though the line of demarcation has been crossed and people's hearts have become hardened, God still pleads for those who disobey him to repent and avoid judgment. This is nothing new; it replicates God's pleadings with Israel before they were exiled, in accordance with the covenantal curses. The ones who are put aside, in terms of being instruments for achieving God's purposes, continue to experience his patience and mercy until the very last moment. Of course, for those who fail to fulfil their assigned task and reject God, the consequence is not merely a loss of status; they also come under judgment for misrepresenting him and for the unrighteousness in which they took part. This is true for the Gentiles as much as it was for Israel.

9:23 in order to make known the riches of his glory for vessels of mercy, which he has prepared beforehand for glory—

Romans 9: When People Try to Justify Themselves

Another question is raised—how are people prepared for glory? Earlier, Paul discussed the redemption that is in Christ Jesus (Rom. 3:21ff.), highlighting Christ's role in undoing the work of Adam (Rom. 5:12ff.). The letter pivots around the exodus of the people of God from Egypt, and then the return from Babylon. Both Old Testament redemptive events show how God, having committed himself to his people in covenant, prepared for their deliverance. He made plans to bring them out of bondage, misery, and shame in order that he might bring them into his glory (Isa. 41:8–16).

Using these powerful Old Testament models, Paul is saying that God will be as glorified by his new covenant people's delivery from exile as he was when he made the ancient people a vessel of honour, delivering them first from captivity in Egypt and then from Babylon. The mercy that was extended to Israel has now been extended to the nations which she considered to be 'vessels of destruction'. Believers from these Gentile people groups, along with believing Jews, have been rescued from exile and brought into the kingdom of God (Col. 1:13–14). Those who thought that they had divine rights to inclusion have been excluded.

9:24 even us whom he has called, not from the Jews only but also from the Gentiles?

God extended his mercy in order to bring about a single covenant community made up of believing Jews and believing Gentiles. The original argument against God having the right to reject or elect as he wished (v. 19) has not been fully developed. Now, Paul returns to his premise, spelling out the background to the calling of the Jews and their salvation history. God's purpose was to gather to himself a people, made up of Jews and Gentiles, who would love him and display his grace and mercy to the whole of creation (Eph. 2:8–18).

9:25 As indeed he says in Hosea "Those who were not my people I will call 'my people,' and her who was not beloved I will call 'beloved.'"

Paul adapts the text of Hosea 2:23. The original passage was from Hosea's life when, tragically, the prophet realized that the child his wife had borne was not his but her lover's. God uses the pain of Hosea to speak of his own anguish. He calls the northern kingdom of Israel 'not my people'. She had broken away from Judah and Benjamin (who stayed loyal to the line of David), and had played the harlot by setting up her own shrines to worship false gods (Hosea 3:1; Ezek. 16:23–34). God said that the children of Israel were not his and separated himself from them by exiling them at the hand of the Assyrians (2 Kgs. 18:11).

Paul now adapts the Hosea passage to speak of the Gentiles, whom God has brought to himself. God honours them with the title 'my people'. The text was originally applied to a people who had forfeited their privilege by joining themselves to other gods—which according to Paul is the same position occupied by everyone who is in Adam. Through Jesus, God is going to accept the repentant children of Adam (believing Gentiles) back into his presence. The use of the quotation expands but does not violate the original message given by the prophet.

9:26 "And in the very place where it was said to them, 'You are not my people,' there they will be called 'sons of the living God.'"

Paul quotes from Hosea 1:10. If he is deliberately emphasizing the 'very place' where the Gentiles will become part of the covenant community, he might have had in mind the prediction of the Gentiles going up to Jerusalem. The prophets saw Jerusalem as the place where the Gentiles would assemble when they sought God (Isa. 2:1–4; 19:24–25). Some think this was the prophecy that motivated Paul to lead a deputation of Gentiles into Jerusalem with an offering for the believers who were suffering through extreme poverty (Rom. 15:25; 1 Cor. 16:1–3). Scholars reason this visit was a symbolic act on Paul's part, fulfilling the predictions of the prophets that the Gentile nations would come up to Jerusalem to worship the Lord.

What is significant is the unquoted opening sentence of Hosea 1:10, 'Yet the number of the children of Israel shall be like the sand of the sea, which cannot be measured or numbered'. This is nothing less than a renewal of the Abrahamic covenant; for just as God had given Isaac back to Abraham from the dead (Heb. 11:19), so now many sons (including Gentiles) were being brought from the dead.

9:27 And Isaiah cries out concerning Israel: "Though the number of the sons of Israel be as the sand of the sea, only a remnant of them will be saved,

As we have already noted, Paul's argument was not about election to salvation, but to service. However, salvation terminology is introduced here as Paul begins his discourse about the condition of Israel in relation to God's saving activity. While the argument moves on to Israel's salvation rather than her call to service, the argument does, of course, continue to be corporate rather than individualistic. It is about Israel's salvation, not about individual salvation. Paul draws on Isaiah 10:22: 'for though your people Israel be as the sand of the sea, only a remnant of them will return. Destruction is decreed, overflowing with righteousness'.

The promise that Abraham would have a multitude of descendants was clearly important to the eighth century prophets. It must have sustained them, assuring them that God was bound by his own oath to save, at the very least, a remnant of Israel. If God allowed the extinction of Israel, his promise to Abraham could never be fulfilled.

Paul, of course, has demonstrated that the true children of Abraham—the children of the covenant—are those who share Abraham's faith in the God who keeps his promises. In the original passage of Isaiah, there is an intended note of distress that only a remnant would be saved; but here, Paul writes out of hope. Despite the sinfulness of Israel, a remnant would still be saved. The emphasis is on the fact that even Israel's rebelliousness could not frustrate the sovereignty of God. This is the first direct mention that a remnant of Israel will be saved, although Paul has been implying it throughout the section since v. 6. By incorporating Isaiah 10:22 into his evidence, Paul is able to show that Gentiles are included in the pilgrim community that returns from exile in Adam.

9:28 for the Lord will carry out his sentence upon the earth fully and without delay."

The final part of the Isaiah 10:22–23 passage makes it clear that God's judgments are final, and that it is he who determines the time of their fulfilment. Throughout history, some have mistaken the longsuffering of God to be a sign of weakness or non-existence. Both conclusions are foolish and dangerous. If his judgment could come on his covenant people with such devastation and ferocity that surrounding nations were aghast (Jer.

22:8; 46:12–13; Ezek. 5:15; 28:19), how foolish it would be to suggest that God would not bring judgment on all who rebel against him (1 Cor. 10:1–11).

9:29 And as Isaiah predicted, "If the Lord of hosts had not left us offspring, we would have been like Sodom and become like Gomorrah."

The fall of Jerusalem at the hands of the Babylonians was so complete that it appeared to be the end of the covenant. It is true that Israel would survive in exile, but what sort of survival would it be? Without the Temple and land, her people were disinherited. In ancient understanding, it was unthinkable for a people to be without their land and their God. Even in modern thinking, nationhood is often thought to be inseparable from a homeland, yet sadly modern-day exile is a reality for many millions of refugees at the beginning of the twenty-first century.

Those who survived the dreadful slaughter following the fall of Jerusalem were exiled to Babylon. Eventually, they came to terms with their new circumstances and started to make a life for their families. Many had worked successfully during the seventy years since their deportation and had been absorbed into Babylonian society. When God called them to return to their homeland, most chose to forsake their inheritance; they stayed in their new home, despite the promise that God would restore the nation after seventy years of exile (Jer. 29:10–14). Any return to the Promised Land was going to cost the Jews; they would have to endure great hardships and, in so doing, deprive their families of the benefits of living in an advanced society. As a result, most rejected God's call to go back. The descendants referred to in Romans 9:29 must be the remnant who continued to believe God's promises given through the prophets. These people recognized that God would fulfil his word. He was a God who kept covenant with his people and who freely gave mercy. They knew that if this had not been so, Israel—like Sodom and Gomorrah—would have ceased to exist.

In mentioning these two notorious cities, Isaiah was acknowledging not merely the necessity for Jerusalem's judgment, but her undoubted oblivion if God had not intervened. Jerusalem not only deserved a similar judgment to Sodom and Gomorrah but doubly deserved it (Gen. 19:24–25, 28). These

Romans 9: When People Try to Justify Themselves

two cities had sinned in ignorance, but the people of Jerusalem had sinned in the face of all the warnings of the prophets and their appeals for them to turn from their sin. Israel's wilful disobedience brought direct shame on God, whose servant she was supposed to be, and whose honour she should have upheld. She was the one who had been called into covenant with God, and it was her rebellion rather than the holiness of God (Lev. 19:2) that the nations of the world had witnessed. Paul skilfully uses the comparison with these two ancient cities to emphasize that no one can accuse God of being unjust for acting in judgment. Indeed, if God is to be accused of anything, it is that he has not given man the judgment he deserves. This judgment has been delayed; and for those who believe, it has been averted at great cost—the cost of his own Son's death (Rom. 8:32).

9:30 What shall we say, then? That Gentiles who did not pursue righteousness have attained it, that is, a righteousness that is by faith;

The irony is obvious. How could it be that those who sought to live according to the law have been rejected, while those who had such little concern have been accepted? Again, Paul is not speaking about individual election, nor is he talking about morality (how some define the 'righteousness of God'), but about how God chooses a people to represent him, to be his servant. The Gentiles have attained righteousness (that is they have experienced God's saving activity) and have been brought into the covenant by God's sovereign choice—not based on works.

For Paul, there is only one saving act of righteousness—and that is Christ's redeeming death. Thus, the term 'righteous' is not limited to moral uprightness, or vindication, before the law. Paul uses the term with the meaning given by Isaiah within the context of redemptive history—it is God's saving activity (Isa. 56:1; cf. Rom. 1:17). God has visited the Gentiles who had not sought him and has brought representatives of all the nations into a covenant that binds them into the promises made to Abraham (Rom. 2:25–29; 4:16–17). They have been redeemed from sin and condemnation and brought into the kingdom of the Son he loves (Col. 1:13–14).

9:31 but that Israel who pursued a law that would lead to righteousness did not succeed in reaching that law.

The ESV has chosen this rendering, out of a range of possibilities, in an attempt to explain a difficult expression. Paul writes literally, 'But Israel did not catch up with the law'. One suggestion is that Paul means Israel was pursuing uprightness through the law but fell short. Paul is not criticizing the Jews for pursuing the law; he simply laments that they have missed its purpose. The law was intended to be the nation's schoolmaster, or 'chaperone', in order to bring the Jews to Christ (Gal. 3:24); it was not to be an end in itself.

9:32 Why? Because they did not pursue it by faith, but as if it were based on works. They have stumbled over the stumbling stone,

Paul's question anticipates the sense of shock he expected believing Jews to experience when they realised the way his argument was developing. Paul has shown that humanity's way of righteousness is not the same as God's. It never has been and never will be—what has always been absent is a living faith in the God of Abraham. He is about to explain that they have fulfilled the scripture that says that they have stumbled over the 'stumbling stone'.

But before considering the stumbling stone text—which comes up again in the next verse—we note that it has been argued by New Perspective theologians that the Reformers misrepresent Paul's understanding of what it meant to be under the law. According to this New Perspective, the Jews never were (certainly not in Paul's time, according to the rabbinical evidence) a people who thought that keeping the law earned them salvation; rather they understood the law to be a gift from God, bestowed upon them after he had accepted them as his covenant people. Their argument concludes with the question, 'If this was their mind-set, how is it that Paul could be interpreted as accusing the Jews of seeking righteousness by the law?' Of course, the question assumes that this is how they did understand the law.

But for Paul, the issue was not how the Jews thought they were made right with God, but how the Gentiles were to be made right with him. Their insistence that the Gentiles had to be circumcised was the acid test. If they really believed their relationship with God was without the law and that the law merely spelled out the covenantal obligations, what right did they have

Romans 9: When People Try to Justify Themselves

to require circumcision of the Gentiles? Their confidence and their understanding were flawed. Like Jonah, who feared that God would be merciful to Nineveh, they were demonstrating how far they were from the true meaning of the covenant. They wanted this grace solely for themselves and sought to protect their unique status by demanding that the Gentiles be circumcised. In other words, they taught that salvation could only be obtained within Judaism. In arguing the necessity of circumcision to get into the covenant they had turned the grace of God into a set of legal requirements. Their understanding of what would save the Gentiles defined how they saw their own salvation; in other words, it was achieved by keeping the works of the law.

But the 'works of the law' were not merely about submitting to the law's 'boundary markers' such as circumcision, food laws and Sabbath observances, for Paul preached to the very people who lived under these markers when he spoke these words in the synagogue at Antioch in Pisidia:

> *Therefore, my brothers, I want you to know that through Jesus the forgiveness of sins is proclaimed to you. Through him everyone who believes is justified from everything you could not be justified from by the law of Moses (Acts 13:38–39).*

This statement clearly shows that some at least (including Paul himself), believed that justification is about being forgiven for transgressing the law. This is evidence against the New Perspective view of the mind-set of Second Temple Judaism and is of equal importance as any text from Intertestamental Jewish Literature. Indeed, it is more so, for the evidence brought to the argument by New Perspective theologians is from other Jewish groups, but this is from the mouth of Paul himself.

9:33 as it is written, "Behold, I am laying in Zion a stone of stumbling, and a rock of offence; and whoever believes in him will not be put to shame."

Paul cites the text that predicted the Jews would stumble as they reject the Messiah king. In its historical setting, Isaiah 28:16 spoke of the coming judgment on Judah and her subsequent exile. The whole section (Isa. 28:11–16) is a key passage for New Testament theology. Isaiah 28:11 is quoted by Paul in 1 Corinthians 14:21, and Isaiah 28:16 (the stone text) is the most quoted Old Testament verse in the entire New Testament. I will argue that

Isaiah 28:15 is part of the background that informs Paul's understanding of what it means to be in Adam (see comments on Romans 10:11). Isaiah is saying that, rather than trusting in alliances with other nations for security—alliances made by the king that would cause the fall of Jerusalem—God would raise up a true Son of David. Those who put their trust in him would be brought out of the exile that had resulted from their forefather's sin. Again, we see Paul staying true to the original meaning of the Scriptures. The argument is that God has raised up the righteous Branch, who brings the sons of Adam out of the exile into which they had been sentenced as a result of the fall.

Further Study: Questions for Romans 9

1. Paul's description of his distress in the opening verses is seen to be modelled on which Old Testament character?

2. What was the concern of this Old Testament character, and does it help us to understand Paul's concern?

3. What examples does Paul give to show that God is not locked into natural human expectations?

4. What ultimately determines what happens?

5. What is the significance of Paul's quote from Isaiah 45 concerning the imagery of the potter and the clay? What is the complaint about?

6. What demonstrated God's greatness in his dealings with Pharaoh?

7. Why did the Jews miss the prize they struggled to gain and why?

Romans 10: Painful Concern

Introduction

In chapter 10, Paul continues to express his deep longing for the salvation of his kinsmen (v. 1). He argues that, while the Jews think that they have been zealous for God, in reality they have been obstinate and disobedient, refusing to submit to the only righteousness that God can accept, the righteousness that is by faith in Jesus Christ (Rom. 10:2–4). Remember, as mentioned earlier, the righteousness of God is primarily a reference to his act of salvation rather than a reference to his perfection. So here Paul is lamenting that the Jews are not prepared to accept the saving work of God in Christ, believing that, unlike the Gentiles, they do not need it. Their pride in being 'people of the book' actually hindered them from discovering what the message of the book (the Old Testament) was all about. By quoting Deuteronomy 30:12–13 in Romans 10:6, Paul demonstrates that the law had always anticipated that righteousness would be a gift given by faith.

Within this Old Testament text, there are references to 'ascending into heaven' and 'descending into the deep'. These phrases—familiar to Paul's Jewish readers—refer to the finding of the law. Paul applies them now to Christ. He can do this with great confidence because the law and the writings of the prophets point to Jesus; their decrees all being fulfilled in him who is the end, or goal, of the Old Testament revelation.

Thus, Christ is to be found. He is not far off but is near to all who call upon him. Paul drives this lesson home by explaining how salvation is to be received, 'if you confess with your mouth that Jesus is Lord and believe in your heart that God raised him from the dead, you will be saved' (Rom. 10:9).

Paul uses the words of Isaiah to describe those who preach the gospel (v. 15), 'How beautiful are the feet of those who preach the good news!' The prophet was speaking about the Jews who, on returning to Jerusalem from

Babylon, rejoiced that God had delivered them from their exile. As they journeyed towards Zion, they brought good news for the Jews who still lived there, that God would comfort, restore, and exalt the ruined city. He would deliver her inhabitants from their shame—even raising up the promised Davidic prince who would bring the remnant into a glorious salvation.

Paul likens the witnessing New Testament believers to the exiles leaving Babylon— pilgrims declaring that all those who hear and believe can share in salvation and come out of their bondage to sin. The summons to declare that Jesus Christ is Lord echoes Romans 1:4, where Jesus the Son of David, through the Spirit of holiness, was proclaimed to be the Son of God by his resurrection from the dead. The New Testament constantly asserts that Jesus is this promised Davidic king. However, before sharing in His glory, the believing community must share in his sufferings (Rom. 8:18).

The few who returned from the Babylonian exile joined the small number of Jewish families that had remained in Jerusalem. Together, they became the remnant through whom God would continue his purposes. Paul writes that there is still a remnant of Jews who have heard God's call and obeyed, but the majority reject the call to join the redeemed community. He is distressed that his unbelieving kinsmen refuse to take their place in the eschatological community and to experience the salvation to which the exodus pointed (Rom. 10:16–21).

10:1 Brothers, my heart's desire and prayer to God for them is that they may be saved.

The Jews considered themselves to be saved and in a right relationship with God because, in the time of Moses, Pharaoh had been overthrown and their ancestors had experienced the exodus. Paul has made it clear in chapter 9 that in clinging to their history and privileges, the Jews are rejecting the eschatological reality to which their historical experiences point. Just as a wedding ceremony is prepared for by means of a rehearsal, so that all in the bridal party can know their parts in the event, so their exodus was a rehearsal for what God was to do for his people in the death of his Son. The tragedy was that the Jews confused the rehearsal with the real event. They concentrated on the fact that they were redeemed from Egypt when they had not been redeemed from sin—the redemption to which the rehearsal had pointed.

Paul had written in chapter 9 of God's mercy in bringing the Gentiles into the covenant community. However, it must be remembered that in the Acts of the Apostles, Paul went to the Jews first with the good news. He visited their synagogues, proclaiming to worshippers that Jesus was the Messiah for whom they had been waiting. Indeed, earlier in the letter, he wrote that the gospel is to the Jew first and also to the Greek (Rom. 1:16).

In this verse, Paul pauses to share his constant burden. He knew the Jews had been blessed with many privileges and that nothing more could be done for them. Yet, despite their unique privileges, they, like the unbelieving Gentiles, were children of the kingdom of darkness. The realization of their condition caused Paul to cry to God.

Paul distinguishes between longing ('my heart's desire') and prayer. It is a fact that sometimes we pray because we know that we should, rather than because we are driven by a burning desire. Paul probably knew the sort of praying that responded to duty rather than compassion. Here, however, he writes that whenever he thinks of his countrymen, he cannot but pray—his heart going out to God for them. The dynamism that drives such prayer is love, and Paul's affection and concern brought him deep distress for the dangerous condition they were in.

How easy it would have been for Paul to wash his hands of any responsibility for his fellow countrymen. They had done everything to silence him; they had planned his death (Acts 9:24), slandered him (Phil. 1:17), and sought to ruin the work he had sacrificed everything for (Gal. 1:6–9). Yet, their eternal welfare was his primary concern. God blesses such a man who gives himself—regardless of the cost—to those who need to hear the good news of Jesus Christ.

10:2 For I bear them witness that they have a zeal for God, but not according to knowledge.

Paul is able to acknowledge the zeal that drives the Jews to silence him. It is the same zeal that had controlled him before his conversion (Acts 8:3). It now led them to go to incredible lengths in their attempts to assassinate him (Acts 23:12–15; 2 Cor. 11:25). They belonged to the chosen nation, with privileges and blessings above all other nations. How could they accept that a Galilean, crucified by the Romans, could possibly be the Messiah of God? It was this utter revulsion that drove them—as it had driven Paul—to persecute the Jewish followers of Jesus (Acts 22:3– 5). While their rejection of Jesus seemed logical, their presuppositions were wrong. They interpreted the promises of God in terms of privilege and innocence, and not in terms of responsibility and guilt.

10:3 For, being ignorant of the righteousness of God, and seeking to establish their own, they did not submit to God's righteousness.

In saying that they did not know the righteousness of God, Paul is not saying that the Jews were ignorant of God's requirements—rather that they had refused to accept what God had provided. This is what alarmed him for he had been like them at one time. He thought that he was pleasing God by his commitment to destroy the church but, instead of pleasing God, he was actually fighting against him.

Before his conversion, Paul could not have accepted that God's righteousness had been made available through the crucifixion of someone at the hands of the Gentiles. To accept that the death of Jesus, sentenced as a common criminal, was part of the purposes of God was something Jews could not countenance. They reasoned that nothing could transcend the events of their history. What could be greater than the revelation of God in saving his people from bondage in Egypt and in bringing them to Sinai, where he revealed himself in glory and majesty? What could be greater than the messages of the prophets and the deliverance from exile in Babylon? The answer to these questions was the resurrection of Jesus Christ from the dead. This alone was able to change Paul from persecutor to disciple, and from destroyer to proclaimer. Until they faced this historic reality, which overshadowed all other demonstrations of God's power and presence, the Jews would continue to reject the message of the cross, preferring to embrace their own righteousness (that is, the experience of salvation through Moses), which actually held them captive in darkness.

10:4 For Christ is the end of the law for righteousness to everyone who believes.

Is Paul actually saying the law has no relevance because its life span is over? Such a suggestion would do nothing but terrify a devout Jew, for the law is an essential part of the covenant. In Jewish thinking, 'no law' meant there was 'no covenant'. The end of the law would mean the end of the unique relationship between the Jewish people and God. This is a point that Paul is well aware of, and it is going to be the thrust of his argument in the next chapter. Here, he is specifically focusing on the law's role in achieving righteousness. Paul is not rescinding the need for righteousness; he is redefining the scope of those who are its recipients, making it clear it is no longer limited to the Jews who alone had the law.

We need to remember that when Paul speaks of 'righteousness', he uses it in the way that the Old Testament prophets, especially Isaiah, used the term. In their writings, 'righteousness' referred to the saving activity of God in delivering his people from exile in Babylon, so that they could return to their inheritance and appear in his presence. This is the argument Paul is making here. It is not only the Jews who are able to come into the presence of God as rescued and forgiven sinners; the Gentiles also are included in this act of salvation. It is not an act of redemption based on the Old Testament acts of God and into which the Gentiles are invited to share (provided they convert to Judaism and come under the law). It is a salvation, or a righteousness, that has come through Christ's death and is available to all who believe. The old law is no longer applicable. There is a new covenant and, therefore, a new law—the law of Jesus, the new husband (Rom. 7:1–6).

Paul is not saying that the ethics of the law have no relevance to Christian living. His concern has to do with the law's role in establishing righteousness. Later in the letter, he says that love is the fulfilment of the law (Rom. 13:8). For many Jews delivered from Egypt, it was the keeping of the law that demonstrated their gratitude to God. But the law, with its high principles, could only regulate outward behaviour. Love regulates the whole life, especially the heart of a man or woman. For the new covenant, the law is inadequate and has to be replaced by the command to love. It is love for

Christ that causes the believer to accept gladly the authoritative law of the new husband, the law of Christ.

However, it is possible that Paul means that Christ is the end of the law in another way as well. We have noted the ongoing priestly theme of the letter. In Romans 8:34, Paul has written, 'Who is to condemn? Christ Jesus is the one who died—more than that, who was raised—who is at the right hand of God, who indeed is interceding for us'. Such a statement concerning Christ's priesthood should not be overlooked. We have already noted that there are strong thematic links between the letter to the Romans and the letter to the Hebrews—there the writer explained that the change of administration (that is, the establishment of a new covenant) meant a change of priesthood and with it a change of law. If this is the background to the statement in Romans 10:4, then Christ is the end of the law because he is the end of the old administration. He is the High Priest of the new one and, in this new administration of grace, the law of Christ replaces the Law of Moses and the priesthood he established.

This suggestion makes good sense in the light of the argument that Paul is about to make for, as we shall see, the question '"Who will ascend into heaven?" (that is, to bring Christ down)' (Rom. 10:6) is better understood as a reference to Christ's ascension than to his incarnation. If the ascension reading is correct, then it directs the reader to consider Christ's priestly role which resulted from his ascension, so that in heaven he now intercedes for his people. Thus, the law has come to an end because a better law (the law of the Spirit of life in Christ Jesus) has been established based on a new High Priest and a new covenant.

10:5 For Moses writes about the righteousness that is based on the law, that the person who does the commandments shall live by them.

Moses describes in this way the righteousness that is by the law, 'the person who does the commandments shall live by them' (Lev. 18:5). At first reading, this verse suggests that Paul is speaking about attaining righteousness by observing the law. This is an understandable interpretation, but it tends to exclude the Old Testament's covenantal dimension of the term 'the righteousness of God'. I have sought to show that there are passages in

Paul's letters which can be read against the background of covenantal nomism (that is, the understanding that the law did not terrify the Jews but was seen as their greatest blessing; a gift from a loving God to his covenant people). If this is so, then the 'righteousness that is based on the law' (v. 5), does not refer to salvation that is secured by its keeping, for it had not been given for that purpose. Indeed, when we recall that righteousness in the Old Testament is not essentially about character but about God's saving activity, we find that Paul is saying that the law does not secure this salvation.

Indeed, in the Leviticus passage that Paul quotes (Lev. 18:5), the thrust is not 'keep the law and you will gain salvation' for the passage implies that the Israelites had already been saved, 'You shall not do as they do in the land of Egypt, where you lived' (Lev. 18:3a). The passage continues, 'and you shall not do as they do in the land of Canaan, to which I am bringing you' (Lev. 18:3b). In other words, to know the fullness of the blessing of salvation, the Israelites now had to live according to the law of God.

Thus, Paul's statement should be read in the same context as Moses' address to Israel; the saving activity of God is brought to completion by his people's response to the teaching of the law. The righteousness of God is initially established in the church (or the lives of believers) by the deliverance that comes through Christ's death. It will be completed when those who have been redeemed are transformed at the appearing of Christ (Phil. 3:21). It must be emphasized that this reading of righteousness (that is in a covenantal context rather than in a legal or forensic setting) still requires the free gift of God's forgiveness. This is because the covenant could not exist unless God was prepared to deal with humanity on the basis of grace rather than on the basis of humanity's ability to fulfil the law. The passage is saying nothing different from Ephesians 2:4–10.

The Greek text of Romans 10:5 begins with the word *gar* ('for') which links vv. 5–9 with the four opening verses of the chapter, where Israel's condition under the law and her attempt to use it to attain righteousness (salvation) have been discussed. Paul is explaining how the law is fulfilled in a totally unexpected, but nevertheless predicted, way in Christ.

10:6 But the righteousness based on faith says, "Do not say in your heart, 'Who will ascend into heaven?'" (that is, to bring Christ down)

Paul quotes Deuteronomy 30:12. Before attempting to unravel the meaning of the passage in its wider Old Testament context (the source to which Paul and the Roman church unquestionably had access), we need to note that, once again, Paul demonstrates a high regard for the context of his Old Testament quotations. The chapters preceding Deuteronomy 30 warned Israel of the danger of not keeping the covenant. If she lived according to its precepts, she would be richly blessed, but if she went after other gods, she would be uprooted from the land and given over to her enemies. While Deuteronomy 28–29 anticipated Israel's unfaithfulness and judgment, resulting in her exile, the nation was also given a promise that she would be restored to her inheritance when she returned to God. As outlined in Deuteronomy 30, the process of turning back would be a national undertaking which required Israel's heartfelt repentance and call to God for mercy and deliverance.

Aware of the value his countrymen placed on the law, Paul sought to show them its limitations. To do this, he turned to another key statement of Moses in Deuteronomy 30:11–14. Paul used the Greek conjunction de ('but') at the beginning of Romans 10:6 to turn the tide of Moses' statement to favour his own argument. While Moses taught the people to keep the law, Paul reasoned that Moses knew this could not be achieved and, because of this, told the people of another means of righteousness. Paul unpacks Moses' statement to show that it speaks of Christ.

Moses' question can be expressed as, 'Who will ascend into heaven to get it [the book of the law] and proclaim it to us so we may obey it?' (Deut. 30:12b). It was addressed to the Israelites before they entered the Promised Land and the question probably echoed their experience at Sinai when Moses, their leader, ascended the Mount for the final time. He carried in his hands the two replacement stone tablets on which the Lord would inscribe the Ten Commandments—the words of the covenant. When Moses descended, he gave the Israelites all the commands the Lord had given him (Exod. 34:1–32).

Romans 10: Painful Concern

In Deuteronomy 30:11–14, Moses told the Israelites not to look for anyone to ascend a mount again in order to receive a new revelation. They were to recognize that God had provided for them through the giving of the book of the law on Sinai. This would stand during their time in the Promised Land and after the return of their descendants from exile. That same word would always be near them—it was in their hearts and would be in the hearts of their descendants because it had been taught since the nation's inception. Moses pronounced that no new teaching or revelation would be needed for Israel—just willingness to obey what had already been given (Deut. 30:10). Paul could bring Deuteronomy 30:11–14 over into his letter because it fitted perfectly the theological framework of God's salvation being accomplished through the new exodus.

Many scholars see that Romans 10:6 speaks of Christ's incarnation—but I suggest that it speaks rather of Christ's ascension into the Father's presence. Paul has brought Deuteronomy 30:12 into an argument replete with quotations from the Old Testament having second exodus themes. I see that the key for understanding Paul's fuller meaning of Deuteronomy 30:12 is this ongoing story of the new exodus. In this new setting, the true Son of David has ascended into heaven from where he sends down the gift of the Holy Spirit to his people. Because of the descent of the Spirit of Christ, no one needs to go up into heaven in order to 'bring Christ down'. He is already with his people by his Spirit. Since Deuteronomy 30:12 is used by Paul to support an argument that brings his readers to the resurrection and ascension of Christ, I am persuaded that Paul has made the text refer to Christ's ascension and glorification There is, of course, a difficulty with interpreting the statement 'do not say in your heart, "Who will ascend into heaven?" (that is, to bring Christ down)' (Rom. 10:6) as a reference to the ascension of Christ. The passage goes on to ask, 'or "Who will descend into the abyss?" (that is, to bring Christ up from the dead)' (Rom. 10:7). Since Jesus' resurrection occurs before not after his ascension, the logical order of the verses seems to suggest that the incarnation, not the ascension, is in view here. Yet even so, evidence for treating Romans 10:6 as the ascension may be found in Ephesians 4:8–10:

> Therefore it says, "When he ascended on high he led a host of captives, and he gave gifts to men." (In saying, "He ascended," what does it mean but that he had also descended into the lower regions, the earth? He who descended is the one who also ascended far above all the heavens, that he might fill all things.)

What this reading of Ephesians 4:8 shows us is that there was a richly developed ascension tradition in the early church. An examination of other New Testament texts suggests this tradition was extensive and formed a major part of the church's teaching. If this is so, grounds are given to return to Romans 10:6 to see if, despite the apparent inappropriate sequence of events, it reflects the same ascension tradition which is found in Ephesians.

Indeed, if this seemingly unusual sequence can be resolved satisfactorily, a typological exegesis would be the most natural reading of Paul's use of Deuteronomy 30:12. The question has to be asked whether the word order is as crucial as is commonly understood or, indeed, has it been correctly interpreted?

It is clear that Moses was a type of Christ and that his ascent of Mount Sinai represented the ascension of the leader of the eschatological new exodus. As a result—if our reasoning is correct—Deuteronomy 30:12, as part of the ascension tradition found in the Old Testament, did not require adaptation to make it fit the church's message. All that was required for referencing Deuteronomy 30:12 in Romans 10:6–7 was a straightforward typological application and reading—a process that has been established as widely practiced by the early church.

Furthermore, Paul may be more careful in his use of the Deuteronomy 30:12 text than has been recognized. It is possible that he is reading back through redemption history and, as he looks back, the most recent events were the ascension of Christ and the gift (or outpouring) of the Spirit (Rom. 10:6). These had been preceded by the death and resurrection of Christ (Rom. 10:7). Viewed in this way, the statement is effectively saying that Easter, the Ascension, and the Pentecost events have been accomplished, and that these events brought an end to the old covenant and the law that expressed it.

If Paul is looking back through the events of salvation history, the apparent awkwardness of the ascension reading of Deuteronomy 30:12 is resolved. He has no need to change the position of the events in the text. He can leave them as they are for their existing order serves his purpose perfectly. He can begin with the climax of the covenant promise—the giving of the Spirit, which was secured by Christ's ascension. In reality it is more than this, for the ascension not only secured the outpouring of his Spirit but also the exaltation of Christ as Lord, in whose presence every knee will eventually bow in submission. Indeed, it is by professing Jesus' Lordship that salvation is given before the Day of Judgment. The importance of this event is laid down in the confession of faith required in Romans 10:9 and this should control the earlier reading of Deuteronomy 30:12.

This proposed reading of Romans 10:6 (that the ascension of Christ and the giving of the Spirit are to be understood by the phrase 'to bring Christ down'), parallels the reading of Ephesians 4:8 where the gift was the promised presence of Christ himself to the believing community (John 14:15–21; 15:26–27). Paul had written of this as the right of the church (Rom. 8:10–17). This ascension and outpouring happened because God raised Jesus from the dead. As a result, there was no need for anyone to descend into the deep to bring Christ up, for this had been accomplished once for all. I suggest for the early church, Deuteronomy 30:12 naturally referred to the ascension of Moses and to his new exodus successor, David. Thus, the great Son of David, who came down in the incarnation, has ascended to heaven, but resides in the person of the Spirit with his people, just as he had promised.

This reading is supported by the conclusion of the section. As noted earlier, this is what Paul's argument is working towards, which is why the quote from Deuteronomy 30:12 is at the heart of his preamble. Romans 10:6–7 leads to the declaration about how to become a member of the new covenant community in v. 9, 'if you confess with your mouth that Jesus is Lord and believe in your heart that God raised him from the dead, you will be saved'. The resurrection of Christ is central to this confession; any reading of Romans 10:6–7 that fails to take this into account is more than likely to miss the point of Paul's discourse. This reading of Deuteronomy 30:12 in

Romans 10:6 directs the Roman church to the one who has replaced David and Moses in the new exodus (Rom. 6:4; 7:4–6; 8:31–39; 1 Cor. 10:6–13; Col. 1:13–14). His conquests have brought about the eschatological new exodus event and with it the creation of a new covenant. With this new covenant, a new law (that is, the gift of the Spirit) has been given. Indeed, we saw in the introduction the massive transition in the Jewish prophetic tradition of the eighth century B.C. in which the future hope of Israel was no longer bound up with Moses but rather with the victory, and ascent, of David's descendant, Jesus Christ.

Thus, the question, 'Who shall ascend into heaven?' is understood to be about receiving the benefits of the work that the glorified redeemer has achieved. It is not about receiving the law (as it was in the case of Moses) but what the law pointed to, that is the fulfilment of the covenant and all of its blessings—not least, the gift of the Spirit. It is because of this that Christ is the end of the law for all who believe (Rom. 10:4; cf. Gal. 3:25; 5:18).

The argument that has been made for the meaning of Romans 10:6 has assumed a new exodus setting of the text. That this is the correct setting can be further demonstrated when the wider context of the text is considered.

10:7 "or 'Who will descend into the abyss?'" (that is, to bring Christ up from the dead).

Paul here considers the second obstacle that Moses said did not need to be overcome by the Israelite people. However, Paul changes the obstacle from the sea to the grave of the Messiah, and so does not strictly follow Deuteronomy 30:13, which says, 'Neither is it beyond the sea, that you should say, "Who will go over the sea for us and bring it to us, that we may hear it and do it?"' Rather, he has, '"Who will descend into the abyss?" (that is, to bring Christ up from the dead)'. It seems that Paul made a connection between Deuteronomy 30:12 and Psalm 107:26—a psalm that recalls the experience of Israel in times of crisis and the subsequent mercy of God. There is widespread agreement that the psalm is a second exodus psalm about Jews returning from exile. Indeed, the Jews used it in the Temple to celebrate God's faithfulness in rescuing the nation from Babylon. Through this liturgical use, it became well known and easy to recall. With this creative merger, Paul has given the words of Moses far greater significance. The one like Moses has not been brought from across the sea but up from the grave to speak God's decisive last word (Heb. 1:1–4). Indeed, the one who has done this is none other than the Son of David (Rom. 1:3), so it is appropriate that the words that bear David's name (Ps. 107) are used to instruct the church in Rome.

In human terms, descending into the deep—the grave—is an impossible and hopeless situation. The most that could be hoped for was that, in some way, the death of Jesus might inspire others to keep faith with what they believe, even to the point of death. But that was not God's intention. Jesus had not been abandoned in the grave by God, so man does not have to go searching for him in the terrifying arena of death. God has acted decisively by raising Jesus from the dead. Jesus is neither limited to heaven nor is he a prisoner of death. He is near to all who would call on him.

Could it be that, in his transformed text, Paul is directing the believers in Rome away from any thought that they needed to travel across the seas to meet with the Messiah? There was no need for them to make a pilgrimage to Jerusalem, and the following verse gives the reason why.

10:8 But what does it say? "The word is near you, in your mouth and in your heart" (that is, the word of faith that we proclaim);

Moses in Deuteronomy 30:14 pronounced that the requirements of the law were clear to any who were truly seeking to know God's ways. When Moses said these words to the Israelites, he was about to leave them. They were soon to cross the Jordan under a new leader, Joshua. Moses assured them that, although he would not be with them to teach them, they knew the message of truth for it was in their hearts. If they sought God with all of their hearts, they would find him, for they had been taught his word.

Paul's reference to the word being in their mouths and in their hearts probably recalls Jeremiah 31:33–34, where God declares that he will put his law into the minds and hearts of members of the new covenant community.

10:9 because, if you confess with your mouth that Jesus is Lord and believe in your heart that God raised him from the dead, you will be saved.

Contrasting with the uncertainties of the legalistic use of the law and the inaccessibility of God is the ringing certainty, 'you will be saved'. But what is required of humanity to secure release from sin and bring the individual into the certainty and assurance for which the human heart longs? It is the simplest thing that can be asked of anyone, 'confess...and believe'.

However, to confess Jesus as Lord was no small thing. The Roman Christians knew it meant confessing that the will of Jesus came before any claims that Caesar or any other supposed deity could make upon them. Life in Rome meant daily confrontations with claims for allegiance, and faith required that, into these situations, confessions of Christ's Lordship were spoken immediately. There was to be no hiding behind some indecisive gesture or turn of phrase that left onlookers uncertain as to what was being proclaimed. The confession had to be clear, unequivocal, and absolute. It was not sufficient to say that Jesus was a lord or a great figure. To confess him as Lord was to say that there was no rival to his authority.

The Lord's will was for the early disciples to be committed to him, even if it cost them their lives. For many Roman Christians this was exactly the price they paid. Just as a bridegroom and bride confess their acceptance of each other, regardless of the circumstances that will face them, so commitment to Jesus as Lord begins at the point of confession. Living with him and for him has to be worked out daily in every detail of life.

Surprisingly, the exhortation is not 'believe and confess', but 'confess and believe'. This was possibly the confessional order required by the apostles, as it followed the sequence given by Jesus to those who claimed allegiance, 'So everyone who acknowledges me before men, I also will acknowledge before my Father who is in heaven' (Matt. 10:32). This cuts through the danger of mere intellectual assent. Indeed, faith is born in the act of confession. In the indifferent West, the implications of this order can easily be missed. This is not so for those who live in hostile parts of the world, where to confess can be the most costly thing a person can do.

10:10 For with the heart one believes and is justified, and with the mouth one confesses and is saved.

Romans 10: Painful Concern

Paul spells out the way God saves people. It is with a simplicity that offends many because it demands no great feat from them. They presume the almighty sovereign Lord ought to be demanding great demonstrations of sacrifice and loyalty to his laws. Instead, Paul writes to the Romans that all he demands is confession of Jesus as Lord, and obedience to him.

Paul is not bypassing the seriousness of sin. He has already spelled out the devastating consequences of it in the early chapters of the letter. He has shown how extremely serious sin is, and how dreadful it will be for any person to give an account before God. However, he has also explained that God has made a way of escape through the death of his Son.

In the first part of the verse, the ESV translators have interpreted the Greek noun *dikaiosunē* as 'justified'. But the passage literally reads, 'for with the heart one believes into righteousness'—or 'you believe, resulting in righteousness'. Thus, one who believes will be made right with God, their Creator, and restored to the relationship for which they were created. The important difference between justification and righteousness is that the former is an event, whereas the latter is a status.

The confessional statement in Romans 10:10 is one that each of the Roman Christian converts would be required to make. While I have argued for a corporate baptismal significance of Romans 6:1–4, and other Pauline baptismal texts, I do not deny the practice of the early church in baptizing those who came to faith (1 Cor. 1:14, 17), as this is clearly evidenced throughout the book of Acts (Acts 2:38, 41, 47– 48; 13:24; 19:5). The New Testament writers saw baptism as the natural way of confessing faith and acceptance of the Lordship of the Saviour, Christ Jesus. Indeed, it was not only the natural way; it was what Jesus commanded (Matt. 28:19).

10:11 For the Scripture says, "Everyone who believes in him will not be put to shame."

Paul demonstrates that this principle of faith is not his own invention. In quoting the prophecy of Isaiah (Isa. 28:16), he is not making use of a text that is unrelated to his theme. The original context of the quotation is about Israel turning from God and entering into a covenant with Môt, the Egyptian god of death (Isa. 28:15, 18). By means of this covenant, Israel sought protection from God's anger. Isaiah promised the people that God would protect those who returned to him; moreover, he would not put them to shame. If Môt, the god of death, could be thought to offer protection to his subjects, how much more could God, the living God, secure his own from the onslaught of Satan?

10:12–13 For there is no distinction between Jew and Greek; for the same Lord is Lord of all, bestowing his riches on all who call on him. For "everyone who calls on the name of the Lord will be saved."

Paul again turns to an Old Testament prophet to support his argument. Joel 2:28 was directed to those who were in exile. The prophet predicted the coming of the Day of the Lord, when the Spirit would be poured out. His prophecy was fulfilled on the Day of Pentecost, when Peter, in his sermon, referred to the same text (Acts 2:21). The Day of the Lord was the day when God raised up his servant, the descendant of David, to bring the captives out of exile (Isa. 52:3–10). Paul, along with all of the New Testament writers, is saying that the Day of the Lord has come. Jesus, the Son of David, has delivered his people from exile.

Joel also declares that anyone who calls on the name of the Lord will become part of the covenant community, and experience deliverance. Again, the invitation is to all unredeemed Jews and Gentiles. Paul stresses the universality of the gospel; the Jews, as far as salvation is concerned, have no favoured status. Their entrance into salvation is the same as that of Gentiles. They must call on the name of the Lord who is rich in mercy.

10:14–15 How then will they call on him in whom they have not believed? And how are they to believe in him of whom they have never heard? And how are they to hear without someone preaching? And how are they to preach unless they are sent? As it is written, "How beautiful are the feet of those who preach the good news!"

Paul asks a series of questions, drawing the Roman believers along his line of reasoning to the point where they recognize how important it is that the message of salvation is proclaimed. Paul's intention is not only to emphasize the need for the gospel to be preached, but also to stress that it is part of the Old Testament picture—it is the fulfilment of God's purposes. God's

Romans 10: Painful Concern

intention has always been to save through preaching the message of salvation.

The quotation is from Isaiah 52:7 and refers to the Jews returning from exile. As we have seen, as they journeyed through the wilderness, they announced to all they met that they were returning home because God had redeemed them. Isaiah described these returning exiles as having 'beautiful feet'. They announced that their exile was over and invited all the Gentiles that they met to journey with them to Jerusalem where they could worship God together. The returning remnant gave this invitation because the prophets had said that, once the exile had ended, the nations would come to Jerusalem to worship the Lord (Isa. 56:6–8; 60:8–16).

This is how Paul envisages the ministry of the church in Rome. Having been delivered from the kingdom of darkness, she journeys towards her heavenly home. As she journeys, she tells everyone she meets—in and beyond the city—that her God has redeemed her. Everyone is invited to join her in her pilgrimage and become part of the witnessing redeemed community at the heart of the Roman Empire.

10:16 But they have not all obeyed the gospel. For Isaiah says, "Lord, who has believed what he has heard from us?"

Isaiah was distressed because, as Jews in Babylon began their journey home, many refused to join the redeemed band (Isa. 53:1). Their refusal was partly due to disbelief that deliverance really was at hand, but also to their unwillingness to identify with the ministry of the Suffering Servant. Many declined to leave the security they had acquired in Babylon. They preferred to stay under the headship of the Babylonian king than return to a disgraced and troubled Jerusalem; to the service of God who had been the nation's judge. It was more comfortable to stay in Babylon than to undertake a demanding pilgrimage; and the enormous task of rebuilding Jerusalem with all its attendant problems and deprivations was equally as daunting.

This is obviously how Paul is using the text, for the first part of the verse is clearly linked with the ministry of the returning exiles in the previous verse. Paul removes Isaiah 53:1 from its Old Testament context (the ministry of the Suffering Servant and the people's refusal to believe the prophets' message) and applies the passage to unbelieving Israel in his own time. Their preference for the security of the old covenant, over the suffering that the new covenant would bring, provides a stark parallel with Isaiah's original message.

In the original context, the description of the Suffering Servant applied to one about whom the kings of the earth could not speak (Isa. 52:15). This is an important clue for identifying the Servant. Aristocrats are rarely moved by the suffering of ordinary people; however, they are alarmed when one of their own suffers. The world saw something of this when members of the Russian royal family were assassinated during the Bolshevik revolution. It sent shivers of fear throughout the royal families of Europe. They realized the same fate could be theirs, and mere mention of the tragedy distressed them.

This is what is happening in Isaiah 53. The Servant is Israel's king, and he is the one the nation had hoped would come in glory to deliver her from Babylon. Instead, she is told that he will be treated like a common criminal. Isaiah sees the Servant's death (that is, the king's death) as a sin offering for rebellious Israel. He goes on to say (Isa. 55:3) that the suffering of the Servant brings the sure mercies of David to those who believe, confirming the royal significance of the Servant figure. While it is important to understand Isaiah 53 in its original context, it has become a key passage by which Christians interpret the death of Jesus—and rightly so. It is their king—the Jewish Messiah—who has died for their salvation.

10:17 So faith comes from hearing, and hearing through the word of Christ.

Paul takes the principles of the returning exiles' ministry and uses them to describe the ministry of the Christian community in Rome. However, the message the New Testament pilgrims carry is far more exalted because they are proclaiming Christ. He is not only the Son of David, leading his people to their inheritance, but he is the one who gave his life as the sacrifice which broke the power of Satan, delivering his people from bondage. Again, Paul emphasizes how important it is that the Christian community should emulate the example of faithful Old Testament saints, and not fail to fulfil her role in the way that Israel had (Jer. 5:11; 31:22; Ezek. 39:23; Hosea 4:12).

Since the message creates faith, Paul sees it as crucial to proclaim it, even though doing so had put his life in danger. He was not so much threatened by the unbelieving pagan world but by the Jews, who were aghast at his betrayal of their heritage and the denial of their unique status as the elect. Religious hatred like this can often spawn violence and injustice as communities defend their perceived purity and privileges. Paul would have none of this, for all of these privileges are meaningless outside of Christ.

10:18 But I ask, have they not heard? Indeed they have, for "Their voice has gone out to all the earth, and their words to the ends of the world."

Paul anticipates that one of the Roman believers, listening to his letter being read, might suggest that perhaps the Jews had never heard the good news. He discounts this by citing Psalm 19:4, where the Psalmist reasons how creation itself disperses the knowledge of God throughout the universe. Paul argues that the creation displays the glory and knowledge of the Creator God. The psalm continues by extolling the Scriptures—the Jews will have known them from childhood and could be led by them in the way everlasting. According to the Psalm, they are perfect, revitalizing, trustworthy, wise, right, joy-giving, radiant, enlightening, sure, righteous, precious, and sweet—and what is more, they are accessible to every Jew. So, because he had the witness of creation, and the Scriptures, no Jew could excuse himself from seeking a right relationship with God.

10:19 But I ask, did Israel not understand? First Moses says, "I will make you jealous of those who are not a nation; with a foolish nation I will make you angry."

What Paul is arguing for is not something new—certainly not something that should take his fellow countrymen by surprise. The apostle appeals to Moses, who was cherished by his countrymen above all other Old Testament figures. Moses warned the Jews that God would make his people envious by giving his attention to the Gentiles (Deut. 32:21). The blessings that God would pour upon them would provoke the Jews to envy.

Deuteronomy 32:21 is one of three citations from Deuteronomy 32 (the Song of Moses) in the letter. In Romans 12:19 Paul cites Deuteronomy 32:35, and in Romans 15:10 he cites Deuteronomy 32:43. It is clear that the Song of Moses was well known to Paul and to the believers in Rome. He expects them to identify with the original passages and their context. In the Song of Moses, Israel was warned about her rebelliousness (Deut. 32:15–18) and threatened that God's judgments would come upon her (Deut. 32:19–25).

Because Israel had provoked God to anger by worshipping false gods, God would provoke Israel to jealousy by taking a people that were not his people in the place of those Jews who, although they were among the chosen people, had failed to repent and believe the gospel. Paul clearly sees this text as a prophecy of the calling of the Gentiles and continues this theme of jealousy into chapter 11.

10:20 Then Isaiah is so bold as to say, "I have been found by those who did not seek me; I have shown myself to those who did not ask for me."

Paul demonstrates that the Jews ought to have realized that the nations would come into a special relationship with God. He quotes from Isaiah 65:2, in which the prophet warned the people that God would be found by those who had not sought him. The Gentiles would not have sought the Lord but for the fact that he revealed himself to them. This was tantamount to saying that Israel, who had been the recipient of this same divine self-disclosure, was no longer the sole benefactor of God's electing grace. Others, whom the Jewish people despised, were to come into the same privileges. No doubt this would cause violent protest from Paul's Jewish kinsmen, but he could respond by asking the question, 'Don't you remember; this is the very same state that we were in when God elected us?' The Jews were also chosen when they were not a people and had no prior claims on God.

10:21 But of Israel he says, "All day long I have held out my hands to a disobedient and contrary people."

The same Scriptures are now used to warn Israel. Despite having the blessings of the covenants, she did not want the intrusion of God into her national life and would not respond when he made his rightful claims upon her. To emphasize his point, Paul cites Isaiah 65:2. Like Hosea, Isaiah depicted God as the husband and Israel as his bride. God had rescued Israel when no one else wanted her, and he secured her life. He nurtured her until she became strong and beautiful, and then took her as his wife. She committed adultery, however, turning to the gods of the surrounding nations. She rejected God's love and spurned his pleas (Ezek. 16:15– 29). This is a picture of Israel that all Jews were familiar with from the writings of the prophets.

But the Jews of Paul's day could not see that they were doing exactly the same as their forefathers. Indeed, they were doing worse. For the love of God had been revealed in a way that was beyond anything the Jews of the Old Testament period could have envisaged. God had sent his beloved Son to die as the Passover victim, to bring them out of their bondage to sin, and to make them the new covenant community—the bride of Christ. The marriage theme is such a part of Jewish understanding that, at every Passover meal, the Song of Songs is read. It speaks of the love between a man and a woman, which points to a far greater love—the love of God for his people. The Passover celebrates the divine marriage, when God took Israel as his bride on the first Passover night.

Thus, Romans 10 pulls together the theme of the exhortation of Moses in Deuteronomy 30:12–13 with the instruction that, when the Israelites return from exile, they are not to search for someone who will represent them before God in the mountain as Moses had done. They are not to send emissaries overseas either to find someone of the calibre of Moses who was brought to the nation by God from beyond the Red Sea. There would be no 'new revelation' from God. He would give his people all that they needed in the person of the prophet who would be raised up from among them. This prophet would be like Moses, and his words were to be obeyed. This is the exhortation which is accompanied with the powerful themes of pilgrimage and deliverance from exile—themes that resonate throughout Paul's letter to the Romans.

Further Study: Questions for Romans 10

1. Why is Christ the end of the law for those who believe?

2. When Moses uttered the words about not going up into heaven to bring the law down, what was the context of his original message?

3. Can you explain the various views about how to understand what ascending into heaven and descending into the deep might mean? Which explanation do you prefer and why?

4. How do individuals enter the new covenant community (how are they saved)?

5. How did God intend to make the Jews jealous, and for what purpose?

6. How does the quote from Isaiah support what Moses had said?

Romans 11: What Will Happen to Israel?

Introduction

In the eleventh chapter, Paul continues to express his concern about the present condition of Israel. He shows that the principle of the 'remnant' is not new but has been part of God's purpose and Israel's history throughout the ages (Rom. 11:1–6), as demonstrated by the Scriptures (Rom. 11:7–10). Paul explains that the rejection of Israel is neither final nor total, but temporary and partial (Rom. 11:11–12); he makes reference to the first-fruits offering (Rom. 11:16), and the grafting of olive branches (Rom. 11:17–21) to illustrate his argument.

These two illustrations are significant as they are both images from exodus material. Instructions for the first-fruit offering of bread were given at Sinai in Leviticus 23:17 when the children of Israel were at the beginning of their journey to the Promised Land. Reference to the olive tree was made in Jeremiah 11:16–17 and in Hosea 14:4–6, where a promise of blessing was given for those who would be brought out of the predicted exile in Babylon.

Thus, the new exodus motif emerges once again in Paul's argument. His reasoning is at two levels. First, he wishes to show that the church is the first-fruit of the new exodus and that creation itself will share in this eschatological event. Second, he wants to demonstrate continuity, in that there has not been a total break with the purposes of God as revealed in the Old Testament. The original, cultivated olive tree, which was not yielding the fruit it should have done, has now been pruned of most of its branches and has new branches (albeit from wild stock) grafted in amongst the remaining old ones. This second picture was given to illustrate that Gentiles from many nations have been brought into the community of faith to receive the blessings promised to Abraham alongside the believing Jewish remnant. These Gentiles are also now Abraham's children by virtue of sharing his faith (Gal. 3:6–9, 26–29). Paul writes to the Jewish and Gentile believers in Rome that originality (the creation of a new covenant people) and continuity (the fulfilment of the Old Testament promises) are distinguishing features of the purposes of God (Rom. 11:22–24).

In the conclusion of the section, Paul insists that unbelieving Jews could still have a place in these purposes. However, they will be accepted on the same terms as all other people. Israel's salvation is conditional (as is that of the Gentiles) on recognition of need and reception of saving mercy (Rom. 11:25–32). This will happen when the deliverer comes from Zion. This reference to the 'deliverer' coming 'from Zion' (Rom. 11:26) is a distinctively Pauline adaptation. The prediction is based on Isaiah 59:20, 'And a redeemer will come to Zion, to those in Jacob who turn from transgression'. It appears Paul does not think the term 'redeemer' is appropriate when writing about Christ's future saving of Israel and so he chooses 'deliverer'.

11:1 I ask, then, has God rejected his people? By no means! For I myself am an Israelite, a descendant of Abraham, a member of the tribe of Benjamin.

Because he had quoted from the prophets who speak about God bringing Gentiles into a special covenant relationship (e.g. Isa. 10:20), Paul feared that some of the Gentile believers in Rome might think they had replaced the Jews as the covenant community. He is careful to show this is not the case. If God could abandon his covenant with the Jewish people, he could not be trusted—and Christian confidence in him would be undermined. If God had given up the Jews, could he not also abandon the Gentile believers in Rome?

Paul begins his response to the claim that God had abandoned the Jewish people by outlining his own Jewish pedigree. Paul always held that he had not compromised his Jewish heritage, even though he now valued it differently. Before he met the risen Lord, when he was on the way to Damascus to arrest followers of Jesus, he hated everything about the new sect known as the Way (Acts 19:23). His encounter with the living Lord changed everything. Paul came to see that Jesus did not destroy his Jewish faith, he fulfilled it. Elsewhere, Paul used his personal testimony as a corrective to possible error; for example, when writing to the Philippian church to warn the believers about the teaching of Judaizers who were pressing for Gentiles to be circumcised (Phil. 3:2–14).

11:2–3 God has not rejected his people whom he foreknew. Do you not know what the Scripture says of Elijah, how he appeals to God against Israel? "Lord, they have killed your prophets, they have demolished your altars, and I alone am left, and they seek my life."

When stating that God has not rejected 'his people', Paul uses the Greek word *sperma* ('seed'). He has used this term in Romans 8:7–9, and the expression clearly has important theological significance—for as we have seen it refers to the promised descendants of Abraham. The point that Paul repeatedly makes is that descent from Abraham is no guarantee of covenant membership—at least, not of the covenant that ultimately matters.

Paul continues his argument by appealing to the Scriptures. This time he considers the era of Elijah (1 Kgs. 19:10, 14), reminding his readers that the prophet thought all had forsaken God. Evidence supporting Elijah's despair was all around him; the Israelite people, now following Baal, had torn down the altars where God was worshipped and were seeking the prophet's life. Nor was this an idle threat, for they had already killed many of God's prophets. It seemed to Elijah that the covenant had been rescinded—Israel's sin had finally brought her relationship with God to an end.

11:4 But what is God's reply to him? "I have kept for myself seven thousand men who have not bowed the knee to Baal."

God told Elijah that even though he could see no obvious evidence to support the LORD's answer, the situation was not hopeless (1 Kgs. 19:18). He was not alone as other prophets had also stayed true to God and been preserved. They were the remnant and the object of God's concern. Who could harm them when under the protection of the living God?

The point Paul is making is that even during one of the worst periods of apostasy in Israel's history, God had still preserved a remnant for himself who remained faithful to him and his covenant. It was a time of famine, so the pressure for the Israelites to worship Baal—the god of fertility—must have been immense. Yet despite the fact that it had not rained for three and a half years, seven thousand refused to bow the knee to Baal. The drought was God's judgment on the sinfulness of Israel, and only when she responded in repentance was the judgment lifted (1 Kgs. 18:39, 45).

11:5 So too at the present time there is a remnant, chosen by grace.

Although it appeared that God's purpose for Israel was thwarted, there was no possibility of this happening as, through his saving grace, God had preserved a remnant for himself. Paul writes that the same thing was true in his day. That Paul reasoned in this way is evidence of a radical change in expectation from the immediate post-Pentecost days when Jews, in their thousands, were entering the kingdom of Christ (Acts 2:36–41; 6:1–7). In those heady days, it must have seemed as though Israel's acceptance of Jesus as her Messiah was imminent. How quickly this optimism changed, and how difficult it was for Jewish believers to accept that Gentiles were coming into the kingdom ahead of their kinsmen.

In seeing the Jews who believed in Jesus as a remnant, Paul makes a comparison with the remnant that refused to worship Baal. The logical conclusion of Paul's argument is that he considers Judaism to be a pagan religion akin to Baal worship— a concept that would have horrified the orthodox Jews. It was pagan because it sought to demand an alternative allegiance from the Jewish people in the face of the claims of their Messiah. It has been suggested that Paul uses this ploy in his letter to the Colossians. In that letter his argument follows the same line of thought—Judaism is a religious system that has rejected the Messiah. In so doing she has become nothing less than pagan. Paul is clearly using this polemic against the Jews in an attempt to provoke repentance (see vv. 13–14).

11:6 But if it is by grace, it is no longer on the basis of works; otherwise grace would no longer be grace.

The believers were not in relationship with God as a result of their own work. Paul introduces the word 'grace', into the argument despite the fact there is no mention of it in the original Old Testament incident involving Elijah. Paul legitimately embellishes the story by the addition of the word 'grace' because the remnant has received far more than those of Elijah's day, for they have now been brought into the Messiah's kingdom. God's remarkable mercy could only be summed up by the term 'grace'—total and absolute unmerited favour. The contrast is clear. While it was God who kept the remnant safe in Elijah's day, because they had remained faithful, so it could be claimed they were rewarded for faithfulness or works. In the new exodus however, the Jews were not in the redeemed community because of their commitment to God, but because of his commitment to them as fallen and defiled sinners. This is why Paul wrote to the Ephesians, 'For by grace you have been saved through faith. And this is not your own doing; it is the gift of God, not a result of works, so that no one may boast' (Eph. 2:8–9).

11:7 What then? Israel failed to obtain what it was seeking. The elect obtained it, but the rest were hardened,

What is tragic in this analysis of Israel's history is that, although driven in her pursuit to please God, she fell far short of the target. Paul argues that those whom the Jews despise—who were never part of the covenant—have received that which they had never sought: a right relationship with God.

Unbelieving Israel has been hardened, just as Pharaoh had been (Exod. 8:32; 9:12) as he sought to stop the Jews from leaving Egypt for the Promised Land. Paul is, in effect, saying that in the early years of the Christian church's pilgrimage, the one who now plays the role of Pharaoh is unredeemed Israel. She is seeking to prevent the people of God from leaving the kingdom of darkness to follow the Davidic Messiah on his triumphant march to the Promised Land. To suggest such a startling reversal of roles would have left any orthodox Jew shocked.

11:8 as it is written, "God gave them a spirit of stupor, eyes that would not see and ears that would not hear, down to this very day."

Paul appeals to the writings of Isaiah (Isa. 29:9–10), in which he warned Jerusalem of her forthcoming judgment. Isaiah warned Jerusalem not to be complacent because her situation was precarious. The reason for the Jews' ill-judged perception of security was because God had given them a spirit of stupor. It was as if they were dazed and unable to reason. God had turned against his own people because they continually rejected his word.

He also appeals to Moses, who in Deuteronomy 29 summoned the Israelites to renew their covenant with God. Despite all that he had done in delivering them from Egypt and in keeping them during forty years of wanderings in the desert, they still had a warped understanding of God. Moses said the Lord had blinded their eyes and stopped up their ears (v. 4), effectively causing them to stumble as if their senses were withdrawn.

Paul is making the point that the present hardening of heart his kinsmen were experiencing was not a unique event—God had acted in judgment against his own covenant people throughout the Old Testament. While the Jews thought the covenant protected them from God's chastening, the Scriptures made it clear that, because they were the covenant people of God, they would be chastised ahead of the Gentiles (Amos 3:2).

11:9–10 And David says, "Let their table become a snare and a trap, a stumbling block and a retribution for them; let their eyes be darkened so that they cannot see, and bend their backs forever."

Now, to add insult to injury, Paul brings the words of their own Messianic king to witness against his unbelieving subjects (Ps. 69:22–23). David's prayer was for God to exact vengeance on his enemies, but here Paul applies David's words to the Jews. Yet his doing so does not represent a misuse of the passage; for in its original setting, the psalm concerns an attempt to overthrow David by members of his own family.

There is another reason why Paul uses David's Psalm. He has been describing how the gospel is the fulfilment of the promises made to David and Abraham. To reject Jesus, therefore, is to reject David and the covenant made with him (2 Sam. 7:5– 16). Hence it is entirely appropriate to apply David's cry in Psalm 69:22–28 to the Jews of Paul's day, for they persecuted their own countrymen who had turned to the Son of David for salvation.

The mention of the 'table' in David's psalm may have a significance that is not immediately obvious. The term was used by Paul in 1 Corinthians 10:21, 'You cannot drink the cup of the Lord and the cup of demons too; you cannot have a part in both the Lord's Table and the table of demons'. This possible link suggests that the term has a cultic significance for Paul. He may be suggesting through the use of 'their table' that the Jewish sacrificial system has become a snare and a trap, preventing the Jews from seeing their need for Christ's death. This is also the thrust of the argument in the letter to the Hebrews. If this suggestion is correct, Paul is saying that David's psalm predicted the obsolescence of the sacrificial system as a means of getting right with God.

11:11 So I ask, did they stumble in order that they might fall? By no means! Rather through their trespass salvation has come to the Gentiles, so as to make Israel jealous.

In responding to his own question concerning the permanence of Israel's fall, Paul answers an emphatic, 'Not at all!' He explains that the very purpose of the Gentiles being brought into the covenant was to provoke Israel to envy. It is doubtful if Paul intended the Roman believers to think this was the only reason for the salvation of the Gentiles, because the rest of Scripture presents a much higher motive—the glory of God himself (Eph. 2:10; 3:10–11). The provocation of Israel to envy is intended to cause the Jews to seek God and so bring him more glory.

11:12 Now if their trespass means riches for the world, and if their failure means riches for the Gentiles, how much more will their full inclusion mean!

The method of argument in this verse was well known in Judaism. If negative events bring positive results, then positive events would bring positive results of a greater magnitude. A modern equivalent would be the question, 'If a sick child can make so many people happy, how much more joy will he bring when made well?'

Paul asks the church in Rome a similar question about his kinsmen, 'if their sin, with its consequential loss of blessing, is the cause of the Gentiles coming into blessing, how much more blessing will overflow to the Gentiles when God graciously, out of his mercy, restores the Jews to their forfeited place in the covenant?' So, Paul anticipates a future for his kinsmen as they turn to the Messiah—their full inclusion. Moreover, this inclusion will not lead to any disadvantage for the Gentiles, but rather greater blessings.

11:13 Now I am speaking to you Gentiles. Inasmuch then as I am an apostle to the Gentiles, I magnify my ministry

Paul addresses the Gentiles in the congregation and reminds them of his status. He is the apostle who has been called specifically to minister to them (Acts 9:15–16; Rom. 1:5). His calling gives him the right to speak with authority. Paul's instruction is not from an academic, detached position; it is the exhortation of a man who is investing his life in bringing the good news to those who were estranged from the covenants of God (Eph. 2:11–13).

11:14 in order somehow to make my fellow Jews jealous, and thus save some of them.

Paul says that part of his ministry to the Gentiles is directed towards his own countrymen. This is a fascinating insight into his mind, and an example of how it has been shaped by the Scriptures. This same desire to jolt Israel out of her sinfulness by showing that the Gentiles are preferred before her is also in the heart of God (Isa. 19:23–25). The use of the term tinas ('some') is telling. Paul is not expecting that the entire nation of Israel will be saved through his ministry. He understands the promise to Abraham was that there will always be a true and saved seed, and his argument flows from this expectation that a remnant—bearing witness to God's faithfulness—will be preserved. These are the Jews that Paul is longing to reach!

11:15 For if their rejection means the reconciliation of the world, what will their acceptance mean but life from the dead?

Paul reasons, in the manner of many rabbis, from the lesser case to the greater. He tells the Roman Gentiles they must not cast the Jewish people off as though they had no further purpose in the plans of God. Indeed, he reasons that the real blessing of mankind through the Jewish people is yet to happen. If casting Israel off brought salvation to the Gentiles, what will her return bring? Paul says it would be wrong and foolish to discount the Jewish people with the assumption that they no longer had any place in the purposes of God.

In saying that the acceptance of the believing remnant would be part of redemptive history, Paul is not describing some future event, as some believe. This imagery of resurrection was used to describe Israel's return from exile (Hosea 13:14—cited in 1 Cor. 15:55; Ezek. 37:1–14; Dan. 12:2). The expression 'life from the dead' echoes Ezekiel 37, where in the vision of the valley of dry bones Israel was resurrected. This spoke, of course, of her return from exile. Its significance for our discussion on Israel's future is that only the remnant came back from exile in Babylon. The majority of the nation remained and continued to suffer the consequences of the covenantal curses—they remained cut off from fellowship with God; for sadly, they chose to remain in a foreign land rather than to be faithful to their calling and the claims of God. If this is the imagery Paul is alluding to, he writes that in turning to the Messiah (and Jews in their many thousands had), Israel is being resurrected from spiritual death; she is at last coming home from exile, returning to God to worship him. The fact that this is a present reality is evidenced by the growing community of Jews who, as a result of God's faithfulness to the covenant he made with Abraham were (and still are) coming to Christ.

We will soon see that Paul expects a great future ingathering of his countrymen into the elect community on a scale never seen before in history. What a glorious finale to human history, when the promises of God will be completely fulfilled so the whole of creation can be in no doubt that he is to be worshipped as the covenant- keeping God!

11:16 If the dough offered as firstfruits is holy, so is the whole lump, and if the root is holy, so are the branches.

In Leviticus 23:9–15 (v. 11 especially), we find that the first-fruits were offered three days after the offering of the Passover sacrifice. In 1 Corinthians 15:3, Paul writes that Jesus rose from the dead 'on the third day in accordance with the Scriptures', and then adds that he is the 'first-fruits of those who have fallen asleep' (v. 20). It is clear Paul places the death of Jesus in the context of the Passover (1 Cor. 5:7), as did the gospel writers, and he interprets its significance from that setting.

When Jewish people offered first-fruits at the harvest, the first of the gathered fruit (or grain) was offered to God to indicate that the rest of the harvest belonged to him. Paul applies this concept to the believing Jews— they are the 'first-fruits'. He writes, in effect, that because Abraham was the first-fruit, the rest of the believing nation is not only offered to God but is also holy. This has nothing to do with her achievements, any more than the

Gentile believers could claim it was their achievements that saved them. God accepted them out of his grace in order to stay faithful to the covenant he had made with Abraham.

Paul now brings to the Gentile believers' attention the image of the olive tree, a long established symbol of Israel (Jer. 11:16–17; Hosea 14:6; Zech. 4:3, 12–14). He has already written about Abraham being the father of all who believe within Judaism and within the nations of the world (Rom. 4:16–17). In making use of the picture of the olive tree, it seems probable that Paul saw its root to represent the promises made to Abraham and its branches to represent his spiritual offspring— believing Jews and Gentiles who are justified and made holy by the same faith as their 'father'.

The purpose was to make him the father of all who believe without being circumcised, so that righteousness would be counted to them as well, and to make him the father of the circumcised who are not merely circumcised but who also walk in the footsteps of the faith that our father Abraham had before he was circumcised. (Rom. 4:11b–12). By arguing in this way, Paul begins to prepare his hearers to view soberly their inclusion in the new covenant community.

11:17 But if some of the branches were broken off, and you, although a wild olive shoot, were grafted in among the others and now share in the nourishing root of the olive tree,

Paul now asks the Christians in Rome to imagine a situation where some of the branches of the olive tree have been broken off. It seems likely that Paul had Jeremiah's description in mind by which he warned the houses of Israel and Judah:

> *The LORD once called you 'a green olive tree, beautiful with good fruit'. But with the roar of a great tempest he will set fire to it, and its branches will be consumed. The LORD of hosts, who planted you, has decreed disaster against you, because of the evil that the house of Israel and the house of Judah have done, provoking me to anger by making offerings to Baal (Jer. 11:16–17).*

Paul will go on to say that the branches were broken off because of unbelief, but at this point in his argument he is more concerned to illustrate the picture of the Gentiles' inclusion in the covenant community, and he uses his readers' knowledge of grafting to achieve this. Paul asks the Roman Gentiles to imagine the situation where an olive grower would break off the many unproductive branches from a cultivated olive tree and, having cut a branch from a wild olive tree, graft it into the cultivated stock among the few remaining productive branches.

This is what God, who is the grower in the illustration, has decided to do. The success of grafting depends upon an ongoing supply of water and minerals being drawn up from the ground by the cultivated root. Paul's point is clear: the very inclusion of the Gentiles in the covenant community is by grace. They are dependent upon the continuance of God's purposes for his ancient people because the root, which transports the nourishing sap, is their 'father' Abraham. They must remember that the covenant made with Abraham, as well as the promises given to the patriarchs and reiterated by the prophets, allow the Gentiles into the grace they now enjoy. Any temptation to reject their believing Jewish brothers and sisters would be a rejection of Abraham himself—the root on which they depend.

While the salvation of the Gentiles has not replaced the salvation of the Jews (the grafted shoot is sharing the same rising sap as the remaining, original branches), the prophets promised their conversion as the consequence of Israel coming into her own inheritance (Isa. 42:1–7). It is interesting that the order expected by the reforming prophets was not fulfilled, because the Gentiles came into the new covenant ahead of the majority of Jewish people. However, their inclusion is still dependent on the promises God made to Abraham and his descendants. This rearrangement of key redemptive and historical events is also found elsewhere in the New Testament. For example, the Gentiles were brought into the covenant without circumcision (Acts 10:44–48; 15:14–21). Also, the Spirit, who was expected to be poured out when Israel was restored to her promised glory, is poured out on the church who has shared in the death of her Saviour. God had returned to his Temple as promised, but it was no longer a building made with hands, it was, as it had always been intended, his people (Ps. 114:2; John 2:18–21; 1 Cor. 6:19–20; Eph. 2:18–20; 1 Pet. 2:4–6; Rev. 21:22–26).

In Jewish expectation, this event was to be the climax of history, at the eschaton. Isaiah 19:19–25, which looks forward to this occasion, is one of the most remarkable passages in the Old Testament relating to the in-gathering of the Gentiles. There we read they will be accepted as nations in their own right, with no suggestion that they will be required to convert to Judaism. Yet here in Romans, the prophetic predictions about the Gentiles' acceptance have been rearranged to show that it happens during redemptive history rather than at its end.

Paul has not only rearranged the order of key Jewish redemptive expectations; he has also changed the order of the illustration. Normally, branches grafted into a stock have superior, desirable features. The old stock, while hardy, is merely used to support and nourish each graft. Paul reverses this situation in his illustration as the root is superior to the grafted branch. It is quite possible that Paul has done this deliberately in order to emphasize, as he has stated earlier, that the Gentiles are dependent on the promises made by God to the Jews. It never is, or was, the other way around.

11:18 do not be arrogant toward the branches. If you are, remember it is not you who support the root, but the root that supports you.

Paul's concern is to stress to the Gentiles that they must not become arrogant towards the believing Jews in the congregation. At the heart of his concern is that the Gentile believers were beginning to look at their Jewish brothers and sisters with disdain, and their arrogance offended him deeply.

He had to warn them their conceit was dangerous. Indeed, esteeming themselves over the Jews in the church would reverberate back down through the generations to Abraham, the Jews' natural ancestor. Paul is concerned that the Gentiles respect the patriarch. He was the one with whom God made his covenant to the eternal benefit of the Gentile nations.

Paul has already written about the patriarch in his letter (Rom. 4:1–3, 12, 13, 16, 18; see also Gal. 3:6, 8, 9, 14, 16; 4:22), and now reminds the Gentiles that as a branch of the olive tree, they do not support Abraham, the root. On the contrary, the Gentiles are totally dependent on the covenant which God entered into with Abraham, and the promises made to him. Paul continues to use this fitting illustration of the olive tree, developing and applying it as the passage unfolds (see v. 24).

11:19 Then you will say, "Branches were broken off so that I might be grafted in."

Paul moves away from the main thrust of his argument so that he can deal with the response he anticipates from his Gentile readers. He expects them to say something like, 'God has put almost all of the Jews out of the covenant community and we have replaced them. We were chosen and grafted into the tree in their place. We are the privileged people and they, the removed branches, have been abandoned'. This was the very attitude of pride which took over the hearts of the Jews in the Old Testament and led to their ultimate downfall (Isa. 25:11).

It is vital for Paul to warn the Gentiles about their attitude as they must not be under any illusion regarding their spiritual security now that they are included in the covenant people. God can treat them in exactly the same way as he treated the Jews—chastening them for their pride and arrogance. The same hand of correction that had fallen on the covenant people of the Old Testament could just as easily fall on them (Exod. 32:1–35; Jer. 11:1–17; 1 Cor. 10:1–22).

11:20 That is true. They were broken off because of their unbelief, but you stand fast through faith. So do not become proud, but fear.

Paul grants the claim of the Gentile believers concerning their status, and also that of the unbelieving Jewish community, as far as the new covenant blessings are concerned. However, he warns them of the danger of arrogance and of not being fearful of the living God, lest they become like the unbelieving Jews and fall under judgment.

The reason Israel was brought under judgment (as is suggested by the term 'broken off') was more than the term 'unbelief' implies—a term which can suggest a period of grave doubt. The term Paul uses is apistia. Surprisingly, it is not found in any of the Old Testament writings and is used only five times in the New Testament (Mark 9:24; Rom. 3:3; 4:20; 11:20, 23; 1 Tim. 1:13). The term can mean 'unfaithfulness', making Israel's removal from the covenant community understandable. She did not merely have a lapse of confidence in God but displayed a rebellious and determined turning away.

The same imagery of branches being lost is used by Jesus in John 15:1–4, where the Lord refers to vine branches being cut off. However, in Romans 11 the branches were 'broken off' (rather than pruned) from the olive tree— not a technique used in tree management. Perhaps Paul envisaged them as being diseased and destroyed as in a storm, as per Jeremiah's prophecy (cited earlier).

In Jesus' analogy, the divine gardener cut the branches that did not bear fruit, but in Paul's illustration the gardener only came into view when he chose to graft in the wild branch. Why was this? Perhaps the answer lies in the term apistia which, as has been noted, can be translated 'unfaithfulness'. In the quotation from the book of Jeremiah, Jews had been unfaithful to God, the nation's 'husband', and had 'turned to the right and to the left' in their worship of false gods. As a result, they had died to him. They had broken covenant with him and could no longer be part of his covenant community. This awful rupture of the covenant led to an appalling consequence—the branches fell. The Jews who were removed from the covenant had, in essence, removed themselves.

It should be noted that when Jesus spoke of branches being removed (John 15:1–8), he used the imagery of the vine. This plant was another well-known description of Israel (Ps. 80:8–18). By means of this imagery, Jesus was effectively saying, 'I am the true Son of God. Unlike most of Abraham's descendants, I am the one whose disciples will bear fruit pleasing to the Divine gardener'. It was a powerful image but not appropriate for Paul's argument, for Jesus was speaking to, and about, Jews. Paul needed a horticultural example where grafting was a common practice because he wanted to illustrate how God was bringing in the Gentiles and joining them to the covenant community. The image of Israel as an olive tree (a tree with which the technique of grafting into old stock was practiced) was well known in the ancient world, and it provided Paul with the picture he needed. Thus, the unfruitful branches were broken off and the Gentiles grafted in.

As an aside, the illustration of the vine and branches used by Jesus in John 15, and which, at first glance seems to be related to Paul's example in this passage, is often misunderstood. The imagery used by Jesus in John 15 has been seen by many to challenge the doctrine of eternal security. This is not the case. In this passage, Jesus was speaking to the Jewish people and not to the church, which his death and resurrection had yet to bring to birth. He speaks at two levels: to the nation of Israel and to the individual Jew. The cutting off and burning of the branches specifically applies to the nation albeit that individuals make up its identity. In the first exodus, such 'breaking off and burning' took place when the wilderness generation came under judgment and could not enter the land of promise. It also happened in the second exodus when the nation was delivered up to the Babylonians and the Jews were deported—cut off from the blessings of the covenant (Ezek. 19:10–14). In John 15, Jesus warned his disciples they were members of another generation that was in danger of such judgment. It soon happened, for Rome destroyed Jerusalem and drove the nation from the land. Thus, we must not read Jesus' words as a direct warning to the individual Christian about his fruitfulness. They are about Jewish apostasy and its consequences.

Paul has already told the Gentiles in Rome not to boast to their Jewish brothers and sisters. Now he tells them, 'do not be arrogant', because he fears this attitude may lead to their own judgment. Paul and the Gentiles would have been familiar with many examples of such arrogance in the Old Testament and of the Lord God's attitude towards it:

> 'For behold, the day is coming, burning like an oven, when all the arrogant and all evildoers will be stubble. The day that is coming shall set them ablaze, says the LORD of hosts, so that it will leave them neither root nor branch' (Mal. 4:1).

When writing to the church in Corinth, Paul was concerned about the attitudes of the believers there also. He warned them in 1 Corinthians 10:12, 'Therefore let anyone who thinks that he stands take heed lest he fall'.

However, Paul's warning to the Gentiles in Rome was not that they would lose their salvation but that they would experience the Lord's discipline. This would be exercised with the intention of bringing them back to him in repentance and renewal. Paul has already implied that not all of the broken branches (the Jews) were discarded or consumed. The gardener (God) clearly preserved them so that he could, if he wished (when the Jews did 'not persist in unbelief' but turned back to God in repentance) graft them in again to the olive tree (the covenant community), so re-establishing his covenant with them. Following our corporate reading, the branches would likely refer to particular generations of Jews. Thus, the promise of branches being grafted in suggests an eschatological harvest of believing Jews that will complete redemptive history.

Finally, in this verse Paul instructs the Gentiles to fear; for unless they revere the Lord, their attitude may bring the Lord's chastisement.

11:21 For if God did not spare the natural branches, neither will he spare you.

Paul presents the inevitable logic of his reasoning with clarity and force. What right has the Gentile believing community to think that it will survive if the natural branches suffered chastisement for the same sin of arrogance? It is too easy for the Gentiles to think they are a special, privileged case whom God will excuse. Once they begin to think in such a way, they are in grave danger of being cast out of the covenant community as a consequence of the Lord's discipline.

11:22 Note then the kindness and the severity of God: severity toward those who have fallen, but God's kindness to you, provided you continue in his kindness. Otherwise you too will be cut off.

It is disturbingly easy to take the grace of God for granted; but Paul reminds his Gentile readers that the character of God has not changed. He is both kind and severe (a term never applied to God or any person elsewhere in the Scriptures). He is kind to those who feel their need and turn to him in humble repentance. On such he pours his love and forgiveness without measure (Rom. 2:4). But he sets himself against those who are proud or arrogant. He has always been such a God. Paul urges the Gentiles to remember this and not presume they have a relationship with a God who changes his character.

Paul's warning still applies today. When Christians become inflated with pride and self-satisfaction, they are in danger of losing the sense of God's graciousness and of falling into a deepening abyss of conceit and obstinacy. The judgment of God on his people is a theme all too rarely heard from the pulpits of twenty-first century Christendom. The modern message focuses on the certainty of forgiveness. In some respects, this is right, but if salvation loses its transforming effect as a result of indifference to what God has done in giving up his own Son to death, there is real danger of his new covenant people coming under a discipline no less severe than the Jewish people experienced and of which the Gentile Christians in Rome were warned. Hence, the awfulness of the warning, 'you too will be cut off'. This warning is not addressed to individuals regarding the loss of their salvation, but to Christian communities whose behaviour may cause them to come under discipline with the subsequent removal of their witness (Rev. 2:5). Similar language was addressed to Israel when she was warned of being cut off by being sent into exile (Deut. 29:18– 29). There, she was chastened until she repented and accepted the call from God to return to her inheritance.

11:23 And even they, if they do not continue in their unbelief, will be grafted in, for God has the power to graft them in again.

Far from God having closed the door to the Jews, Paul asserts they also can come into the blessings of the new covenant—not on the basis of merit, or ancestry, but on the same basis as Abraham, by faith. It is unbelief (unfaithfulness) which has caused the Jews to be cut off from their glorious destiny; but this destiny will be restored to them as soon as they exercise the same faith as their illustrious ancestor.

11:24 For if you were cut from what is by nature a wild olive tree, and grafted, contrary to nature, into a cultivated olive tree, how much more will these, the natural branches, be grafted back into their own olive tree.

Paul now brings his illustration of the olive tree to an end. His closing point is a further warning to the Gentile believers. It is as easy for God to reverse the position they are boasting about as it is for him to restore believing Jews to their former place within the covenant community. Even in horticulture, it would be more fruitful, reliable, and easy to graft a previously cultivated branch back into its old cultivated tree than to graft in a branch from a wild tree. Paul must have left his Gentile hearers in no doubt that their inclusion in the community was purely of grace. He had, indeed, chosen a very effective and telling illustration!

11:25 Lest you be wise in your own sight, I do not want you to be unaware of this mystery, brothers: a partial hardening has come upon Israel, until the fullness of the Gentiles has come in.

Paul calls the inclusion of the Jews back into the covenant community a 'mystery'. This term is used elsewhere to describe the inclusion of the Gentiles (Eph. 3:4–6). A 'mystery' in biblical terms is not a puzzle. It is used to speak of something that could never be known unless God revealed it. As an expression of his grace, and according to his own wishes, he reveals his mystery and purposes to all sorts of people, regardless of their intelligence or station in life.

Too often, wrong attitudes emerge in the lives of Christian people because they fail to see God's greater plan. When the picture of God's saving purposes is out of focus, spiritual life can be damaged. Theological distortions are of grave concern as, instead of believers developing attributes that reflect the character of God, they are spiritually 'defaced' and exhibit characteristics that are more like their former father, the devil (John 8:39–44). The tragedy of this truth litters the pages of church history. For this reason, Paul does not want his hearers to be ignorant of this mystery.

As we have seen, in speaking of Israel's salvation as being dependent on the in- gathering of the Gentiles, Paul has reversed Jewish expectation. The Old Testament clearly shows that the blessings of the new covenant will come to the Gentiles following the in-gathering of the Jewish people (Isa. 42:1; 49:6; 49:22; 56:7; 62:2; 66:12; Ezek. 38:23; Mic. 4:2; Mal. 1:11). Paul says they have come in ahead of the Jews because Israel has rejected the Messiah. Consequently, the Jews must now wait for the blessing of the Gentiles to be completed before the nation can enter into the promises made to Abraham. No wonder the Jewish community had great difficulty in coping with Paul. Not only did he insist that the Gentiles should not be made

Romans 11: What Will Happen to Israel

to undergo circumcision, he also taught they were now the conduit for Israel's blessing!

11:26 And in this way all Israel will be saved, as it is written, "The Deliverer will come from Zion, he will banish ungodliness from Jacob";

The first question the text raises is whether 'in this way' is a correct translation of *houtos*. It has been suggested it should be translated 'only then' or 'and so'. The second question is, 'who is Israel in this passage?' Is Paul still thinking of spiritual Israel as discussed in Romans 2:28–29 and 4:11–12, that is, Jews and Gentiles who share the same faith as Abraham? If so, then he refers only to those who believe and are the true sons of Abraham. Or is Paul using the term to denote the nation of Israel, giving his words their national and historical meaning?

It is difficult to avoid the conclusion that Paul meant the latter because of what he goes on to write in Romans 11:28—how can the members of spiritual Israel, the true sons of Abraham, be described as 'enemies' in relation to the gospel? But if we take it to be the nation of Israel another question is raised—is Paul saying that all of the nation of Israel will be saved? This question is difficult to answer, but it could be resolved if the term 'all' is intended to convey all believers in Christ in the nation.

In seeking to understand the scope of 'all Israel', it is helpful to recognize that the term when used in the Old Testament does not include every Jew but a large number of representative Jews (1 Sam. 18:16; 28:4; 2 Sam. 3:21).

This section concerning Israel's calling is notoriously difficult to unravel, so, it will be helpful to give careful attention to Paul's use of Isaiah 59. Unfortunately, the situation is complicated by the fact that he follows neither the Hebrew nor the Greek text of the LXX. Clearly, Paul's alteration of the Isaianic text requires attention.

First, we should note that the Hebrew text says, 'And a redeemer will come to Zion, to those in Jacob who turn from transgression' (Isa. 59:20). However, Paul alters the text, writing, 'The deliverer will come from Zion; he will banish ungodliness from Jacob'. Why has he made these changes? It may be he wants to emphasize that the salvation which the deliverer will bring is not a salvation for the Jews alone. Paul may be writing, in effect, that the deliverer is more than a national figure. He is the Saviour of all men, he does not come 'to Zion' but 'from Zion', he is the Jewish Messiah coming to the remnant to save his people, including those in the Gentile world. This fits in perfectly with what we have noted and with contemporary scholarship. Paul did not abandon his Jewish heritage but stayed within its boundaries as he expounded the gospel for the Gentile world.

But there is another possibility. In writing that the deliverer will come 'from Zion', it could be Paul is implying that he is coming to those who do not make Zion their hope, leaving behind those who stress that Zion is the place of salvation. In other words, Paul writes that salvation is not found in Zion but comes 'from Zion' to those who know that there is no salvation in the institutions of Judah.

The image of the Messiah coming to the Israelite people of faith who are nonetheless outside of Zion (that is, not depending on its institutions), fits the picture drawn in the letter. These people are the believing Jews who wait for the return from exile, the eschatological exodus of the people of God. They recognize there is another Jerusalem (see Gal. 4:24–27; Heb. 12:22; Rev. 21:1–2) to which they must come and have no confidence in national achievement or historical privilege. Indeed, they recognize that they are outside of Zion (their heavenly home) as they make their pilgrimage; and it is from there (the heavenly Zion) that the deliverer comes. The argument is about the salvation of the Jews. It suggests they share the same faith as the Gentile believers among whom they dwell, for they also await the coming of the deliverer. If this is the perspective of Paul's argument, then by 'all Israel' he understands believing Israel who—with all believing Gentiles— comprises the true seed of Abraham, the ones who will be saved. Although the argument Paul makes in this passage has nothing to do with Gentile believers, we know that he sees them to be part of spiritual Israel by what he has already written in the letter (Rom. 2; 4; 9:6).

This line of exegesis is supported by Paul's use of Isaiah 52:7 in Romans 10:15. The original setting of the Isaianic passage was the return of the exiles when they proclaimed to all who wanted to hear that God had redeemed them from bondage. The task of the remnant was to encourage the Gentiles to join them on their pilgrimage. This task has been transferred to the church, which is made up of the remnant of Jews and Gentiles. It is her task, while on her eschatological pilgrimage, to encourage others to join her and experience the grace of God's redeeming love.

If this is a correct understanding of the way that Paul has adapted the Old Testament scripture, it suggests that the true people of God are still to enter Zion and that Paul's alteration of the Old Testament is intended to point to this fact. Moreover, Paul goes on to quote from Jeremiah 31:33 (Rom. 11:27). This is, of course, a promise regarding the new covenant, suggesting that his argument is not about the Parousia but the coming of the gospel. Whoever is the intended focus of the adjusted prophecy's fulfilment, it is clear that the deliverer will transform the lives of those he has come to—'he will banish ungodliness from Jacob' (see conclusion of Romans 11). From the quote borrowed from Isaiah, the Roman Gentiles would have known that 'ungodliness' (a term only used by Paul) would have been 'turned away from Jacob' when those in Jacob repented of their sins (Isa. 59:20).

Before moving on to Romans 11:27, we need to note that Paul—in keeping with the rest of the New Testament—has avoided calling Jesus 'the redeemer', preferring instead to use the term 'deliverer'. This is especially significant here for it would have been natural to follow the Hebrew text. But this is in keeping with his Paschal theology where the term redeemer has been dropped in preference for the more definitive title 'firstborn'. Paul, as do the other New Testament writers, keeps in step with this Paschal theology.[12]

From this discussion, it appears that Paul cannot bring himself to say national Israel has been abandoned but that the conditions of her acceptance are the same as the Gentiles. She will only be restored through the salvation that Christ has made possible through his death and resurrection. 'All Israel' therefore has two meanings. First, it refers to all believing Jews; second, to all the sons of Abraham (Jewish and Gentile

---

[12] See Holland, *Contours,* pp. 237–291.

believers). Paul, it would seem, is quite fluid in the way he uses the term. What it does not refer to is the nation of Israel.

11:27 "and this will be my covenant with them when I take away their sins."

Paul continues to make use of the Isaianic quote by combining the first phrase of Isaiah 59:21 with the sense of Isaiah 59:20b. It is also clear that Paul instinctively looks to the prophecy of a new covenant (Jer. 31:33–34), which promised that Israel's sins would be forgiven. This is significant, for this promise was made to the Jews in exile. If Paul is exercising his usual respect for the original context of the passage he quotes, the application has to be to those who are exiled from Zion. Indeed, the promise originally made by Jeremiah was not to all the Jews—most stayed in Babylon, refusing to respond to the call to return to Zion. Such people excluded themselves from this new covenant. The promise was not for those who refused the hardships of the return but for those who responded in faith and went back to their homeland—despite those hardships—in order to serve and worship their God.

It does not take much imagination to see the New Testament parallel. The 'exile' is not separation from the earthly Zion but from the heavenly one. Those living in the earthly Zion are the ones who refuse the call to faith, and the challenge to leave behind all that is precious to them. Those to whom the deliverer comes are the ones who find no comfort in Zion with its nationalism and hardness of heart. They wait for their deliverer to appear and lead them to the heavenly Zion for which their hearts long. So, the statement 'when I take away their sins' was equivalent to 'when I bring them out of exile', for it was because of their sins that they had been cut off from their inheritance.

11:28 As regards the gospel, they are enemies for your sake. But as regards election, they are beloved for the sake of their forefathers.

Paul has already used the term echthroi ('enemies') in his letter. Indeed, he included himself in the term when describing God's saving activity on behalf of his people in Romans 5:10. He wrote, 'For if while we were enemies we were reconciled to God by the death of his Son, much more, now that we are reconciled, shall we be saved by his life'.

Romans 11: What Will Happen to Israel

So, Paul sees that God's enemies are Jews who have not been reconciled to him, and this seems to be the sense of the term in Romans 11. Paul is not intending to convey the sense that the Jews are hated as far as the gospel is concerned but, at this point in their history, they are loved less (or, to use a better term, 'behind') the believing Gentiles, who have been reconciled to God and brought into the kingdom ahead of them.

Yet, even though this is so, it is only a temporary situation. The Jews are loved on account of the patriarchs, and their election has not been put aside. Paul has been at pains to stress how the new covenant has redefined Israel, and this redefinition has not abrogated the promises made to the ones with whom God had made the preparatory covenant. It is the fulfilment of these ancient covenants made with Abraham (Rom. 4:1–25) and David (Rom. 1:3) that brings blessing to the Gentiles and for which they should be eternally grateful.

11:29 For the gifts and the calling of God are irrevocable.

Regardless of what the Roman Gentile believers think about his explanation of the Jews' standing, Paul reminds them that ultimately their status is not dependent on human consent. It is settled by a sovereign God whose decisions cannot be challenged. This is true of God's right to bestow gifts to humanity and his right to exercise his prerogative in choosing who he will save and in what order.

We need to keep in focus the fact that Paul is not discussing individual election but that of people groups, namely Jews and Gentiles. This does not alter the fact that, elsewhere, the same principle is applied to individuals (Acts 13:48).

11:30 For just as you were at one time disobedient to God but now have received mercy because of their disobedience,

Upon hearing Paul's letter read to the gathered church, the Gentile believers in Rome were reminded that there was a time when they also were disobedient to God and enemies of the cross of Christ. Indeed, at the opening of his letter, Paul exposed the fact that he knew of the depraved behaviour and ongoing disobedience of those who are now believers. Romans 2:1–16 must have made very uncomfortable listening for some.

But, despite their disobedience, the Gentiles had received mercy when they responded in repentance to the gospel, which was extended to them as a result of God's grace. Paul writes, 'through whom we have received grace and apostleship to bring about the obedience of faith for the sake of his name among all the nations, including you who are called to belong to Jesus Christ' (Rom. 1:5–6).

Had the Gentiles in the congregation been listening carefully to the letter as it was being read to them, they would have known their call came about because of the disobedience of the Jews. Paul had already reminded them of the words of the prophet Hosea (Hosea 2:23) in Romans 9:24–26 that God would call them 'my people' who were not his people and 'my loved one' who was not his loved one.

11:31 so they too have now been disobedient in order that by the mercy shown to you they also may now receive mercy.

Paul clearly sees that responsibility accompanies the mercy which has been extended to the Gentiles. They are obliged by divine grace to bear witness to the unbelieving Jews so that they too may hear the good news of God's saving activity in Christ, repent, and be reconciled to the God of their fathers.

It might seem strange that Paul says the Jews will receive mercy because of the mercy that the Gentiles have received, but this is not so strange when it is appreciated that, once again, his frame of reference is the prophetic word of the Old Testament. The prophets had said the Gentiles would be brought into the covenant community, and that God would provoke the Jews to jealousy by calling a people he had not formerly known to be his people (Rom. 9:25). The Gentiles were actually being used to provoke the Jews—to make them realize that their unbelief was denying them the blessing of fellowship with God.

Of course, such an argument on its own would not win the Jews to Jesus the Messiah—the Gentiles would need to demonstrate that they had turned from their sin and disobedience to serve the living God in the very way that the Jews had been called to do. Rather than being the cause of boasting, the calling of the Gentiles brought with it an awesome responsibility to live as the servants of God.

11:32 For God has consigned all to disobedience, that he may have mercy on all.

There is no limit to the 'all' in this statement. All the children of Adam—whether descendants of Abraham or not—who actively disobey the command of God (that is those who are outside of Christ) are under judgment (Rom. 3:22–24). It can no longer be said that God gives Israel privileges over the Gentiles. Indeed, all her privileges have come to an end in terms of her special relationship with him. She is now in the same position of danger as the Gentiles. She must turn to her God in repentance and, like them, seek the same kindness and mercy.

11:33 Oh, the depth of the riches and wisdom and knowledge of God! How unsearchable are his judgments and how inscrutable his ways!

Paul has come to the end of his presentation on the equality of Jews and Gentiles before God. The first eleven chapters of his letter have argued for this equality on theological grounds—the next section will argue for it in practice. At this point of transition, Paul pauses. He is not able to conclude his argument without reflecting on the wonder of what he has been presenting. His heart rings with praise and thanksgiving to God, and he writes the longest doxology of any in his extant writings. This brief, concluding section is possibly a key passage in an unexpected way. It shows us that Paul not only knew his theology but was overwhelmed by its message and by the wonder of the God about whom it spoke. Paul is a powerful example to those of us who love theology, that such a love can never be a substitute for loving God himself.

Paul declares the depth of the richness of God's knowledge. The term 'depth' is used throughout the Scriptures to denote those areas that are beyond human inspection (e.g. Prov. 18:4; 1 Cor. 2:10; Phil. 1:9). In his letter, Paul has argued for God's right to make decisions that people may not approve of. He would not be God if he had to seek the endorsement of humanity for his decisions and actions. Because he is uniquely omniscient, no one should challenge his wisdom. How dare we, in our foolishness, question the judgments and decisions of the Lord God! God's judgments are at a depth that man cannot fathom, and his actions, therefore, are always going to be beyond what man can comprehend.

11:34 "For who has known the mind of the Lord, or who has been his counsellor?"

While there is an echo of Job 15:8 in this verse, Paul clearly relies on Isaiah 40:13, which he also uses in 1 Corinthians 2:16, 'For who has understood the mind of the Lord so as to instruct him? But we have the mind of Christ'. The questions are rhetorical and asked not because Paul was expecting an answer (he and his hearers knew that the answer was 'no one'); rather, he intended that his argument should remove any complacency.

The original text in Isaiah 40 celebrated the wonder of God who announced that he would deliver his people from exile in Babylon. The declaration by Isaiah was to answer those who challenged the prophet's message by claiming there was no possibility that God would bring Israel back home to Zion. No one would have advised God to act in this way as it was contrary to all that the nation deserved. However, instead of casting her off forever, God was working to redeem Israel and re-establish the relationship she had rejected. Of course, what Isaiah declared about God redeeming his people from bondage in Babylon pales into insignificance when we recall the length to which God went to redeem his new covenant people from bondage to Satan. He did this so that he could bring his people home to the heavenly Jerusalem. I have argued that the letter to the Romans is set within a new exodus framework, and here, in the closing section of the theological discussion, Paul again uses new exodus passages from Isaiah. The presence of Isaiah's oracles is a clear reminder of the importance of this eighth century prophet's perspective and the many predictions and comforts he brought to Israel in that crucial period of her history. Paul's use of the prophet of the second exodus underlines the continuity of these great themes and promises that have been, and are being, fulfilled in Christ.

Paul asserts the impossibility of any man being able to instruct God, 'who has been his counsellor?' To think that we can manage, understand, and advise God in a way that satisfies our puny, fallen, darkened minds is both arrogant and foolish. God is not beholden to humanity. He does not have to seek human approval for his decisions and goals. He is the Creator who answers to no one, yet he is not a capricious God. He is the God who redeems and saves those who call on him. The sufferings of creation are not the result of his affliction but the consequence of humankind's fall. Into this sin-cursed existence, God has come in the person of Jesus, to bring life and immortality by means of the gospel (2 Tim. 1:10). His judgments are unsearchable and his paths beyond finding out.

This has been the thrust of Paul's argument throughout his letter to the Romans. Humanity has given itself over to sin (Satan). As a result of this covenant relationship with Satan, humanity is in exile; there is nothing people can do to annul this relationship and reverse its consequences. The quotation from Isaiah is a comment on the theology of the letter over which the previous verse has burst into gratitude and praise. The attention of such a God to the well-being and deliverance of his people is a source of unspeakable comfort (Isa. 40:1).

11:35 "Or who has given a gift to him that he might be repaid?"

The quote is difficult to identify with any certainty, but it is possibly based on Job 41:11. This section of Job concludes a long, searching debate between Job and his so-called comforters, finally ending with God's challenge to Job as to his right to question the Creator. Job responds with a hymn of intense praise, which glorifies God for his wisdom, power, and might.

The point Paul is making is that no mere human can understand God's ways; it is only as God reveals himself that people can possibly begin to understand their own insignificance and frailty. There is nothing we can give to God; we need to receive everything from him. The relationship is not one of equals, and yet, incredibly, God desires to treat us as though we are equals. In the light of God's perfection, majesty, and power, the redemption of humanity is beyond anything that could have been contemplated. 'Where,' asks Paul, 'has this salvation come from?' He answers, 'From the heart of God himself'.

11:36 For from him and through him and to him are all things. To him be glory forever. Amen.

The human race deserves nothing but judgment and condemnation from God; they are guilty and totally helpless. All of God's gracious dealings with redeemed men and women, Jew or Gentile, are because God has purposed to do 'all things' for them:

And we know that for those who love God all things work together for good, for those who are called according to his purpose. For those whom he foreknew he also predestined to be conformed to the image of his Son, in order that he might be the firstborn among many brothers. And those whom he predestined he also called, and those whom he called he also justified, and those whom he justified he also glorified (Rom. 8:28–30).

Thus the 'all things' are those things that pertain to salvation. Paul can only respond, 'to him be the glory forever! Amen'.

Further Study: Questions for Romans 11

1. What evidence does Paul give to show that God has not rejected his chosen people?

2. How would you define what Paul calls 'the remnant'?

3. What truth does Paul demonstrate by citing a series of examples?

4. How has salvation come to the Gentiles and what is one of the purposes of this process?

5. How will the Jews be reconnected with God?

6. What does Paul tell the Gentiles to beware of?

Romans 12: What an Incredible Transformation!

Introduction

Paul has now concluded the theological section of his letter in which hugely important issues have been patiently yet decisively presented. However, Christian living is not only about understanding theology but also about living it out, and it is to this that Paul now turns. God saved his people to serve him in truth and holiness, qualities which Israel tragically failed to display. Living as faithful servants is obligatory, for we have been saved from the awful judgment that awaits those who are not in Christ. Like the Jews in the exodus who benefitted from the death of the lamb, the church is saved as a result of the death of its Paschal sacrifice (1 Cor. 5:7), Jesus the firstborn and redeemer (Col. 1:15). Because of this, 'there is therefore now no condemnation for those who are in Christ Jesus' (Rom. 8:1). As a result of Israel's exodus from Egypt she was called to be a priestly people, and this, Paul says, is now the calling of the church.

12:1 I appeal to you therefore, brothers, by the mercies of God, to present your bodies as a living sacrifice, holy and acceptable to God, which is your spiritual worship.

By using the word 'therefore', Paul is effectively saying, 'In light of what I've written, this is how you should respond'. This does not refer to the material of chapter 11 alone (where Paul explained the role of the Jews in the purposes of God) but to the argument that has gone on from the beginning of the letter. Throughout the letter, Paul has focused on the history of God's saving activity, showing the believers that Jesus, the Son of David, has fulfilled all the predictions of the Old Testament prophets, bringing salvation to those who looked to the living God. Despite Israel's rebellious history, God's many promises, and the examples of how he acted in history, show that he would continue to have compassion on them and be merciful to them (Isa. 63:9; Neh. 9:31). It is into this mercy that the Gentiles have now been brought, sharing with those in Israel who have true faith. By appreciating that the first eleven chapters of the letter provide the background for the exhortation of chapter 12, we can understand more clearly what motivated Paul's appeal. The prophets had, albeit implicitly, anticipated the death of Jesus. His death was nothing other than the great eschatological Passover. Paul discussed this in Romans 3:21– 26, and the ramifications of this awful event overshadow the rest of the letter. In the original Passover, the Jewish firstborn sons were spared death because lambs were slain on their behalf. These firstborn sons were then claimed by God as priests and were set apart to represent the nation in worship (Exod. 13:2; 22:29b). God then provided an alternative arrangement, allowing the Jewish families to keep their firstborn sons by substituting the tribe of Levi for them (Num. 3:12–13). The Levites acted in their place as the priesthood of the nation. Regardless of this arrangement, God named those who had been spared (indeed the whole nation) his 'firstborn', calling them all to a ministry of priestly service (Exod. 4:22–23; 19:6).

This is Paul's argument. He has explained how through the death of Jesus— God's beloved son and firstborn of all creation—the church has been spared. No spotless lamb was killed in her place but, as with the Egyptian families, the victim of judgment was their elder brother (Rom. 8:3–4, 29). Note the theme of redemption throughout chapter 8 in which the life of the firstborn was surrendered. Jesus, by his death, has become his people's redeemer.

The death of Jesus means that believers have been set free—released from bondage and impending judgment. Just as those Jews who were spared the judgment of the first Passover were claimed by God as priests, so, through the great Passover when Christ died, God has claimed those he had spared as his own priestly people. All the redeemed of the Lord were henceforth called to be a holy nation and a royal priesthood (1 Pet. 2:5, 9). This priestly theme is part of the exodus, second exodus and the new exodus. Not only was Israel redeemed to be God's bride but also his priestly people. Isaiah 61:10 describes the condition of restored Israel not only in terms of being the bride of God also in terms of their becoming his priestly people:

I will greatly rejoice in the LORD; my soul shall exult in my God, for he has clothed me with the garments of salvation; he has covered me with the robe

Romans 12: What an Incredible Transformation

of righteousness, as a bridegroom decks himself like a priest with a beautiful headdress, and as a bride adorns herself with her jewels (Isa. 61:10).

This is the background of Paul's appeal to the Roman believers that they offer themselves as a living sacrifice. That was precisely what the priesthood was meant to be in the Old Testament—the people were to be a living sacrifice. This is the basis of Christian living for all believing people. It is not a call for special classes of Christians such as 'full-time' and 'cross-cultural workers'. Such distinctions were never suggested in the New Testament. All Christians are full-time, because they have been fully redeemed; and the implications of this are far reaching for the way they live their lives. What we expect from certain 'categories' of Christians is no different from what God expects of all his people. As priests of the living God, believers are called to minister in intercession as well as instruction, for the priests of the Old Testament formed a teaching community (2 Kgs. 17:27; 2 Chr. 15:3; 17:7; Ezek. 44:21–23). The New Testament knows nothing of a division between laity and ordained as all believers are priests of God (Rom. 15:16; 1 Pet. 2:5; Rev. 1:6). All are called to serve by making Christ known, being totally committed to this task because they have been redeemed and are not their own. When Paul urges the Roman believers to yield their bodies, he is not limiting his appeal to the dedication of their physical bodies. His appeal includes the whole of their persons and could legitimately be translated as 'present yourselves' (Rom. 6:13–14). This is not playing with words, for scholars who have studied the way the ancient Jews used the term sōma ('body') have shown that it was used differently by the Greeks for whom it mostly meant 'physical body'. However, for the Jews it was a term that embraced the whole of the person—it encompassed mind, emotions, will, and physical being.

Thus, Paul's appeal is for the Roman believers to be totally and completely dedicated to God, recognizing that they belong to the one who has given his Son for their forgiveness and salvation. If, when listening to the letter being read to them, they grasped the enormity of what God had done for them in Christ, Paul's appeal for dedication would have been met with ready assent from the assembled congregation. It is understandable for Paul's exhortation to be seen as an individualistic, introspective appeal to all the believers in Rome to live holy lives which can be offered to God as individual living sacrifices. The picture this conjures up is of Roman believers striving to live holy lives in the context of their families and social responsibilities within the city. They come together to be strengthened and helped through the teaching of the Scriptures and the celebration of the Lord's Supper so that they are prepared for the more important task of living their independent, sacrificial lives in the days ahead.

However, Paul is saying more than this. The nuances of individual and corporate vocabulary are lost in many modern translations. As the believers listened to the letter being read, they would have heard the appeal more like this, 'present your bodies (pl.) as a living sacrifice (sing.), holy and acceptable to God, which is your (pl.) spiritual worship'. Paul had already addressed them corporately in Romans 6:12 'Let not sin therefore reign in your (pl.) mortal body (sing.)'. I think what Paul is saying to the believers in Rome goes something like this, 'Remember how I told you earlier in the letter that God rescued you from bondage to sin through the death of his Son and gave life to you through his Spirit? In response to his mercy and grace, I urge you to offer yourselves to him as a corporate sacrifice. You are all equally part of Christ's church. You are all children of Abraham, and despite the differences that have divided you in the past and made you suspicious of each other (I hope you now know that these must stop), you are to recognize that God has accepted you all. So, you are all called to priestly service, Jew and Gentile alike, and you are all to offer yourselves in order to make the church in Rome a living sacrifice. And I want this offering to be a sacrifice that God can accept. In other words, the church must be spotless and without blemish. This means that you all must be holy—conformed to the image of his Son—and you must be united. If, as a church, you make an offering to God of this quality (and, after all the things that he has done for you, this is surely not too much to ask), you will bring him great pleasure and be effective in his service.'

Since sacrifices were offered in the Temple by priests, Romans 12:1 suggests that Paul saw priestly ministry as continuing in the New Testament church. This is indeed how the early church saw her service, for when they chose seven of their number to serve as deacons, the apostles prayed and laid hands on them (Acts 6:6). When Barnabas and Saul were set apart to do their missionary work among the Gentiles (Acts 13), the elders also laid hands on them in the manner of setting priests apart. Later in this letter (Rom. 15:15–16), Paul writes, 'because of the grace given me by God to be a minister of Christ Jesus to the Gentiles in the priestly service of the gospel of God, so that the offering of the Gentiles may be acceptable, sanctified by the Holy Spirit'. Paul is clearly saying that as a New Testament priest his responsibility is to make the gospel known to the Gentiles. It is through his proclamation that Gentiles will believe and become proclaiming priests in turn, so becoming part of the 'offering acceptable to God'. Of course, while the priesthood of the New Testament draws from the imagery of the Old Testament institution, it remains distinctive, since it is not about offering physical sacrifices but rather spiritual ones. Also, unlike the Old Testament priesthood, which was exclusive, the New Testament priesthood is all-inclusive. Every believer, regardless of ethnicity, and no matter what position in society, or gifting in the church, is a priest.

In our verses Paul did not use the term *pneumatikos* ('spiritual') but *logikos* ('logical' or 'reasonable'), and so he actually writes, 'This is your reasonable (or logical) service'. So, Paul says that in light of God's faithfulness, the gift of the Spirit, and the taking of the church as his bride 'your (pl.) reasonable (sing.) service (sing.)' is to be a living sacrifice. Again, there is a corporate dimension to this phrase—all the believers contributing to the single, united, acceptable, holy offering to God that is the redeemed community, that is the church in Rome. All the believers are to see that, as a church, their priestly act of service was the reasonable response to God's undeserved mercy, and that all are responsible for maintaining the church's integrity as a holy and pleasing sacrifice. This interpretation is supported by what Paul says in Romans 15:16 where he speaks of his own calling, 'to be a minister of Christ Jesus to the Gentiles in the priestly service of the gospel of God, so that the offering of the Gentiles may be acceptable, sanctified by the Holy Spirit.'

12:2 Do not be conformed to this world, but be transformed by the renewal of your mind, that by testing you may discern what is the will of God, what is good and acceptable and perfect.

Another way of saying 'do not be conformed to this world' is to say, 'do not let the world mould you'. The Roman church had two options. It could either allow God to mould it by submitting to the Spirit, to God's word as revealed in the Old Testament, and to its leaders (including Paul) as they interpreted and taught the Scriptures, or it could allow Roman society to shape it as it had done before their conversion.

The tragedy is that this moulding of lives often takes place unnoticed. Values are disseminated throughout popular culture, being expressed through media, science, non-Christian families, friends, and work colleagues. They change people imperceptibly. Regardless of how noble our societies may appear, Paul would urge, 'Brothers and sisters, do not conform any longer'. The values believers embrace are to be based on those of another kingdom—the one that Christ rules.

In saying this, Paul is not urging believers to be less than human. Culture is an expression of man's creativity. It is a gift from God and part of the enriching experience of life. His concern for the Roman Christians is that the city's prevailing culture is anti-God; an instrument by which he can be deposed from the throne of the church's heart and mind. He wants the believers to control its influence. In Philippians 4:8, he writes, 'Finally, brothers, whatever is true, whatever is honourable, whatever is just, whatever is pure, whatever is lovely, whatever is commendable, if there is any excellence, if there is anything worthy of praise, think about these things'. We are to reject what is base, crude, false, and unkind as part of our refusal to be moulded by the world (Rom. 6:13–14).

When Paul uses the term 'world' in the phrase, 'do not be conformed to this world,' it has a particular meaning. It speaks of the activities of people from which God is excluded. This is the way the Apostle John used the word (e.g. 1 John 2:15), and the usual meaning of the term 'world' in his gospel is 'humankind,' (e.g. John 3:16).

The condition of unredeemed humanity ('being in the flesh') is a result of Adam's disobedience to God's commands. The scriptures say that there is a spiritual war raging between God and Satan (Dan. 10:12–14; Mark 3:23–29; 4:15; 2 Cor. 10:1; Eph. 6:10–18; Rev. 12–17) into which humankind, through

Adam, has been drawn. Their decision to reject God's offer of mercy leaves them bound in covenant to Satan, and the life they live 'in the flesh' reflects the character of the federal head they have chosen.

For those who embrace God's mercy, the death of Christ—their 'firstborn'—breaks this covenantal binding, setting them free to enter into covenant with Christ (Rom. 7:1–4). However, Christ's redeemed people on earth are still living in the world, interacting with many who are 'in the flesh' and feeling the pull of their old allegiance to it. Their minds need to be constantly renewed, and this can only be achieved when they take the message of Scripture seriously and evaluate everything in its light. Only when they do this will they see the significance of the issues that face them. Paul urges the church in Rome to seek such a Christ-centred world-view.

Paul urges the church to be 'transformed by the renewal of your (pl.) mind (sing.)'. He continues to be concerned for its corporate identity and witness (see also Eph. 2:16; 4:17–32; Col. 3:5–17), urging a renewal that comes from submission to the word of God. A renewed mind will enable the church to test and evaluate the issues it faces in Roman society, as well as discern God's will. No promises are made that the church would be given direct revelation of God's will in the way Paul had experienced. The believers would discover the sort of life that God wanted them to live as they gathered to listen to the Scriptures being explained by the ministry gifts given to the church. It is likely that Paul speaks of the renewing of the church's mind in contrast to what he has said in Romans 1:28 about those who 'did not see fit to acknowledge God', of whom he writes, 'God gave them up to a debased mind to do what ought not to be done'.

The renewing of the church's mind, therefore, is a rediscovering of God's perspective by a community of people who value the retention of his word and values. The effectiveness of a church that is renewed in this way is described by Paul in his letter to the Philippian church:

> *Do all things without grumbling or questioning, that you may be blameless and innocent, children of God without blemish in the midst of a crooked and twisted generation, among whom you shine as lights in the world, holding fast to the word of life (Phil. 2:14–16a).*

Paul describes God's will as 'good and acceptable and perfect'. Some understand this statement to speak of Paul's conviction that there is a perfect, unique plan for the life of every Christian. If Paul believed this, supporting texts would be needed to confirm this view. However, in this statement he is addressing the church. This is clearly indicated by his urging of the Roman believers to 'present your bodies'. By doing this, the church will come to know God's perfect will. I would question whether there is an individual plan for a believer's life. Verses that are usually appealed to in support of such a conviction are not normally about the experience of the individual but of the church. The 'plan' is for the people of God collectively, and it is the responsibility of each Christian to strive to fulfil his part in it. God's will is that the community will fulfil its role as a servant of the Lord, bringing knowledge of him to those who are in darkness.

Statements which indicate that the will of God may be known are found elsewhere in Paul's writings (1 Thess. 5:18; Eph. 5:17; Col. 3:15). When it is remembered that these letters are addressed to churches and not individuals, 'his will' is found to have a corporate perspective. The letters speak of the churches' corporate experience of the peace of God as evidence of his will being revealed. The plan is for the people of God as a whole, and it is the responsibility of each Christian to seek to fulfil his part in the corporate plan so that the community will be a faithful servant of the Lord, bringing the knowledge of God to those who are in darkness, under the control of Satan, and living in the flesh. Just as God told Moses to 'Speak to all the congregation of the people of Israel and say to them, "You shall be holy, for I the LORD your God am holy"' (Lev. 19:2), so Paul speaks to the Roman church. Just as all the children of Israel were asked to be holy, so every member of the Roman congregation had to put the teaching into action and live out the challenge before the pagan world.

The question must be asked, 'How does the church know God's will?' First, his will can be known from the Scriptures (Ps. 119:7–112; Prov. 3:5; Rom. 15:4). The Scriptures make clear what God's plan is for his people, and it is in them that we find how the church was led in its mission in the early years. Although Paul says that Christ is the end of the law for those who believe (Rom. 10:4), it is clear that he constantly referred to the Old Testament and used it as an inspired tool as he taught the early church. Second, his will can be known through the Holy Spirit who guides and prompts the church to fulfil her mission (Acts 13:2; 16:7). In addition to these foundational means of knowing God's will, there is the counsel of mature believers who are able to give advice in the light of Scripture and their knowledge of the leadings of the Holy Spirit in similar circumstances. However, these 'secondary means' are subjective in nature and can easily be misinterpreted. Because of this, secondary means must never be heeded if they are contrary to the clear message of Scripture.

12:3 For by the grace given to me I say to everyone among you not to think of himself more highly than he ought to think, but to think with sober judgment, each according to the measure of faith that God has assigned.

The direction of the appeal changes in this verse, for Paul now addresses the individual believers using his apostolic status, saying, 'For by the grace given to me I say...'

In his appeal to the believers, Paul is effectively saying, 'If apostles are called not to become conceited, then so are you'. Elsewhere, Paul highlights the danger of people having over-inflated opinions of themselves. Such people are, 'slanderers, haters of God, insolent, haughty, boastful...though they know God's righteous decree that those who practice such things deserve to die' (Rom. 1:30, 32), and he also says that an overseer, 'must not be a recent convert, or he may become puffed up with conceit and fall into the condemnation of the devil' (1 Tim. 3:6). Conceit is a serious sin. It was the root of Satan's rebellion, for in aspiring to be like God, pride entered his heart.

Exercising an over-inflated self-opinion is a sin that is all too easy to commit, and Paul felt obligated to write to the congregation about this sensitive matter. Seducing Christians to seek their own advancement at the expense of others is one of Satan's most effective ploys. When writing to the church in Philippi, Paul urged the believers to 'do nothing from selfish ambition or conceit, but in humility count others more significant than yourselves...Have this mind among yourselves, which is yours in Christ Jesus' (Phil. 2:3, 5).

God is not as concerned about our gifts as about his grace being manifest in our lives. Conceited Christians can so easily become Absaloms in their local churches (2 Sam. 15:1–4), despising and passing judgment on church leaders. Often this sort of criticism comes from hearts that have failed to think of themselves with sober judgment and where the interests of others are subjugated to their own. Perhaps Paul had heard reports about such believers in the church in Rome and was concerned about the damage that they could do to its witness (Rom. 14:10). Perhaps he had in mind the bringing together of the Jews and Gentiles in the birth of the Roman church and was appealing to the two communities not to think more highly of themselves than they should. He goes on in the letter to say 'live in harmony with one another. Do not be haughty, but associate with the lowly. Never be wise in your own sight' (Rom. 12:16). Certainly, this understanding maintains the corporate dimension of the letter.

The reference to 'the measure of faith' could be understood in one of three possible ways. First, the measure of faith could refer to the amount of faith or trust that a person has. If this is what Paul meant, he is in danger of driving vulnerable believers to continual self-analysis and deprecation, particularly in the presence of those with faith to 'move mountains'.

Second, the measure of faith could refer to the degree of faithfulness that the believers have, for that is how faith is evident. If this is correct, then Paul is writing that the believers ought to assess themselves in light of their commitment to Jesus Christ. Without such commitment, their gifts might prove to be a liability leading to boastfulness and conceit. This sort of meaning is behind Paul's warning to Timothy not to appoint a young, unproved convert—no matter how talented—to the role of overseer or elder as he may become conceited and fall under judgment (1 Tim. 3:6). Sadly, history is strewn with examples of those who once ran well as young Christians but who were 'promoted' within their churches too early. This was something that Paul feared could even happen to himself (1 Cor. 9:27).

Third, the measure of faith could refer to zeal for the gospel. Paul uses it in this way in his second letter to the Corinthians, where he says:

Romans 12: What an Incredible Transformation

> *Not that we dare to classify or compare ourselves with some of those who are commending themselves. But when they measure themselves by one another and compare themselves with one another, they are without understanding. But we will not boast beyond limits but will boast only with regard to the area of influence God assigned to us, to reach even to you. For we are not overextending ourselves, as though we did not reach you. For we were the first to come all the way to you with the gospel of Christ. We do not boast beyond limit in the labours of others. But our hope is that as your faith increases, our area of influence among you may be greatly enlarged, so that we may preach the gospel in lands beyond you, without boasting of work already done in another's area of influence. 'Let the one who boasts, boast in the Lord'. For it is not the one who commends himself who is approved, but the one whom the Lord commends. (2 Cor. 10:12–18)*

If this is the correct meaning, Paul is encouraging the believers to measure themselves in the light of the sacrifice they have made for the sake of the gospel. Such people know, of course, that the sacrifice is never adequate when compared to the one made to save them from sin. But lest there be any who might boast about the opportunities they have for service, Paul goes on to expand his teaching on the body, its gifts, and the honour given to its members. He does this to put every form of Christian service into its right perspective.

12:4 For as in one body we have many members, and the members do not all have the same function

Paul now prepares to tell the Roman believers how they can make sober judgments of themselves. He is going to remind them of the gifts God has given them. It will be through their ministry that the church will know how to renew her mind. Once again, he draws their attention to the corporate reality of their situation. No gift is given for the recipient's sake, but for the benefit of the believing community.

Paul has used the imagery of the body to describe the church in his first letter to the Corinthians (1 Cor. 12, 14). 'Body of Christ' imagery comes naturally from the concept of the divine marriage, which—as we have seen—is threaded throughout the argument of the letter to the Romans. The church is the 'bride of Christ'. Just as the body of a bride belongs to her husband, the church (the new covenant community) becomes the body of

Christ. Note that the same language is used in Ephesians 5:25–26, where clearly both marital and new exodus themes are alluded to.

Paul not only applies this imagery to the worldwide church but also to the local church. He sees each believing community to be the witnessing 'body of Christ' in its particular locality (1 Cor. 1:2; 1 Thess. 1:1). In preparation for using 'body of Christ' imagery, Paul reminds the believers of the makeup of the human body. He will soon use this analogy to illustrate the corporate body, the church—to which they belong.

Paul's initial point is that there is diversity among the members of the human body, each member having a particular role in its healthy functioning. It is obvious to all that the body will be impeded in health and vitality if certain of the members fail— if, for example, the eyes could no longer see, the ears no longer hear, or the tongue no longer speak.

12:5 so we, though many, are one body in Christ, and individually members one of another.

Paul then applies this simple illustration to the church, which is comprised of many believers to form one body; and just as in the human body, there is diversity among its members. This diversity is fundamental to the understanding of the status and dignity of individual believers. In 1 Corinthians 12 and 14 Paul argues this principle more fully, his main thrust being that hidden parts of the body are often the most important while obvious parts, despite attracting the greatest attention, are of less consequence for its on-going maintenance. It is more disastrous if the brain malfunctions than if an eye is lost.

Paul stresses the unity of the local body of Christ. He does not write that each member belongs to Christ, which they obviously do by virtue of being 'in Christ,' but that 'each member belongs to all the others'. This is a beautiful way of expressing a church's interdependence and unity. Gifts are given for the building up of the local body of Christ. Although given to individuals, they are not for their blessing but for the benefit of the whole body.

Many believers think that they have been denied gifts; but this is not so. All gifts given to the church are for the sake of all. They are given in order that everyone can be built up so that, corporately, believers can progress in an understanding of God's purposes and love, to the end that he will be glorified in the church.

The believer's transformation into the image of Christ does not concern the individual; just as it was not individual Jews who made the pilgrimage from exile back to the Promised Land, but groups of Jews. In other words, the return was only achievable when he was part of the pilgrim community. It was highly unlikely that his individual return from Babylon could be achieved, but corporately it was possible.

In the same way the transformation of the individual believer is achieved as he recognizes that he goes on a pilgrimage to the heavenly home with other believers in the church. Together they encourage each other as they benefit from the gifts God has given them. Indeed, in Paul's thinking, being renewed in the image of Christ is the corporate concept of the church becoming like its saviour (Eph. 4:20–24; Col. 3:10).

12:6 Having gifts that differ according to the grace given to us, let us use them: if prophecy, in proportion to our faith;

In v. 3, Paul spoke of the grace that had been given to him. Now he applies the giving of grace to the Roman church. He is clearly concerned that the believers grasp the truth that there are different gifts bestowed on believers in the church through God's grace. A failure to appreciate this can lead to divisions as a result of petty jealousies and rivalries.

Many Christian fellowships have been divided over gifts because of pride, jealousy, and hurt. The danger of division is avoided when it is understood that God has given gifts according to his will. They are not inherited talents whose distribution is governed by genetic makeup. However, despite these gifts having a divine origin, churches often select leaders on the basis of talent, personality, status, and family, seeing these as indicative of divine gifting. Such appointments may place churches in danger of damage from pride and ambition.

Paul begins to specify gifts that are given by the Spirit. He does not mention that these gifts are the gifts of the Spirit as he does in his first letter to the Corinthians (1 Cor. 12:8–11). Here, the gifts are simply the gifts that God has bestowed. This is an indication of Paul's 'Trinitarian' understanding—for although this is not a term that Paul actually uses, his understanding of God as a Trinity is found in the way that he often attributes Old Testament descriptions of God to either Christ or the Spirit (e.g. 1 Cor. 8:6; 2 Cor. 13:14. See also Phil. 2:10–12, where the quotation from Isa. 45:23b originally applied to God).

When Paul encourages the gift of prophecy, he qualifies its use by saying 'let him use it in proportion to his faith'. This exhortation is unlikely to refer to the confidence the recipient has in his powers of oratory, as that would promote self- confidence and lead to arrogance. The term 'faith' is likely to mean 'faithfulness,' as discussed earlier. A church should only encourage the gifts of its members when it sees them living in faithfulness to Christ. The exercising of gifts without the appropriate grace leads a church into a spiritual minefield.

Prophesying was clearly a common ministry in the early church. The New Testament prophets' responsibility was to apply the word of God. This had been the function of the prophets in the Old Testament. They did not bring a new revelation to Israel but constantly reminded them of the covenant of which they were part. That is not to deny that they occasionally predicted the future or that they developed themes that had previously been known only in part. However, their main task was to remind the people that because of the covenant, God made claims upon them. Their preaching was essentially a reiteration of the promises and warnings of the covenant in which Israel was urged to walk obediently (Isa. 40:1–5; Jer. 34:1–10; Hosea 14:1–3; Amos 5:4–5).

This was no less the function of the New Testament prophets. Their gift was to direct the church to the Old Testament Scriptures, which spoke prophetically about the coming age. They were able to draw from those Scriptures to spell out the obligations of the new covenant and urge the church to fulfil them. In this, God would be glorified; and, in turn, he would respond in blessing. Although the church was given teachers (v. 7), the

Romans 12: What an Incredible Transformation

prophet's ministry also included teaching. It is possible that the prophet spoke with more authority—the Spirit of God empowering his message. Because of this, the word of God came to the people with a sense of 'the Holy Spirit says' (Acts 13:2; 21:11).

It is clear from the first Corinthian letter that Paul thought highly of the gift of prophecy—a gift which he said was for believers (1 Cor. 14:22), 'The one who speaks in a tongue builds up himself, but the one who prophesies builds up the church' (1 Cor. 14:4).

12:7 if service, in our serving; the one who teaches, in his teaching;

The gift of serving is the next gift listed by Paul. While it is difficult to know exactly what he had in mind regarding this gift (and in 1 Corinthians 12:5 he states that there are different kinds of service), it is of interest that Paul placed serving between prophesying and teaching, suggesting that its place in church life was of great importance. It has often been thought that 'serving' refers to the meeting of practical needs within the local church and amongst needy believers in other churches. When he wrote the letter, Paul was on his way to Jerusalem with a gift for those who were suffering from poverty, and he describes his anticipated visit as being 'in the service of the saints' (Rom. 15:25). In his first letter to the Corinthians, Paul commended to them the household of Stephanas because of their 'service to the saints' (1 Cor. 16:15–17).

The role of deacons in the early church has often been linked with the gift of 'serving' (1 Tim. 3:10, 13) as has the general expression of concern that believers show for one another within a fellowship (Rom. 12:9–11; Gal. 5:13). In his letter to the Ephesians, Paul says that apostles, prophets, evangelists, pastors, and teachers have been given to the church 'to equip the saints for the work of ministry, for building up the body of Christ,' (Eph. 4:12). While we shall consider the outworking of 'works of service' later in the chapter, an alternative understanding of the gift of 'serving' may be of interest.

At the opening of his letter, Paul assured the believers of his prayers by writing, 'For God is my witness, whom I serve with my spirit in the gospel of his Son, that without ceasing I mention you always in my prayers, asking that somehow by God's will I may now at last succeed in coming to you' (Rom. 1:9–10). Moreover, in Romans 15 he wrote that he was 'a minister of Christ Jesus to the Gentiles in the priestly service of the gospel of God...In Christ Jesus, then, I have reason to be proud of my work for God' (Rom. 15:16–17). It is, therefore, possible that Paul saw the gift of serving— the second gift in his Romans list—to be the proclamation of the gospel, that is the gift of evangelism (Eph. 4:11–12).

Support for this view is found in the letter to the Corinthians. Paul—who sees his work as priestly ('serving at the altar' rather than at tables)—wrote that those who preach the gospel should receive their living by it (1 Cor. 9:13–14). In his second letter to the church, he reminded the Corinthians that he had served them by

'preaching the gospel of God' (2 Cor. 11:7–8). Finally, the letter to Timothy states, 'in accordance with the gospel of the glory of the blessed God with which I have been entrusted. I thank him who has given me strength, Christ Jesus our Lord, because he judged me faithful, appointing me to his service' (1 Tim. 1:11–12).

It is clear that those who did the work of evangelism exercised other gifts in the church. Philip—one of the seven deacons in Acts 6:1–6—became known as 'Philip the evangelist' in the town of Caesarea (Acts 21:8–9), and Timothy—who was urged to devote himself to preaching and teaching in Ephesus (1 Tim. 4:13–14)—was encouraged to 'do the work of an evangelist' (2 Tim. 4:5). Thus, if the gift of service is evangelism, Paul sees the proclamation of the gospel to be one of the foundational gifts to the church, and this may explain its prominent position in his list—a position not so suitable for its traditional meaning of menial labour.

Teaching is the next gift to be mentioned. It may refer to the catechizing of new converts, enabling their understanding of basic Christian truths, or to its more public ministry to the gathered church. Whatever the form of teaching received by the Roman church; Paul commends the believers' whole-hearted obedience to it. As a result of teaching, they had been set free from sin and had become servants to righteousness (Rom. 6:17–18). Paul appreciated how vital teaching was for the health of the church. It would prepare the congregation for service, build its members up in the knowledge of God and bring them to maturity (Eph. 4:11–14).

Teaching was a gift that the apostles exercised when they taught the young church in the days following Pentecost (Acts 2:42). Indeed, they recognized the danger of neglecting the gift when the practical needs of the infant church pressed upon them. So, after the church had chosen seven wise, spirit-filled men from the congregation, and the apostles had set them apart to ensure that the social needs of the believers were not overlooked, they gave themselves to prayer and teaching. The results were remarkable (Acts 6:1–7).

Like the apostles, many Christian leaders feel the pressure of being expected to do a wide range of tasks in their congregations to the neglect of their teaching ministries. The consequence of yielding to such pressure is that believers are not well taught and are left exposed to false teachings. As a consequence, the word does not spread in the locality and the leaders are left exhausted. Even the Roman congregation, with its obedient assent to the teaching it received, had to be warned against its exposure to false teaching (Rom. 16:17–19).

Those who have responsibility for teaching in a church need mentors like Jethro who, on drawing alongside Moses, saw the pressure he was under and suggested the appointment of officials to lighten his load. Moses was then free to teach decrees and laws to the people as well as to settle major disputes (Exod. 18:17–26). The New Testament shows that church leaders need to be part of a leadership team, which provides a forum for mutual support and understanding within the church. So, we find Paul urging Titus to appoint elders in every town (Titus 1:5). Such men, like the apostles, corporately bore the load, each contributing his particular gift(s) to the building up of the church for which they were responsible.

The support, understanding, and mutual encouragement necessary in church leadership cannot be provided by inter-church fraternalism alone, however valuable this may be. The New Testament does not recognize the 'one-man ministry' that characterizes many churches. The ministry within a church comes from all the people of God, and their collective gifts that make

Christian service possible. The church, of course, requires leadership to oversee the ministry in which the believing community is engaged, but this leadership is the community's servant rather that its dictator.

Timothy was told not to neglect his gifts of preaching and teaching but to be diligent in their use. He was also told to watch his life and doctrine closely. It is clear that 'the knife can be blunted' through sin and laziness, to the detriment of the preacher and the congregation he serves.

12:8 he one who exhorts, in his exhortation; the one who contributes, in generosity; the one who leads, with zeal; the one who does acts of mercy, with cheerfulness.

Paul now urges those in the congregation with a gift of exhorting to exercise their gift. The NIVTM and other modern translation have 'encourage', although the Greek noun paraklēsis could also mean 'comfort,' and this was how the term was used in some New Testament passages (Acts 15:22–31; Eph. 6:21–22). It is the same term that Jesus used when he described the ministry of the Holy Spirit, 'And I will ask the Father, and he will give you another Helper' (John 14:16). Paul himself benefited from encouragement. Barnabas whose name means 'the son of encouragement,' befriended Paul as a new convert, introducing him to the leadership of the church in Jerusalem (Acts 9:27). Moreover, he was Paul's co-worker on his first missionary journey during their time in Antioch (Acts 11:26). In his second letter to the Corinthian church, Paul told the believers that he and Timothy had been 'comforted' by Titus and the church in Corinth at a very difficult time in their ministry (2 Cor. 7:5–7), and, in a sensitive letter to Philemon, he expressed his gratitude for the encouragement he had received from Philemon's love for the saints (Phlm. 1:4–7).

But is this what Paul had in mind when writing about the gift of encouragement? It is possible that ESV is correct in translating paraklēsis as 'exhort'. This would fit neatly into Paul's list as it is the gift that follows prophesying, serving (evangelizing), and teaching—all gifts concerned with the ministry of the word. Encouraging by means of exhortation can be done by members of the congregation. For example, the believers in Thessalonica were urged to 'encourage one another' about the coming of the Lord (1

Thess. 4:13–18; 5:11). However, it is probable that the gift refers to a more public ministry of encouragement (Acts 13:14–52; 14:21–22; 1 Cor. 14:3; 1 Thess. 2:1–3; 2 Tim. 4:2; Titus 1:7–9). The following is written to Timothy, 'Until I come, devote yourself to the public reading of Scripture, to exhortation, to teaching' (1 Tim. 4:13).

To conclude, if the gift of encouragement is a public ministry, its exercising in a congregation would reflect the ministry of the Godhead to his people—God encouraging them through the Scriptures he has given for their edification (Rom. 15:4–5).

The next gift in the list—'one who contributes'—is usually seen to refer to the support of needy believers. Paul's desire is that this gift be exercised 'in generosity'—the Greek carrying the idea of giving without reservation. The idea is of a bountiful generosity that springs from a desire to help those in need. Paul uses the verb metadidōmi—which can be translated 'impart,' 'share,' or 'give'—on three other occasions in his letters. The phrase in Romans 12:8 would perhaps be better understood as 'he who imparts or shares the things of God and himself, with the result that believers are encouraged and established in their faith'. This understanding reflects the ministry of Jesus to his disciples. He shared with them the good news and gave himself for their blessing and establishment. Elsewhere Paul has written:

> And he gave the apostles, the prophets, the evangelists, the shepherds and teachers, to equip the saints for the work of ministry, for building up the body of Christ, until we all attain to the unity of the faith and of the knowledge of the Son of God, to mature manhood, to the measure of the stature of the fullness of Christ (Eph. 4:11–13).

Next Paul addresses himself to the leaders of the congregation. If leadership is their gift, they must lead 'with zeal'. It is no surprise that leadership is listed with gifts that benefit the work of the gospel in the local church. Its diligent exercise is crucial, as ineffective leadership results in an undisciplined church where lives are damaged.

The leadership of a local church was the prerogative of elders who were set apart for the task (Titus 1:5). Their appointment was not to be made in haste, as the scrutiny of their lives was essential (1 Tim. 3:1–7; 5:22; Titus

1:6–9). Their work was extremely demanding. In writing to the Thessalonian believers, Paul urged them saying, 'We ask you, brothers, to respect those who labour among you and are over you in the Lord and admonish you, and to esteem them very highly in love because of their work. Be at peace among yourselves' (1 Thess. 5:12–13). It was demanding because their ministry involved preaching and teaching—with all of the resulting pastoral needs of people seeking to apply what they had heard—as well as the oversight of the church's affairs (1 Tim. 5:17; Titus 1:9). In addition to these demands, all their dealings had to be conducted with a godly attitude (1 Pet. 5:1– 3).

Finally, in the Romans verse under consideration, Paul writes to the believers 'the one who does acts of mercy, with cheerfulness'. It is difficult to be certain who Paul is referring to as recipients of mercy, what the gift entailed, and who exercised it.

The term translated 'does acts of mercy' can also mean 'has or shows mercy or pity'. Paul used this term when speaking of the Lord's mercy in 1 Corinthians 7:25, and in Philippians 2:27 when speaking of God's mercy to the sick Epaphroditus. The Romans text is Paul's only reference to mercy being extended by and to a believer. The same term is used in Matthew 5:7 when Jesus promises that God will show mercy to the merciful, and in Matthew 18:33 when the wicked servant in the parable was rebuked for not showing mercy; Jesus equating mercy with 'forgiving your brother from the heart'. In addition, Jesus spoke of the rich man, in torment in hell, asking Abraham to show mercy to him (v. 24).

So, while the term can be used to speak of forgiveness, it is also used to speak of compassion to the needy and it is likely that this meaning is the context for 'acts of mercy' in Romans 12:8. This gift would have been exercised, at the very least, by deacons in the church—people who were set apart for the task of dealing with pressing social concerns in the fellowship so that the prophets, evangelists, teachers, pastors, and elders could give full attention to exercising their gifts (Acts 6:1–6; 1 Tim. 3:8–13). Perhaps Paul had the deacons in mind when he wrote this to the church in Rome. He urged that the gift of showing mercy be carried out with 'cheerfulness'. This reflects the wisdom of the book of Proverbs, which says, 'A joyful [cheerful] heart is good medicine, but a crushed spirit dries up the bones' (Prov. 17:22).

Romans 12: What an Incredible Transformation

In summary, in Romans 12:6–8, Paul encourages the prophets, evangelists, teachers, preachers, pastors, elders, and deacons to exercise their gifts in the church in Rome. Like Timothy, they would probably exercise more than one gift, fulfilling their calling so that together they would be able 'to equip the saints for the work of ministry, for building up the body of Christ, until we all attain to the unity of the faith and of the knowledge of the Son of God, to mature manhood, to the measure of the stature of the fullness of Christ' (Eph. 4:12–13). What a powerful, public display of a living sacrifice to God in Rome that would be!

In Romans 12:9–21, Paul returns to his concern that the believers in Rome should live holy lives as priests of the living God (v. 1), so that they can offer to him a church that is 'a living sacrifice, holy and pleasing'. He has urged all of the believers to evaluate their lives seriously and honestly (Rom. 12:3; Matt. 7:1–5), reminding them of the gifts that God has given the church (Rom. 12:6–8). As they benefit from these, Paul hopes that the corporate body of believers will rise to the challenge to renew its mind.

In the passage we are now considering, Paul begins to tell the church how it can stop conforming to the world and become a transformed believing community. His appeal echoes the teaching of Jesus in his Sermon on the Mount (Matt. 5–7). Indeed, it seems possible that Paul is here applying this teaching of Jesus to his disciples to the context of the local church (Matt. 7:24–27; Eph. 2:22).

Paul begins his exhortation by introducing its theme—'let love be genuine'. His desire is that the greatest fruit of the Spirit will be demonstrated in the believers' lives. This will transform the church in Rome, affecting those within the fellowship and those outside in the wider community.

When the believers heard this passage read, they would have taken from it a challenging pattern for individual living. While Paul's exhortation in chapter 12 is to individuals in the congregation, it must be remembered that his emphasis throughout the letter has been the church—the body of believers. Although his desire was that the lives of the individual believers would be built up (Rom. 15:2; 1 Thess. 5:11), his greatest desire was that the local church would be built up to become a 'dwelling place for God by the Spirit' (Eph. 2:22).

12:9 Let love be genuine. Abhor what is evil; hold fast to what is good.

Paul begins his exhortation with the theme of 'genuine love'. The adjective anupokritos ('genuine' or 'without hypocrisy') is related to the verb *hypokrinesthai* ('to answer'). It was used to speak of the reply an actor gave on stage and was associated with the pretence of the performer in his role. Affection that is a pretence of friendship is odious (1 John 4:20–21). It is the very opposite of Christian love, which must be the expression of genuine concern.

In his letter to the Galatians, Paul wrote that agapē ('love') was one of the fruits of the Spirit (Gal. 5:22), and in his first letter to the Corinthians, he described the transformed attitudes of people who display this love (1 Cor. 13:4–8a). In 1 Corinthians 13:13, he says that it is the greatest spiritual fruit that we can exhibit, reflecting the love that God has for his people (Rom. 5:8). Indeed, it is the essence of God himself, for he is its source (Rom. 5:8; 1 John 4:7–19). So, how do the believers in Rome love in sincerity? Paul goes straight to the point by telling them to engage their wills.

God's standard is clear—he hates evil (Amos 5:14–15; Ps. 97:10). Those who would have fellowship with him must share his concern and values. Despite the values of those around, the Roman believers must be concerned about pleasing God alone (Rom. 12:21).

The Christians in Rome were to abhor evil within their hearts and any expression of it in society. If the church had access to the gospel of Matthew (as has been suggested), the believers would know from Jesus' Sermon on the Mount that in being recipients of evil as a result of their allegiance to Christ, they must not hate the evil-doers but take encouragement from the fact that persecution will bring blessing. While hating what is evil, the believers were told to 'hold fast to what is good'. The phrase suggests a desperate situation, like a drowning man in a storm clinging to a beam of wood and feeling so weak that he does not know how he can survive. All he must do is keep on clinging! The problem is that this interpretation places

Romans 12: What an Incredible Transformation

all the responsibility on the believer to keep hold of what is good, despite all the pressures that buffet him.

The word translated 'hold fast' can be translated 'join yourself to,' 'join closely together,' or 'unite'. It is the same term used by Paul in 1 Corinthians 6:16–17 where he writes, 'Or do you not know that he who is joined to a prostitute becomes one body with her? For, as it is written, "The two will become one flesh". But he who is joined to the Lord becomes one spirit with him'. In light of this usage it is possible that Paul is saying that the believers must hold fast to relationships that are good. They are to commit themselves to the Lord and his people, which is what the next verse advocates.

12:10 Love one another with brotherly affection. Outdo one another in showing honour.

The exhortation to be devoted to one another in brotherly affection is an outworking of the sincere love of v. 9. Paul uses philadelphia ('brotherly affection' or 'love') in one other letter:

> *Now concerning brotherly love you have no need for anyone to write to you, for you yourselves have been taught by God to love one another, for that indeed is what you are doing to all the brothers throughout Macedonia. But we urge you, brothers, to do this more and more (1 Thess. 4:9–10).*

Being devoted to one another is not a directive to accept everything that a fellow Christian does. Such mindless acceptance will not bring glory to God but will be an opportunity for Satan to exploit. God was devoted to the Jewish people throughout the long history of the Old Testament—but that commitment resulted in tough action. He not only spoke against them when they were breaking his commandments but also warned them that he would use the armies of mighty Babylon to wield the sword when they repeatedly refused to hear and obey his word. So, being devoted to one another may mean the leaders of the church exercising 'tough love' in situations where the word of God is being rejected or ignored. Such 'tough love' was prescribed by Paul for the church in Corinth when it refused to deal with a case of incest (1 Cor. 5–6) and is seen in the warnings that Jesus gave the churches in the book of Revelation (Rev. 2:1—3:22).

Paul now tells the believers to 'outdo one another in showing honour'. Honouring one another would have been hard enough for the Jewish and uncircumcised Gentile believers in Rome but honouring each other above themselves would have seemed well-nigh impossible. Another challenge for the believers would have been the honouring of disadvantaged brothers and sisters in the congregation. This would have been particularly challenging for those in leadership positions. However, in his letter to the Corinthians, Paul leaves us in no doubt as to God's wishes in this matter (1 Cor. 12:22–26).

It would have been a crushing command for the believers but for the fact that God had sent his Spirit into their hearts (Rom. 8:15), bringing with him a different set of values from the ones they had lived by (Rom. 8:9, 12–13; Gal. 5:16–26).

12:11 Do not be slothful in zeal, be fervent in spirit, serve the Lord.

Paul has just exhorted the believers to be devoted to each other in brotherly love and to honour each other above themselves. He now exhorts them to maintain their zeal. A believer's first rush of excitement on discovering the glorious reality of God's love can easily become fossilized. An improvement in living standards (resulting from a more disciplined lifestyle) can become the purpose of life and an intellectualization of new-found faith can replace the warmth of first love. The zeal of loving and serving Christ can disappear like the morning dew—it happened to Israel's love for God (Hosea 13:3), and sadly it happens to Christians' love for Christ (Gal. 1:6; 2 Tim. 4:10; Rev. 2:4).

The ESV translation of this verse gives the impression that Paul is exhorting the church to be 'zealous'. Certainly, being zealous was a characteristic of his people, the Jews. In Romans 10, Paul testifies that the Jews display zēlos ('zeal') in the defence of their faith (v. 2), and in his letter to the Philippians he writes retrospectively of himself, 'as to zeal, a persecutor of the church' (Phil. 3:6). However, in this verse he uses the term *zeontes* for 'diligence' or 'earnestness' (literally 'boiling in spirit'). So, the opening phrase of v. 11 would be better translated 'never be lacking in diligence or earnestness'.

Perhaps Paul is referring to what he has just written—urging the believers to be fervent, with no hint of laziness, in their devoted love and preference for each other. But how can the believers maintain fervour? Paul has given the answer in the earlier part of his letter. By reflecting on who Christ is, and what God has done for them through his death, their hearts will be moved (Rom. 8:1–3). This means that the believers must put themselves under the authority of the Scriptures, for these were written for their instruction (Rom. 10:14b, 17; 15:4).

12:12 Rejoice in hope, be patient in tribulation, be constant in prayer.

Paul writes to the believers in Rome telling them that they should 'rejoice in hope'. He has already written sublimely about this theme in the opening verses of chapter 5.

The future for the Roman Christians is so glorious that joy ought to characterize their lives. No matter what happens—and appalling persecution was soon to come—their hope remains a sure certainty. Loss of status, health, wealth or friends could not affect their certainty, for their inheritance is laid up in heaven (1 Cor. 2:9; 1 Pet. 1:4–5). Only the Christians in Rome could rejoice in what lay ahead. For everyone else, death would be the entrance into God's presence where they will be judged. For the Christians, it will be altogether different. Instead of this frightening scenario, death will be their glorious entrance into the Lord's presence and into joy unspeakable. The Christians' hope should permeate their lives so that they are characterized by joy (Ps. 16:11; John 16:20; Rom. 14:17; 15:13; 1 John 1:4).

Paul writes that they should be 'patient in tribulation'. Should any of the believers be experiencing tribulation, much of Paul's letter would prove to be an enormous comfort and encouragement. The patience in tribulation that Paul desired the church to have is rooted in her hope in the Lord Jesus Christ. This hope marked out the believers in Thessalonica. Paul wrote to the church there, commending the believers for their patience in tribulation (1 Thess. 1:3b; 2 Thess. 1:4).

Being 'constant in prayer' was essential if the believers were to be patient in tribulation and joyful in hope. Prayer is about committing ourselves and the things that concern us into the hands of God. When we are confident that our lives are in his hands, we can know the sort of confidence that these verses speak about. When we are confident in the unchanging dependability of God's covenant love, we are empowered to face the problems of life (Rom. 5:1ff.; Jas. 1:2–8; 1 Pet. 4:12–16). It is then that we can share in the Psalmist's experience, and we shall not fear what people will do to us (Ps. 27:1–3).

Prayer is the natural expression of spiritual life. When Paul was conquered by the realization that Jesus was the Christ who had been raised from the dead, spiritual life flowed through his soul. When Ananias was told by the angel to go to Paul and pray for the restoration of Paul's sight, Ananias was told 'he is praying' (Acts 9:11). Spiritual life begins with prayer, and prayer upholds it. The Acts of the Apostles demonstrates that just as prayer was vital to Jesus (cf. Matt. 14:23; 26:36; Luke 3:21; 5:16; 6:12; 9:28), so it was to the church he left behind (Acts 1:14; 2:42; 3:1; 6:4; 12:5; 16:13–16).

If the believers in Rome are not constant in prayer, there will be no possibility of them living lives that will corporately make their church a living sacrifice, and no possibility that they will patiently bear the awful tribulations yet to come.

12:13 Contribute to the needs of the saints and seek to show hospitality.

One of the characteristics of the early church that made an impact on the unconverted was their care for one another (Acts 2:44–45; 4:32–35; 6:1–4). This sprang from their brotherly love and was expressed in many ways. Here, Paul identifies a specific aspect of care—that of contributing to those in need. This was a ministry that he benefited from himself when the church at Philippi sent him financial aid while he was in chains (Phil. 4:10, 14–16, 18). How encouraging it must have been for the people of Rome to see wealthy Christians being concerned for those Christians who had very little—if anything—of this world's goods.

The gospel abolishes all sorts of barriers. The removal of social distinctions is because believers are loved and valued by the God who has made them in his own image. They know that only the death of Jesus was sufficient to redeem them from the kingdom of darkness and the guilt of sin, and that the cost of this redemption underscored the value God placed on them all.

Romans 12: What an Incredible Transformation

This injunction to care for one another regularly appears in the New Testament (Acts 24:23; Gal. 6:10; Eph. 4:28; Phil. 2:25; 1 Tim. 6:18; Heb. 13:16). The apostle clearly could not conceive of a believing community not giving care towards those who were in need, as his letters to the Corinthians make abundantly clear (1 Cor. 16:1–4; 2 Cor. 8–9). It is thought by some that there is the possibility of a veiled hint that the Roman church was providing for the destitute members of the impoverished Jerusalem church. Hospitality was an important demonstration of the gospel in the days of the early church (3 John 1:3–8). As Christian workers moved around the empire, there were few places where they could stay safely. The inns were not the most desirable of places and would expose itinerant preachers (such as Tychicus in Ephesians 6:21–22) to physical and moral danger. When writing his letter, Paul tells the believers about the hospitality that he had received in the home of Gaius (Rom. 16:23) and commends Phoebe to them for their help and hospitality when she arrives (Rom. 16:1–2). When writing to Timothy about the eligibility of widows for church help, the author says that one of the conditions was their giving of hospitality (1 Tim. 5:10), and John commends Gaius for his hospitality to fellow workers in the gospel (3 John 1:5–8). From the above citations it is possible to get the impression that hospitality was merely given to itinerant preachers and visitors from afar, but Peter encourages the practice of willing hospitality within the local church (1 Pet. 4:9).

12:14 Bless those who persecute you; bless and do not curse them. Rejoice with those who rejoice, weep with those who weep.

Paul here extends the principles of Christian living to the area of personal persecution. At first sight, it seems that v. 14 should be located before v. 17, a verse which introduces a section concerning the pressure from hostile relationships. Sadly, it appears that Paul sees the need to advise faithful believers in Rome about their response to persecution within the church (Rom. 2:1; 14:10–13). Paul was writing out of personal experience, many in the wider church opposed him. Some of his greatest opponents were former Jews who saw him as a betrayer of all that was eternally true; a betrayer of what God had given to Moses. These 'believing' Jews—including some circumcised Gentiles—would have applauded Paul if he had led the Gentiles into the fold of Judaism through their submission to circumcision. The hatred that his non-compliance generated is difficult to appreciate but is evident throughout his letters and the Acts of the Apostles (Gal. 6:12; 1 Thess. 2:13– 16; Acts 21:20–22; 23:12–22).

In urging the believers to bless those who persecute them, Paul was not asking them to abandon principles of justice. In Romans 13:1ff., he will explain the God- appointed role of rulers for maintaining justice, and in 1 Corinthians 6:1–8 he urges believers to seek arbitration concerning their disputes from the church leadership. There is no suggestion that we have to abandon justice within the church in order to bless others. Indeed, a characteristic of the early church was its anxiety to uphold the laws of the state. By asking the Roman believers to bless their enemies, Paul was effectively saying that they should pray for them—not seek their humiliation or destruction (Matt. 5:44).

The object of all discipline must be that the offender is restored to fellowship and welcomed back with all the forgiveness that God gives to repentant sinners. The Scriptures do not ask us to do anything more than what God would do himself. He forgives only when there is genuine repentance, and when he has to punish, he never delights in its implementation. Likewise, Christians can only forgive those who have wronged them when there is genuine repentance. Where there is no repentance, there can be no forgiveness, and the resulting pain can be hard to bear for the Christian who has been wronged. Clearly the Christian should always want reconciliation and be ready to forgive. However, when someone is consistently abused or exploited, and if the church fails to intervene, Paul indicates elsewhere that the state has been appointed to correct such injustices. Paul had found himself in this very position when he appealed to Caesar for the settlement of a dispute. When some of the Jewish leaders in Jerusalem—opposed to the message about Jesus and the resurrection—sought to have Paul murderously 'silenced' he was forced to appeal to the state for protection.

12:15 Rejoice with those who rejoice, weep with those who weep.

It may be that Paul is referring to the normal events in life when he invites the believers to rejoice with fellow believers; events such as births and marriages within the church. However, he usually uses the term 'rejoice' in the context of suffering and hope—suffering for Christ and hoping in him (cf. Phil. 2:17–18; 4:4–7; Col. 1:24). This reflects the teaching that Jesus gave to his disciples in the Sermon on the Mount (Matt. 5:10–12; Luke 6:22–23) and is in agreement with Peter's teaching (1 Pet. 1:6–9; 4:12–16 where Peter uses a term meaning 'rejoice' or 'exult').

When writing to the Philippians, Paul contemplated the possibility of martyrdom and invited the believers to rejoice with him, 'I am glad and rejoice with all of you. So you too should be glad and rejoice with me' (Phil. 2:17b–18). This passage reflects his exhortation to the believers in Rome to rejoice with each other.

How could this work out in practice in the local church? Perhaps Paul was exhorting the Christians to rejoice with those who, despite the sufferings that they were experiencing, were rejoicing in the Lord. The believers are not being advised to draw alongside those who are suffering as 'Job's comforters' but as encouragers, pointing the sufferers to the great hope that awaits them all. 'Let us rejoice and exult and give him the glory, for the marriage of the Lamb has come, and his Bride has made herself ready' (Rev. 19:7).

Paul then writes that the believers should 'weep' with those who weep. This is a true mark of sincere love for a fellow believer. The tears are not the fabricated ones of the mourners in the home of Jairus' daughter in Luke 8, or of the professional mourners who followed Jesus to Golgotha (Luke 23:27–31). They come from a spirit that has been deeply troubled and moved at the suffering of another (John 11:33– 36, 38).

Paul was unashamed at showing his emotions (2 Cor. 2:4; Phil. 3:18). He recalls the tears he had shed while with the church in Ephesus (Acts 20:17–19, 31). On bidding the elders of the church a final goodbye before going to Jerusalem, he and the elders wept (Acts 20:36–38). When writing to Timothy, the author recalled Timothy's tears (2 Tim. 1:4), and the writer to the Hebrews records the tears that Jesus shed throughout his life as he prayed (Heb. 5:7).

What Paul asks of the believers in Rome is that they do not rush to comfort and encourage the broken-hearted with words alone, but that they show their deep sorrow by entering into the pain of their fellow believers. Then, words such as Isaiah 61:1–3 can have their place:

> *The Spirit of the Lord GOD is upon me, because the LORD has anointed me to bring good news to the poor; he has sent me to bind up the brokenhearted, to proclaim liberty to the captives, and the opening of the prison to those who are bound; to proclaim the year of the LORD's favor, and the day of vengeance of our God; to comfort all who mourn; to grant to those who mourn in Zion-- to give them a beautiful headdress instead of ashes, the oil of gladness instead of mourning, the garment of praise instead of a faint spirit; that they may be called oaks of righteousness, the planting of the LORD, that he may be glorified (Isa. 61:1–3).*

12:16 Live in harmony with one another. Do not be haughty, but associate with the lowly. Never be wise in your own sight.

The ESV translation 'live in harmony with one another' leads us to assume that Paul is commenting on the previous verse. Unfortunately, this is a misleading translation of phronountes. It means 'be of the same mind' (literally, 'think the same thing') as one another. This appeal underscores the importance of the believers meeting together to hear the Scriptures explained.

The related term phroneomai ('being of one mind') has identical roots with phronountes ('mind' or 'mind-set') which appears often in Scripture. Paul has already written in his letter about the importance of a right mind. He has mentioned the 'debased mind' of unredeemed humanity (Rom. 1:28–32; 8:6–7) and has reflected on his pre-conversion experience (Rom. 7:21–25). Elsewhere, he has written about having the mind of the Spirit (Rom. 8:6). Matthew records the rebuke of Peter by Jesus who discerned that Peter did not, at that stage, have in mind the things of God (Matt. 16:23). However, it appears that after conversion the renewed mind can become corrupt again, especially when exposed to false teachings. So, Paul warns the church in Ephesus about some of its community with unspiritual minds wreaking havoc in the church (Acts 20:28–31). The sanctification of the mind in this way is not an option for believers. In replying to a question posed by a Pharisee, who asked what the greatest commandment was, Jesus answered, 'You shall love the Lord your God with all your heart and with all your soul and with all your mind. This is the great and first commandment' (Matt. 22:37–38).

Paul then addresses the matter of pride and conceit in the church. There was clearly much evidence of this—Jews looking down on uncircumcised Gentiles, circumcised Gentiles (who called themselves Jews) looking down on uncircumcised Gentiles, and believing Gentiles looking down on unconverted Jews as discarded branches of the olive tree. The mind of Christ was not much in evidence in this situation, and the issues of pride and conceit had to be addressed if the church was to be a light to the nations.

These two sins do more to damage the fellowship of God's people than almost any other. The tragedy is that those who commit them are often unaware of the damage that they are doing, and when approached are deeply offended. The proud and conceited have normally achieved success in life and feel it is their right to pass judgment on others, especially when they perceive them to be hindering the progress of the work into which they themselves invest resources and time (3 John 1:9–10). In other words, pride and conceit is a particular danger to those who have been promoted to leadership within the Christian community. How dangerous this is. The very ones who should be examples of the grace of Christ can so easily be the cause of offence to new, struggling believers.

12:17 Repay no one evil for evil, but give thought to do what is honourable in the sight of all.

Paul is deeply concerned about the possibility of revengeful acts of evil taking place within the church in Rome. The Law of Moses commanded that if someone found his neighbour's animal out of its confines and in danger of getting hurt, the animal had to be delivered safely back to its owner even though the neighbour might have previously harmed the one who found the animal (Deut. 22:1–3). The Scriptures are realistic in recognizing how feuding—which results from taking revenge— incalculably damages the parties involved as well as other members of the community.

In saying that they must do what is right in the eyes of everyone, Paul is effectively saying that their actions must be open to scrutiny—and appreciate the danger of doing things that are lawful but that give a wrong impression. Paul is not so naive as to suggest that we can please everyone or do what everyone considers right. After all, he was criticized by many for what they saw as his radical acceptance of uncircumcised Gentiles. Many of the world's leading social reformers have had to stand against what their peers considered right because of the flaws they discerned. If we find ourselves in conflict with prevailing values that are morally wrong, we must make sure that we are not open to the accusation of doing wrong to achieve right. For Paul—and the other New Testament writers—the end never justifies the means if those means are against what Scripture teaches. The means we employ to take our stand have to be ones that God himself would condone.

12:18 If possible, so far as it depends on you, live peaceably with all.

Strain in relationships—even between believers—is recognized in this verse. Paul knows that despite all of his exhortations, tensions do occur within the Christian community as well as outside (Phil. 4:2–3). Here, he urges his readers to do all they can to ensure that they are not responsible for the breakdown of peace.

12:19 Beloved, never avenge yourselves, but leave it to the wrath of God, for it is written, 'Vengeance is mine, I will repay, says the Lord'.

The greatest danger in being wronged is of becoming a double victim. If we were to respond by taking revenge, then we will have taken our case out of the hands of God in order to exercise our own authority. While it is a natural instinct, it is one that must be brought into subjection to Christ. Jesus was wronged more than any yet did not take matters into his own hands. He committed himself to his Father and suffered for the unjust. Once we take matters into our own hands, we cease to be God's servants and people through whom he can reveal himself. His power is never revealed through his people's sin but through his people's obedience and, if necessary, weakness. Paul writes to the believers in Rome that they are to leave revenge to God. He references Deuteronomy 32:35, 'Vengeance is mine, and recompense, for the time when their foot shall slip; for the day of their calamity is at hand, and their doom comes swiftly' (see also Lev. 19:18).

The Roman Christians can be confident in the knowledge that the judge of all the earth will do right. Before God acts on their behalf, he will offer the same mercy to those who offended them as he did to the believers before they responded to his mercy. If this mercy is rejected, he will act in judgment at the time of his choosing (Rom. 2:5, 8; 1 Thess. 1:10).

12:20 To the contrary, 'if your enemy is hungry, feed him; if he is thirsty, give him something to drink; for by so doing you will heap burning coals on his head'.

The believers are not only to leave their case in the hands of God (who will avenge and repay as he sees fit) but are to do good to those who do evil to them. While responding in like manner justifies the behaviour of those who have done wrong, acts of kindness disarm them, leaving them confused and vulnerable. For such people, this is more painful than revenge.[13]

Some find a contradiction in Paul's teaching. He urges the Romans not to take revenge into their own hands, and yet says that by doing good to their enemies burning coals are heaped on their heads. But Paul is perhaps counselling believers to recognize that revenge will only confirm the attitude and not change the character. By kindness, their enemies can be made so uncomfortable that they can no longer bear it.

However, there is a possible alternative meaning within this text and that echoes the Old Testament. Live coals are a symbol of purging (Isa. 6:6–7) and were part of Isaiah's preparation for the service God was calling him to. It is possible that Paul is saying the outcome of the kindness of the believers is the salvation of their enemies who will then be brought into God's service and counted among his redeemed.

---

[13] The quotation Paul uses here is from Proverbs 25:21ff. (LXX).

12:21 Do not be overcome by evil, but overcome evil with good.

Paul's concern is that the church's testimony is not lost. The church is to overcome evil with good. This is the way God has conquered us and disarmed our hostility toward him.

Further Study: Questions for Romans 12

1. How do lives and services get offered up to God?

2. How has the church become a priestly community?

3a. What sort of things will result from our not thinking of ourselves more highly than we ought?

3b. What factors could hinder this in the Roman church? Are there lessons in this for the modern church?

4. What are the characteristics of a healthy church?

5. What should be the dominant characteristic of the believing community? How can you help it characterise the fellowship you are part of?

Romans 13: What Shall We Do with the Law?

Introduction

Having instructed the Romans in the preceding section about their priestly calling (Rom. 12:1–2), and the need to maintain their zeal (Rom. 12:11), Paul turns to the issue of earthly rule. There has always been a tendency throughout the church's history to claim an authority for itself that exceeds what God intended. Here Paul, clearly aware of that danger, instructs the church in Rome regarding her duties to assist the servants of the state in their God-given calling to promote the good of the people of the empire, and to maintain law and order. Paul not only calls the Roman believers to respect the state and its servants, but to live pure and good lives that mark them out as the people of Christ in a dark and failing society.

Despite the trend to see Paul as a political activist, this key passage clearly shows that Paul had no such ambition. In fact, Paul valued his own Roman citizenship and used the privileges it gave him to ensure that he had a fair trial by appealing to Caesar (Acts 25:10–11). No doubt this was not just about his own survival, he had been told (Acts 9:15) that he was to carry Christ's name 'before the Gentiles and their kings'. This was clearly a driving force for his whole ministry.

13:1 Let every person be subject to the governing authorities. For there is no authority except from God, and those that exist have been instituted by God.

By using *pasa psuche* ('everyone must submit') Paul emphasizes the importance of willing acceptance of the rulers' claim to authority over the Roman believers. The authorities are to be obeyed not only because they have the power to punish, but because their authority has been conferred on them by God. They are his appointed agents to govern.

Paul uses the term 'authorities' in different ways in his writings. He applies it to men such as the chief priests (Acts 26:12; 1 Cor. 9:12 [translated 'right'];

2 Cor. 10:8), and to spiritual powers (Acts 26:18 [translated 'power']; Eph. 1:21; 2:2 [translated 'kingdom']; 3:10; 6:12; Col. 1:13 [translated 'domain']; 2:10; 2:15).While Paul rarely applies the term to the state, this is generally accepted to be his application in Romans 13, the authorities being civil rulers who hold the sword on God's behalf.

If 'authorities' in Romans 13 is a reference to civil rulers, then we can assume that Paul is here drawing on his understanding of the Old Testament. It was God who appointed Saul (1 Sam. 9:16) and David (1 Sam. 16:1) as Israel's kings. Indeed, the coronation Psalms show that the king was the servant (son) of God (Ps. 2:7). Importantly, it was not only the Jewish kings who were seen to be God's agents but also pagan kings. Cyrus, the Persian king, was referred to as 'his anointed' and his 'chosen,' whom God summoned, exalted, and strengthened (Isa. 45:1–5). Paul would thus be staying within the Old Testament perspective; no matter how evil the world, God controls the nations.

This Old Testament background would provide the reason for Paul's appeal to Christians to recognize that a regime soaked in paganism and violence (with the ensuing moral consequences) was, nevertheless, the God-appointed government in Rome. When its laws did not conflict with their calling as Christians, the Roman believers were to give it due honour and homage.

Recently, an alternative understanding of 'authorities' in Romans 13 has been put forward. It is argued that local churches did not always separate from the local synagogues perhaps because they afforded protection to the believers, and that this was the situation in Rome. This meant that Jewish worshippers and Jewish believers in Jesus mixed with each other when they came to the synagogues for worship. Such a situation was not unknown in Judaism as Jews themselves embraced different messiahs and actively sought to persuade their countrymen of the credentials of their chosen 'anointed' ones. This relative openness witnesses to the diversity of the Jewish synagogue system, as does the fact that visitors were encouraged to share with the congregation messages of exhortation, of news, or some other matter (Acts 13:5, 15; 14:1; 17:10–12; 18:4; 19:8). However, a major cause of friction in many synagogues was that the followers of Jesus were

Romans 13: What Shall We Do with the Law?

bringing the message of a crucified Messiah to the congregations. In addition, they were introducing uncircumcised Gentiles as men with equal rights as the orthodox Jews. Indeed, not only did these Jewish followers of Jesus argue for the inclusion of uncircumcised Gentiles into the covenant community, they argued that, unless law-observing Jews believed in Jesus, they were excluded from the covenant community! This historical setting has been used to argue that the 'governing authorities' of v. 1 are not representatives of the Roman state but of the synagogue.

This recently argued understanding has Paul pleading for the Gentile believers to accept the authority of the Jewish leadership of the synagogue because God has appointed it. If this is the setting of the exhortation, the problem is no longer how the believers relate to the state but to the religious leadership. Paul is appealing for respect, but not at the cost of compromise.

13:2 Therefore whoever resists the authorities resists what God has appointed, and those who resist will incur judgment.

The outcome of Paul's reasoning is predictable. If the governments (civil or religious) are the appointed agents of God, to rebel against them is to rebel against the God who appointed them. This is a remarkable position to take if Paul is referring to civil authorities, as many of the believers in Rome were slaves. Their distressing conditions were often due to the greed, ambition, and ruthlessness of the mighty Roman Empire, so it would be more than understandable if some of them bitterly resented their masters. As with the earlier exhortation not to take revenge (Rom. 12:19), this exhortation would have cut right across their instincts for justice.

Paul is as clear on this issue as he was about revenge; rebellion would leave the believers open to judgment. Such judgment might be meted out by the authority using its might and power in suppression, or it might be meted out by God for rejecting the authority he had ordained. While this latter suggestion is a possibility, the argument that follows suggests that Paul has the judgment of the former in mind.

13:3 For rulers are not a terror to good conduct, but to bad. Would you have no fear of the one who is in authority? Then do what is good, and you will receive his approval,

Paul was not idealizing rulers as men who always acted with the purest of motives. He was not naive. He knew the intrigues of political manoeuvring in the synagogue and in the state, and how the innocent were often victims of miscarriages of justice, suffering because their legitimate grievances were ignored. How should the Roman Christians respond should these be the prevailing circumstances? While Paul does not address this here, it is hard to believe that he would urge his readers to give blind obedience. On such occasions, they will have to take a stand that may prove very costly.

The questions must be asked, 'When a ruling authority is corrupt, does it cease to be God's instrument?' and moreover, 'do Christians have a responsibility to join with others to bring such a tyranny to an end?' These are questions that Paul does not address, and so the answers to such questions must be sought by examining other scriptures to see what principles they provide. Paul had the same attitude to these matters as Jesus. We are to 'render to Caesar the things that are Caesar's and to God the things that are God's' (Matt. 22:15–22, cf. Rom. 13:6).

13:4 for he is God's servant for your good. But if you do wrong, be afraid, for he does not bear the sword in vain. For he is the servant of God, an avenger who carries out God's wrath on the wrongdoer.

The one in authority—be he the leader of the synagogue or the head of the state— is God's servant; and his responsibility is to seek the good of the citizens in his care. Of course, authorities should not only punish wrongdoers in order to protect the weak but should commend and nurture those who do well.

If Paul had the Roman civil authorities in mind, then the believers who lived within their jurisdiction ought to be grateful for how much Rome (God's servant) had bequeathed to them in terms of legal and religious privilege. However, they had to be aware that any civil authority could also punish wrongdoing. Paul warns his readers that if they do wrong, they must not think that they will be exempt from punishment.

If Paul meant that the synagogue rulers were God's servant, then he would have in mind the good done by them in, for example, religious, moral, legal, and educational matters. The reference to the synagogue ruler bearing the sword is not a problem in this context as the synagogue was the legal centre of the Jewish community and the place where punishment was meted out on those who violated its laws. Paul himself had represented such a ruling authority, brandishing the sword on behalf of the high priest (Acts 9:1–2; Gal. 1:13–14). Indeed, after his conversion on the Damascus road he became the recipient of its judgment; however, such an interpretation is not likely to be correct if it sees the synagogue eldership as having the right to take life.

The reference to the sword is possibly from Deuteronomy 32:41, where God threatens to take his sword and wreak vengeance on his adversaries. This is supported by the fact that Paul has already quoted from the chapter. He quotes Deuteronomy 32:21 in Romans 10:19 and Deuteronomy 32:35 in Romans 12:19. The threat of God taking the sword against his enemies suggests that Paul sees those who profess faith and yet disobey as enemies of the Lord. This is not a new perception for Paul—he has spoken of Israel as a nation of unbelievers and having become effectively God's enemy, and suffering judgment by his hand. He warned the Corinthians of this danger of coming under their Lord's discipline in 1 Corinthians 10:1–10 and threatened it in 1 Corinthians 5–6.

13:5 Therefore one must be in subjection, not only to avoid God's wrath but also for the sake of conscience.

Paul underlines two reasons for obeying the authorities. The first is the fear of God's wrath and the second is for the sake of conscience. It might seem strange that Paul mentions fear as a motive. Indeed, he not only lists it but puts it before conscience. We live in an age when psychologists tell us never to use fear as a motive. The fact is that society, having yielded to such advice, is returning to the dark ages in terms of social behaviour. Scripture has no hesitation in spelling things out as they are; and for most, including Christians, fear of punishment in this life and the next affects them deeply. We should not be afraid of an emotion that is part of human experience and which can save us from harm.

13:6 For because of this you also pay taxes, for the authorities are ministers of God, attending to this very thing.

As has been mentioned, Paul asserts the principle taught by Jesus that we should 'render to Caesar the things that are Caesar's and to God the things that are God's' (Matt. 22:21b). Because the authorities are God's servants, he has ordained that people should support them. If Paul sees the authorities as the state, then those who work full time in the upholding of social order should be provided for by means of taxation. Paying taxes would then be as much an act of giving to God as paying 'tithes'. The former would be for the administration of society's needs, the latter for the administration of the gospel. Paul sees nothing wrong in officials being paid fairly for the work they do—theirs is a high calling, ensuring the smooth and just running of affairs. They should be paid appropriately to avoid corruption.

13:7 Pay to all what is owed to them: taxes to whom taxes are owed, revenue to whom revenue is owed, respect to whom respect is owed, honour to whom honour is owed.

Paul extends the principle of what is owed to governing officials to what is owed to those in daily life. He tells the Romans that they are to settle all their debts—no matter to whom they are indebted. Debt can cripple the conscience. Moreover, when left unpaid it can cause devastation to those who depend on its repayment. All too often, those who live in abundance hold on to what is not theirs, leaving the ones who are owed with the problem of coping with the unpaid debts. It is especially inappropriate for Christians not to settle debts (Jas. 5:4–5). The Old Testament has much to say about this (Deut. 24:10–13; Job 24:3; Prov. 20:16; Ezek. 33:15), and there is no doubt that it is from this source that Paul draws his ethical principles.

Debts are owed by the Roman believers in monetary and non-monetary terms. Paul writes to them that they are to pay appropriate debts of respect and honour to all in authority. If those who have been given responsibilities by God fulfil them in a way honouring to him, they deserve due recognition. Paul would expect the Roman believers to apply this principle to their civil, synagogue, and church lives, recognizing and respecting the work done in the latter by its prophets, evangelists, teachers, pastors, elders, and deacons (1 Tim. 3:8; Titus 1:7; 3:2; Heb. 13:7, 17; 1 Pet. 5:5).

Romans 13: What Shall We Do with the Law?

This debt of gratitude owed by the Roman believers to their officials could be usefully heeded by churches today. We live in an age of criticism and cynicism, where often the expression of gratitude is of less importance than a demand to entitlement. Many churches would be transformed if members of their congregations took to heart Paul's exhortation to the believers in Rome and paid debts of gratitude to those who, often voluntarily, seek to care for their souls.

13:8 Owe no one anything, except to love each other, for the one who loves another has fulfilled the law.

The exception to the rule regarding the repayment of debts is the debt of love, which can never be settled. The 'one who loves another has fulfilled the law' is probably a reference to the love of God—the 'debt' of the law is a debt that only Christ has met.

13:9 For the commandments, 'You shall not commit adultery, You shall not murder, You shall not steal, You shall not covet,' and any other commandment, are summed up in this word: 'You shall love your neighbour as yourself'.

Paul reminds the believers of the commandments that relate to the treatment of others, reinforcing the permanence of these laws. They express the bottom line for Christian behaviour. If a believer loves someone, he cannot sin against that person in ways the commandments forbid. Love is a higher principle than law. What the law commands is the beginning of the expression of love, not its limit.

The commandment 'you shall not commit adultery' continues to be the key to every stable marriage. While the world treats sexual morality as a private affair, it recognizes that the betrayal of a partner is inexcusable, and that it provides immediate grounds for divorce. In this case, natural justice reflects divine justice. Adultery not only sins against God and the partner, but the extended family (especially the children). Scripture is uncompromising in speaking out against sexual immorality because it destroys the fabric of lives. It robs families of security, trust, and dignity, and casts them into a darkness with which little can compare.

Jesus extended this commandment to attitudes of the heart. He warned that whoever looked at a woman and lusted after her had already committed adultery with her as far as God was concerned (Matt. 5:27–28). Such high standards are not out of touch with the pain that women feel when they see their husbands' lingering glances at other women. Such glances attack their security and self-worth.

Murder is another act that is universally recognized as wrong. While there are grounds for a state taking a life to protect its population against an aggressor, reason can become warped, justifying executions for the wrong cause. The Jesuits, in their South American mission, put people to death on the pretext that their souls would be saved. The Crusaders did the same thing in the Islamic states during the Middle Ages. Jesus gave the commandment against murder a spiritual dimension by saying that hating a person is as bad as physically harming him (Matt. 5:21–22). Peoples, characters, and reputations can be put to death just as much as the body can, and Jesus applied the commandment beyond the limits of the Mosaic Law.

The command 'you shall not steal' is clear. We are not to take from individuals, companies, or governments. Stealing does not only involve tangible things. It can be taking time from an employer as well as stealing a person's good reputation through gossip and slander.

Coveting is the desire to have what belongs to someone else. This does not mean that we are forbidden to admire a possession of another person and resolve to acquire the same through legitimate means. It means that jealousy—the twin sister of covetousness—must never be in our hearts. We ought to be glad that others have been blessed with possessions even if we are not able to own them. This is not a hopelessly impossible ideal. Its attainment begins with valuing spiritual blessings above material ones.

Paul writes that these and other commandments are summed up in the principle of loving our neighbour as ourselves. It is one of the great commandments that Jesus gave in response to the scribes' attempt to catch him out. The other is that we love God with all our hearts (Mark 12:29–30). While Paul cites the command to love from Leviticus 19:18b (a command relating specifically to loving fellow Jews), he is not restricting his command to ethnic Israel. For Paul, as well as for Jesus, 'my neighbour' is all humanity.

13:10 Love does no wrong to a neighbour; therefore love is the fulfilling of the law.

When Paul writes that 'love does no wrong to a neighbour,' it seems that anything causing pain or sadness cannot spring from love. However, Paul often said very direct and even hurtful things (2 Cor. 6:14–18; Gal. 2:14; Phil. 3:2), indicating that there are times when keeping quiet harms a person more than the initial distress caused by speaking out. In other words, there are times when we have to see the long term good of our neighbour and act with that in mind. There can be no greater good than a person's acceptance into heaven. Incalculable harm can be done by believers keeping silent concerning the remedy for sin for fear of causing their neighbours any distress.

The same principle applies when someone steals from us, attacks our property, or violates us in any way. Paul is not saying that we should disregard the law's support or protection. Indeed, a Christian should hope that the moral welfare of the guilty party will be served by facing the seriousness of the wrong that he or she has done. In other words, Paul's injunction not to harm a neighbour is about dealing justly with them. There should be no thought of stealing from them, slandering, or hurting them in any way. Regardless of their colour, creed, or status, they are to be treated with respect and dignity at all times. This concern for equality and justice comes from the Old Testament, where Israel was told to protect the vulnerable; not only orphans and widows, but strangers (immigrants) and economic casualties (Exod. 22:21–27). They were to be accepted as those made in the image of God and those for whom the Lord would plead the cause if they were violated.

This sort of reasoning can be extended to other areas of Christian living. The principle Paul is emphasizing is that we have no right to judge someone whom God has accepted. The moment we think that we are more acceptable to God is the moment we cease to appreciate his free grace. To grade Christians in terms of favour is to fall into serious error. We are all accepted on exactly the same grounds, by God's free grace and mercy. The purposes of the law are that people give to God the love and honour he deserves and that they give to others—who are made in God's image—the love and respect they deserve. Love means dealing with others in the way that God deals with us. This is the fulfilment of the law.

13:11 Besides this you know the time, that the hour has come for you to wake from sleep. For salvation is nearer to us now than when we first believed.

Paul emphasizes that faith in Christ is not only expressed in ideals and doctrines but in the life the Roman believers lead (Rom. 12:1–21; 13:9–10). Their actions must flow from an understanding of their current situation in Rome. They must not be content with comfort but alert to the fact that others in the city are in mortal danger and in need of rescuing from God's coming judgment. Paul urges the believers to wake from slumber and buy up the opportunities of serving Christ in the city (cf. Eph. 5:8–20). The call to 'wake from sleep' is a direct quote from Isaiah 60:1, where the people were told that God was coming to bring them salvation. It is, of course, a text that has new exodus significance. The original context was God's call to Israel to prepare herself for her return pilgrimage to Jerusalem.

It is imperative that the believers in Rome spread the knowledge of God so that it might shine in the hearts of those in the city who will believe, bringing them forgiveness and salvation (Acts 26:18). This task demands that they put aside 'works of darkness' (v. 12) as unbelievers will only take the gospel seriously when they see it being lived out with integrity by the believers.

13:12 The night is far gone; the day is at hand. So then let us cast off the works of darkness and put on the armour of light.

Elsewhere, Paul has written that the Christian needs to put on the full armour of God in order to bear a good witness (Eph. 6:11). This is an echo of Isaiah 59:16–17, where the prophet recounts the coming of the redeemer to Zion, fully armed and equipped for his saving work. Because of this divine intervention, the remnant was released to make its journey to the promised inheritance—the city of Zion.

Romans 13: What Shall We Do with the Law?

The Old Testament citations (and especially Isaiah 60:1, which was considered in Romans 13:11) suggest that Paul understands believers to be involved in a pilgrimage (see also Rom. 5:1ff.; 8:32ff.; 10:14–15). They can only progress on their pilgrimage as they fulfil the responsibility of living as children of light. This understanding supports the idea that Paul constructed his letter to the Romans around Israel's experience of coming out of bondage and shame. This visual aid from the history of Israel is fulfilled in the church, the true inheritor of the promises of God (Gal. 6:16).

The exhortation to put on the armour of God was originally spoken to Israel; while the individual Christian may apply it to himself, it is nevertheless an exhortation to the community. Isaiah 59:9–10 speaks of captive Israel being in darkness and knowing nothing of justice. Paul follows this theme in Romans 13:12–13. He urges his readers not to fall into the same sins that Israel fell into on her pilgrimage (Isa. 59:2–8, 12–15; cf. 1 Cor. 10:1–13), when she involved herself in orgies, drunkenness, sexual immorality, debauchery, dissension, and jealousy. Paul used very similar language in 1 Corinthians 10:6ff., when he warned the Corinthians that God would act to discipline them as he had disciplined the children of Israel. The setting of the exhortation in the Corinthian letter was the wilderness wanderings. We have seen that Paul is able to use material from the Egyptian and Babylonian exoduses to illustrate what God has done for his people through the death of Christ, 'our Passover'. This typology continues to be the key to interpreting Paul.

13:13 Let us walk properly as in the daytime, not in orgies and drunkenness, not in sexual immorality and sensuality, not in quarrelling and jealousy.

When Paul writes 'let us walk properly as in the daytime,' he is saying that he and the Roman believers must be open to public scrutiny. He identifies with them, saying that he and they should live transparent lives, doing nothing of which they would be ashamed. For example, the Roman Christians should not be involved in 'orgies'. The term refers to secret rites and rituals in the worship of pagan gods, especially Bacchus.

Repeated 'drunkenness' is also forbidden (cf. 1 Cor. 5:11). In 1 Corinthians 6:10, Paul lists drunkards as people who will not inherit the kingdom of God.

This is a warning to believers in an age when alcohol is readily available and much consumed. While it cannot be denied that wine was the accepted refreshment of the New Testament world, we must recognize Scripture's warning of its misuse; it can bring the strongest man to destruction (Gen. 9:21; Prov. 20:1; 1 Tim. 3:3; Titus 2:3). In the Greek text, the phrase translated 'orgies and drunkenness' may suggest an act of drunken revelry rather than two distinct practices.

Paul urges the Roman believers not to be involved in sexual immorality. Again, this is a sin that is as prevalent in modern society as it was in the ancient world. Sex, which is both powerful and beautiful, is God's gift to mankind. It brings incredible joy and comfort when contained within the realm of a true and permanent relationship between a man and a woman. We live in an age when traditional forms of morality have largely been abandoned. Indeed, the pain and psychological and emotional damage caused by broken relationships has not yet reached its high-water mark in society. This is not how God intended it to be; he wants sex to be the evidence of genuine love and total trust. If these are present in a relationship, it is difficult to see why anyone should deny the partner the protection that the legal status of marriage gives.

'Quarrelling' means to habitually reject the views of others. It is the product of self- assurance, conceit, and pride. There are times when it is right to question the views of others if there is going to be reform, but Paul is not dealing with such legitimate questioning. Indeed, Paul himself was 'guilty' of dissention when he proclaimed the gospel of Christ in the synagogues. Paul is concerned, rather, with the unhelpful dissent caused simply because of differences over legitimate alternative policies. Sadly, we often find such dissension in churches, for example when people think the pastor's ministry is over and they seek to influence others in support of his removal. This has happened throughout history, and no less in biblical history. It is even more tragic when people who were once used by God become the centre of dissension. Such examples are Miriam and Aaron, who tried to replace—or, at the very least, share leadership with—Moses, their brother (Num. 12).

'Jealousy' is a state of heart and mind that causes much suffering. It is often hidden under a veneer of respectability. It ruins relationships, twists truth, and excuses gross injustices. To succumb to jealousy's enticements is to be a prisoner of a ruthless mistress.

13:14 But put on the Lord Jesus Christ, and make no provision for the flesh, to gratify its desires.

The lifestyle of the people of God is to be different from that of the world. While there are notable exceptions, the sins Paul has listed are those which gratify the 'flesh'. As we have seen, sarx ('flesh') has a range of meanings reflecting the weakness of humanity. Paul sees Christians as continuing in their fallen creaturely weakness. While this does not necessarily equate to sinning, it probably does in this verse. Paul is exhorting the Roman Christians not to gratify the flesh in actions that are typical of unredeemed humanity. They are to wait patiently and live sober lives as they look for the completion of their redemption when Christ returns.

In exhorting the Roman believers to 'put on the Lord Jesus Christ', Paul is appealing to the church community to live a Christ-like life. God's people are to 'put on' (NIVTM 'clothe yourselves') with Christ Jesus. The scriptural basis of this appeal is taken from Isaiah 60:1, where Israel was commanded to awake from her sleep and prepare for her second exodus. This Old Testament text echoes in the background as Paul warns the church to awake from slumber because her salvation is nearer now than when she first believed (v. 11). Thus, new exodus imagery continues to drive the argument. The church is to live in such a way to be fit for the coming of the divine bridegroom—an event that Isaiah 62:1–5 foretold. Paul is still employing corporate language here (see Eph. 4:24; Col. 3:10). Moreover, the language of clothing is found throughout the Old Testament. It refers to preparation for doing evil (Ps. 73:6) or good (Ps. 45:3; Isa. 51:9) as well as the transformation of people through life events (Job 8:22; Ps. 30:11; 35:26; 109:29; 132:16; Isa. 52:1; 61:10).

Further Study: Questions for Romans 13

1. What are the exceptions for not submitting to the authorities?

2. Who has appointed the authorities and for what reasons?

3. What does non-compliance with just laws of society imply?

4. What is it that God's commandments direct us to?

5. What reason does Paul give to strive to be obedient citizens?

6. Why must Christians wake from their present slumber?

Romans 14: Caring for the Weak

Introduction

Paul begins this section by appealing for the weak and the strong to accept each other. In view of the discussion he had about the division between Jews and Gentiles in chapter 9–11, it is likely that this same division is that referred to in this section. This is made even more likely by the mention of food and holy days, the very issues that divided the Jewish and Gentile believers in the church at Rome.

Paul stresses that we are all accepted because Christ has died (Rom. 14:9, 15), and that no one should be quick to judge because we are all to be judged by God (Rom. 14:10–12). Paul makes the startling claim that if one causes another to stumble because of his attitude, he sins against Christ himself (Rom. 14:20). Paul says that the principle which must be applied is whether a person has a clear conscience about what they do. If their conscience is clear, and their actions are not forbidden, nor harm other believers, they are free to continue their chosen course. Thus, Paul puts down a mark for the importance of Christian freedom.

14:1 As for the one who is weak in faith, welcome him, but not to quarrel over opinions.

In all Christian congregations there are people from different backgrounds who have had different experiences. At this point in the letter, Paul is concerned with the difference that exists between each believer's individual measure of faith, and about the attitudes they should adopt towards each other as a result of these differences. Exactly who Paul has in mind when addressing this exhortation is not clear as the definition of those with weak or strong faith does not necessarily fall along Jewish/Gentile lines. He clearly sees himself as one of the strong but argues that such as he must follow the example of Jesus to support the weak (Rom. 1:3; cf. Phil. 2:5–9).

In any community there are those who are full of confidence and opinion. Others are far less robust and may be hesitant to the point of causing themselves pain in their uncertainties. The 'weak' are not necessarily ignorant of Christian doctrine, but struggle to work out its consequences and implications. It is all too easy for those who are 'strong' to become frustrated with those who do not share their self- confidence. In a community where all must be taken seriously and their opinions respected, there is always tension. Paul speaks into such a situation, for differences of opinion and conviction can cause rift and division.

He urges those who are strong in faith to make sure their confidence does not damage weak believers. They are to do this by not passing judgment on them. Paul is anxious that each Christian should respect the consciences of other Christians so that things are not pressed on them of which they are unsure. What a model Paul is presenting! God does not want a church full of successful and confident people. He wants a church to be full of believers with different natures and characters so that, as they care for each other's needs, the world will see how they love one another. This love is not to be like that of the tax collectors (Matt. 5:46) but like the love of God who, in his infinite power and wisdom, comes alongside frail and uncertain believers, working to help them grow and embrace certainties. Imposing stronger 'faith' on a weak believer results in a false discipleship where the belief systems of others are accepted by those who do not understand their foundations. The divine example must be the guide, as the letter to the Philippians demonstrates. In that letter, Paul used a beautiful piece of poetry—probably adapted as a hymn—to speak of the example of Christ (Phil. 2:6–11). This understanding of who the strong are runs contrary to the view of some scholars hold who see the description as a reference to numerical superiority.

14:2 One person believes he may eat anything, while the weak person eats only vegetables.

Paul presents two extremes of faith. One is of a Christian who has no conscience about what he eats. The other belongs to one who is deeply distressed over issues relating to meat and who, therefore, is vegetarian. There is no suggestion in the Scripture that vegetarianism was an issue, so

Romans 14: Caring for the Weak

it is probable that Paul has believers in mind, like the ones in Corinth, who are deeply concerned with the meat's origin (1 Cor. 10:23–32). In Rome, it appears that some of the believers are taking the rather extreme measure of only eating vegetables in order to ensure that they do not unknowingly eat meat that had been offered to idols.

14:3 Let not the one who eats despise the one who abstains, and let not the one who abstains pass judgment on the one who eats, for God has welcomed him.

Paul raises an issue that was a common problem in the early church. The Christians lived in societies where pagan gods were worshiped daily, the meat of the sacrificed animals being sold on to market traders. Consequently, it was almost impossible to be certain that meat bought in the marketplace was free from association with idol worship. Those who converted to Christ from idolatry knew the significance of such offerings. They were the means of celebrating fellowship with the forces of darkness, and the meat of such sacrificed animals was the property of the deities who had been worshiped. 'How,' such Christians asked, 'could a believer eat such food?' They reasoned that it could only be by sinful compromise, offending God and rupturing fellowship with him. While Paul believes that idols have no objective reality or existence (1 Cor. 8:1–8), he realizes nevertheless that eating meat sacrificed to them is a cause of great difficulty for some. He explains that there is a reality of demons exploiting idols and enslaving those who worship them.

Here, in Romans 14:3, Paul lays down an important principle of Christian tolerance. It is all too easy to see one's own position as superior. The matter under consideration was the eating or abstaining from certain meats. Those who ate them saw themselves as more robust and stronger in faith than those who abstained; those who abstained saw themselves as more spiritual and sensitive to the will of God than those who ate. Both believed that they were the ones concerned for the glory of God.

14:4 Who are you to pass judgment on the servant of another? It is before his own master that he stands or falls. And he will be upheld, for the Lord is able to make him stand.

Paul stresses the inappropriateness of intruding into somebody else's relationship with God. His argument is clear, 'What right have you got to judge someone whom God has accepted?' If some of the Roman believers were to claim that they knew things about another believer of which God was ignorant, it would be the height of arrogance in the face of his omniscience, for he knows all things. Paul's point is that when God accepts a believer, that person becomes God's responsibility. Judgment in such matters is not for fellow believers to exercise—for God has never assigned such authority to them. A pressing reason for Paul writing this letter was because such a presumption was in danger of ripping the church apart.

14:5 One person esteems one day as better than another, while another esteems all days alike. Each one should be fully convinced in his own mind.

Paul moves from the issue of meat-eating and applies the same principle to another matter that was straining the relationship between Jewish and Gentile believers in Rome. Some believed that certain days were more holy than others and ought to be observed by following rules that had developed around them. Others did not see any intrinsic sacredness in these days, for God was with them in all the affairs of life and not just in 'holy affairs'. Such Christians could not see why they should be forced to keep days as holy when the whole of life was holy.

The subtle thing about the choice Paul made in raising these examples is that the eating of meat (because of possible pagan links) distressed the Gentile believers but the non-observance of certain 'holy' days distressed the Jewish believers. He carefully selected issues that gave both parties an insight into the pain of being abused, misunderstood, or rejected. It is this contrast of experiences—highlighted in the following verse—that suggests it is the Gentile believers who are referred to as the weak in the matter of the eating of meat.

14:6 The one who observes the day, observes it in honour of the Lord. The one who eats, eats in honour of the Lord, since he gives thanks to God, while the one who abstains, abstains in honour of the Lord and gives thanks to God.

As is Paul's practice, he restates the essence of the argument. The attitude of the believers' hearts is the real issue. The argument Paul is making is similar to that found in 1 Corinthians 8–10, but there are significant differences between the two situations and their associated problems. In Corinth, some were exercising their freedom by eating idol meat in the pagan temple itself. To weaker believers this suggested participation in fellowship with the demons that hid behind the idols. However, in Rome the issue does not appear to be as complicated. Possibly the situation was different because, with a strong Jewish community (estimated between 20,000 and 50,000 at the time of Claudius' edict ejecting Jews from Rome), kosher butchers were well established and provided the assurance that the meat on sale had not had contact with idol temple worship. Obviously, we have no idea how many such butchers survived the edict—possibly the majority were expelled. Nevertheless, it is reasonable to suggest that if there was ongoing trade from Gentile converts who preferred kosher meat because of its unpolluted source, some businesses would have been taken over to meet the demand.

14:7 For none of us lives to himself, and none of us dies to himself.

Paul stresses that no one is a free agent. We all have responsibilities to someone else—a husband has responsibilities to his wife and the wife has responsibilities to her husband, a father to his children and the children to their father, an employee to his employer and the employer to his employee. This said, all of us are responsible to God, and our lives and deaths are significant to him. Christ has died to save us, and our death is the means by which we enter into his immediate presence. Both life and death serve the purposes of God for his children. We are, therefore, responsible to him in both life and death. To use the Psalmist's words, 'Where shall I flee from your presence?' (Ps. 139:7).

14:8 For if we live, we live to the Lord, and if we die, we die to the Lord. So then, whether we live or whether we die, we are the Lord's.

No matter what experiences life may bring to Paul and the believers in Rome, he reminds them that they are kept by Christ. There may be things that happen that are the opposite of what they want, but Paul encourages them that their status cannot be threatened for they are 'the Lord's'. Paul is saying that God uses the whole range of human experience to teach us about his faithfulness and bring believers to maturity in Christ (see comments on Rom. 5:1–8; 8:35ff.). In viewing life from this perspective, distressing experiences become part of the teaching process by which God prepares his people for heaven.

The experience of the community is prominent in Paul's thinking—a fact evidenced by the repeated use of the pronoun 'we'. Theirs is a corporate experience that comes from sharing in the death of Christ (see comments on Rom. 6:1–5) and exists because of their membership of the covenant community. It is essentially covenantal and corporate, flowing from the work of the Messiah and his Spirit.

14:9 For to this end Christ died and lived again, that he might be Lord both of the dead and of the living.

The reason for Christ's death, resurrection, and ascension was the restoration of creation—especially humankind—to its original position of subjection to his Lordship. Through Adam's sin, the cosmos had not merely come under the curse of God's judgment but had passed into the 'control' of Satan. However, the death and resurrection of Jesus terminated that relationship just as Adam's disobedience had ruptured the relationship between creation and God.

The restoration of all things to their pre-fallen condition is known by theologians as 'recapitulation,' when the control of all things—created and uncreated—will be handed back to Christ. Sadly, not all people will know this return to blessedness. Humankind, made in the image of God, has been given extraordinary dignity in that God's salvation is not forced upon it; salvation is offered but not imposed. Humankind is invited to exercise their right to respond. Without that response they remain in the kingdom of darkness and outside of the transformation. They have denied salvation for one simple reason: they have chosen to remain in the kingdom of darkness—the body of sin. They remain in Adam, and they are responsible for the consequences that flow from that state of alienation.

The declaration that Jesus is Lord would have been seen as an affront to the Emperor. Caesar not only claimed absolute rights over his subjects, he claimed to be the son of God. This claim of divinity impacted many in the empire, especially those in the state's direct employment. They demonstrated their allegiance to him by offering sacrifices. There were times when this practice of honouring Caesar as the incarnate god was demanded of all citizens of the empire. Consequently, submission to the Lordship of Christ placed the Roman Christians in real danger of rousing the state's anger and experiencing its punishment. Paul is not declaring a political manifesto in this statement—he is declaring a theological truth. Nevertheless, such truth inevitably has implications in many aspects of life, including in its political dimension.

14:10 Why do you pass judgment on your brother? Or you, why do you despise your brother? For we will all stand before the judgment seat of God;

Paul's question 'why do you?' makes the charge personal. He does not write a generalization such as 'we ought not to judge,' but addresses the conscience of the believers who gathered to hear the letter read to them.

The issue raised is that of judging and despising fellow Christians. Paul stresses that they are not only undesirable actions, but actually sinful ones. Judgment usurps God's authority. This will become clear on the Day of Judgment when all will stand before him—not only those who have been condemned by judgmental spirits but also those who have exercised such judgment. The implication seems to be that the one who was unjustly judged will become the accuser and the one who was the self-righteous accuser will be the one charged.

Of course, in writing this, Paul would not want to imply that Christians should not express concern when people are behaving badly, but rather that such concerns should be expressed in a spirit of love. Christ made it clear that, when a believer sins, those in close contact ought to encourage them to repent (Matt. 18:15). When this fails, it is the church's responsibility to bring discipline (Matt. 18:16–17; 1 Cor. 5:2–5). What is different in these cases from the ones dealt with in Romans 14 is that Paul is dealing with matters of conscience regarding ceremonial law. The discipline of believers takes place when moral laws have been broken.

14:11 for it is written, 'As I live, says the Lord, every knee shall bow to me, and every tongue shall confess to God'.

Paul concludes his argument with a quotation from Isaiah 45:23. The way he uses this scripture to support his argument demonstrates how Scripture determined his world-view. Isaiah had said these words in God's name and Paul was able to bring the principles behind them to bear on the problems that existed in the Roman church. Paul is anxious that his converts develop this biblical mind-set, and that they learn to put all of the issues of life—whether personal and trivial, or international and crucial—into the framework of biblical revelation and thinking (cf. Rom. 12:1–2). When Israel failed to do this in the Old Testament (negotiating her place among the nations instead), she was swallowed up with compromise (Isa. 31:1–3). However, when she embraced the world-view proclaimed by the prophets, she triumphed, and God's name was glorified (Isa. 66:10–22).

14:12 So then each of us will give an account of himself to God.

At this point, Paul stresses personal responsibility. As we have seen earlier, we have to be careful not to apply to the individual what is only true of the church. However, while it is true that the church has a corporate responsibility, Paul unequivocally speaks to the individual members of the Roman congregation. He makes it clear that each believer has to put into action what he has been taught. If he fails to do so, he will bear his own guilt on the Day of Judgment. This shows that Paul expects a judgment for the believer (2 Cor. 5:10). This does not relate to salvation but to his life following conversion to Christ.

What Paul has in mind is the damage done to believers within a fellowship by the behaviour of fellow Christians. This is not an isolated passage dealing with this matter—it is clear that there was an ongoing concern in church leadership over this issue (Acts 15:5–21; 21:20–21). The church of the twenty-first century also needs to heed this warning. All too often, sensitive believers avoid fellowship with professing local churches because they, or others they know, have been dealt with harshly and uncaringly within them.

Christ does not deal with them in such a way. He is the good shepherd who gives his life for his sheep (John 10:11). When church ideals are in conflict with the compassion and love of Christ, they must be questioned. This is not suggesting that churches abandon standards, but that they must hold them in the context of Christ's compelling love and not in terms of a destructive legalism which promotes self-righteousness and self-satisfaction.

14:13 Therefore let us not pass judgment on one another any longer, but rather decide never to put a stumbling block or hindrance in the way of a brother.

We should not pass judgment on others over matters that are not crucial to our relationship with God. Not only is judgment negative but it puts a stumbling-block in the way of those who are being criticized. Such hindrance to their progress is no small thing. The Christian life is likened to a pilgrimage towards our spiritual home, and criticism can discourage others on their pilgrimage, deflecting them from the road that Christ has called them to walk. For that reason, it is sin.

14:14 I know and am persuaded in the Lord Jesus that nothing is unclean in itself, but it is unclean for anyone who thinks it unclean.

Paul states his position clearly. He describes himself as one who is 'in the Lord Jesus'. In doing this, he identifies himself with the status of every other believer. He is not seeking to lord it over the believers but appeals to them on equal terms.

This conciliatory posture was not always adopted by Paul. When the objective truth of the gospel was at stake, he was very assertive (Gal. 2:14). However, he does not take this confrontational position with the Roman believers, and for good reason. This was not an issue of gospel truth or apostolic authority.

Paul's position remains true to the one taken in the earlier part of the chapter. No food is intrinsically unclean. God has given all food as a gift— even food offered in sacrifice to demons is intrinsically clean. However, if a believer is unable to thank God for providing such food—believing it to be unclean—he ought not to eat it. In writing this, Paul was handling the 'weaker' believers in Rome with great sensitivity. The eating of meat was a serious issue for them, causing them (they thought) to become psychologically and spiritually 'unclean'.

In this example, Paul demonstrates his love for Christ and the people of God. He not only tells the weaker in faith not to eat meat but, in his letter to the Corinthians, he says that if in the eating of meat, a brother or sister is offended, the stronger in faith should stop doing so, even though it was his God-given right (1 Cor. 8:13). Here is a demonstration of the pastoral heart. In his tenderness, Paul thinks of others above himself. He stands with the weaker believers, and even though his theological reasoning dismisses their views, his love and respect for them does not allow him to march away from the argument as the victor and indulge himself in his legitimate freedoms.

How different churches would be if they recognized the legitimate diversity of views as well as the folly of imposing views on others who have not been persuaded of their perspective. When people are pressurized to conform to expressions of personal preferences rather than the clear directives of Scripture, their growth is inevitably stunted. There are many things that are good but are not the essence of the gospel—such practices as keeping certain days as holy, upholding good and sensible health principles, and other social norms that societies throw up as 'best practice'. It is amazing how Christians can confuse their cultural heritage with 'Christian norms' and assume that the former is an essential non-negotiable part of the gospel.

14:15 For if your brother is grieved by what you eat, you are no longer walking in love. By what you eat, do not destroy the one for whom Christ died.

Paul takes his advice a step further. Earlier, he had been concerned about the weaker believer and his unease about eating meat previously offered to idols. Now he widens the issue. He tells those with robust consciences that if their eating of meat causes others to stumble, they affect the faith of those who see danger and defilement in eating in such a way. They are no longer acting in love for, in insisting on their rights, they are in danger of destroying the ones for whom Christ has died.

This is an amazing assertion. These 'stronger' believers had seen themselves as mature and liberated members of the church. Paul is effectively saying, 'If you are mature, then behave as such. Put the needs of the weaker believer as a priority in your lives. It has cost Christ his life to bring this believer into fellowship with himself. Do you dare drive him away as a consequence of demanding your right to practice your freedom?' Such a perspective seriously challenges what most of us understand as Christian maturity. Rather than being strong and arguing for one's own point of view, Christian maturity is about servanthood and following Christ in his self-denial (Phil. 2:1–15).

14:16 So do not let what you regard as good be spoken of as evil.

What does Paul refer to when he writes that they should not let what they 'regard as good be spoken of as evil?' It could be argued that it refers to their freedom to eat meat. That certainly has been the flow of the argument. However, it could also be argued that it is a preparatory statement, for in the following verse, he pleads that the members of the church recognize that there is something much bigger than their own interests—the kingdom of God. Indeed, he goes on to show how these contentious issues fall into their proper place when seen in the context of the reign of God.

This exhortation needs to be heard and obeyed by the people of God in the twenty- first century. Christian communities can be divided over matters that are of little significance when seen in light of the issues about which God is concerned. Personal preferences and prejudices can be dressed up as the most spiritual of arguments to justify pressurizing others into accepting them. Such attempts to 'defend the truth' demonstrate a lack of spirituality, for the love that pervaded Paul's appeal is missing. The absence of love is not rectified by blind devotion to a doctrinal system, no matter how correct and orthodox it might be (1 Cor. 13:1–13).

14:17 For the kingdom of God is not a matter of eating and drinking but of righteousness and peace and joy in the Holy Spirit.

The kingdom of God has not been explicitly mentioned until now, despite the fact that the whole of the letter has been dealing with the subject. The Son of David was predicted to be the inaugurator of the kingdom, and he had come in the person of Jesus (Rom. 1:3). The letter is centred on the ethnicity of the kingdom, its composition of Jews and Gentiles, and the problems that this 'new man' (Eph. 2:15) experiences. Paul is clearly distressed that the church is caught up with matters that divide. The apostles met to give authoritative guidance to the Gentiles (Acts 15:6– 29), but the evidence suggests that the instructions fell on the deaf ears of many Jewish believers (Acts 21:20–21).

14:18 Whoever thus serves Christ is acceptable to God and approved by men.

Paul's use of the definite article with 'Christ' (which is unfortunately omitted in many translations, including ESV) indicates that the term is being used in a titular way. This confirms that Paul's use has this Messianic significance and that it had not been lost in the Gentile mission. This confirms the correctness of reading the letter in light of the Old Testament expectations regarding Israel's long promised Messiah king, who is the Christ; references throughout the letter to the term 'Christ' are correctly read as Messianic in meaning and significance.

It is typical of Paul to write that serving the preference of others serves Christ; it is pleasing to God (Phil. 2:1–15), as Christian living should not fight for rights but strive for unity. It respects the uncertainties and fears of others and is concerned to see them grow into Christ. It is all too easy to think we are serving Christ when motivated by the prejudices of our own hearts and not by his Spirit. How easy it is to confuse the two! How many dreadful mistakes have been made by people who have claimed they were doing God's will while causing the name of Christ to be brought into disrepute? When we serve Christ out of the motive of caring for others, we bring delight to the heart of God and an acknowledgment by others that we are not motivated by bigotry or narrow-mindedness.

14:19 So then let us pursue what makes for peace and for mutual upbuilding.

The term 'peace' is used earlier in the letter where Paul refers to 'peace with God' (Rom. 5:1; 8:6). Those who are at peace with him are obliged to be at peace with other believers as this promotes 'mutual upbuilding'. This clearly suggests that imposing one's view on another is not to be tolerated.

Great effort is needed to enter into the thinking and fears of other people. If we do not take the trouble to appreciate where they come from—in terms of the experiences and traditions that mould their understanding—we have little hope of treating them with respect. Without such effort, we are effectively saying that others have to be made in our image—something that is not only dangerous but blasphemous. The only one who has the right to someone in his own image is God himself.

Without understanding how our differences have come into existence, we can never be instruments of peace and attain mutual edification. Demanding conformity to our own particular understanding of secondary issues divides rather than unites. Indeed, it is important that we understand why we hold our own views, lest we canonize the tradition into which we were converted or which we have adopted.

14:20 Do not, for the sake of food, destroy the work of God. Everything is indeed clean, but it is wrong for anyone to make another stumble by what he eats.

Paul returns to the issue of eating meats. He has no difficulty in upholding the Jewish view that all proscribed food is clean, for it is the provision of the gracious Creator God. However, he is not limiting himself to proscribed food. Paul is saying that all food is clean—something with which Peter had to come to terms (Acts 9:9– 16). But Paul is equally clear that what God has declared clean can easily become the instrument of Satan, for the insistence of 'true understanding' and the practice of one's own rights can lead to the destruction of a weaker believer's faith.

What is sinful is not the eating of meat, but the arrogant manner in which it is done. The abuse of freedom demonstrated is irresponsible and nothing to do with the truth and love of God but is rather about the arrogance of the offender. How easily that which is good can divide and offend, causing the work of God to be destroyed in a sensitive soul. No amount of arguing about their supposed lack of 'spirituality', or about the sovereign grace of God to care for his own, will diminish the responsibility that we carry for causing others to stumble. No one defended Christian freedoms more than the Apostle Paul; yet here he is, pleading for the unity that Christ prayed for, and making it clear that there is no compromise in the giving of high regard and attention to those who are in need of sympathy and support.

14:21 It is good not to eat meat or drink wine or do anything that causes your brother to stumble.

Not only is it better but it is necessary. The motive of love for fellow believers makes abstinence from what is legitimate something that is God-honouring and God- glorifying. It is not the other way around as is often argued by advocates of so-called biblical freedom. Freedom is not given so that we may suit ourselves; rather, freedom is given so that we can share in the immense privilege of advancing the kingdom of God—making his love known to his people and to those who are outside of the covenants of promise. It is to be used to reveal the tenderness of the one who is the good shepherd. Freedom is to be restrained for the sake of those who would feel trampled on and despised by those who consider themselves to be stronger. By forgoing their freedom to eat meat, the Roman believers will show how much they love their brothers and sisters.

Unexpectedly, Paul raises the issue of drinking wine. In light of the fact that drinking wine was widespread—only drunkenness is condemned in the Scriptures—many assume that this reference points to a pagan ritual that took place in the Temple. However, in light of what Paul has written to the believers, it seems probable that he was advising the believers to consider the effect of wine on fellow believers. As today, some will have enjoyed drinking to excess and will have tried to curb their dependence on wine since their conversion. Paul's advice is to abstain from drinking wine in a situation that might upset fellow Christians who have perhaps struggled with a history of personal abuse.

14:22 The faith that you have, keep between yourself and God. Blessed is the one who has no reason to pass judgment on himself for what he approves.

Paul clearly sees that theological correctness can be morally deficient if it is used to score points. However, there are issues that a believer can keep in his heart. According to the text, certain things can be pondered without being published.

There is clearly a pastoral dimension to this teaching. One of the elements is the ability to judge how different Christian truths should be presented and when their implications, as far as Christian living is concerned, should be pressed. Just as there are stages in human development from infancy to adulthood, so there is progression for the Christian. This does not deny that some people develop more rapidly than others, but it does mean that a wise believer should take this into account when dealing with a young Christian.

Does the phrase 'blessed is the one' refer to God's blessing on those who behave in accordance with their conscience, or is it merely Paul's approval of those who act in such a way? Its close proximity to the statement about keeping truth private ought to guide our understanding. It would seem that Paul is saying that the ones who are blessed are those who know that they have struck the right balance. They know that they are not condemned by their conscience. It would, therefore, seem that the blessedness is that of a clear conscience.

14:23 But whoever has doubts is condemned if he eats, because the eating is not from faith. For whatever does not proceed from faith is sin.

In contrast to the man who has a clear conscience and is blessed, the one who goes against his conscience is condemned. It follows that in this case, being condemned is not referring to God's condemnation, but the condemnation of the conscience.

However, such self-condemnation leads to God's condemnation, for action that 'does not proceed from faith is sin'.

Further Study: Questions for Romans 14

1. What do the opening verses warn against? Do you ever find yourself doing this?

2. Who do you think the 'strong' and the 'weak' are in this passage? List your reasons for holding this view. List what you think might be Paul's concerns in this area for the church you belong to?

3. 'Each one of you should be fully convinced in his own mind' (v. 5b). What sort of issues should Christians reflect on in the twenty-first century in your own culture?

4. Although the letter is corporate in its arguments, Paul warns about being pressured by other people's opinions. Can you give modern examples of how this still happens?

5. What does criticism eventually do?

6. What is the source of Christian liberty?

7. What is the one event that every believer will share and conform to?

8. What does Paul urge the believers to make up their minds about?

Romans 15: When All is Going Well

Introduction

The chapter continues the theme followed in the preceding chapter. Believers should not fight for their rights but consider the needs of others, especially the needs of those who are weak in their faith. In doing this they are following the example of the one they say they serve (Rom. 15:3–4).

Paul goes on to show that this acceptance was foretold by the prophets, a fact that suggests that those who are the strong, who need to be urged to accept the weaker believers, are the Jews. Such a citation is especially suited to them in their reluctance to give up their Jewish understanding of what God requires, which tended to be mostly about ritual participation. Their mutual acceptance was to be of the same kind as they have received from Christ, who had every right to reject us all because of our uncleanness.

Paul reflects on his ministry, which is not one of salvaging humanity to a second-rate status but of the restoration of men and women to the privileged position of being priests of God. He sees his own ministry to be priestly (Rom. 15:16), and it is into this ministry that the Gentiles have been brought.

Paul expresses the desire that he will be able to visit them on his way to Spain, where he wants to plant the church of Christ (Rom. 15:28). He tells of his plans to visit Jerusalem with the gift provided by the Gentile churches. He solicits prayer for this endeavour which he knows is dangerous because of the hatred some hold towards him for defending Gentile freedom (15:31).

15:1 We who are strong have an obligation to bear with the failings of the weak, and not to please ourselves.

I have argued that Paul was addressing the Jewish believers about this issue in Romans 14; therefore, this verse is not a change of argument but an application of what he was saying. If this is so, then the one who is not eating out of faith is not the Gentile who is going beyond what his conscience allows, but the Jew who is going beyond what love allows.

15:2 Let each of us please his neighbour for his good, to build him up.

The pastoral heart of Paul shines through again as he appeals to the believers. He is anxious that they learn to be more concerned for the needs of others rather than their own rights and freedoms. The respect and love believers give each other complement the teaching ministry of the church by strengthening them in their faith. Indeed, formal teaching can be undone if the members of the congregation do not live out the realities to which they have been exposed, thus grieving the Holy Spirit, as well as 'weaker' believers. While the translators of the ESV understand 'build him up' in v. 2 to apply to the individual, the term regularly refers to the community in Paul's other writings (1 Cor. 14:5; Eph. 4:12, 29).

In the introduction to the commentary, I suggested that Paul's reason for writing the letter was to give the Romans guidance over the issues that were causing divisions in other churches. The Jewish-Gentile relationship was at the centre of most of the early church's problems. This suggestion seems to be confirmed in this penultimate chapter. Paul is constantly appealing to his countrymen to accept the Gentiles; the Jewish people, as the Lord's servants, had been appointed to bring the light of the good news to the nations. They are to be servants to the Gentiles—not preferring themselves over the ones they serve (Phil. 2:2–4).

15:3 For Christ did not please himself, but as it is written, 'The reproaches of those who reproached you fell on me'.

Paul appeals to the great example of Christ in accordance with the apostles' teaching (2 Cor. 8:9–15; Phil. 2:1–11; Heb. 12:1–3; 1 Pet. 2:21–25), for when arguments fail, examples often triumph. The example of the Son of God, who offered up his life for those who hated and killed him, has transformed more lives than arguments have ever done. Christ was not only an example because he relinquished his own will, but because he subjected himself to the violence and rejection of humankind in all of its ugly brutality. Very soon, those authorities that crucified Jesus would turn on the Roman believers themselves. They will become another example of a vessel chosen for privilege becoming a vessel fitted for wrath.

Paul's point is clear—we have an obligation to follow Christ's example if we dare to call ourselves his disciples. He put others before himself. The citation from the Old Testament is Psalm 69:9 (LXX), and it is used elsewhere in the New Testament (Mark 15:36; Luke 23:36; John 19:29; Rev. 13:8). It is significant that, rather than alluding to the actual events in the life of Christ that demonstrate his self-giving, Paul goes back to the Old Testament for his support. There can be little doubt that the suffering referred to in the psalm is seen by Paul to speak prophetically of the passion of Christ. We can only speculate about why he avoided making direct reference to the life of Jesus. It is not that he rejected any desire to know anything about the earthly Jesus, as some have argued from 2 Corinthians 5:16. The reference there to not wanting to know Christ after the flesh probably means that he did not want to interpret his life from any nationalistic Messianic perspective as he would have done before his conversion.

15:4 For whatever was written in former days was written for our instruction, that through endurance and through the encouragement of the Scriptures we might have hope.

The importance of the Jewish Scriptures for the fledgling church cannot be exaggerated. The Jewish believers and the God-fearers were steeped in them because they had no other sacred writings (the New Testament only existed as an emerging collection). The Old Testament gave them the theological framework by which they interpreted the significance of the life, death, and resurrection of Jesus. However, it was not only the life of Jesus that was interpreted through the lens of Old Testament expectation; their experiences were as well.

We have seen in the introduction to the commentary how widespread Paul's use of the Scriptures was in his thinking and writing. He was not unique. The same Old Testament perspective permeated the thinking of the entire church. This is evident from the way Paul presented his argument—his readers were expected to understand the context of references and significance of echoes. If our presentation of Romans has been correct, the whole of this Epistle exemplifies this undergirding dependence.

The reference to having hope is significant, for Paul has written in Romans 5:1–5 that hope is the fruit of the Spirit. Without the outworking of the word and Spirit, the early church's living hope cannot be experienced. It was the Spirit who applied the promise of the Old Testament to the fledgling church and it is he who continues to apply the same, with its New Testament fulfilment, to the church of today. Any Christian community which does not keep the word and the Spirit in balance is in danger of having a deficient understanding and experience of God's grace.

15:5 May the God of endurance and encouragement grant you to live in such harmony with one another, in accord with Christ Jesus,

Paul prays out of personal experience. There are here no platitudes uttered from the safety of a distant administrative centre, rather this was written by a man who is in the heat of battle, and desires for the church in Rome to share in what he knows of God's sustaining grace and encouragement.

He prays not only for endurance but also for God's encouragement. As these two blessings flow into the believers' lives, they will become united in heart and mind; together gladly submitting to Christ. This unity will lead them to serve one another as Paul has encouraged them to do in Romans 15:1.

15:6 that together you may with one voice glorify the God and Father of our Lord Jesus Christ.

This is the goal of the gospel. The ultimate purpose of God in saving people for himself is that they might corporately demonstrate the character and wisdom of their Saviour (Eph. 3:10–13). It is no more wrong of God to desire to be acknowledged by those he has saved than for parents to want to hear expressions of love and joy from their children. It is not a selfish obsession, because God is the God of love who rejoices in the overthrow of evil and the recovery of his creation from sin's captivity. According to the Westminster Catechism, humanity's chief end is to glorify God and enjoy him forever.

15:7 Therefore welcome one another as Christ has welcomed you, for the glory of God.

The 'therefore' shows that Paul's appeal is based on the preceding verses; there he explained that our goal—because of the effects of the gospel—is to follow the example set by Christ. Christian relationships are not an optional extra to discipleship. They are an essential part of the Christian life for, when lived out as God intends, they bring him praise. For the believer, there can be no greater reason for pursuing Christian reconciliation and mutual encouragement than this. As this reason was given in the previous verse, its repetition indicates the importance of accepting one another.

I have claimed that the letter to the Romans is a pastoral letter about Jewish/Gentile relationships. Here, in this verse, Paul makes his final appeal for the acceptance of the Jewish Christians by the Gentile Christian community and the Gentile Christians by the Jewish Christian community. His appeal sums up his plea made since Romans 14:1; a plea based on the theological argument of Jewish and Gentile equality as discussed in chapters 1–12. This understanding is endorsed by the next verse, which emphasizes the Gentiles' acceptance into the new covenant community.

However, it must be noted that it is wrong to consider Paul's appeal as a demand to overlook sinful actions in the quest for peace. When a man took his father's wife in the Corinthian church (1 Cor. 5:1–13), Paul did not urge the congregation to accept him—he threatened that he would discipline any who behaved in such a way. He made it clear that such behaviour violated the commands of God; even the pagans drew the line at such behaviour. Respecting the weak did not mean tolerating issues that violated the moral law of the Old Testament. The Roman believers were to accept one another in the way that Christ accepted them— without reservation and out of immeasurable grace. The example of Christ is a far greater influence than a theoretical discussion of acceptance and has inspired the reconciliation of people over the centuries who otherwise would never have known the restoration of relationships.

15:8 For I tell you that Christ became a servant to the circumcised to show God's truthfulness, in order to confirm the promises given to the patriarchs,

The phrase 'I tell you,' introduces a solemn doctrinal pronouncement. In this verse, there is an echo of Isaiah 42:1–9, where the servant establishes justice on the earth (v. 4) and is made a light for the Gentiles (v. 6). As a result, the blind are given their sight, captives are delivered (v. 7), and idols are exposed as valueless (v. 8).

Servanthood had been Israel's calling, but she failed to fulfil her role. Now the servant church has been called to fulfil the task that Israel refused to do by bringing good news to those in darkness. Paul clearly sees Jesus, the Christ, to be the one who would bless the Gentiles, fulfilling the promise made to Abraham, Isaac, and Jacob (Gen. 22:18; 26:4; 28:14).

15:9 and in order that the Gentiles might glorify God for his mercy. As it is written, 'Therefore I will praise you among the Gentiles, and sing to your name'.

The reason for the Gentiles being evangelized is that God will be glorified as a result of his saving mercy towards them. In other words, the whole of creation is to acknowledge that God is a merciful and gracious God. People, who had long been in the clutches of Satan and deceived regarding God's nature, will see that they had believed the lie.

While the purpose of the gospel is to bring salvation and not judgment, those who reject its message will suffer the consequence of turning away from the Saviour. Those who welcome the news of God's grace will be transformed, becoming the instruments by which his grace is magnified. Paul demonstrates that this has been God's purpose throughout history and cites Psalm 18:49 to illustrate its biblical basis.

15:10 And again it is said, 'Rejoice, O Gentiles, with his people'.

Further evidence is given for the welcome the Gentiles are to receive. Paul quotes from the song of Moses (Deut. 32:43), which was composed in the closing days of his life as he prepared to bless the tribes of Israel. The song warned the Jews of the character of God—he would punish their rebellion and be vindicated among the nations. The passage Paul quotes is a call to the nations to recognize that God is just and righteous in all his dealings, not allowing even his elect to be excused for their wrongdoing.

Although the original song did not explicitly state that the Gentiles would be brought into the covenant community, this is the logical deduction. Moses' song does not finish with the judgment of the Jews and the praise of the Gentiles but with the promise that God will take vengeance on his enemies and make atonement for his land and his people. But God's call to the nations to rejoice suggests they are going to share in the blessing of Israel's restoration. Those who oppose his people, however, will come under judgment, as the scripture says, 'Rejoice with him, O heavens; bow down to him, all gods, for he avenges the blood of his children and takes vengeance on his adversaries. He repays those who hate him and cleanses his people's land' (Deut. 32:43). The song is, in effect, a summary of the history that Paul has been outlining in the letter, showing how Israel missed the purpose of her calling, and how the Gentiles have been brought in to bring glory to God. The choice of the text is clearly no coincidence, especially as its conclusion is that Israel will be saved.

15:11 And again, 'Praise the Lord, all you Gentiles, and let all the peoples extol him'.

Paul adds a further Old Testament text to his argument. This time it is Psalm 117:1. The two-verse psalm is a summons to the nations to worship the Lord in praise of his love and faithfulness. At face value, it is a plea from the Jewish community to the Gentiles to join in the worship of God. It presupposes—in line with Paul's reasoning (and other parts of the Old Testament, see Isaiah 19:23–25 and Deuteronomy 32:31)—that there is no priority among them, for the exhortation is to 'praise the Lord...all you people'.

15:12 And again Isaiah says, 'The root of Jesse will come, even he who arises to rule the Gentiles; in him will the Gentiles hope'.

Most modern scholars divide the prophecy of Isaiah into sections composed by different authors. However, as far as New Testament authors were concerned the prophecy had only one author, and they developed their arguments from that perspective.

Paul quotes from Isaiah 11:1, 10, which predicts the conversion of the Gentiles. This text was understood by the early church to anticipate later second exodus texts, which are prolific in the book of Isaiah. So, once again, we find Paul's use of the Old Testament has strict regard for the original setting of the texts. His use of the Old Testament is mostly confined to demonstrating how they have been spiritually fulfilled through the exodus that Christ has achieved for his people.

In saying that Jesus was to rule over the Gentiles (NIVTM 'nations'), Paul is making a significant political statement. Many in Rome must have hoped desperately that no representative of the Imperial household was present when this statement was read out. It was a direct challenge to the power of the state to say that God would raise his Christ above the nations, and all would bow to him. The verse illustrates how the gospel can clash with the political realm, because what fallen leaders seek can be diametrically opposed to what God desires—the establishment of righteousness. Neither the prophecy itself, nor the way Paul used it, were intended to be political, but merely statements concerning the fulfilment of God's saving activity. For this reason, it is unwise to suggest, as some do, that Paul was deliberately critiquing the Roman Empire.

15:13 May the God of hope fill you with all joy and peace in believing, so that by the power of the Holy Spirit you may abound in hope.

Paul adds his own prayer to the Scriptures that he has quoted. It is a beautifully crafted prayer that expresses the most important need of the believers in Rome. He calls God the 'God of hope,' echoing the previous verse. He does not change the prospects of life so that they become less gloomy but gives hope to humanity in sin when, humanly speaking, there is no hope (Eph. 2:14–18).

When Paul asks God to fill believers with 'all joy and peace' as they trust in him, there is no doubt that he saw emotion to be a key factor in Christian experience and development. He was not looking to produce intellectual 'know-it-alls' in Rome, but a community of believers with a loving heartfelt appreciation of the God who had saved them. Unless our intellectual understanding is transformed into overwhelming joy and peace, we must question the nature of our spiritual understanding. Joy and peace are not the products of intellectual attainment but come from trusting in God. Here is the beautiful simplicity and profoundness of the gospel. While it has engaged some of the finest minds in attempts to penetrate its truths, treasures, and benefits, the fact is that all these blessings are offered equally to all—even to children—for God is a God who meets all who respond to him in simple faith.

Paul wants the believers to overflow with hope by the power of the Holy Spirit, reflecting the hope of the Gentiles (v. 12). Its abundance in their lives will be the result of the Spirit's work. Already he has written to them about the Holy Spirit pouring love into their hearts (Rom. 5:5), inspiring a hope which does not disappoint. Because of this powerful work of God by his Spirit, Paul dares to pray that they will overflow with this hope.

Since hope affects the way they live and confront the problems of life they will need an abundance of it in the years ahead, for Nero—driven by his evil and deranged mind—will turn the capital into a burning inferno. He will blame the city's destruction on the infant church, and the believers—having been made the scapegoat of a madman—will suffer unspeakable cruelty for their faith in Christ.

15:14 I myself am satisfied about you, my brothers, that you yourselves are full of goodness, filled with all knowledge and able to instruct one another.

Some see vv. 14–16 as key to the exhortatory discourse of Romans. Paul encourages the members of the church by praising the quality of their lives. His praise of the Roman church is not with an ulterior motive. He is not like those public speakers of the ancient world who flattered their audience with an eye on the rewards they would receive. Paul is realistic about their moral achievements and knows that they are far from perfect. The point is that he sees that the Romans would allow the Spirit to fulfil his ministry in their lives. If they are full of goodness, they will behave towards each other with love and respect. If they have true knowledge, they will understand how knowledge without love counts for nothing (1 Cor. 13:2).

The believers in Rome were equipped to instruct each other; this would mean that Gentiles would teach Jews as well as vice versa. It was this ministry of teaching that the Jews believed was their unique calling, but it had led to pride and arrogance. The Gentiles were not as competent in teaching as their Jewish brothers and sisters because they had less knowledge of the Old Testament promises. However, well- instructed

Gentiles would acquire this theological perspective and would be competent to address Jewish pride. Gentiles would exhort Jewish believers, and this would not be because they had usurped the Jew's historic role, but because they had been called to such a ministry by Abraham's God.

15:15 But on some points I have written to you very boldly by way of reminder, because of the grace given me by God

The apostles believed their responsibility was to keep reminding the church of her inheritance in Christ (2 Pet. 3:2; 1 John 5:13; Heb. 12:1–3), and Paul acknowledges that he has written 'very boldly'. This may indicate his awareness of the sensitive nature of the issues he has raised. He is certain that problems will not go away unless they are confronted and resolved by a clear understanding of the history of salvation. By showing how God has accepted the Jews he has been able to demonstrate that the calling of the Gentiles is not a distortion of the law, but its very principle.

15:16 to be a minister of Christ Jesus to the Gentiles in the priestly service of the gospel of God, so that the offering of the Gentiles may be acceptable, sanctified by the Holy Spirit.

Paul describes his ministry in terms of it being a priestly duty. We have noted in Romans 12:1 that the priests in the Old Testament were appointed to represent the firstborn, taking their place in the ministry based in the tabernacle. God claimed all of Israel's firstborn for himself, the sons being designated to be God's priests. The term leitourgos ('minister') is often used of the Levite in the LXX. Paul has not been released from the obligation to serve God; rather he, like all other redeemed people, is obliged to serve God with his whole life. Indeed, it is because Jesus— God's firstborn—has been delivered up to death that Paul is required to serve as a priest. It is the only response he can make to the God who has spared him through the giving up of his own Son as the Passover sacrifice (1 Cor. 5:7b).

The Jewish nation's priestly duty had been to bring the light of the knowledge of God to the nations, but she failed miserably. Paul sees himself as called to fulfil this work so that the Gentiles might be brought into the blessings of the covenant. Their conversion is, therefore, the goal of his ministry. He knew it would happen because the Scriptures predicted it (Gen.

12:3; Isa. 2:2–3; 11:10; 19:21–25), and he had been commissioned to the task by the risen Christ (Acts 26:17–18).

The Holy Spirit must sanctify the Gentiles to make them acceptable. Paul is not speaking of individual Gentiles being brought into the covenant through personal response and faith; he is viewing them as a group, for prosphora ('offering') is singular. This parallels Israel's sanctification when she was brought out of bondage (Isa. 50:8; 53:11).

While this new exodus of God's people has been achieved through the cross, it is the Holy Spirit who has brought about their unity with Christ. The same Spirit applies this saving work to individuals as he circumcises their hearts and gives them the experiential status required for membership in the new covenant community. By this circumcision they are brought into their already-secured inheritance and can make offerings that are acceptable to God.

The phrase 'so that the offering of the Gentiles may be acceptable' suggests they are being brought into the same ministry as the believing Jews. They are also part of the holy nation, the New Testament priesthood, and it is their responsibility to share the good news with those they meet. In the New Testament, all those who have been redeemed through Christ, their Passover, are priests to God.

It has been pointed out that, while Paul uses priestly terminology for his work of evangelism, he never uses this terminology when speaking of those who preside in worship or lead in the celebration of the Eucharist (the Lord's Table). It was later generations of Christians who reintroduced the Old Testament order, despite the fact that the New Testament had clearly seen this to have been fulfilled in Christ (Heb. 10:11–18). Indeed, the institution of the 'Lord's Supper' was nothing more than the Christian version of the Passover, when 'Christ, our Passover, was sacrificed for us' (1 Cor. 5:7). Any later developments of 'real presence' or other 'sacramental significance' would not have been in the minds of Jesus or the apostles. This is made clear when we question the widely-held view of Hellenism as a key for interpreting the New Testament, and instead read the New Testament out of the Old Testament. As there is no evidence of sacramentalism in the Old

Testament sacrificial system, and the writers of the New Testament were soaked in its theology, we need to question such understanding of the celebration of the Lord's Supper. Once the inauguration of the Lord's Supper was removed from its original setting of the Passover, the parameters of its significance were lost, and the door was opened to an understanding that was not part of the original celebration.

15:17 In Christ Jesus, then, I have reason to be proud of my work for God.

For Paul, there could be no greater privilege than being a servant of God. This was not being said by a man who had lived a life of ease because of privilege, but by one who had experienced immense suffering because of his loyalty to Jesus Christ.

15:18 For I will not venture to speak of anything except what Christ has accomplished through me to bring the Gentiles to obedience—by word and deed,

In saying that he 'will not venture to speak,' Paul can be understood in one of two ways. He may be saying that he is not competent to speak beyond his own experience of ministry, so purposely limiting himself to this. Alternatively, he might be stressing that he has nothing about which to boast. It is God alone who can take glory for what has been achieved. In light of the context, it is probably the latter interpretation that expresses Paul's intention.

15:19 by the power of signs and wonders, by the power of the Spirit of God—so that from Jerusalem and all the way around to Illyricum I have fulfilled the ministry of the gospel of Christ;

While Paul rarely speaks of involvement in miraculous ministry (2 Cor. 12:12), his companion, Luke, reported on it more freely (Acts 13:4–12; 14:8–10; 16:16–18; 25– 34; 19:11–20). It is much wiser to let others report on the blessings God has given to our service rather than getting caught up in the cult of self-promotion. Such a cult robs Christ of his glory.

Paul writes, 'from Jerusalem and all the way around to Illyricum'. Illyricum is part of the Balkan region, which was once known as Yugoslavia. This statement creates a problem because there is no record of Paul ministering in this region. Some have concluded that Illyricum is intended to represent the western limit of the eastern part of the Roman Empire. If this is so, then Paul is claiming that he has evangelized the whole of the Empire apart from Italy and the west. This interpretation, however, presents its own problem. It was not physically possible for Paul to have preached everywhere in such a vast area. The most plausible understanding is that Paul has preached in its chief centres, confident in the knowledge that others have radiated out from them with the gospel message.

A better translation of the phrase 'the gospel of Christ' is 'the gospel about Christ'. This has been the thrust of exposition throughout this commentary, for the letter is about Jesus, the Son of David (Rom. 1:3), who is the Christ.

15:20 and thus I make it my ambition to preach the gospel, not where Christ has already been named, lest I build on someone else's foundation,

Paul sought to evangelize regions where no one had gone. One such region was to the west of Italy, that is Spain. While his intended visit to Italy would serve to strengthen the church in Rome as he shared fellowship with them (Rom. 1:11–12), his main purpose was to make the visit a stepping-stone to the west (cf. Rom. 15:24). Even though he avoided building on other people's foundations, it would seem that he saw no reason not to exercise an evangelistic ministry while passing through regions on his way to his intended field of ministry (Rom. 1:15).

15:21 but as it is written, 'Those who have never been told of him will see, and those who have never heard will understand'.

In citing Isaiah 52:15 (LXX), Paul is not justifying his efforts to take the gospel to the unreached but justifying his view of himself as part of the servant ministry. Here, it is sufficient to note that he deliberately applies to himself a text that speaks of the suffering Servant. For Paul, there is no doubt that Christ fulfils this ministry to the nations, bringing about their forgiveness and reconciliation to God. Nevertheless, as my comments on Romans 1:1 suggest, the application of Servant passages was not limited to Christ by the early church. She saw herself as continuing this ministry—overwhelmed with the privilege and responsibility of making the gospel known.

15:22 This is the reason why I have so often been hindered from coming to you.

If we go outside Paul's letter to the Romans, we find examples of him acknowledging how Satan hindered him at times (e.g. 1 Thess. 2:18). However, in this verse, Paul is not suggesting that Satan had prevented him from visiting Rome. The reasons for the delay must have been the various ministries in which he was involved (vv. 19–20), for he was constantly stretched. In light of his principles and goals, it was vital for him to identify his priorities (Rom. 1:14–16; 15:23–33). He had to be sensible and plan his work ahead, endeavouring (though not always succeeding) to keep to time schedules (cf. Acts 20:16; 2 Cor. 1:15ff.; Titus 1:5). Thus, 'this is the reason' indicates that Paul has given an account of the Gentile mission (see Rom. 15:1–22) he has been involved in so that those in Rome could understand what had occupied his time and energies. It was these noble activities that had delayed his long-desired visit to Rome.

15:23 But now, since I no longer have any room for work in these regions, and since I have longed for many years to come to you,

It is evident that Paul had not evangelized all the regions of Asia, so what does he mean by such a statement? It can only be that he saw his ministry to be pioneering—preparing ground and establishing congregations that would take the gospel to the unreached regions of Asia. As a result of this strategy, there were no more places for him to go.

Paul wants to move into Spain and employ the same 'relay' strategy there, setting up congregations with the expectation that the gospel would diffuse throughout the nation by means of the believers' testimonies. With this strategy, the infant church expanded rapidly—and it still does where such a plan of action is implemented! Too often in the West we lack Paul's missionary vision—we major on his doctrine but ignore his practice. As a result, the transforming gospel is not heard, and people are left in darkness. The church cannot call itself apostolic if it does not put into practice the apostolic example. Upholding the apostles' doctrine is essential, but it's equally important to follow their practice too.

Romans 15: When All Is Going Well

15:24 I hope to see you in passing as I go to Spain, and to be helped on my journey there by you, once I have enjoyed your company for a while.

It is unlikely that Paul was able to achieve his goal of ministering in Spain as we know he was arrested in Jerusalem after writing this letter (Rom. 15:25). From Jerusalem, he was taken to Rome at his own insistence that he be tried under Roman law in front of Caesar (Acts 25:11; 28:16). He chose this in order to thwart the malicious intentions of those Jews who plotted his death (Acts 23:12–30).

While there is no evidence that Paul fulfilled his plan to evangelize Spain, some argue that he was released from house-arrest in Rome and continued on to Spain, being rearrested sometime later. Subsequently, he was brought back to Rome where, according to Christian tradition, he was beheaded at Tre Fontane Abbey (that is Three Fountains Abbey), during the reign of Nero (about 65 A.D.).

When Paul writes 'I hope...to be helped on my journey,' he uses the verb propemphthēnai, which is often translated 'escorted by'. It has been suggested that he is looking for more than financial or material support; Paul hopes the Roman believers will share with him in the mission he plans in Spain by sending representatives to work with him. This was not so that he would have company on the journey; rather it became Paul's practice to involve established churches in his outreach work to those areas yet to be evangelized (Acts 13:1–3; 2 Cor. 8:22ff.; Phil. 2:25–30; 2 Tim. 4:9–13). By this strategy, Paul gives us the model for training Christian workers. Like Jesus, he discipled them by means of his own example (1 Tim. 1:15–16; 2 Tim. 2:2–3; 3:10—4:2).

15:25 At present, however, I am going to Jerusalem bringing aid to the saints.

Some say Paul does not appeal to the believers in Rome for funds to support the suffering believers in Jerusalem because he wished the gift to be from churches he had established. This is hardly likely to be the reason as, at the time of writing, he was travelling in the opposite direction to Rome, on his way to Jerusalem. It would have been unrealistic for Paul to invite the Roman believers to contribute to the gift. His letter—written in Corinth—

would have had to have been delivered speedily to Rome in order for a collection to be made. This would then have had to be transported quickly across or around the Mediterranean and given to Paul and his party who were on their way to Jerusalem. It is more realistic to think that Paul was asking the Roman believers to pray that the gift would be acceptable to the Jews. This was important because of the strain between the Jewish and Gentile sections of the Jerusalem church for, despite the immense suffering of their brothers and sisters, the Judaizers would be tempted to press for the gift to be rejected, fearing it would defile the community.

The suggestion that Paul sought to 'buy' legitimacy for his Gentile mission through the presentation of the gift is not acceptable. This proposal misses the fact that the Jerusalem Council had already endorsed his mission (Acts 15). What Paul's action does is to remind us of the practical ways in which the unity of the church can be promoted. His theological knowledge was being given expression; by means of this tangible display of concern Paul was able to underscore the unity that Christ had brought about through his death.

The gift for the poor saints in Jerusalem was a priority for Paul. This was no ordinary gift. If it had been, he would have entrusted it to others and made his way to Rome, and then Spain, without such a detour. Paul saw the gift as a vital expression of the unity of Jews and Gentiles in the gospel. Establishing this principle was so important that it took priority over his consuming passion of making Christ known in regions beyond. Some have seen the delegation that Paul led to Jerusalem to be an expression of the prophetic promise that the nations would come to Jerusalem to worship the Lord (Isa. 2:1–5).

15:26 For Macedonia and Achaia have been pleased to make some contribution for the poor among the saints at Jerusalem.

The term hoi ptōchoi ('the poor') became a technical term for the pious who were often oppressed and economically deprived (1 Cor. 16:3; 2 Cor. 8:19). However, there is no reason to see it being used here in this technical sense, as Paul says that the contribution is for the poor among the saints. Some believe the Jerusalem church was vulnerable to famine conditions. It has been argued that its members had used their resources to support those believers who had stayed on in Jerusalem after Pentecost. They remained in the city in order to take advantage of apostolic instruction before returning to their homes throughout the Empire. While there was clearly great generosity, it is probably claiming too much to say that it left the church members impoverished and without the means of coping with famine. The poor are found in every society, and the church in Jerusalem would have been no exception.

Following the council of Jerusalem (Acts 15), the apostles urged Paul not to forget the poor, and this request brought ready agreement (Gal. 2:10). 2 Corinthians 8:8–15 refers to the same collection as mentioned in Galatians, and shows his ability to manage this important project, and his lack of embarrassment in asking for money in order to care for those in need. While he was unabashed in seeking support for others, he was reluctant to seek it for himself (Phil. 4:10–20), preferring to tent make (Acts 18:3) rather than be misunderstood (1 Cor. 9:1–18). The mention of Macedonia and Achaia indicates how far from Jerusalem the contributors lived and how Paul taught the Gentile churches of their debt to the Jewish believers as the ones who brought them the good news.

It is clear from the request made by the apostles at Jerusalem—and the willing practice of Paul—that caring for the physical needs of people is not a deviation from gospel ministry but a vital expression of it. It is a sad situation when professing Christians are reluctant to support the practical relief of the destitute while priding themselves on being disciples of Christ. It should be noted that Paul's efforts are directed toward the poor. That does not exclude compassion toward the unbelieving poor, but it underscores the need of the believing poor, who often suffered more because they were believers.

15:27 For they were pleased to do it, and indeed they owe it to them. For if the Gentiles have come to share in their spiritual blessings, they ought also to be of service to them in material blessings.

The willing response of the Gentile churches must have been a great encouragement to Paul in his desire to see the two sections of the church learn to respect and accept each other. Their response flowed from the sense of debt they had to the Jewish believing community. Paul spells out what that debt is: they have shared in the spiritual blessings of the old covenant community. This is not to say, of course, that the Jewish nation had been delighted by the way God had blessed the Gentiles through the gospel of Christ—as we have seen most Jews deeply resented them for claiming to be the true inheritors of the Abrahamic blessings.

Paul's comment about the Gentiles having shared 'in their spiritual blessings' refers either to the nation of Israel or to the remnant community (the Jewish church). The nation had been given the promises and borne the hope of their fulfilment throughout long years of suffering. Tragically, she had rejected the one to whom these promises pointed. The remnant, however, recognized and welcomed the bringer of salvation (Luke 2:25–38), and had accepted its mission to make his salvation known to the nations. However, while the Gentiles owed a great debt to the Jewish remnant there are good grounds for saying they also owed one to the entire Jewish nation, for it was used by God as an incubator for the gospel promises. Without Jewish history and the theology that grew out of it, it would be impossible to understand the message of God's redeeming activity for creation.

15:28 When therefore I have completed this and have delivered to them what has been collected, I will leave for Spain by way of you.

Although *karpos* ('fruit') is in the text, the ESV translation has omitted a reference to it; NIVTM has, 'So after I have completed this task and have made sure that they have received this fruit, I will go to Spain and visit you on the way'. The language of receiving the fruit is unusual, some suggesting that it has ceremonial roots. If this is correct, it suggests that Paul anticipated a formal handing over of the gift for the poor in Jerusalem. This fulfilled the promise he had made to the Jerusalem Council as recorded in Galatians 2:10. No doubt Paul hoped the gift would be presented in a community setting, with the consequent public recognition in Jerusalem of the care and concern of distant Gentile believers. Paul was prepared to use every means to get across the message of unity between believing Jews and Gentiles. This gave the gift a higher priority, which is probably why he wanted to take it himself rather than send it with others.

As we have seen, Paul expected to follow the visit to Jerusalem with a visit to Rome on his way to Spain, where he planned to start church-planting. We know from the Acts of the Apostles that his pathway was going to be anything but straightforward. In Jerusalem, he was beaten and almost lynched, then put on trial before the high priest and successive Roman governors. He endured a dangerous and eventful voyage to Rome where he was detained under house-arrest for two years, awaiting his appeal to Caesar. Did Paul have any inkling of what was going to happen to him as he approached Jerusalem? Certainly, he was aware of dangers facing him there (Rom. 15:31) and was warned by Agabus of his impending imprisonment (Acts 20– 21). How different the cause of the gospel would have been if the early believers had risk-assessed their missionary endeavours and not accepted the challenge to take the gospel to the furthest corners of the earth.

15:29 I know that when I come to you I will come in the fullness of the blessing of Christ.

Paul's assurance that he would visit the Roman church 'in the fullness of the blessing of Christ' could express one of the following understandings.

First, Paul did not consider himself to be unique, bringing to the believers something they did not already have. He anticipated he would receive from them the same gospel fellowship he would bring. He expresses his confidence that believers experience the presence of Christ when they meet together (Matt. 18:20). He had verbalized the same expectation of Christ's presence in another setting when he instructed the Corinthians to gather in the name of Jesus in order to deliver one of their members over to Satan (1 Cor. 5:4). As Paul would not be with them, it is clear that he did not see his presence to be necessary for Christ to be with them. The heritage of believers meeting together with their Lord is still the privilege and inheritance of the church today.

A second possible understanding of the verse is that Paul thought he was bringing blessings that only an apostle could impart. Clearly, the apostles had a unique authority in the early church, and the visit from such a representative of Christ would inevitably be anticipated with excitement over the blessing that would accompany such a visit.

15:30 I appeal to you, brothers, by our Lord Jesus Christ and by the love of the Spirit, to strive together with me in your prayers to God on my behalf,

Here, we have mention of the three members of the Godhead who the church would later describe as 'the Trinity'. Just how Paul intended this statement to be understood is not clear. What is generally agreed by scholars is that the understanding of God as triune developed slowly in the thinking of the early church and that too much weight must not be placed on early texts.

However, despite the prevailing opinion, a case can be made that the church used Trinitarian language earlier than is supposed. It has been argued that the Christology of the New Testament is not titular (that is, understanding who Christ is by analysing his titles such as Son of Man, Last Adam, and Messiah) as previous generations had supposed, but functional (understanding Christ's person by focusing on what he has achieved). If this is correct, there is reason to believe the church grasped the uniqueness of Christ early in her existence. She certainly recognized his death as the means by which God had redeemed his creation which is something no creature could do (Rom. 8:18–25).

Paul's request for prayer gives some insight into the agony he went through in his attempts to reconcile the two wings of the church. His appeal to 'strive together' indicates his concern. He knew his life was in constant danger because of the intense hatred some Jews had towards him. He covets the prayers of the Roman believers that the visit he was about to make might achieve the goal for which he longed. The danger Paul was willing to face in going up to Jerusalem shows his concern for the Jewish believers and the unity of the church. This concern, no doubt, expresses his knowledge that Christ had specifically prayed for the unity of his people (John 17:11). Divisions amongst believers ought to be the very last option, not the first knee-jerk reaction, to disagreements.

15:31 that I may be delivered from the unbelievers in Judea, and that my service for Jerusalem may be acceptable to the saints,

Romans 15: When All Is Going Well

We can only imagine the intensity of feeling that built up as Paul approached Jerusalem. He was urged by Christians on his journey not to put himself in danger (Acts 21:7–14). The prophecy given by Agabus (Acts 21:10–11) would have taken all hope of a peaceful outcome from his heart, but he still continued with his visit. Paul was putting his life on the line for the sake of achieving a better understanding and acceptance of the Gentile believers by the Jewish church. There can only be one reason for such commitment: Paul believed that what he was doing was of vital importance for the work of the gospel. Such an example must surely condemn us for taking our unity in Christ so lightly!

Despite the fact that this was such an important issue for Paul, the book of Acts says very little about whether he achieved his goal. He appears to have presented the collection, or been in the act of presenting it, when Jews from Asia caused a riot and dragged him from the Temple (Acts 24:17; 21:27). The relative silence on this point in Acts suggests this aspect of the visit was not successful (possibly Luke chose to avoid mentioning it in case it caused distress). If this is so, Paul had again experienced what many pastors repeatedly encounter—God's people, while claiming to have the highest ideals as their motives, undo the work of God by showing intolerance to other believers. Of course, Paul also expresses the opposite concern. He is aware how some people can become dictatorial and harsh in their role as leaders (Acts 20:26–27).

15:32 so that by God's will I may come to you with joy and be refreshed in your company.

Paul was to visit the Roman believers soon, but in circumstances he did not envisage when writing these words. A short time later, he was arrested (Acts 24–27), detained in prison, and went through several trials in Judea and Caesarea. Having asserted his legal rights as a Roman citizen, Paul was taken to Rome under escort. Here, he was given great opportunities to witness while under house arrest, awaiting Caesar's pleasure to try him (Acts 28:16–31).

15:33 May the God of peace be with you all. Amen.

The simplicity of these words cannot relate the profoundness of the reality. Paul prays for the Roman believers to share in what he has experienced for himself (Phil. 4:9). Soon, these very people were going to need to know the God of peace as a living reality. Some would be burned to death as human torches in the gardens of Nero for his amusement, while others were to entertain the depraved Roman crowds by having their limbs ripped apart by lions in the Colosseum. This small Christian community had no idea that its testimony would inspire countless millions of Christians to be faithful to Christ, some even to death.

There has been ongoing debate among scholars as to whether Paul actually concluded his letter at this point—they see chapter 16 as not being part of the original letter to the Romans but added at a later date. Those who favour this displacement theory claim the doxology at the end of chapter 16 was originally at the end of chapter 15. This is supported by a manuscript dated around 200 A.D. Other manuscripts have the doxology after Romans 15:33 and Romans 14:23, while two ninth century manuscripts and a derivative one from the fourteenth century omit it entirely. One of these manuscripts does, however, leave a space at the end of chapter 14, suggesting there may have been something that the copyist intended to insert. However, not all scholars accept this interpretation. Indeed, there is a growing minority that accepts the location of chapter 16 as it is in most manuscripts.

Further Study: Questions for Romans 15

1. What is the great example that should motivate Christian behaviour?

2. What is the relevance of the Scriptures for the church?

3. What does the fact that Christ became a servant imply?

4. According to this chapter, what is the purpose of the believer's life?

5. Why is it important not to pass judgment on others?

6. Is ones claim to liberty the final word in behaviour? If not, why not?

7. What should Christians strive together for?

Romans 16: Catching up on Friends

Introduction

Paul wishes to send greetings to a list of Roman believers, even though it is thought by most that he had not founded or visited the church in Rome. For this reason, some doubt that this chapter belongs with this letter, but to another letter that had been sent to a church whose members were well known to Paul.

There is, however, evidence suggesting that its location is not misplaced. When writing to churches he had founded, it was unusual for Paul to mention people by name. For example, there is a notable absence of names in his letters to the Corinthians, Galatians, Philippians, and Thessalonians, churches which Paul had planted on his missionary journeys. The nearest passage that is similar to the ending of the letter to the Romans is Colossians 4:15–17. These are verses in the concluding chapter of a letter written by Paul to a church he had not founded (see Col. 1:6–8). So, it is a possible pattern Paul which adopts; not giving personalized greetings to churches he planted but giving them to churches founded by others. If this evidence is reliable, it would be fair to conclude that Paul did not found the church in Rome because he greeted almost thirty named believers at the close of his letter.

What does Paul hope to achieve with this familiarity? Perhaps he wants to establish a relationship with them that would profit his mission to Spain, or perhaps he simply has the well-being of the congregation in mind. The names suggest that most of the believers greeted by Paul are Jews. Indeed, some of them have been key workers with him in past missionary endeavours. In writing to a church which was in danger of rejecting its Jewish roots, Paul may be anxious for the Gentile believers to welcome and honour his kinsmen; after all, some of them had come to Christ before him and had ministered to his needs with dedication and kindness (one is described as 'a mother' to him). A positive response to the commendations would help to prevent the threatened rift between the two sections of the Roman congregation.

His appeal is similar to the one made to the Gentile churches to provide for the needs of the saints in Jerusalem. In Rome, however, the need among the Jews is not merely practical but emotional, social, and spiritual. The Roman Gentiles are to care for these worthy representatives of the Jewish believing community, and, as an expression of their compassion, they are to share their material prosperity with those who had shared their spiritual heritage (hinted at in Romans 15:26–27).

Since it is acknowledged by most that Paul had yet to visit Rome, how did he know the people he greeted in Romans 16:3–16? We know that Claudius, the Roman Emperor, had expelled the Jews from the city in 49 or 50 A.D. This was the reason Priscilla and Aquila were absent from Rome and in Corinth (Acts 18:1–3). They were able to go back to Rome after the death of Claudius. No doubt before their return, Priscilla and Aquila would have talked with Paul about the key believers in Rome as well as the problems they faced within, and outside, their congregations.

If we accept this reasoning about Priscilla and Aquila, we must accept the possibility that Paul met other believing Jews from Rome in his travels, drawing close to many of them. Many of these would have returned to Rome—along with Priscilla and Aquila—when the way became clear. Others would have gone to Rome for different reasons. Phoebe, from the church in Cenchrea, seems to have had financial independence and was able to travel for personal or business reasons. It is possible that she was the one entrusted to deliver Paul's letter to the Roman believers.

Another possible explanation for Paul's knowledge of the congregation is that his parents lived in Rome before moving to Tarsus, leaving behind family in the city. If this is what happened, Paul's wider family would be a source of information about the church in Rome.

16:1 I commend to you our sister Phoebe, a servant of the church at Cenchreae,

Romans 16: Catching Up on Friends

Cenchreae (or Cenchrea) is one of the two ports of Corinth, the capital city of Southern Greece (formerly the Roman province of Achaia). As Corinth is thought by many to be the place where Paul wrote his letter (see below on 16:23), it is likely that Phoebe is its bearer. The following verse suggests she was a wealthy woman, so it is possible that she was visiting Rome for business reasons, and that she agreed to deliver Paul's letter for him. Her background was not Jewish—as indicated by her pagan name. Possibly, she was one of those converted through Paul's Corinthian mission.

While some translate *diakonos* as 'deaconess' many doubt Paul intended to suggest that Phoebe held an office in the Cenchrean church. It is possible the term was used to denote a function rather than an office. If this is correct, then the term indicates that she functioned as a servant of the church, giving support to those in need. Such a functional significance of diakonos must equally apply to male deacons, their description not being that of an office in the church but of a ministry they exercise on the church's behalf.

16:2 that you may welcome her in the Lord in a way worthy of the saints, and help her in whatever she may need from you, for she has been a patron of many and of myself as well.

Paul's commendation of Phoebe is a model of diplomacy. He reminds the Romans of their status. They are saints, the people of God. Just as God welcomes people into his family, they are to welcome Phoebe. Paul asks them to help her in whatever way she needed while she fulfilled the reason for her visit to Rome. This could be by giving spiritual support as well as the practical help of hospitality—something Paul has already exhorted the believers to do (Rom. 12:13).

The affection shown to Phoebe by her home church in Cenchrea is obvious from Paul's commendation. She had helped many, including Paul himself. Such selfless people are vital for the life of the church, for they exercise an essential pastoral gift for the Christian community. Pastoral ministry is not the exclusive ministry of the 'pastor' as the Spirit gives this gift more widely in the church for the blessing of God's people.

16:3 Greet Prisca and Aquila, my fellow workers in Christ Jesus,

Like Paul, Priscilla and Aquila were Jews with Roman names. They had settled in Corinth after being expelled from Rome under the edict made by the Emperor Claudius. This affected all the resident Jews in the city. In Corinth, Priscilla and Aquila met Paul, who worked with them for eighteen months. It was during this time that he established the Corinthian church (Acts 18:1–3).

After this, Priscilla and Aquila moved with Paul to Ephesus (Acts 18:18). Here, they used their gift of hospitality in opening up their home to Apollos, who had come to the city. They exercised a pastoral gift too, taking time to help him have a clearer understanding of the way of God (Acts 18:24–26).

In time, they returned to Rome where they opened up their home to believers again. If it is true that Paul had never visited the city, Priscilla and Aquila would have been vitally important as ambassadors for him, telling the church of all they had observed of the apostle as they worked alongside him. No doubt, having returned to Rome, they continued in their trade of tent making.

After living in Rome for a period of time, the couple travelled back to Ephesus, opening up their home to all the believers. The Ephesian church met there under the oversight of Timothy (1 Cor. 16:19; 2 Tim. 4:19). Whenever the couple are named, Priscilla is normally mentioned before her husband (Acts 18:18, 26; 2 Tim. 4:19).[14] This order is unusual in ancient writings, perhaps implying her greater contribution to Christian work or her higher social status.

16:4 who risked their necks for my life, to whom not only I give thanks but all the churches of the Gentiles give thanks as well.

We have partial knowledge of the sufferings Paul experienced in Corinth and Ephesus—the two cities where we know he worked alongside Priscilla and Aquila. Indeed, most of them are mentioned incidentally when Paul felt the need to give his credentials as an apostle (Acts 19:29–40; 1 Cor. 15:30; 2 Cor. 11:23b–33). We have no details of how Priscilla and Aquila risked their lives,

---

[14] For the reverse order, see Acts 18:2; 1 Cor. 16:19.

but it is evident from what Paul writes that their devotion to him and to other believers was widely known and highly valued.

The reference to 'the churches of the Gentiles' has led some to suggest that there were Gentile churches meeting separately from Jewish churches. However, in the light of Paul's insistence on the acceptance of each group by the other, it does not seem likely that he would encourage separate congregations.

16:5 Greet also the church in their house. Greet my beloved Epaenetus, who was the first convert to Christ in Asia.

Again, we find Priscilla and Aquila giving hospitality, for a church is meeting in their home in Rome. There were probably a number of 'house churches' scattered throughout Rome (Rom. 16:14–15), in keeping with the common practice of the early church (Col. 4:15; Philemon 2). Church buildings did not become common until the fourth century. It is quite possible that the believers in Rome continued to meet in the synagogue as well, but their unique identity as followers of Christ would eventually bring this relationship to an end.

Epaenetus is greeted with warm affection. Paul describes him literally as 'the first- fruits of Asia'. Again, Paul uses Paschal (Passover) imagery—the first fruits being brought from the fields three days after the sacrifice of the Passover lamb (Lev. 23:11). It was not the harvest crop that Paul had in mind but the Levitical priesthood (evidenced by references to priestly ministry in Romans 12:1–2; 15:16), which was given as a token that God claimed not only the firstborn but the whole nation. Epaenetus was the first from that region who had become a priest of the new covenant.

16:6 Greet Mary, who has worked hard for you.

Mary is an unknown member of the Roman church. We do not know if she was Jewish or Gentile, for her name was common in both communities. She is representative of the millions whose devotion and service are the backbone of the churches to which they belong. The reference to her having worked very hard for the Roman believers suggests she had laboured with

Paul and had rendered a service to the apostolic team on behalf of the Roman church (cf. Phil. 2:25–30).

16:7 Greet Andronicus and Junia, my kinsmen and my fellow prisoners. They are well known to the apostles, and they were in Christ before me.

Andronicus and Junia appear to have been a married couple, the latter name being a common Roman name for women. The use of the term 'kinsmen' (some translations have 'relatives') reveals either that these two people were part of Paul's extended family or that they were fellow Jews whom he knew well.

Many are reluctant to concede that Paul may have had relatives in Rome, possibly due to the prevailing opinion that Paul had neither visited nor founded its church. He certainly had family who were sympathetic to him as a Christian (Acts 23:12– 22), and while it is true that he was from Tarsus (in modern Turkey), there is no reason why Christian members of his family could not have travelled west to settle in Rome. Indeed, as has been mentioned, his immediate family may well have been citizens of the city of Rome, leaving the wider family in order to settle in Tarsus where Paul was raised.

Andronicus and Junia were 'well known to the apostles'—the term 'apostle' does not necessarily always refer to the twelve, for the term was used in a wider sense in the early church (Acts 14:4, 14; 2 Cor. 11:13–15; 12:11ff.). We can deduce wives accompanied their husbands on their missions and were recognised for their work among the apostles. God's calling, equipping, and employing of married women in the service of the church should perhaps be revisited by some. Andronicus and Junia were 'in Christ' before Paul, being part of the original Jewish church. They had worked and suffered alongside Paul as he took the gospel to the Gentiles. We have seen throughout the letter that Paul regularly uses the expressions 'in the Lord' or 'in Christ'. These phrases speak of membership of the Messianic community, which exists because the Spirit has united believers with Christ in his death.

The mention of a second couple to whom Paul sends greetings hints at the importance of married couples to the early church's missionary endeavours.

Romans 16: Catching Up on Friends

It was not only that they gave each other support (1 Cor. 9:5)—no doubt compensating for each other's weaknesses—but they were able to work in situations where a single person, such as Paul, could not operate or would have difficulty. Of course, there are also ministries that single people can do that married people would find equally very difficult. Sadly, some married believers neglect the fact that they are commanded first to give themselves to their family responsibilities. In failing to do this they dishonour Christ rather than glorify him. Single people do not have this particular distraction and are able to engage in work that married people should not even consider (1 Cor. 7:32–35). Thus, both the married and the single have their own special gifting that expresses the will of the same Lord who gives gifts to his people as he wills.

16:8 Greet Ampliatus, my beloved in the Lord. Greet Urbanus, our fellow worker in Christ, and my beloved Stachys.

Ampliatus is a slave name. We can only guess how Paul knew a slave living in Rome. It is possible that his master, along with his household, had moved to Rome, or that his freedom had been gained through a process of manumission, leaving him free to travel. Paul's affection for Ampliatus is unashamedly expressed! It must have been a great encouragement to slaves in the early church to know they were valued by their Christian brothers and sisters. Loving people for their own sakes rather than for their status or influence is an important testimony to the power of the gospel and the love of Christ.

16:9 Greet Urbanus, our fellow worker in Christ, and my beloved Stachys.

Urbanus is another member of the Roman congregation with a slave name. The status of being a fellow-worker in Christ must have given dignity and self-respect to one who Virgil referred to as nothing other than a talking tool. It would seem that Urbanus worked alongside Paul in his missionary endeavours. We know nothing of Stachys other than that Paul regarded him with affection. Indeed, Paul describes him as 'beloved,' which suggests that he knew Stachys very well.

16:10 Greet Apelles, who is approved in Christ. Greet those who belong to the family of Aristobulus.

The reference to Apelles's testing suggests that he has endured something beyond the normal. We have no other reference to him, but no doubt such a commendation must have encouraged him greatly. Aristobulus might be the grandson of Herod the Great, who was a friend of the Emperor, Claudius. While Paul makes no mention that Aristobulus had become a Christian, the reference suggests that a number of his household had become believers.

16:11 Greet my kinsman Herodion. Greet those in the Lord who belong to the family of Narcissus.

Again, we have Paul referring to a kinsman (see comment on v. 7), but the greeting gives little away about Herodion. Indeed, the virtual silence supports the view that he was a blood relative as there seems little point in Paul isolating one of his many countrymen in Rome in order to send such a brief greeting.

Narcissus is not greeted personally, so he is probably head of a household with believing members. It is of interest that Narcissus was the name of a famous person in Rome in the middle of first century CE. He was a freed man who had risen to an exalted position under Claudius. This aroused great jealousy in many Romans citizens, to the point that, after Claudius' death, he was provoked to commit suicide. If this Narcissus is the man referred to in this verse (and many assume he is), his untimely death would have put the Christians in his household in a very dangerous position through association.

16:12 Greet those workers in the Lord, Tryphaena and Tryphosa. Greet the beloved Persis, who has worked hard in the Lord.

The warmth and appreciation of these greetings cannot be ignored by those who claim that Paul was a misogynist. Whatever one thinks about Paul's statements concerning the subjection of women to their husbands, it is clear that he had a high regard for his female colleagues. Indeed, it could perhaps be argued that the reason many women carry far too many responsibilities in churches and on the mission field is because men have not been equally as willing to respond to the challenge.

16:13 Greet Rufus, chosen in the Lord; also his mother, who has been a mother to me as well.

Rufus is a Latin name. Since it is possible that the gospel of Mark was written for the Roman church, the Rufus mentioned in Mark 15:21—a son of Simon of Cyrene— may be the same person.

The greeting gives us an insight into the support that Paul received from the mother of Rufus. Possibly, his recollection goes back to when Rufus and his mother joined his apostolic band. Perhaps she met his needs as a mother would have done, caring for her own son at the same time. This would have been very important to Paul as, unlike other apostles, he did not have a wife to help him. Being welcomed into a Christian family is a source of joy and comfort for thousands of unmarried Christian workers. Such hospitality is a ministry that enriches many single people (Acts 18:1– 3).

If the identification of Rufus as a son of Simon of Cyrene is correct, it follows that his mother was from Cyrene. It seems likely that, following the death of Simon, Rufus and his mother left Cyrene and served Paul's apostolic band in its missionary work. Notice the presence of Lucius from Cyrene in the fledgling church in Antioch (Acts 13:1). At some point after the death of Claudius, Rufus and his mother (who were Jews) moved to Rome, where they became part of the body of believers.

16:14 Greet Asyncritus, Phlegon, Hermes, Patrobas, Hermas, and the brothers who are with them.

Again, we have a list of unknown acquaintances. Both Origen and Eusebius link Hermes with the early Christian writing, 'The Shepherd', although this identification has been contested by modern scholarship.

16:15 Greet Philologus, Julia, Nereus and his sister, and Olympas, and all the saints who are with them.

Extending the greeting to 'all the saints who are with them' suggests that the named believers are the heads of Christian households. Perhaps they are the leaders of house-church groups in Rome.

16:16 Greet one another with a holy kiss. All the churches of Christ greet you.

A kiss had long been a form of greeting by men in the ancient world (Luke 7:45). Paul's exhortation to the believers in Rome was that it should be a holy kiss. This probably means that they should greet one another as holy in the Lord, as fellow members of the new covenant community. They were to welcome one another, extending the acceptance that Christ had given them. When Paul wrote to believers in Corinth and Thessalonica, he exhorted the believers similarly (1 Cor. 16:20; 2 Cor. 13:12; 1 Thess. 5:26), while Peter urged the Jews of the dispersion to greet each other with a kiss of love (1 Pet. 5:14). In whatever culture we find ourselves, the practice of greeting fellow believers ought to be a joyous, welcoming, and encouraging one. Paul sends the greetings of the churches to the believers. As the recognized apostle to the Gentiles, he was able to represent churches even though he had not founded or had contact with them all.

16:17 I appeal to you, brothers, to watch out for those who cause divisions and create obstacles contrary to the doctrine that you have been taught; avoid them.

This sudden denunciation of some of the congregation seems odd in view of the appeal Paul has made in chapter 14 that the Roman believers accept one another. This is one of the reasons that some have claimed the chapter does not belong to the original Roman letter but is part of another letter written by Paul.

However, such a closing exhortation to believers to be on their guard is found in some of Paul's other letters (cf. 1 Cor. 16:22; Gal. 6:12ff.; Phil. 3:18ff.), suggesting that contention for the gospel went on within congregations as well as outside. It is not clear what specific problem among the Roman believers Paul had in mind— perhaps he was thinking of Jews who were trying to persuade the Gentiles they needed to be circumcised, or of other groups who were rejecting his exhortation to accept one another. If the latter case is true, Paul urges the church to reject those who are jeopardizing the unity of the believing community. A similar exhortation is found in 2 Corinthians 6:14–18. Traditionally, this passage has been seen to instruct believers not to marry unbelievers. However, in recent years it has been recognized that Paul is telling the Roman Christians to keep separate from those who seek to usurp authority in the church and nullify his influence. If this conclusion is correct, then the two passages are addressing the same issue.

16:18 For such persons do not serve our Lord Christ, but their own appetites, and by smooth talk and flattery they deceive the hearts of the naive.

It is better to translate koilia as 'bellies' rather than 'appetites'. It would seem from such a direct reference to food that the agitators are those who are contending for their right to eat what they wish. If this is correct, they could be the Jews who see no harm in eating meat sacrificed to idols, or in putting their freedom ahead of serving the weaker believers. Their teaching is right theologically, but it has been taken outside of the dimension of love and it has become motivated by a desire to exercise rights.

The problem with identifying 'such persons' as Judaizers is there is no suggestion they used flattery. Their belief that they conformed to the law would suggest that their argument would be direct and confrontational. However, it might be that they had developed a more tactful approach to win over the Gentiles—this seems to have been happening in Colossae (Col. 2:8, 16–18). The identification of the various groups that Paul contended with is an ongoing problem for scholarship.

16:19 For your obedience is known to all, so that I rejoice over you, but I want you to be wise as to what is good and innocent as to what is evil.

The news of the Roman believers' obedience was spoken of in other churches. It must have been a real encouragement to others to know there was such a congregation of believers in the capital city of the empire. The response of the faithful in Rome is not described as belief but obedience (Rom. 1:5). This does not deny that the message received was about faith in God, but obedience to the message believed was considered by Paul to be a hallmark of faith. As a result of their response, Paul experienced overflowing joy that God's word was transforming lives in Rome.

However, despite his joy, Paul writes that he wants the believers to be spiritually mature, wise, and innocent. He wants them to recognize instinctively what God is doing; in other words, he wants them to be wise about what is good. Rather than having personal experience of evil, he wants them to be ignorant of it (Phil. 4:8). This desired innocence is underlined in the next verse, where reference is made to the serpent who beguiled Adam and Eve. Paul is concerned that the innocence of the Roman believers might leave them vulnerable to smooth talkers.

16:20 The God of peace will soon crush Satan under your feet. The grace of our Lord Jesus Christ be with you.

The Greek has 'the Satan' and this term is found elsewhere in the New Testament (Matt. 12:26; Luke 10:18). But what does Paul mean by this? He could be referring to those he sees as the servants of Satan, who seek to undermine the work of God among the Romans. If this is correct, then Paul expects these troublemakers to come under some form of judgment.

The expression, 'the grace of our Lord Jesus Christ', is used regularly by Paul. It denotes the outpouring of God's free love through his Son upon his people. Grace is more than love. It speaks of the love between those in a covenant relationship— one in which they have vowed to protect and care for each other. It is best illustrated by the love between a husband and wife, which excludes all others and sacrificially strives for each other's blessing and happiness. Paul is praying the Roman believers will be conscious of this unconditional love with which God has blessed them. It is a love that burns in a believer's heart, transforming everything.

16:21 Timothy, my fellow worker, greets you; so do Lucius and Jason and Sosipater, my kinsmen.

Paul concludes his own greetings so that he might convey those of his companions. Timothy had worked with Paul from his earliest days in the faith (Acts 16:1–4; 17:14ff.; 18:5; 19:22; 20:4ff.; 1 Cor. 16:10ff.; Phil. 2:19–24; 1 Thess. 3:2, 6). He was clearly a key worker and is regularly mentioned by Paul in his letters.

For comment on Paul's kinsmen (NIVTM 'relatives') see the discussion on Romans 16:7. While Lucius may be a variant of Luke, the name does not refer to the Gentile physician, as Lucius was a Jew, being a kinsman or relative of Paul. It is possible that he is Lucius of Cyrene, who worked alongside Paul as one of the band of prophets and teachers in the church in

Antioch (Acts 13:1). This Lucius had come to Antioch as a result of the persecution following Stephen's death, and had spoken to the Jews and Greeks in the city about the Lord Jesus. Despite this serious situation, Lucius, and those with him, knew great blessing on their ministries and the church expanded significantly. As a result, Paul was brought to Antioch to help Barnabas teach the new believers (Acts 11:19–26).

Jason may be the resident of Thessalonica who gave hospitality to Paul when he stayed there for three weeks. Because Paul took the opportunity each Sabbath day to explain the Scriptures regarding Jesus in the synagogue, jealous Jews precipitated a riot, subjecting Jason to frightening harassment (Acts 17:1–9).

16:22 I Tertius, who wrote this letter, greet you in the Lord.

It appears that at this point in the dictation of the letter, Paul allowed Tertius to send his own greeting to the believers in Rome. It seems he regularly dictated his letters, possibly necessitated by failing eyesight or another condition that made writing difficult (Gal. 6:11; Philemon 19), however this may not have been the case, for many in Paul's day commonly enjoyed the support of a secretary or an amanuensis.

16:23 Gaius, who is host to me and to the whole church, greets you. Erastus, the city treasurer, and our brother Quartus, greet you.

Not only did Gaius give hospitality to Paul but his home seems to have been used by the church for its gatherings. His name was Roman, and he was obviously wealthy, having a home large enough for the 'whole church' to meet in and 'enjoy'.

It is normally accepted that Paul's letter was written in Corinth, so it is assumed this was Gaius's home city. In the letter to Timothy, Paul mentions 'Erastus stayed (or remained) in Corinth' (2 Tim. 4:22). The fact that greetings are sent from Erastus in our verse alongside those of Gaius, reinforces the idea that Gaius was indeed living in Corinth. Erastus was the city's treasurer (or steward), and this suggests that he enjoyed a comfortable standard of living. Clearly, there were some in the Corinthian church who were among the 'elite' of society (implied by 1 Cor. 1:26). There is another reference to an Erastus. He is described as one of Paul's helpers who was sent by Paul to Macedonia with Timothy (Acts 19:22). These two helpers were sent ahead to prepare the churches' collections for the needy saints in Jerusalem. If this Erastus is the Erastus of Romans 16, he would fulfil this role superbly, being the treasurer of Corinth! Quartus is someone about whom we have no other information. One can assume he was a believer, perhaps known to the Roman believers.

16:24 May the grace of our Lord Jesus Christ be with all of you. Amen. (NIVTM — footnote)

The ESV omits this verse which is found in a range of Greek texts. It is included in (amongst others) the New American Standard Bible, The American Standard Version and The King James Version. The Greek manuscripts that omit the statement tend to be the older manuscripts, and because of this some translators prefer to omit it from their translation. I offer the following comments without intending to endorse any particular textual view or attempt to explain to the reader the statement's omission from the ESV. Having greeted those he knows or has heard of in Rome, Paul concludes his letter by reminding his readers that the message keeping them is the same as that preached to the Old Testament covenant community. It has, at last, been brought to completion, for the message of God's grace is being preached to all nations. This was Israel's calling and service. She was to bring the nations into the community that was set apart to be the bride of God.

16:25 Now to him who is able to strengthen you according to my gospel and the preaching of Jesus Christ, according to the revelation of the mystery that was kept secret for long ages

This verse begins with what is known as the closing formula. The conclusions found throughout Paul's letters have been carefully studied and found to reflect the theology found earlier in the letter. In this conclusion, Paul speaks of the gospel having gone to the nations. This is a clear reflection of the theme is argued for in chapter 4—that Abraham is the father of many nations.

Since the gospel is not only about saving people from God's judgment but also about making them into the people God wants them to be, the term stērizō ('strengthen') is used. The goal of the gospel is to bring people into the kingdom of God where they will love and serve him as they live holy lives.

When Paul says, 'my gospel,' he is not suggesting that his gospel is any different from that of the other apostles. All of the indications are that he received the content of his gospel from those who had gone before. He was never hesitant to acknowledge his dependency. By referring to 'my gospel,' he echoes his calling to apply the good news to the Gentiles. Paul had worked hard to keep them from having to accept the normal Jewish initiation rites of circumcision and dietary laws. In doing this, he had insisted the Gentiles were not obliged to become Jews in order to be reconciled with God. This defence of Gentile liberty made many Jews—even believers—suspicious of him. Some hated Paul so much for what they considered was betrayal of true faith that they sought to kill him. It is this distinctive application of the good news that enables Paul to speak of 'my gospel'. Thus, his reference to not having received his gospel from men (Gal. 1:12) probably means that he came to see, without any human aid, that the Gentile believers were not to be circumcised and that on this issue hung the essence of the gospel; it is acceptance without the works of the law.

The proclamation of the gospel revealed the 'mystery'. This technical term denotes that the purposes of God cannot be known other than when God reveals them. God's purpose is to bring his creation back under his control, having redeemed it through the death of his Son. In this new creation there is no longer a division between Jew and Gentile as both are united in Christ to form one new man. This act of redemption glorifies God before the whole of his creation and extends his honour. In turn, this leads to the chief end of humanity—the worship of their Creator.

16:26 but has now been disclosed and through the prophetic writings has been made known to all nations, according to the command of the eternal God, to bring about the obedience of faith

Paul cannot separate the preaching of the gospel and, by implication, its content from the prophetic writings. This was not the result of human planning but of the command of God. It is no wonder that the gospel is sometimes called 'the gospel of God'.

16:27 to the only wise God be glory forevermore through Jesus Christ! Amen.

It is fitting that Paul finishes his letter in this way, for it was the purpose of his life. He sought through everything he did to honour God and bring others to love and serve him. This is what the letter to the Roman believers is about. He has shown them they are a redeemed people with an obligation to live no longer for their own pleasure or enjoyment. Indeed, they were not even to live as model citizens of the Roman Empire but as members of the kingdom of God. Their calling was to submit themselves to what God required and to seek his glory.

Paul says that God is glorified through Christ Jesus. This is not only saying that Christ has glorified God, but that God is honoured and glorified as we embrace what he has done through Christ's death and resurrection and to live in light of the claims made by his Son.

This closing section gathers together the themes from the earlier part of the letter and brings them to a glorious conclusion.

Paul's purposes have been to encourage the Roman church and to persuade her believers of the certainty concerning their future. This will prove to be essential, for days will soon unfold when the might and pride of the Roman Empire will be unleashed against her in an attempt to wipe the Christian community from the face of the earth. Recalling Paul's words will bring unspeakable comfort to thousands of Christians in the city and empire of Rome. Yet, while many will lose their lives, others will be attracted to the Christ as a result of witnessing willing deaths. Instead of the church dying, it will grow, and eventually see the demise of the decadent state.

The historic realities of suffering and the seemingly meaningless triumph of evil over good must make us wary of interpreting Paul's statements about suffering in too simplistic a way. Paul did not write these words to assure those who are at ease in this life that God would look after their interests.

He wrote to those who were about to be deprived of the most basic human rights, and who knew they could lose everything they owned, including life itself. For these Roman believers—whose testimony in the face of appalling suffering will win the admiration of the most sceptical of historians—Paul's words will prove to be the comfort that enables them to see a far greater treasure and to strive for a far more glorious citizenship. They will, indeed, prove the promise that God has given them 'all things' (Rom. 9:28–39).

And so, we come to an end of commenting on the letter to the Romans. While it is a letter to a particular church, written two thousand years ago, the church of today needs its message no less.

May we be helped to live out the life of Christ in the twenty first century, for God's honour and glory!

Further Study: Questions for Romans 16

1. Find how many of Paul's relatives are mentioned in the chapter.

2. List the people Paul depended on and identify how they supported him.

3. List the terms that are strongly relational in the chapter.

Bibliography

Agersnap, S., *Baptism and the New Life: A Study of Romans 6.1–14* (Oakville, CT: Aarhus University Press, 1999)

Albright, W. F., and Mann, C. S., *Matthew* (Garden City, NY: Doubleday, 1971) Aletti, J. N., 'L'argumentation Paulinienne en Rm. 9.' *Bib* 68 (1987), pp. 41–56

Aletti, J. N., 'Rm. 7:7–25 encore une fois: enjeux et propositions', *NTS* 48:3 (2002), pp. 358–76

Allison, D. C. Jr., 'Jesus and the Covenant', *JSNT* 29 (1987), pp. 57–78.

Anderson, B. W., *The Eighth Century Prophets: Amos, Hosea, Isaiah, Micah, Proclamation Commentaries* (Philadelphia: Fortress Press, 1978)

Anderson, C., 'Romans 1:1–4 and the Occasion of the Letter: The Solution to the Two Congregation Problem in Rome', *TJ* 14 (1993), pp. 2–40

Ashton, J., *The Religion of Paul the Apostle* (New Haven; London: Yale University Press, 2000)

Aune, D., 'Human Nature and Ethics in Hellenistic Philosophical Traditions and Paul: Some Issues and Problems', in *Paul in His Hellenistic Context*, edited by T. E. Pedersen, pp. 291–312 (Minneapolis: Fortress, 1995)

Badke, W. B., 'Baptised into Moses—Baptised into Christ: A Study in Doctrinal Development',

EvQ 60 (1988), pp. 23–29

Bailey, K. E., 'St Paul's Understanding of the Territorial Promise of God to Abraham. Romans 4:13 in its Historical and Theological Context', *NESTTheolRev* 15 (1994), pp. 59–69

Ballentine, G. L., 'Death of Jesus as a New Exodus', *RevExp* 30 (1962), pp. 27–41

Balsdon, J. P. V. D., *Roman Women: their History and Habits* (London: Bodley Head, 1963)

Barclay, J. M. G., 'Paul and Philo on Circumcision: Romans 2:25–29 in Social and Cultural Context', *NTS* 44:4 (1998), pp. 536–56

Barr, G. K., 'Romans 16 and the Tentmakers', *IBS* 20:3 (1998), pp. 98–113

Barrett, C. K., *A Commentary on the Epistle to the Romans* (London: A. & C. Black, 1957)

Barrett, C. K., *From First Adam to Last: a Study in Pauline Theology* (London: A. & C. Black, 1962)

Barth, M., *Ephesians: The Anchor Bible* (Garden City, N.Y: Doubleday, 1974)

Bauckham, R., *The Climax of Prophecy* (Edinburgh: T. & T. Clark, 2000)

Baxter, A. G., and Ziesler, J. A., 'Paul and Arboriculture: Romans 11:17–24', *JSNT* 24 (1985), pp. 25–32

Beale, G. K., *The Book of Revelation*: *A Commentary on the Greek Text: The New International Greek Testament Commentary* (Grand Rapids: Eerdmans, 1999)

Beale, G. K., 'Did Jesus and His Followers Preach the Right Doctrine from the Wrong Texts? An Examination of the Presuppositions of Jesus' and the Apostles' Exegetical Method' *Them* 14:3 (1989), pp. 89–96

Bechtler, S. R., 'Christ, the *Telos* of the Law: The Goal of Romans 10:4', *CBQ* 56:2 (1994), pp. 288–308.

Beet, J. A., *Commentary on St. Paul's* Epistles to the *Corinthians* (New York: Macmillan, *1882*)

Bekken, Per Jarl, 'The Word is Near You: A Study of Deuteronomy 30:12–14' in *Paul`s Letter to the Romans in a Jewish Context*. Beihefte zur Zeitschrift fur die Neutestamentliche (Berlin: Walter de Gruyter, 2007)

Bell, R. H., 'Rom. 5:18–19 and Universal Salvation', *NTS* 48:3 (2002), pp. 417–32

Belli, F., 'Un'allusione a Is. 50:8–9 in Rm. 8:31–39', *RBB* 50:2 (2002), pp. 153–84

Berkley, T. W., *From a Broken Covenant to Circumcision of the Heart: Pauline Intertextual Exegesis in Romans 2:17–29,* SBL Dissertation Series 175 (Atlanta: Society of Biblical Literature, 2000)

Best, E. A., *Commentary on the First and Second Epistles to the Thessalonians* (London: Black, 1977)

Best, E. A., *A Critical and Exegetical Commentary on Ephesians*, *The International Critical Commentary* (Edinburgh: T. & T. Clark, 1998)

Best, E. A., *The Letter of Paul to the Romans* in The Cambridge Bible Commentary: New English Bible (Cambridge: Cambridge University Press, 1967)

Best, E. A., *One Body in Christ: A Study in the Relationship of the Church to Christ in the Epistles of the Apostle Paul* (London: SPCK, 1955)

Betz, H. D., *Galatians: A Commentary on Paul's Letter to the Churches in Galatia*

(Philadelphia: Fortress, 1979)

Betz, H. D., 'Transferring a Ritual: Paul's Interpretation of Baptism in Romans 6' in *Paul in His Hellenistic Context*, edited by Troels Engberg-Pedersen (Minneapolis: Fortress, 1995), pp. 84– 118

Bird, M. F., *The Saving Righteousness of God: Studies on Paul, Justification and the New Perspective* (Eugene, OR: Wipf & Stock, 2007)

Bird, M. F., and Preston M. P., *The Faith of Jesus Christ: Exegetical, Biblical, and Theological Studies* (Peabody: Hendrickson, 2009)

Black, M., 'The Pauline Doctrine of the Second Adam', *SJT* 7 (1954), pp. 170– 79 Black, M., *Romans, New Century Bible* (London: Oliphants, 1973)

Black, M., 'The "Son of Man"' in the Old Biblical Literature', *ExpTim* 60 (1948–1949), pp. 11– 15

Blauw, J., 'Paul as a Pioneer of Inter-Religious Thinking', *Studies in SID* [Kampen] 7 (1997), pp. 66–75

Bligh, J., 'Baptismal Transformation of the Gentile World', *HeyJ* 37:3 (1996), pp. 371–81

Blocher, H., *Original Sin: Illuminating the Riddle, New Studies in Biblical Theology* (Leicester: Inter-Varsity Press, 1997)

Bockmuehl, M., '1QS and Salvation in Qumran' in *Justification and Variegated Nomism,* vol.

2. Wissenschaftliche Untersuchungen zum Neuen Testament, edited by D. A. Carson, P. T. O'Brien, and M. A. Seifrid (Grand Rapids: Baker Academic, 2001), pp. 343–59

Boers, H., 'Jesus and the Christian Faith: New Testament Christology since Bousset's Kyrios Christos', *JBL* 89 (1970), pp. 450–56

Boers, H., 'The Structure and Meaning of Romans 6:1–14', *CBQ* 63:4 (2001), pp. 664–82

Bornkamm, G., *Paul* (trans. by D. M. G. Stalker) (London: Hodder & Stoughton, 1971)

Bornkamm, G., 'The Revelation of Christ to Paul on the Damascus Road and Paul's Doctrine of Justification and Reconciliation: A Study in Galatians 1', in

Reconciliation and Hope: New Testament Essays on Atonement and Eschatology Presented to L. L. Morris on His 60th Birthday, edited by R. Banks (Exeter: Paternoster, 1974), pp. 90–103

Bowker, J., 'The Son of Man', *JTS* 28 (1977), pp. 19–48 Braaten, C. E., 'Romans 12:14–21', *Int* 38:3 (1984), pp. 291–96

Brewer, D. I., 'The Use of Rabbinic Sources in gospel Studies', *TynBul* 50 (1999), pp. 281–98 Broyles, C. C., *Psalms* (Peabody: Hendrickson, 1999)

Bruce, F. F., *The Epistle of Paul to the Romans*: *An Introduction and Commentary* (London: Tyndale, 1963)

Büchsel, F. art, 'θυμός' *TDNT* 3:168.

Budd, P. J., *Numbers: Word Biblical Commentary* (Waco: Word Books, 1984) Bultmann, R., *Neueste Paulusforschung Tru* (Tubingen, 1936)

Bultmann, R., *Theology of the New Testament* (London: SCM, 1952)

Bultmann, R., 'Ursprung und Sinn der Typologie als hermeneutischer Methode', *TLZ* 75 (1950), pp. 205–12

Burke, T. J., *Adopted into God's family: Exploring a Pauline Metaphor* (Downers Grove, IL: InterVarsity, 2006)

Byrne, B., 'Rather Boldly (Rom 15:15): Paul's Prophetic Bid to Win the Allegiance of the

Christians in Rome', *Biblica* 74 (1993), pp. 83–96

Byrne, B., *Sons of God—Seed of Abraham: A Study of the idea of the Sonship of God of all Christians in Paul against the Jewish Background (*Ana Bib 83 Rome: Biblical Institute, 1979)

Caird, G. F. B., 'The Descent of Christ in Ephesians 4:7–11', *SE* 2 (Berlin: Akademia, 1964), pp. 535–45

Caird, G. F. B., *New Testament Theology* (Oxford: Oxford University Press, 1994) Calvin, J., *Romans* (Edinburgh: The Calvin Society, 1850)

Campbell, D. A., 'The Atonement in Paul', *Anvil* 11:3 (1994), pp. 237–50

Campbell, D. A., *The Deliverance of God: An Apocalyptic Rereading of Justification in Paul (*Grand Rapids: Eerdmans, 2009)

Campbell, D. A., 'Romans 1:17—A Crux Interpretation for the ΠΙΣΤΙΣ ΧΡΙΤΟΥ Debate', *JBL* 113:2 (1994), pp. 265–85

Campbell, W. S., 'The Freedom and Faithfulness of God in Relation to Israel', *JSNT* 13 (1981), pp. 27–45

Campbell, W. S., *Paul and the Creation of Christian Identity: Library of New Testament Studies* (Edinburgh: T. & T. Clark, 2006)

Campbell, W. S., 'The Rule of Faith in Romans 12:1—15:13', In *Pauline Theology Vol. 3 Romans* (Minneapolis: Fortress, 1995), pp. 259–86

Carbone, S., 'Israele nella Lettera ai Romanai', *RivistBib* 41:2 (1993), pp. 139–70

Carson, D. A., *'Christological Ambiguities in the Gospel of Matthew'* in Christ the Lord: Studies in Christology presented to Donald Guthrie, edited by H. H. Rowdon (Leicester: InterVarsity, 1982), pp. 97–114

Carson, D. A., *The gospel According to John* (Downers Grove, IL: InterVarsity, 1991)

Casey, M., *From Jewish Prophet to Gentile God: The Origins and Development of New Testament Christology* (Cambridge: Clarke, 1991)

Casey, R. P., 'The Earliest Christologies', *JTS* 9 (1958), pp. 253–77

Cervin, R. S., 'A Note Regarding the Name 'Junia(s)' in Romans 16:7', *NTS* 40:3 (1994), pp. 464–70

Chadwick, H., 'All Things to All Men (1 Cor. IX:22)', *NTS* 1 (1955), pp. 261–75

Charlesworth, J. H., 'A Caveat on Textual Transmission and the Meaning of Abba: A Study of the Lord's Prayer', in *The Lord's Prayer and Other Prayer Texts from the Greco-Roman Era*, edited by J. H. Charlesworth, M. Harding, and M. Kiley, (Valley Forge, PA: Trinity, 1994), pp. 1–14

Chilton, B., 'Romans 9–11 as Scriptural Interpretation and Dialogue with Judaism' *ExAud* 4 (1988), pp. 27–37

Chilton, B., and P. Davies, 'The Aqedah: A Revised Tradition History', *CBQ* 40 (1978), pp. 514– 46

Coleman, T. M. 'Binding Obligations in Romans 13:7: A Semantic Field and Social Context',

TynBul 48 (1997) 307–27.

Court, J. M., 'Paul and the Apocalyptic Pattern' in *Paul and Paulinism: Essays in Honour of C.K. Barrett*, edited by M. D. Hooker and S. G. Wilson, (London: SPCK, 1982), pp. 57–66

Cousar, C. P., 'Paul and the Death of Jesus', *Int* 52 (1998), pp. 38–52

Coxon, P., 'The Paschal New Exodus in John: An Interpretive Key with Particular Reference to John 5–10', Unpublished PhD thesis submitted to the University of Wales, St. David's College, 2010

Cozart, R., 'An Investigation Into the Significance of the Promise of a New Exodus of Israel in the Letter to the Ephesians' Unpublished PhD thesis submitted to the University of Wales, Trinity Saint David's College, 2011.

Cranfield, C. E. B., *The Epistle to the Romans* vols. 1 & 2 (Edinburgh: T. & T. Clark, 1975, 1979)

Cranfield, C. E. B., 'Has the Old Testament Law a Place in the Christian Life? A Response to Professor Westerholm', *IBS* 15:2 (1993), pp. 50–64

Cranfield, C. E. B., *Romans: A Shorter Commentary* (Grand Rapids: Eerdmans, 1985)

Cranfield, C. E. B., 'Some Observations on Romans 8:19–21' in *Reconciliation and Hope*, edited by R. Banks (Exeter: Paternoster, 1974), pp. 224–30

Cullmann, O., *Baptism in the New Testament* translated by J. K. S. Reid (London: SCM, 1950)

Cullmann, O., *The Christology of the New Testament* translated by S. C. Guthrie and A. N. Hall (London: SCM, 1959)

Cullmann, O., *The State in the New Testament* (London: SCM, 1957)

Dahl, N.A., 'The *Atonement*: An Adequate Reward for the Akedah? (Rom 8:32)' in Neotestamentica et Semitica, ed. E. Earle Ellis and Max Wilcox (Edinburgh: T. & T. Clark, 1969), pp. 15–27

Davies, R. E., 'Christ in Our Place: The Contribution of the Prepositions', *TynBul* 21 (1970), pp. 71–91

Davies, R. P., 'Passover and the Dating of the Aqedah', *JJS* 30 (1979), pp. 59–67 Davies, W. D., *Jewish and Pauline Studies* (Philadelphia: Fortress, 1955)

Davies, W. D., 'Paul and the People of Israel', *NTS* 24 (1977), pp. 4–39 Davies, W. D., *Paul and Rabbinic Judaism* 2nd ed. (London: SPCK, 1955)

Davila, J. R., 'The Old Testament as Background to the New Testament', *ExpTimes* 117:2 (2005), pp. 53–57

Davila, J. R., *The Provenance of the Pseudepigrapha*: Jewish, Christian, or Other? Supplements to the Journal for the Study of Judaism (Leiden: Brill, 2005)

De Jonge, M., 'The Earliest Christian Use of Christos: Some Suggestions', *NTS* 32:3 (1986), pp. 321–43

De Lacey, D. R., 'Image and Incarnation in Pauline Christology: A Search for Origins', *TynBul* 30 (1979), pp. 3–28

DeMaris, R. E., 'Funerals and Baptisms, Ordinary and Otherwise: Ritual Criticism and Corinthian Rites', *BibToday* 29 (1999), pp. 23–34

Denova, R. I., 'Paul's Letter to the Romans 13:1–7: The Gentile-Christian Response to Civil Authority', *Enc* 53:3 (1992), pp. 201–29

Derrett, J. D. M., *Law in the New Testament* (London: Darton, Longman & Todd, 1970)

Derrett, J. D. M., 'You Abominate False Gods; But Do You Rob Shrines? (Rom. 2:22b)', *NTS*

40:4 (1994), pp. 558–71

Dillon, J. R., 'The Priesthood of St Paul, Romans 15:15–16', *Worship* 74:2 (2000), pp. 156–68

Dodd, C. H., *According to the Scriptures: The Substructure of New Testament Theology* (London: Nisbet, 1952)

Dodd, C. H., *Essays in New Testament Studies* (Manchester: Manchester University Press, 1953)

Dodd, C. H., *The Interpretation of the Fourth gospel* (Cambridge: Cambridge University Press, 1953)

Donaldson, T. L., 'The Curse of the Law and the Inclusion of the Gentiles: Galatians 3:13–14', *NTS* 32 (1986), pp. 94–112

Donaldson, T. L., *Paul and the Gentiles: Remapping the Apostle's Convictional World* (Minneapolis: Fortress, 1997)

Donaldson, T. L., 'Riches for the Gentiles (Rom. 11:12): Israel's Rejection and Paul's Gentile

Mission', *JBL* 112 (1993), pp. 81–98

Donfried, K. P., 'A Short Note on Romans 16' in *The Romans Debate*, edited by K. P. Donfried (Edinburgh: T. & T. Clark, 1991), pp. 44–52

Donne, B. K., *Christ Ascended* (Exeter: Paternoster, 1983) Downing, J., 'Jesus and Martyrdom', *JTS* 14 (1963), pp. 279–93

Dozeman, T.B., *God at War: Power in the Exodus Tradition* (New York: OUP, 1996)

Driver, J., *Understanding the Atonement for the Mission of the Church* (Scottdale, PA: Herald, 1986)

Dunn, J. D. G., '1 Corinthians 15.45. Last Adam, Life Giving Spirit' in *Christ and Spirit in the NT, Studies in honour of C. F. D. Moule*, edited by Lindars. B. and Smalley SS (Cambridge: Cambridge University Press, 1973), pp. 127–46

Dunn, J. D. G., *Baptism in the Holy Spirit* (London: SCM, 1970)

Dunn, J. D. G., *Christology in the Making. An Inquiry into the Origins of the Doctrine of the Incarnation* 2nd ed. (London: SCM, 1989)

Dunn, J. D. G., *The Epistle to the Galatians*, Black`s New Testament Commentary Series (Peabody: Hendrickson, 1993)

Dunn, J. D. G., *Jesus and the Spirit: A Study of the Religious and Charismatic Experience of Jesus and the First Christians as Reflected in the New Testament* (London: SCM, 1975)

Dunn, J. D. G., editor, *Jews and Christians: The Parting of the Ways, A.D.70 to 135; the Second Durham Tubingen Research Symposium on Earliest Christianity and Judaism (September 1989)*, Wissenschaftliche Untersuchungen Zum Neuen Testament: Vol. 66, (Tubingen: Mohr, 1992)

Dunn, J. D. G., *The New Perspective on Paul: Collected Essays.* Wissenschaftliche Untersuchungen zum Neuen Testament (Tubingen: Mohr Siebeck, 2005)

Dunn, J. D. G., 'Paul's Understanding of the Death of Jesus' in *Reconciliation and Hope*, essays presented to L. L. Morris on his 60th birthday, edited by R. Banks (Exeter: Paternoster Press, 1974), pp. 125–41

Dunn, J. D. G., *Romans 9–16* (Waco: Word, 1988)

Dunn, J. D. G., *The Theology of Paul the Apostle* (Edinburgh: T. & T. Clark, 1998)

Dunn, J. D. G., *Unity and Diversity in the New Testament: An Inquiry into the Character of Earliest Christianity* 2nd ed. (London: SCM, 1990)

Dunn, J. D. G., 'Who Did Paul Think He Was? A Study of Jewish-Christian Identity', *NTS* 45:2 (1999), pp. 174–93

Durham, J. I., *Exodus* (Waco: Word Books, 1987)

Du Toit, A. B., 'Die Kirche als doxologische Gemeinschaft im Romerbrief', *Neot* 27 (1993), pp. 69–77

Earnshaw, J. D., 'Reconsidering Paul's Marriage Analogy in Romans 7:1–4', *NTS* 40 (1994), pp. 68–88

Edwards, J. R., *Romans* (Peabody: Hendrickson, 1992)

Elliott, J. K., 'The Language and Style of the Concluding Doxology to the Epistle to the Romans', *ZNW* 72 (1981), pp. 124–30

Ellis, E. E., 'II Cor V.1–10 in Pauline Eschatology', *JNTS* 111 (1959), pp. 211–24

Ellis, E. E., 'A note on 1 Cor. 10:4', *JBL* 76 (1957), pp. 53–56

Ellis, E. E., *Paul and His Recent Interpreters* (Grand Rapids: Eerdmans, 1967)

Ellis, E. E., *Paul's Use of the Old Testament* (Edinburgh: Oliver & Boyd, 1957)

Ellis, E. E., *Prophecy and Hermeneutic in Early Christianity* (Grand Rapids: Eerdmans, 1978)

Ellis, E. E., 'Traditions in 1 Corinthians', *NTS* 32:4 (1986), pp. 481–502

Emerton, J. A., 'The Origin of the Son of Man Imagery', *JTS* 9 (1958), pp. 225–42 Engberg-Pedersen, T., *Paul and the Stoics* (Louisville, KY: Westminster John Knox, 2000)

Eskola, T., 'Paul, Predestination and 'Covenantal Nomism'—Re-assessing Paul and Palestinian Judaism', *JSJ* 28 (1997), pp. 390–412

Esler, P., 'Ancient Oleiculture and Ethnic Differentiation: the Meaning of the Olive-Tree Image in Romans 11', *JSNT* 26 (2003), pp. 103–24

Espy, J. M., 'Paul's 'Robust Conscience' Re-Examined', *NTS* 31 (1985), pp. 161–88

Fee, G. D., 'Christology and Pneumatology in Romans 8:9–11', in *Jesus of Nazareth, Lord and Christ: Essays on the Historical Jesus and New Testament Christology,* edited by J. B. Green and M. Turner (Grand Rapids: Eerdmans, 1994), pp. 312–31

Fee, G. D., *God's Empowering Presence: The Holy Spirit in the Letters of Paul* (Peabody: Hendrickson, 1994)

Finger, R. H., 'Was Julia a Racist? Cultural Diversity in the Book of Romans', *DS* Chicago 19:3 (1993), pp. 36–39

Fitzmyer, J. A., 'The Consecutive Meaning of ΕΦ'Ω in Romans 5:12' *NTS* Vol. 39:3 (1993), pp. 321–39

Fitzmyer, J. A., *Romans: A New Translation with Introduction and Commentary* Anchor Bible (New York: Chapman, 1993)

Foerster, W., 'εἰρήνη', *TDNT* 2:400–420

Ford, D., 'What about the Trinity?' in *Meaning and Truth in 2 Corinthians,* edited by F. Young and D. Ford (Grand Rapids: Eerdmans,1987), pp. 255–60

Ford, J. M., 'The Son of Man Euphemism?', *JBL* 87 (1969), pp. 189–96

Fretheim, T. E., *Exodus* (Louisville: Westminster John Knox, 1991)

Friedbert, N, *Indicators of Typology within the Old Testament: The Exodus Motif*

(Frankfurt/M., Berlin, Bern, Bruxelles, New York, Oxford: Wien, 2001)

Friesen, G., and J. R. Maxson, *Decision Making and the Will of God: A Biblical Alternative to the Traditional View* (Portland, OR: Multnomah, 1980)

Fuller, R. H., *The Foundations of New Testament Christology* (London: Lutterworth, 1965) Furnish, V. P., *The Moral Teaching of Paul* (Nashville: Abingdon, 1979)

Gager, J. G., 'Functional Diversity in Paul's Use of End Time Language', *JBL* 84 (1970), pp. 325–37

Gagnon, R. A. J., 'The Meaning of ὑμῶν τὸ ἀγαθόν in Romans 14:16', *JBL* 117:4 (1998), pp. 675–89

Gagnon, R. A. J., 'Why the 'Weak' at Rome Cannot be Non-Christian Jews', *CBQ* 62 (2000), pp. 64–82

Garlington, D. B., 'The Obedience of Faith in the Letter to the Romans. Part III: The Obedience of Christ and the Obedience of the Christian', *WTJ* 55 (1993), pp. 87–112

Garlington, D. B., 'Romans 7:14–25 and the Creation Theology of Paul', *TJ* 11:2 (1990), pp. 197–235

Garnet, P., 'Atonement Constructions in the Old Testament and the Qumran Scrolls', *EvQ* 46 (1974), pp. 131–63

Gaston, L., 'Israel's Enemies in Pauline Theology', *NTS* 28:3 (1982), pp. 400–423

Gathercole, S. J., 'A Law unto Themselves: The Gentiles in Romans 2:14–15 Revisited', *JSNT*

23:3 (2002), pp. 27–49

Gathercole, S. J., *Where is Boasting? Early Jewish Soteriology and Paul's Response in Romans*

1–5 (Grand Rapids: Eerdmans, 2002)

Getty, M. A., 'Paul and the Salvation of Israel: A Perspective on Romans 9–11', *CBQ* 50:3 (1988), pp. 456–69

Giblin, C. H., 'Three Monotheistic Texts in Paul', *CBQ* (1975), pp. 527–47

Ginzberg, L., *The Legends of the Jews* (Philadelphia: Jewish Publication Society of America, 1925)

Given, M. D., 'Restoring the Inheritance in Romans 11:1', *JBL* 118 (1999), pp. 89–96 Glancy, J., 'Israel vs. Israel in Romans 11:25–32', *USQR* 45:3/4 (1991), pp. 191–203

Goldingay, J., *Psalms vol 2:42–89* (Grand Rapids: Baker Academic, 2007)

Goppelt, L., *Typos: The Typological Interpretation of The Old Testament in the New* translated by D. H. Madvig (Grand Rapids: Eerdmans, 1982)

Goulder, M.D., *The Psalms of the Return (Book 5, Psalms 107-150): Studies in the Psalter, 4, Journal for the Study of the Old Testament Supplement.* (Sheffield: Sheffield, 1998)

Gray, G.B., *A Critical and Exegetical Commentary on Numbers, International Critical Commentary* (Edinburgh: T. & T. Clark, 1903)

Grech, P., 'The Old Testament as a Christological Source in the Apostolic Age', *BibToday* 2 (1975), pp. 127–45

Green, G. L., *Jude and 2 Peter* (Grand Rapids: Baker, 2008)

Green, G. L., *The Letters to the Thessalonians* (Grand Rapids: Eerdemans, 2002) Gulley, N. R., 'Ascension of Christ' in *ABD* 1:472–74

Hahn, F., *The Titles of Jesus in Christology, their History in Early Christianity* (New York: World Publishing, 1969)

Hall, D. R., 'Romans 3:1–8 Reconsidered', *NTS* 29 (1983), pp. 183–97

Hamerton-Kelly, R. G., 'Sacred Violence and the Curse of the Law (Galatians 3.13). The Death of Christ as a Sacrificial Travesty', *NTS* 36 (1990), pp. 98–116

Hanson, A. T., *New Testament Interpretation of Scripture* (London: SPCK, 1980) Harman, Alan, *Psalms* (Fearn: Christian Focus, 1998)

Harris, M. J., *Jesus as God: the New Testament use of Theos in Reference to Jesus* (Grand Rapids: Baker, 1992)

Harris, W. Hall III., *The Descent of Christ: Ephesians 4:7–11 and Traditional Hebrew Imagery*, Arbeiten zur Geschichte des Antiken Judentums und (Leiden: E. J. Brill, 1996)

Hays, R. B., 'Adam, Israel, Christ' in *Pauline Theology, Vol. III, Romans*, Edited by Hay, D. M. and Johnson, E. E. (Minneapolis, MN: Fortress, 1995)

Hays, R. B., *The Conversion of the Imagination: Paul as Interpreter of Israel's Scripture* (Grand Rapids: Eerdmans, 2005)

Hays, R. B., *Echoes of Scripture in the Letters of Paul* (New Haven, CT: Yale University Press, 1989)

Hays, R. B., 'Have we found Abraham to be our Father According to the Flesh? A Reconsideration of Rom 4:1', *Nov T* (1985), pp. 76–98

Hays, R. B., 'ΠΙΣΙΣ and Pauline Christology: What is at Stake?' in SBL Seminar Papers, edited by E. H. Lovering Jr. (Atlanta: Scholars Press, 1991), pp. 714–29

Hays, R. B., '"Who Has Believed Our Message": Paul's Reading of Isaiah" in *New Testament Writers and the Old Testament: An Introduction*, edited by J. M. Court (London: SPCK, 2002)

Hellholm, D., 'Die argumentative Funktion von Romer 7:1–6', *NTS* 43:3 (1997), pp. 385–411

Hendriksen, W., *Exposition of Paul's Epistle to the Romans: Vol.1: Chapters 1–8* (Grand Rapids: Baker, 1981)

Hengel, M., *The Atonement: The Origins of the Doctrine in the New Testament* (Philadelphia: Fortress, 1981)

Hengel, M., *The Son of God, The Origin of Christology and the History of Jewish-Hellenistic Religion* translated by J. Bowden (London: SCM, 1976)

Herrmann, J. art, 'ἱλασμός', *TDNT* 3:301-310

Hester, J. D., *Paul's Concept of Inheritance: A Contribution to the Understanding of Heilsgeschichte,* Scottish Journal of Theology, occasional papers (London: Oliver & Boyd, 1968)

Hill, D., *Greek Words and Hebrew Meanings. Studies in the Semantics of Soteriological Terms*

(London: Cambridge University Press, 1967)

Hills, J. V., 'Christ was the Goal of the Law: Romans 10:4', *JTS* 44:2 (1993), pp. 585–92 Hodge, C., *A Commentary on Romans* (Grand Rapids: Eerdmans, 1886)

Hoehner, H. W., *Ephesians: An Exegetical Commentary* (Grand Rapids: Baker Academic, 2002)

Holland., T., 'A Case of Mistaken Identity: The Harlot and the Church (1 Corinthians 5–6)', *ATI* 1 (2008), pp. 56–68, http://atijournal.org/ATI_Vol1_No1.pdf

Holland., T., *Contours of Pauline Theology* (Fearn, Scotland: Christian Focus, 2004)

Holland., T., *The Paschal New Exodus Motif in Paul's Letter to the Romans with Special*

Reference to its Christological Significance (PhD diss., University of Wales, 1996) Hooker, M. D., 'Adam in Romans 1', *NTS* 6:3 (1960), pp. 297–306

Hooker, M. D., 'Further Notes on Romans 1', *NTS* 13 (1967), pp. 297–306

Hooker, M. D., 'Interchange in Christ', *JTS* 22:2 (1971), pp. 349–61

Hooker, M. D., *Paul: Apostle to the Gentiles,* St Paul's Lecture given at St Botolph's, Aldgate on November 16th, 1989

Hooker, M. D., 'Paul and 'Covenantal Nomism' in *Paul and Paulinism: Essays in Honour of C.*

K. Barrett, edited by M. D. Hooker and S. G. Wilson (London: SPCK, 1982), pp. 47–56 Horst, J., 'μελη', *TDNT* 4:555–68

Howard, J. K., 'Into Christ: a Study of the Pauline Concept of Baptismal Union', *ExpTim* 79 (1968), pp. 147–51

Howard, J. K., 'Passover and Eucharist in the Fourth gospel', *SJT* 20 (1967), pp. 329–37 Jansen, F. J., 'The Ascension, the Church and Theology', *TToday* 16 (1959), pp. 17–29

Jeremias, J., *New Testament Theology* (London: SCM, 1971)

Jeremias, J., *The Prayers of Jesus*. Philadelphia: Fortress, 1967

Jewett, R., 'Ecumenical Theology For the Sake of Mission' in *Pauline Theology*, vol. 3, edited by D. M Hay and E. E. Johnson (Minneapolis: Fortress, 1995), pp. 80–108

Jeremias, J., *Paul's Anthropological Terms: A Study of their Use in Conflict Settings*. Arbeiten zur Geschichte des Antiken Judentums und (Leiden: Brill, 1971)

Jeremias, J., *Romans: A Critical and Historical Commentary* (Minneapolis: Fortress, 2006) Johnson, A. R., *Sacral Kingship in Ancient Israel* (Cardiff: University of Wales Press, 1967)

Johnson, B. C., 'Tongues: A Sign for Unbelievers?—a Structural and Exegetical Study of 1 Corinthians XIV 20–25', *NTS* 25 (1978/79), pp. 180–203

Johnson, D. G., 'The Structure and Meaning of Romans 11', *CBQ* 46 (1984), pp. 91–103

Johnson, L. T., *Reading Romans: A Literary and Theological Commentary* (New York: Crossroads, 1997)

Karlberg, M. W., 'Israel's History Personified: Romans 7:7–13 in Relation to Paul's Teaching on the Old Man', *TrinJ* 7 (1986), pp. 68–69

Karris, R. J., 'Romans 14:1—15:13 and the Occasion of Romans' in *The Romans Debate*, edited by K. P. Donfried (Peabody: Hendriksen, 1991), pp. 65–84

Käsemann, E., *Exegetische Versuche und Besinnungen I.* (Gottingen: Vandenhoeck & Ruprecht, 1965)

Käsemann, E., Commentary on Ro*mans* (Grand Rapids: Eerdmans, 1980)

Kay, B. N., *The Thought Structure of Romans with Special Reference to Chapter 6* (Austin, TX: Scholar Press, 1979)

Keck, L. E., 'Christology, Soteriology, and the Praise of God (Romans 15:7–13)' in *The Conversation Continues: Studies in Paul and John in Honour of J. Louis Martyn*, edited by R.

T. Fortna and B. R. Gaventa (Nashville: Abingdon, 1990), pp. 85–97

Keck, L. E., 'Towards the Renewal of New Testament Christology', *NTS* 32 (1986), pp. 362–377

Keck, L. E., 'What Makes Romans Tick?' in *Pauline Theology*, vol. 3, edited by D. M. Hay and

E. E. Johnson (Minneapolis: Fortress, 1995), pp. 3–29

Kee, H. C., 'Christology and Ecclesiology. Titles of Christ and Models of Community', *SBL*

Seminar Papers, pp. 227–42

Keesmaat, S. C., 'Exodus and the Intertextual Transformation of Traditions in Romans 8:14–30', *JSNT* 54 (1994), pp. 29–56

Keesmaat, S. C., 'Paul and His Story: Exodus and Tradition in Galatians', *Horizons in Biblical Theology* 18.2 (*1996*), pp. *133–68*

Kelly, J. N. D., *The Epistles of Peter and of Jude* (Black: London, 1990)

Kennedy, A. A., *Saint Paul's Conception of the Last Things* (London: Hodder and Stoughton, 1904)

Kidner, D., *Genesis* (Leicester: InterVarsity, 1967)

Kidner, D., 'Sacrifice—Metaphors and Meaning', *TynB* (1982), pp. 119–36

Kim, S., 'The Mystery of Rom. 11:25–26 Once More', *NTS* 43:3 (1997), pp. 412–29

Kirby, J. C., *Ephesians: Baptism and Pentecost—An Inquiry into the Structure and Purpose of the Epistle to the Ephesians* (London: SPCK, 1968)

Kirkpatrick, A. F., *The Book of Psalms* (Cambridge: Cambridge University Press, 1910)

Klein, W. W., *The New Chosen People: A Corporate View of Election (*Eugene, OR: Wipf & Stock, 2001)

Klijn, A. F. J., 'The Study of Jewish Christianity', *NTS* 20 (1974), pp. 119–31

Kline, M. G., 'The Old Testament Origins of the gospel Genre', *WTJ* 1.38 (1975), pp. 1–27 Knox, J., *Life in Christ: Reflections on Romans 5–8* (Greenwich, CT: Seabury, 1961)

Knox, W. L., *St. Paul and the Church of the Gentiles* (Cambridge: Cambridge University Press, 1939)

Kosmala, H., 'The Bloody Husband', *VT* 12 (1962), pp. 14–28 Kramer, W., *Christ, Lord, Son of God* (London: SCM. 1966)

Kraus, Hans-Joachim, *Psalms 60–150* (Minneapolis: Fortress, 1993)

Kreuzer, S., 'Der den Gotlosen rechtfertigt (Rom. 4:5). Die fruhjudische Einordnung von Gen. 15 als Hintergrund fur das Abrahambild und die Rechtfertigungslehre des Paulus', *TheolBeitr* 33:4 (2002), pp. 208–219

Krimmer, H. *Romer-Brief* (Stuttgart: Hänssler, 1983)

Kroger, D., 'Paul and the Civil Authorities: An Exegesis of Romans 13:1–7', *AsiaJournTheol* 7:2 (1993), pp. 344–66

Kummel, W. G., *The Theology of the New Testament according to its Major Witnesses: Jesus—Paul—John* (London: SCM, 1974)

Kuss, O., *Der Römerbrief* (Regensburg: F. Pustet, 1963-1978)

Laato, T., 'Paul's Anthropological Considerations: Two Problems' in *Justification and Variegated Nomism*, vol. 2. Wissenschaftliche Untersuchungen Zum Neuen Testament, edited by D. A. Carson, P. T. O'Brien, and M. A. Seifrid (Grand Rapids: Baker Academic, 2001), pp. 343–59

Lagrange, P. M. J., *Saint Paul Epitre aux Romains* (Paris: Gabalda, 1950)

Lambrecht, J., 'Paul's Christological Use of Scripture in 1 Cor. 15:20–28', *NTS* 28:4 (1982), pp. 502–27

Landy, F., *Hosea, Readings: A New Biblical Commentary* (Sheffield: Sheffield Academic Press, 1995)

Lane, W. L. 'Covenant, the Key to Paul's Conflict with Corinth', *TB* 33 (1982), pp. 3–29

Laurer, S., 'Traces of a gospel Writing in 1 Corinthians 1 to 7: Rediscovery and Development of Origen's Understanding of 1 Corinthians 4:6b', PhD diss., University of Wales, 2010 Leaney, A. R. C., '1 Peter and the Passover: An Interpretation', *NTS* 10 (1963/64), pp. 238–51

Lee, Y. L., *Pilgrimage and the Knowledge of God* Unpublished PhD diss., University of Wales, Lampeter, 2007

Leenhardt, F. J., *L'epitre de Saint Paul aux Romains* (Geneva: Labor et Fides, 1981) Lemico, E., 'The Unifying Kerygma of the New Testament', *JSNT* 33 (1998), pp. 3–17

Levinson, J. D., *The Death and Resurrection of the Beloved Son. The Transformation of Child Sacrifice in Judaism and Christianity* (New Haven: Yale University Press, 1993)

Lincoln, A., *Ephesians* (Dallas: Word, 1990)

Lincoln, A., 'From Wrath to Justification' in *Pauline Theology*, vol. 3, edited by David M. Hay and E. Elizabeth Johnson (Minneapolis: Fortress, 1995), pp. 130–59

Little, R. C., *Mission in the Way of Paul: Biblical Mission for the Church in the Twenty-First Century* (New York: Peter Lange, 2005)

Longacre, R. E., and W. B. Wallis, 'Soteriology and Eschatology in Romans', *JETS* 41:3 (1998), pp. 367–82

Longenecker, B. W., 'Pistis in Romans 3:25—Neglected Evidence for the "Faithfulness of Christ"?', *NTS* 39:3 (1993), pp. 478–80

Longenecker, R. N., *Galatians* (Waco: Word, 1990)

Longenecker, R. N., 'Prolegomena to Paul's Use of Scripture in Romans', *BBR* 7 (1997), pp. 145–68

Lyall, F., 'Roman Law in the Writings of Paul—Adoption', *JBL* 88 (1969), pp. 458–66

Maartens, P. J., 'The Relevance of "Context" and "Interpretation" to the Semiotic Relations of Romans 5:1–11', *Neot* 29 (1995), pp. 75–108

Maartens, P. J., 'The Vindication of the Righteous in Romans 8:31–39: Inference and Relevance', *HvTSt* 51:4 (1995), pp. 1046–87

MacGregor, G. H. C., 'Principalities and Powers: The Cosmic Background of Paul's Thought',

NTS 1:2 (1954/55), pp. 17–28

Macintosh, A. A., *A Critical and Exegetical Commentary on Hosea* (Edinburgh: T. & T. Clark, 1997)

Mackay, J. L., *Exodus: A Mentor Commentary* (Fearn, UK: Christian Focus, 2001)

Maddox, R., 'The Function of the Son of Man according to the Synoptic gospels', *NTS* 15 (1968–1969), pp. 45–74

Maddox, R., 'The Function of the Son of Man in the gospel of John' in *Reconciliation and Hope, New Testament Essays on Atonement and Eschatology, Presented to L. L. Morris on His 60th Birthday*, edited by R. Banks (Exeter: Paternoster, 1974), pp. 186–204

Maile, J. F., 'The Ascension in Luke-Acts', *TynB* 37 (1986), pp. 29–59

Maillot, A., L'Épître aux Romains. Épître de l'œcuménisme et théologie de l'histoire (Paris: Centurion, 1984)

Malherbe, A. J., *The Letters to the Thessalonians* (New York: Doubleday, 2000)

Malick, D. E., 'The Condemnation of Homosexuality in Romans 1:26–27', *BibSac* 150:599 (1993), pp. 327–40

Manek, J., 'The New Exodus in the Book of Luke', *NovT* (1955), pp. 8–23.

Manson, T. W., 'Romans', *PCB*, pp. 940–53

Manson, T. W., 'St. Paul's Letter to the Romans—and Others' in *The Romans Debate*, edited by K. Donfried (Minneapolis: Augsburg, 1977), pp. 1–16

Manson, T. W., *The Teaching of Jesus: Studies of Its Form and Content*. 2nd ed. (Cambridge: Cambridge University Press, 1935)

Marsh, J., *The Fullness of Time* (London: No Publisher, 1952)

Marshall, I. H., 'Living in the "Flesh"', *BibSac* 159:636 (2002). pp. 387–403

Marshall, I. H., *The Origins of New Testament Christology* (Leicester: InterVarsity, 1976)

Marshall, I. H., 'Palestinian and Hellenistic Christianity: Some Critical Comments', *NTS* 19:2 (1973), pp. 271–87

Martin, J. P., 'Kerygma of Romans', *Int* 25:2 (1971), pp. 308–28

Martin, R. P., *Colossians: The Church's Lord and the Christian's Liberty* (Exeter: Paternoster, 1972)

Mays, J. L., *Psalms, Interpretation, a Bible Commentary for Teaching and Preaching* (Louisville: Westminster John Knox, 1994)

McKay, C., 'Ezekiel in the NT', *CQR* 162 (1961), pp. 4–16

McKelvey, R. T., *The New Temple: The Church in the New Testament* (London: Oxford, 1969) McNeile, A.H., *The Book of Numbers* (Cambridge: University Press, 1911)

McKnight. S., *A New Vision for Israel: The Teachings of Jesus in National Context* (Grand Rapids: Eerdmans, 1999)

McWhirter, J., *The Bridegroom Messiah and the People of God: Marriage in the Fourth gospel*. Society for New Testament Studies Monograph Series (Cambridge: Cambridge University Press, 2006)

Meggitt, J. J., 'The Social Status of Erastus (Rom. 16:23)', *Nov Test* 38:3 (1996), pp. 218–223

Meissner, S., 'Paulinische Soteriologie und die "Aqedat Jitzchaq"', *Jud* 51 (1995), pp. 33–49

Metzger, B. M., 'The Punctuation of Rom. 9:5', in *Christ and Spirit in the New Testament: in Honour of Charles Francis Digby Moule*, editors B. Lindars and S. Smalley (Cambridge: Cambridge University Press, 1973), pp. 95–112

Metzger, B. M., *The Text of the New Testament* 3rd ed. (New York: Oxford University Press, 1992)

Meyer, B. F., 'The Pre-Pauline Formula in Rom. 3:25–26a', *NTS* 29 (1983), pp. 198–208 Michael, O., *KEK* (Gottingen: Vandenhoeck & Ruprecht, 1957)

Millard, A. R., 'Covenant and Communion in First Corinthians', in *Apostolic History and the gospel: Essays Presented to F. F. Bruce on His Sixtieth Birthday,* edited by W. Gasque and R. P. Martin (Exeter: Paternoster, 1970), pp. 242–48

Miller, J. C., *The Obedience of Faith, the Eschatological People of God, and the Purpose of Romans* (SBL Dissertation Series, 177) (Atlanta: SBL, 2000)

Mitton, L. C., *Ephesians: New Century Bible Commentary*, ed. Matthew Black (London: Marshall, Morgan, and Scott, 1973)

Molland, E., *Das Paulinische Evangelion: Das Wort und die Sache* (Oslo: Jacob Dybwad, 1934)

Monte, W. D., 'The Place of Jesus' Death and Resurrection in Pauline Soteriology', *SBT* 16 (1988), pp. 39–97

Moo, D. J., *The Epistle to the Romans* (Grand Rapids: Eerdmans, 1996)

Moo, D. J., '"Law," "Works of the Law" and legalism in Paul', *WTJ* 45 (1983), pp. 73–100 Morris, L. L., *The Apostolic Preaching of the Cross* (London: Tyndale, 1955)

Morris, L. L., *The Atonement: Its Meaning and Significance* (Leicester: InterVarsity, 1963)

Morris, L. L., *The Epistle to the Romans* (Leicester: InterVarsity, 1988)

Morris, L. L., 'The Meaning of *Hilasterion* in Romans 3:25', *NTS* 2 (1955), pp. 33–43

Morris, L. L., 'The Passover in Rabbinic Literature', *AusBR* 4 (1954/55), pp. 57–76

Moule, C. F. D., *An Idiom Book of New Testament Greek* (Cambridge: Cambridge University Press, 1979)

Moule, C. F. D., 'The Influence of Circumstances on the use of Christological Terms', *JTS* 10 (1960), pp. 247–64

Moule, C. F. D., *The Origin of Christology* (Cambridge: Cambridge University Press, 1977) Moule, C. F. D., *The Sacrifice of Christ* (London: Hodder & Stoughton, 1956)

Moule, H. C. G., *The Epistle of Paul the Apostle to the Romans with Introduction and Notes* (Cambridge: Cambridge University Press, 1903)

Muilenburg, J., 'The Son of Man in Daniel and the Ethiopic Apocalypse of Enoch', *JBL* 79 (1960), pp. 197–209

Muddiman, J. A., *Commentary on the Epistle to the Ephesians, Black's New Testament Commentaries* (London: Continuum, 2001)

Munck, J., *Christ and Israel: An Interpretation of Romans 9–11* (Philadelphia: Fortress, 1967)

Munck, J., 'Jewish Christianity in Post-Apostolic Times', *NTS* 6:2 (1959), pp. 103–16 Munck, J., *Paul and the Salvation of Mankind* (London: SCM, 1959)

Murray, J., *The Collected Writings of John Murray, Vol 2: Lectures in Systematic Theology* (Edinburgh: Banner of Truth, 1977)

Murray, J., *The Epistle to the Romans* (vols. 1 & 2) (London: Marshall, Morgan & Scott, 1967)

Nanos, M. D., 'The Jewish Context of the Gentile Audience Addressed in Paul's Letter to the Romans', *CBQ* 61:2 (1999), pp. 283–304

Nanos, M. D., *The Mystery of Romans: the Jewish Context of Paul's Letter* (Minneapolis: Fortress, 1996)

Nida, Eugene A., and Louw, Johannes P., *Lexical Semantics of the Greek New Testament: A Supplement to the Greek-English Lexicon of the New Testament Based on Semantic Domains* (Atlanta: Scholars, 1992)

Ninow, F., *Indicators of Typology within the Old Testament: The Exodus Motif* Friedensauer Schriftenreihe—Reihe A Theologie (Frankfurt-am-Main: Peter Lang, 2001)

Nixon, R. E., *The Exodus in the New Testament* (London: Tyndale, 1963)

North, J. L., '"Good Words and Faire Speeches" (Rom. 16:18 AV): More Materials and a Pauline Pun', *NTS* 42:4 (1996), pp. 600–614

Noordtzij, A., *Numbers: Bible student`s commentary* (Grand Rapids, MI: Zondervan Pub. House, 1983)

Nwachukwu, M. S. C., *Creation-Covenant Scheme and Justification by Faith: A Canonical Study of the God-Human Drama in the Pentateuch and the Letter to the Romans* (Rome: Editrice Pontifica Universita Gregoriana, 2002)

Nygren, A., *Commentary on Romans* (London: SCM, 1958)

Olyott, S., *The gospel as It Really Is: Paul's Epistle to the Romans Simply Explained* (Darlington: Evangelical, 1979)

O'Neill, J. C., *Paul's Letter to the Romans* (Harmondsworth: Penguin, 1975)

Oster, R. E., 'Congregations of the Gentiles (Rom 16:4): A Culture-Based Ecclesiology in the Letters of Paul', *ResQuar* 40 (1998), pp. 39–52

Owen, J., *Temptation and Sin* (Indiana: Sovereign Grace, 1958)

Pamment, M., 'The Kingdom of Heaven according to the First gospel', *NTS* 27 (1981), pp. 211–32

Pate, C. M., *Adam Christology as Exegetical and Theological Substructure of II Corinthians 4:7—5:21* (Lanham, MD: University Press of America, 1991)

Perrin, N. A., *Modern Pilgrimage in New Testament Christology* (Philadelphia: Fortress, 1974)

Petersen, N. R., *Rediscovering Paul: Philemon and the Sociology of Paul's Narrative World* (Philadelphia: Fortress, 1985)

Peterson, A. K., 'Shedding new light on Paul's Understanding of Baptism: A Ritual-Theological Approach to Romans 6', *StudTheol* 52 (1998), pp. 3–28

Peterson, D., 'Worship and Ethics in Romans 12', *TynBul* 44:2 (1993), pp. 271–88 Pierce, C. A., *Conscience in the New Testament* (London: SCM, 1955)

Piper, J., *The Future of Justification: A Response to N. T. Wright* (Nottingham: InterVarsity, 2008)

Powers, D. G., *Salvation through Participation. An Examination of the Notion of the Believers' Corporate Unity with Christ in Early Christian Soteriology* (Leuven: Peeters, 2001)

Procksch, O., art "λύω", *TDNT* 4:328-335

Punt, J. Paul, 'Hermeneutics and the Scriptures of Israel', *Neot* 30:2 (1996), pp. 377–426

Ra, K. U., 'An Investigation of the Influence of the Paschal—New Exodus Motif on the Description of Christ and His Work in the gospel of John (chapters One to Four)' Unpublished PhD thesis submitted to the University of Wales, St. David's College, 2009

Raisanen, H., 'Paul's Conversion and the Development of His View of the Law', *NTS* 33 (1987), pp. 404–19

Rancine, J. F., 'Romains 13:1–7: Simple Preservation de l'ordre Social?' *EstBib* 51:2 (1993), pp. 187–205

Rapinchuk, M., 'Universal Sin and Salvation in Romans 5:12–21', *JETS* 42:3 (1999), pp. 427–41

Reasoner, M., *The Strong and the Weak: Romans 14:1—15:13 in Context* (Cambridge: Cambridge University Press, 1999)

Reumann, J., 'The Gospel of the Righteousness of God: Pauline Reinterpretation in Rom. 3:21–31', *Int* 20 (1966), pp. 432–52

Richardson, A., *An Introduction to the Theology of the New Testament* (London: SCM, 1958)

Ridderbos, H., 'The Earliest Confession of the Atonement in Paul (1 Cor. 15:3)' in *Reconciliation and Hope: Essays Presented to L. L. Morris on His Sixtieth Birthday*, edited by

R. Banks (Exeter: Paternoster, 1974), pp. 76–89

Ridderbos, H., *Paul: An Outline of His Theology* (Grand Rapids: Eerdmans, 1975) Riesenfeld, H., art "ὑπερ", *TDNT* 8:507–16

Robichaux, K. S., 'Christ the Firstborn', *AffCr* 2 (1997), pp. 30–38

Robinson, D. W. B., 'Towards a Definition of Baptism', *RTR* 34 (1975), pp. 1–15 Robinson, J. A. T., *Wrestling with Romans* (London: SCM, 1979)

Rogerson, J. W., 'Corporate Personality', *A.D.B* 1:1156–157

Rogerson, J. W., 'The Hebrew Conception of Corporate Personality: A Re-examination', *JTS* 21 (1970), pp. 1–16

Rosenberg, R. A., 'Jesus, Isaac and the Suffering Servant', *JBL* 84:4 (1965), p. 381–88 Rosner, R. S., *Paul, Scripture & Ethics: A Study of 1 Cor. 5–7* (Leiden: Brill, 1994)

Rosen-Zvi, I., 'The school of R. Ishmael and the origins of the concept of Yeser hara' (The Evil Inclination)', *Tarbiz* 76 (2006-2007), pp. 1–2

Rowley, H. H., *The Faith of Israel: Aspects of Old Testament Thought* (*Sprunt Lectures*) (London: SCM Press, 1956)

Russell, W., 'The Apostle Paul's Redemptive-Historical Argumentation in Galatians 5:13–26', *WTJ* 57:2 (1995), pp. 333–57

Ryan, J. M., 'God's Fidelity to Israel and Mercy to All', *TBT* 35:2 (1997), pp. 89–93

Sahlin, H., 'The New Exodus of Salvation according to St. Paul' in *The Root of the Vine: Essays in Biblical Theology*, edited by A. Fridrichsen (Westminster: Dacre, 1953), pp. 81–95

Sahlin, H., 'Adam-Christologie im Neuen Testament', *ST* 41 (1987), pp. 11–32 Sampley, J. P., *Paul in the Greco-Romans World* (Harrisburg: Trinity, 2003)

Sanday, W. and Headlam A., *A Critical and Exegetical Commentary on the Epistle to the Romans* (Edinburgh: T. & T. Clark, 1902)

Sanders, E. P., *Paul* (Oxford: Oxford University Press, 1991) Sanders, E. P., *Paul and Palestinian Judaism* (London: SCM, 1977)

Sandnes, K. O., '"Justification by Faith"—An Outdated Doctrine? The "New Perspective" on Paul—A Presentation and Appraisal', *Theology & Life* 17–19 (1996), pp. 127–46

Sandy, W., and Headlam, A., *A Critical and Exegetical Commentary of the Epistle to the Romans* (Edinburgh: T. & T. Clark, 1902)

Sass, G., 'Rom 15:7–13—als Summe des Romerbriefs gelesen', *EvT* 53 (1993), pp. 510–527

Schaefer, J. R., 'The Relationship between Priestly and Servant Messianism in the Epistle to the Hebrews', *CBQ* 30 (1968), pp. 359–85

Schillebeeckx, E., *Jesus: An Experiment in Christology,* translated by H. Hoskins (New York: Seabury, 1979)

Schnackenburg, R., *Baptism in the Thought of St. Paul: A Study in Pauline Theology,* translated by G. R. Beasley-Murray (Oxford: Basil Blackwell, 1964)

Schneider, B., 'The Corporate Meaning and Background of 1 Cor. 15:45b—O Eschatos Adam eis Pneuma Zōiopoioun', *CBQ* 29 (1967), pp. 450–67

Schoeps, H. J., *Paul: The Theology of the Apostle Paul in the Light of Jewish Religious History* (London: Lutterworth, 1961)

Schoeps, H. J., 'The Sacrifice of Jesus in Paul's Theology', *JBL* 65 (1946), pp. 385–392

Bibliography

Schrange, W., *Der erste Brief an die Korinthen 1*. Teilband, 1 Kor. 1:1—6:11 (Benziger: Neukirchener, 1991)

Schrange, W., *Der erste Brief an die Korinthen 2*. Teilband, 1 Kor. 6:12—11:16 (Benziger: Neukirchener, 1995)

Schreiner, T. R., *Circumcision: An Entree into 'Newness' in Pauline Thought* (PhD diss., Fuller Theological Seminary, 1983)

Schreiner, T. R., 'Did Paul Believe in Justification by Works? Another Look at Romans 2', *BullBibRes* 3 (1993), pp. 131–55

Schreiner, T. R., 'Does Romans 9 Teach Individual Election unto Salvation? Some Exegetical and Theological Reflections', *JETS* 36 (1993), pp. 25–40

Schreiner, T. R., 'Paul's View of the Law in Romans 10:4–5', *WTJ* 55 (1993), pp. 113–35 Schreiner, T. R., *Romans* (Grand Rapids: Baker, 1998)

Schreiner, T. R., 'πνεῦμα', *TDNT* 4:435

Schreiner, T. R., 'The Son of Man', *JBL* 79 (1960), pp. 119–129

Schweizer, E., *Lordship and Discipleship* (Naperville: Allenson, 1960) Scott, J. M., 'Adoption, Sonship', in *DPL*, pp. 15–18

Schreiner, T. R., *Adoption as Sons of God: An Exegetical Investigation into the Background of* ΥΙΟΘΕΣΙΑ *in the Pauline Corpus* (Tubingen: Mohr-Siebeck, 1992)

Scroggs, R., *The Last Adam: A Study in Pauline Anthropology* (Oxford: Blackwell, 1966)

Seifrid, M., 'Romans' in *Commentary on the New Testament Use of the Old Testament,* edited by G. K. Beale and D. A. Carson (Grand Rapids: Baker Academic, 2007), pp. 607–94

Shepherd, M. H., *The Paschal Liturgy and the Apocalypse* (London: Lutterworth, 1960)

Sherlock, C., *The Doctrine of Humanity* (Leicester: InterVarsity, 1996)

Shin, C. S., 'New Exodus Motif in the Letter to the Hebrews' (PhD diss., University of Wales, Lampeter, 2007)

Shogren, G. S., 'Presently Entering the Kingdom of Christ: the Background and Purpose of Col. 1:12–14', *JETS* 31 (1988), pp. 173–80

Shum, Shiu-Lun, *Paul's Use of Isaiah in Romans: A Comparative Study of Paul's Letter to the Romans and the Sibylline and Qumran Sectarian Texts. Wissenschaftliche Untersuchungen zum Neuen Testament* (Tubingen: Mohr Siebeck, 2002)

Siegert, F., *Argumentation Bei Paulus, Gezeigt an Rom. 9–11*. Wissenschaftliche Untersuchungen Zum Neuen Testament 34 (Tubingen: Mohr, 1985)

Skehan, P. W., *Studies in Israelite Wisdom and Poetry* (Washington, DC: Catholic Biblical Association, 1971)

Smiles, V. M., 'The Concept of 'Zeal' in Second Temple Judaism and Paul's Critique of it in Romans 10:2', *CBQ* 64:2 (2002), pp. 282–299

Smith, G., 'The Function of "Likewise" (ΩΣΑΥΤΩΣ) Romans 8:26', *TynBul* 49 (1998), pp. 29–38

Smolarz, S. R., *Covenant and the Metaphor of Divine Marriage in Biblical Thought: A Study with Special Reference to the Book of Revelation* (Eugene, OR: Wipf & Stock, 2010)

Snodgrass, S. G., 'Is the Kingdom of God about Eating and Drinking or Isn't It? Romans 14:17', *NovTest* 42:3 (2000), pp. 521–525

Song, Y. M., and J. S. Du Rand, 'The Story of the Red Sea as a Theological Framework of Interpretation', *VE* 30(2), Art. 337

Stählin, G., 'απαξ', *TDNT* 1:381–384

Stanley, Christopher D., *Arguing with Scripture*: *The Rhetoric of Quotations in the Letters of Paul* (London: T. & T. Clark, 2004)

Strauss, M.L., 'The Davidic Messiah in Luke-Acts: The Promise and its Fulfillment' in *Lukan Christology*, *Journal for the Study of the New Testament Supplement* (Sheffield: Sheffield Academic Press, 1995)

Stendahl, K., 'The Apostle Paul and the Introspective Conscience of the West', *HTR* (1963), pp. 199–215

Stott, J. R. W., *The Message of Ephesians*: *God's New Society* (Leicester: InterVarsity, 1979)

Stowers, S. K., 'Paul's Dialogue with a Fellow Jew in Romans 3:1–9', *CBQ* 46 (1984), pp. 707–722

Stowers, S. K., *A Rereading of Romans* (New Haven: Yale University Press, 1994)

Strickland, W., Jr., W. C. Kaiser, D. J. Moo, W. A. Van Gemeren, and S. N. Grundy, *Five Views on Law and gospel* (Grand Rapids: Zondervan, 1996)

Strom, M., *Reframing Paul: Conversations in Grace and Community* (Downers Grove, IL: InterVarsity, 2000)

Stuart, D. K., *Hosea-Jonah, Word Biblical Themes* (Dallas: Word Books, 1989)

Stuhlmacher, P., *Paul's Letter to the Romans: A Commentary* (Louisville, KY: Westminster John Knox, 1994)

Stuhlmacher, P., 'The Theme of Romans', *ABR* 36 (1988), pp. 31–44

Stuhlmacher, P., and E. R. Kalin, *Reconciliation Law and Righteousness: Essays in Biblical Theology* (Philadelphia: Fortress, 1986)

Talbert, C. H., 'Non-Pauline fragment at Romans 3:24–26', *JBL* 85:3 (1966), pp. 287–96 Talbert, C. H., *Romans* (Macon, GA: Smyth & Helwys, 2002)

Taylor, V., *The Atonement in the New Testament Teaching* 2nd ed. (London: Epworth, 1954) Taylor, V., *The Epistle to the Romans* (London: Epworth, 1955)

Thielman, F., 'The Story of Israel and the Theology of Romans 5–8' in *Pauline Theology*, vol. 3, editor by David M. Hay and E. Elizabeth Johnson (Minneapolis: Fortress, 1995), pp. 169– 96

Thiselton, A. T., *Hermeneutics: An Introduction (*Grand Rapids: Eerdmans, 2009)

Thiselton, A. T., *The Hermeneutics of Christian Doctrine* (Grand Rapids: Eerdmans, 2007)

Thiselton, A. T., *The Living Paul: An Introduction to the Apostles Life and Thought* (Downers Grove, IL: InterVarsity, 2009)

Tobin, T. H., 'What Shall We Say That Abraham Found? The Controversy behind Romans 4', *Dia* 35:3 (1996), pp. 193–198

Torrance, T. F., *Theology in Reconstruction* (London: SCM, 1965)

Trumper, T. J. R., 'From Slaves to Sons!', *Foundations* 55 (2006), pp. 17–19 Tsumura, D. T., 'An OT Background to Romans 8:22', *NTS* 40:4 (1994), pp. 620–621

Turner, M., *The Holy Spirit and Spiritual Gifts Then and Now* (Carlisle: Paternoster, 1996) Turner, N., *Grammatical Insights into the New Testament* (Edinburgh: T. & T. Clark, 1965) Turner, S., 'The Interim, Earthly Messianic Kingdom in Paul', *JSNT* 25:3 (2003), pp. 323–42

Udoeyop, E. A., 'The New People of God and Kingdom Fruitfulness: An Exegetical and Theological Study of the Parable of the Wicked Tenants in Matthew 21:33–46 and its Significance for a Corporate Hermeneutic' (PhD diss., Queen's University Belfast, 2006)

Van der Horst, P. W., 'Only then will All Israel be Saved: A Short Note on the Meaning of καὶ οὕτως in Romans 11:26', *JBL* 119:3 (2006), pp. 521–525

Vermes, G., 'Redemption & Genesis XXII. The Binding of Isaac and the Sacrifice of Jesus.' In *Scripture and Tradition in Judaism* (Leiden: Brill, 1961), pp. 193–227

Vleugels, G., 'The Jewish Scriptures in Galatians and Romans', Brussels: *Analecta Bruxellensia*, vol. 7 (2002), pp. 156–163

Wagner, J. R., 'The Christ, Servant of the Jews and Gentiles: A Fresh Approach to Romans 15:8–9', *JBL* 116:3 (1997), pp. 473–485

Wagner, J. R., *Heralds of the Good News: Isaiah and Paul 'In Concert' in the Letter to the Romans* (Supplements to Novum Testamentum, 101) (Leiden: Brill, 2002)

Wanamaker, C. A., *The Epistle to the Thessalonians: A Commentary on the Greek Text* (Grand Rapids: Eerdmans. 1990)

Warnack, V., 'Taufe und Heilsgeschehen nach Rom. 6', *ALW* 111:2 (1954), p. 259

Warnack, V., 'Die Tauflehre des Römerbriefes in der neueren theologischen Diskussion', *ALW* 2 (1958), pp. 274–332

Watts, R. E., *Isaiah's New Exodus and Mark, Wissenschaftliche Untersuchungen Zum Neuen Testament* (Tübingen: Mohr, 1997)

Webb, W. J., *Returning Home; New Covenant and Second Exodus as the Context for 2 Corinthians 6:14—7:1*. JSNTSupp 85 (Sheffield: JSOT Press, 1993)

Wedderburn, A. J. M., 'Adam and Christ: An Investigation into the Background of 1 Corinthians XV and Romans V:12–21' (PhD diss., Cambridge University, 1970)

Wedderburn, A. J. M., 'The Theological Structure of Romans 5:12', *NTS* 19 (1973), pp. 339–354

Weima, J. A. D., 'The Pauline Letter Closings: Analysis and Hermeneutical Significance', *BullBibRes* 5 (1995), pp. 177–97

Westerholm, S., *Israel's Law and the Church's Faith* (Grand Rapids: Eerdmans, 1988)

Westerholm, S., *Perspectives Old and New on Paul: The "Lutheran Paul" and his Critics* (Grand Rapids: Eerdmans, 2004)

Whelan, C. F., 'Amica Pauli: The Role of Phoebe in the Early Church', *JSNT* 49 (1993), pp. 67–85

Whiteley, D. E. H., 'St. Paul's Thought on the Atonement', *JTS* 8 (1957), pp. 240–255 Whiteley, D. E. H., *The Theology of St. Paul* (Oxford: Oxford University Press, 1964)

Whitsett, C. G., 'Son of God, Seed of David: Paul's Messianic Exegesis on Romans 1:3–4', *JBL* 119:4 (2000), pp. 661–81

Wifall, W., 'Son of *Man*—A Pre-Davidic Social Class?', CBQ 37 (1975), pp. 331–40 Wilckens, U., *Der Brief an die Romer*, 3 vols (Benziger/Neukirchener, 1978, 1980, 1982)

Wilder W. N., *Echoes of the Exodus Narrative in the Context and Background of Galatians 5:18* (Studies in Biblical Literature, Vol. 23) (New York: Peter Lang, 2001)

Williams, S. M., 'The "Righteousness of God" in Romans', *JBL* 99 (1980), pp. 241–290 Winger, M., 'The Law of Christ', *NTS* 46:4 (2000), pp. 537–46

Winter, B., *Seek the Welfare of the City: Christians as Benefactors and Citizens* (Grand Rapids: Eerdmans, 1994)

Witherington, B., III., *Grace in Galatia: A Commentary on St. Paul`s Letter to the Galatians* (Grand Rapids: Eerdmans, 1998)

Witherington, B., III., *Paul's Letter to the Romans: A Socio-Rhetorical Commentary* (Grand Rapids: Eerdmans, 2004)

Wood, J., 'The Purpose of Romans', *EvQ* 40:4 (1968), pp. 211–219

Index of Biblical References

Genesis

2:15–17	184, 206
2:16–17	144
3:1–3	217
3:5	54
3:14–19	146
3:15	98
3:17–19	218
9:21	368
12:1–3	234
12:1–4	228
12:1–9	8, 95
12:2–3	120, 178
12:3	48, 115, 226, 397
12:3b	226
12:7	116
15:1–20	108
15:1–21	8
15:2–4	120
15:2–6	251
15:5	106, 120
15:6	96, 97, 98, 100, 105, 107, 109, 116, 120, 127
15:6–18	96
15:8	95, 120
15:13–14	49, 132
15:18	134
16:1–4a	120
16:9–11	251
16:13	60
17:1–14	117
17:1–27	8
17:4–5	91, 121
17:4–5, 16	121
17:8	117
17:11	116
17:16–18	121
17:17	121
18:10	252
18:18	97
19:24–25, 28	268
20:13	122
22:1–19	128
22:1–2	123
22:3	123
22:5	123
22:6–8	122
22:14	126
22:17ff	46
22:18	91, 392
25:1–4	251
25:6	251
26:4	91, 392
28:3	250
28:3–4	250
28:13–14	250
28:14	392
42:13	131
49:10	248

Exodus

1:8–22	8
2:1–10	9
2:23	138
3:10	228
4:21–23	259
4:22	214, 245, 246, 324
4:22–23	245, 324
4:23	38
7:2–4	259
8:19	260
8:32	299
9:12	299

9:15–16	258, 259	56:1	47
9:16	40	**Leviticus**	
9:20	260	16:13–14	85
9:29–35	61	18:3b	279
11:3	260	18:5	278, 279
12:7	102	18:6ff.	22
12:21–24	9	18:3a	279
12:26	154	19:1	80, 176, 355
12:27	89	19:2	269, 330
13:2	324	19:3ff.	22
13:8	154	19:16	80
13:14–16	201	19:18	355
14:4ff.	259	19:33–34	74
14:13	47	20:3ff.	22
14:17–18	134	20:7	178
14:31	163	21:14	135
15:2	47	23:9–11	210
15:11	246	23:9–15	303
15:22	131	23:11	413
16:13–16	229		
18:17–26	339	**Numbers**	
19:6	324	1:53	139
19:7–9	134	3:12–13	324
22:21–27	365	6:26	42
22:29b	324	8:11	35
23:1–9	65	9:13–14	74
23:7	110	25:10–13	97
24:8	10		
32:1	103, 171, 175, 185, 307	**Deuteronomy**	
32:1, 8b	175	4:37	40
32:1, 4, 8	185	9:29	163
32:1–35	307	10:16	26, 72
32:1–6	103	14:1	246
32:8	175	21:22–23	34
32:11	40	22:1–3	353
32:32	244	24:10–13	362
33:12–17	103	25:5–10	211
33:18	246	30:6	26
34:1–10	103	30:10	281
34:1–32	280	30:12	273, 280, 281, 282, 283, 284, 293, 428
34:20	201	30:12b	280
40:34	245	30:15, 19	206
52:10	47	30:15–16	178, 207

Index of Biblical References

30:17–19	10	18:11	266
32:1–35	84	25:1ff.	11
32:6	246	25:18–20	131
32:15–18	292		
32:19–25	292	**2 Chronicles**	
32:21	291	3:1	126
32:43	392, 393	5:11–14	134
		6:42	42
Joshua		7:1–3	134
1:2	131	15:3	325
23:1–16	178	17:7	325
		34:21	242
Judges			
6:23	42	**Ezra**	
		2:1	131
Ruth		3:7ff	12
3:12	211	9:7	184
4:1–8	211		
		Nehemiah	
1 Samuel		4:1ff.	12
9:16	358	9:2, 34	184
10:1	14	9:6	117
10:20–24	9	9:31	323
16:1	358		
16:13	14	**Esther**	
18:16	313	5:2	135
26:9–11	112		
28:4	313	**Job**	
		1:6	38
2 Samuel		8:22	369
3:21	313	19:11	22
7:4–17	234	24:3	362
7:5–16	38	31:1–40	22
7:11–16	248		
7:11–17	111	**Psalm**	
11:1–27	113	2:7	38, 215, 358
15:1–4	332	2:8	38, 117
		5:9	81
1 Kings		10:7	81
12:1ff.	10	16:11	347
18:39, 45	298	19:7–14	191
19:10, 14	297	24:1–2	117
19:18	297	27:1–3	348
		30:8–12	235
2 Kings		30:11	369
17:1–20	11	31:1–5	22
17:27	325		

33:12–15	69	139:7	375
33:13–15	60	**Proverbs**	
35:26	369	2:22	52
36:1	81	3:5	330
37:28	42	3:21–26	22
44:4–8	184	18:4	319
44:8–12	232	20:1	362, 368
44:10–11, 22	232	20:16	362
44:13–16	232		
44:17–19	232	**Isaiah**	
44:23–24, 26	233	1:9	17
45:3	369	1:29	47
51:3–6	77	2:1–4	266
51:11	40	2:1–5	11, 46, 119, 402
69:13	138	2:2–3	397
69:22–23	300	4:4	52
69:22–28	300	6:6–7	355
71:15	83	8:14	17
73:6	369	9:1–7	11
76:10	79	9:2–7	248
80:8–18	308	9:6–7	11
81:8–12	55	9:7	13, 35
82:6	38	10:20	242, 252, 296
85:8	42	10:22–23	17
85:13	83	10:27–28	249
88:4–5, 10–12	235	11:1	11, 47
96:1–5	117	11:1–10	234
97:10	344	11:1–5	35
98:1–6	48	11:10	397
98:2	83	11:11	11
100:1–5	48	11:16	242
102:23–24	235	19:16–25	234
106:8–10	40	19:19–25	41, 115
109:29	369	19:21–25	397
110:1–4	136, 231	19:23–25	11, 46, 91, 302
114:2	305	19:24–25	266
116:3–4	235	20:3	34
119:7–112	330	22:22	35
119:16, 151–52, 158–60, 162, 167	70	23:4	47
		24:23	47
119:129–36	191	25:11	307
121:6	236	26:16–18	218
132:16	369	28:11–16	271

Index of Biblical References

28:15, 18	287	48:1	22
28:16	17, 287	48:16–18	222
29:6	52	48:20–21	11, 47
29:9–10	299	49:3, 6	227
29:10	17	49:6	47, 312
29:16	263	49:6–7	11
29:22	47	49:8	138
30:14	263	49:20–21	186, 211
31:1–3	378	49:22	312
32:1	110	49:22–23	11
33:9	47	50:1–2	211
37:24	34	50:1–8	186
37:32	242	50:8	397
40:1	17, 134, 321, 336	50:9–10	132
40:1–5	134, 336	51:1–3	222
40:3–5	216	51:5–11	84
40:5	163, 246	51:7	247
40:13	17	51:9	369
40:26	40	52:1	369
41:8–16	265	52:1–12	11, 47
41:8–9	34	52:3–10	288
42:1	34, 131, 137, 138, 222, 261, 305, 312	52:5	17
		52:7	11, 17, 35, 47, 206, 227
42:1–4	115, 131	52:7–10	11
42:1–7	305	52:10	47
42:1–9	234	52:15	17, 290
42:5–7	46	53:1	17, 289
42:6–7	41	53:8	52
42:13–14	138	53:11	132, 397
42:13–16	222	54:1–8	12, 211
43:1	192	54:5	192
43:7	88	54:13	206
44:1	22	54:14	84, 103, 110
44:3	11, 27, 131, 200, 212	55:3	35, 37, 290
44:22	192	55:3–4	11
44:28	260	55:13	11, 39
45:1	83, 247, 259, 358	56:1	47, 83, 269
45:1–5	358	56:3	11
45:9	263	56:3–8	46
45:9b	262	56:6–7	41
45:13	83	56:6–8	289
45:23b	336	56:7	312
45:25	103, 131	58:8	103, 131, 134

59:2–8, 12–15	367	16:21	40
59:7–8	17, 81	18:4–6	263
59:20	313, 315	18:6–7	260
59:21	11, 131, 200, 212	19:3	22
60:1–2, 13	131	21:8	211
60:1–3	234	22:8	268
60:3, 10	11	23:5	248
60:8–14	19	25:11	221
60:8–16	289	29:10–14	268
61:1–2	11	30:9	248
61:1–3	11, 14, 200, 212, 352	31:3	11, 226, 234, 316
61:3	84	31:9	246
61:10	12, 230, 325, 369	31:22	290
62:1	103	31:29	61
62:1–2	84, 110	31:31–34	11, 101, 234
62:2	312	31:33–34	316
62:4–5	12, 186, 211	33:4–26	234
62:5	192	33:14–17	11
62:11–12	228	33:15–16	38
63:5	81	33:17	248
63:9	323	34:1–10	336
63:10	40	39:8	52
64:8	263	46:12–13	268
65:2	17, 216, 218	51:7	138
65:13–15	34	**Lamentations**	
65:17	216	1:9–22	184
65:23	218	2:20–22	184
65:25	216	3:22	262
66:1–2	40	**Ezekiel**	
66:1–22	218	5:15	268
66:10–22	378	16:1–14	155
66:12	312	16:8	182
66:15	52	16:9	155
66:18	246	16:15ff	10
66:22	216	16:23–34	266
Jeremiah		16:26–58	185
4:4	72, 101	16:59–60	101
5:11	290	18:2	61
9:23–24	131	19:10–14	309
9:24	90	28:19	268
10:19–22	184	33:15	362
11:1–17	307	34:1–16	50
11:16–17	304		

Index of Biblical References

34:23	248	3:1	22
34:25	206	3:2	64, 116, 148, 245, 300
36:22–32	234	5:4–5	336
36:24	11, 200, 212	5:14–15	344
36:26–27	11	5:14–27	158
37:1–14	302	9:11–12	38
37:1–4	11		

Jonah

3:10	48

37:26	206		
38:23	312		
39:23	290		

Micah

4:2	312
4:9–10	218
7:7–10	184
7:15	11

39:29	27	
43:4	131	
44:21–23	325	
45:18–25	205	

Daniel

7:18	42
10:12–14	328
12:2	302

Habakkuk

2:4	50

Zephaniah

3:13	242

Hosea

1:10	91, 246, 263, 266
2:2	182, 227, 249, 265, 318
2:14	11
2:14–16	203
2:16, 19	12
2:23	227, 249, 265, 318
3:1	10, 266
4:1	22, 185, 290
4:12	290
6:7, 10	142
11:1	38, 215, 246
11:9–11	101
12:9	11
13:3	346
13:14	40, 302
14:1–3	336
14:6	304
4:15–5:7	185

Haggai

1:13–14	12
2:3–9	12

Zechariah

3:8–9	12
4:3, 12–14	304
6:12–14	38
12:10	42

Malachi

1:11	312
3:1	12
4:1	309

Matthew

1:1–17	248
3:1–6	24
3:3	16
3:6	152
3:7	51
3:17	39
5:5	117
5:10–12	136, 351
5:21–22	364

Joel

2:28	137, 208, 288
2:28–29	137

Amos

5:21–48	22
5:27–28	364
5:44	350
5:46	372
6:9–13	213
7:1–5	343
7:24–27	343
10:32	286
12:26	420
14:23	348
15:19–20	55
16:16	15, 38
16:23	352
17:3–4	14
18:15	377
18:15–17	22
18:16–17	377
18:20	405
19:16–22	22
19:27–30	234
21:44	46
22:1–14	203
22:1–4	186
22:15–22	360
22:21b	362
22:37–38	353
22:41–45	231
25:1–13	186
26:36	348
27:54	38
28:18	226, 227
28:18–20	227
28:19	40, 154, 234, 287
28:19–20	234

Mark

1:3	16
3:23–29	328
4:15	328
9:24	307
10:38	152
10:45	169
12:10	46
12:29–30	364
15:36	389

Luke

1:46–55, 67–79	231
2:8–38	231
2:25–38	404
3:4	16
3:7–8	104
3:10ff.	22
3:16	152
3:21	348
3:23–38	248
4:5–6	166
4:18–19	16
5:16	348
6:12	348
6:22–23	351
6:24–26	65
7:1–10	61
7:45	418
8:12	22
9:28	348
9:62	104
10:18	420
12:21	104
12:50	152
14:15–24	186
14:26	255
18:18	62
19:11–27	178
20:17	46
22:15–16	85
23:27–31	351
23:36	389
23:38	13
24:48–49	38

John

1:12	257
1:13	115
1:23	16
2:18–21	305
2:19	86, 248
3:1–2	61

Index of Biblical References

3:1–8	62	6:1–4	348
3:16	62, 104, 328	6:1–6	338, 342
3:16, 36	62	6:1–7	298, 339
3:27–30	186	6:4	348
3:36	51	6:6	327
4:23–24	50	7:51–58	88
5:24	62	8:3	152, 275
6:32–70	75	8:14–17	209
6:40	62	8:26	212
8:39–44	312	8:34–38	24
8:44	159	8:36	152
10:11	169, 379	9:1–2	361
10:28	62	9:11	348
10:33–39	40	9:15	302, 357
12:23	134	9:15–16	302
14:15–21	22, 283	9:16	235
14:16	340	9:23	48
15:26	38	9:24	275
15:26–27	283	9:26–27	243
16:13	38	9:27	340
16:20	347	10:17–23	61
17:3	62	10:22	68
17:11	406	10:44–18	209
19:29	389	10:44–48	305
Acts		10:45	137
1:14	348	10:45–46	223
2:1–4	134	11:11–18	78
2:4–8	223	11:19–26	421
2:17–18, 33	137	11:26	340
2:21	288	12:5	348
2:36–41	298	13:1	341, 401, 417, 421
2:38	24, 127, 152, 287	13:1–3	212, 401
2:38–41	24, 127	13:2	331, 337
2:40–41	22, 104	13:5, 15	358
2:41	250	13:14–52	341
2:42	339, 348	13:38–39	254, 271
2:44–45	348	13:38–41	102
3:1	348	13:38–52	116
4:4	250	13:48	317
4:10	169	14:1	358
4:11	46	14:4, 14	414
4:23–31	136	14:19	243
4:32–35	348	14:21–22	341

14:22	62, 213	20:28–31	353
15:1–2	19	20:36–38	351
15:5–21	378	21:7–14	407
15:6–9	214	21:8–9	338
15:12–35	239	21:10–11	407
15:14–21	305	21:11	337
15:15–21	78	21:17–26	19
15:16–17	14	21:20–21	378, 382
15:22–31	340	21:20–22	350
15:28	212	21:27	407
16:1–4	420	21:27–32	244
16:7	331	23:12	48
16:7–10	212	23:12–15	276
16:13–16	348	23:12–22	350
16:14	68	23:12–30	401
16:14–15	61	24:17	407
17:1–9	421	24:23	349
17:10–12	358	25:10–11	357
17:14ff.	420	25:11	401
17:30–31	60	26:12	357
17:31	69	26:15–18	174
18:1–3	410, 412	26:17–18	47, 397
18:3	403	26:18	51, 358, 366
18:4	358	28:16	401
18:5	420	28:16–31	407
18:9	212	28:30	21
18:18	412		
18:18, 26	412	**Romans**	
18:21	44	1:2	26, 82, 146, 199, 352
18:24–26	412	1:3	26, 30, 53, 86, 88, 136, 201, 231, 248, 249, 285, 317, 331, 371, 382, 399
19:2	209, 296, 412, 422		
19:6	223	1:3–4	53, 249
19:8	358	1:4	46
19:9	244	1:5	302, 318, 419
19:22	420, 422	1:5–6	318
19:23	296	1:7	22
19:29–40	412	1:9–10	338
20:2	44, 157, 186, 353, 407	1:11–12	399
20:4ff.	420	1:14–16	400
20:16	400	1:15	399
20:17–19, 31	351	1:16	148, 196, 275
20:26–27	407	1:16–18	148
20:28	157, 186, 353	1:16–31	196

Index of Biblical References

Reference	Pages
1:17	64, 269
1:18–32	143, 264
1:28–32	352
1:29–31	82
1:30, 32	331
2:1	349
2:4	310
2:5, 16	51
2:5, 8	355
2:8	60
2:12–16	144
2:13	167
2:14–16	116
2:17	90
2:23	90
2:24	17
2:25–29	91, 269
2:28–29	25, 26, 69
3:3	307
3:4	167
3:15–17	17
3:19–20	254
3:20	167
3:21	25, 27, 37, 40, 46, 66, 74, 136, 139, 146, 153, 199, 200, 231, 265, 447
3:21ff.	30
3:21ff.	40
3:21ff.	139
3:21ff.	231
3:21ff.	265
3:21–25	25, 27, 136
3:21–26	53, 66, 74, 101, 153, 200, 205
3:22–24	319
3:23	64, 102, 110, 133
3:24	167
3:25	86, 444
3:26	128, 167
3:28	167
3:30	167
4:1–25	317
4:1–3, 12, 13, 16, 18	306
4:2	167
4:5	167
4:7	105, 106
4:7–8	105
4:9	131
4:11–12	17
4:11b–12	304
4:16	125, 304
4:16–17	269, 304
4:18	131
4:19	131
4:20	131, 307
4:23–24	125
4:25	88, 114, 125, 132, 134
5:1	23, 66, 90, 104, 116, 119, 131, 133, 153, 159, 167, 190, 208, 213, 265, 348, 367, 376, 382, 428
5:1ff.	213
5:1ff.	348
5:1ff.	367
5:1–11	153
5:1–4	208
5:2	131
5:3	25, 213
5:3–5	25
5:5	159, 206, 395
5:6	131
5:6–8	131, 223
5:8	159, 344
5:9	128, 131, 167
5:12	23, 66, 90, 265
5:12ff	66
5:12ff.	66
5:12ff	90
5:12ff.	90
5:12ff	265
5:12ff.	265
5:13	119
5:13, 20	254
5:15	159
5:17	116, 190
5:17–19	116

5:18–19	104	8:17, 29	87
5:20	158, 183	8:18	201, 226, 274, 406
6:1ff.	153	8:18–25	201, 406
6:1–4	128, 171, 208	8:19–25	39
6:4	134, 154, 284	8:25–39	25
6:6	151, 187, 189, 195	8:28–30	322
6:7	104, 182, 230	8:29	201
6:13–14	325, 328	8:30	167
6:17–18	338	8:30–39	201
7:1–2	185	8:31	222, 225
7:1–4	202, 211, 329	8:31–39	222, 284
7:1–6	204	8:32	269
7:2	190, 204, 352	8:33	167
7:4	104	8:34	223
7:4–6	203, 284	8:35–39	153, 208
7:10	102	9:1–5	65, 116, 144, 241
7:12	82	9:4	83
7:21–25	352	9:6–13	263
8:1	38, 39, 87, 153, 168, 200, 201, 210, 212, 220, 222, 226, 229, 274, 283, 323, 346, 347, 406	9:6–17	241
		9:8	215
		9:14–24	241
		9:17	61, 242
8:1–3	347	9:17–18	242
8:3	39, 40, 199, 201, 208, 222, 223, 225, 269, 324	9:25	242, 244, 318
		9:25–26	263
8:3, 32	136	9:25–29	244
8:3–4, 29	324	9:25–33	242
8:5	199	9:27–28	17
8:5–7	199	9:28–39	425
8:6	199, 352, 382	9:29	17
8:6–7	352	9:33b	17
8:9	38, 134, 227, 346	9:33a	17
8:9–11	134	10:1–4	83
8:9, 12–13	346	10:2–4	273
8:10–17	283	10:4	284, 330
8:11	200, 210, 212, 220, 222	10:5–15	234
8:13	168, 200	10:6	278, 281, 282
8:13–25	168	10:7	281, 282
8:14, 19	38	10:9	24, 255, 273
8:15	38, 153, 346	10:9–11	255
8:15–17	38, 153	10:9–15	24
8:16–17	200	10:11	17
8:17	38, 87, 229	10:12–13	127

Index of Biblical References

10:12–18	104	14:10–13	349
10:14b, 17	347	14:11–12	167
10:14–15	153, 227	14:14–17	19
10:15	17	14:17	347
10:16	17, 274	14:20	371
10:16–21	274	15:2	17, 18, 80, 266, 337, 343, 387, 399, 401
10:21	17	15:3–4	387
11:1–6	295	15:4	36, 83, 330, 341, 347
11:7–10	295	15:4–5	341
11:8	17	15:13	347
11:11–12	295	15:15–16	327
11:11–24	25	15:16	35, 43, 325, 338, 387
11:16	295	15:16–17	338
11:17–21	245, 295	15:21	17
11:20, 23	307	15:23	18, 80
11:22–24	296	15:23–24	80
11:25	242, 296, 440	15:23–33	400
11:25–32	296	15:24	399
11:26	17, 244, 296	15:25	266, 337, 401
11:26–27	17	15:28	387
11:27	315	15:31	405
11:33–34	17	15:32	44
11:33–36	257	16:1ff.	23
12:1	23, 25, 35, 43, 227, 332, 357, 359, 366, 378, 411	16:1–2	349
12:1ff.	23	16:5,16	157
12:1–2	25, 35, 227, 357, 366	16:14–15	413
12:1–21	366	16:17–19	339
12:3	343	16:23	349, 444
12:6–8	343	16:25–26	37

1 Corinthians

12:9–11	337
12:11	357
12:13	411
12:16	332
12:19	359
12:21	344
13:1–7	63
13:8	277
13:9–10	366
14:9	162, 371
14:9, 15	371
14:10	51, 332, 371
14:10–12	371

1:2	25, 37, 49, 157, 169, 253, 334, 421
1:3	42
1:11–17	171
1:14, 17	287
1:23	37, 49, 169
1:26–31	253
2:4	38
2:6–16	234
2:9	50, 216, 347
2:10	319
2:14	37

2:16	320	10:1–11	268
3:1–9	171	10:1–13	36, 153, 262, 367
3:8	66	10:1–14	171
4:6	83	10:1–22	307
5:1–13	391	10:1–4	40, 152, 153, 171
5:1–8	262	10:1–6	83, 199
5:2–5	377	10:2	152, 373
5:3–5	175	10:3ff.	22
5:3–8	161	10:6–13	284
5:4	405	10:6–14	22
5:6–8	172	10:19–22	55
5:7	75, 87, 89, 128, 153, 172, 200, 202, 303, 323, 396, 397	10:20, 25–32	19
		10:23–32	373
5:7b	396	11:29–32	212
5:7–8	75, 172	12:7–13	38
5:11	367	12:8–11	336
6:1–2	148	12:10, 30	223
6:1–3	168	12:12, 27	165
6:1–8	350	12:13	152, 153
6:2	117, 153, 186, 228	12:22–26	346
6:9–10	55	13:1–13	381
6:9–11	161	13:2	395
6:10	367	13:4–8a	344
6:11	153	14:3	341
6:15–17	187	14:4	337
6:16–17	345	14:4–28	223
6:19–20	305	14:5	388
6:20	186	14:22	337
7:25	342	15:3	30, 161, 177, 210, 412
7:25–28	23	15:12–34	171
7:32–35	415	15:20	143, 210, 441
8:1–8	373	15:20–28	143, 441
8:4	19	15:22	23
8:4–7	19	15:24–25	62
8:6	249, 336	15:30	412
8:13	380	15:37–58	177
9:1–18	403	15:42–55	134
9:5	415	15:54	132
9:12	357	15:55	302
9:13–14	338	16:1–3	266
9:27	332	16:1–4	349
10:1ff	134, 152, 170	16:3	402
10:1–10	161	16:10ff.	420

16:15–17	337	11:2	186, 203, 225, 244, 276, 412
16:19	412	11:7–8	338
16:20	418	11:13–15	45, 414
16:22	418	11:16–33	235
		11:23b–28	232
2 Corinthians		11:23–29	225
1:2	12, 37, 42	11:23b–33	412
1:8–9a	232	11:24	244
1:15ff.	400	11:25	276
1:20	12, 37, 42	11:28–29	206, 244
2:4	351	11:28–33	232
2:4, 13	206	11:31	243
3:7–18	244	12:7–10	213
3:9	49	12:11ff.	414
3:13–16	37	12:12	398
3:18	38, 227	13:12	418
4:4	54, 232	13:14	336
4:4–10	232		
4:7–18	236	**Galatians**	
4:8	232	1:3	42, 156, 158
5:10	66, 167, 378	1:4	41, 51, 82, 101
5:14–15	162	1:6	45, 275, 346
5:16	389	1:6–9	45, 275
5:17	24, 217	1:12	423
5:19	107	1:13–14	361
5:20	38	1:18–20	243
5:21	66, 204	2:1–10	243
6:1–10	174	2:2–5	42
6:4–10	232	2:10	403, 404
6:8–10	232	2:14	365, 379
6:8–9	232	2:15	71, 99
6:14–18	365, 418	2:15–16	99
6:18	38	3:1–5	100
7:5–7	340	3:2	38
7:13	44	3:6	99
8:1	157, 402	3:6, 8, 9, 14, 16	306
8:9–15	388	3:6–7	100
8:19	402	3:6–9, 26–29	295
8:22ff.	401	3:13	66, 74, 96, 101
10:1	328, 333	3:14	100, 156
10:5	237	3:16	98, 109, 252
10:8	358	3:19	98, 102, 109
10:12–18	333	3:22	102

3:24	114, 118, 270	2:8	110, 265, 299
3:25	284	2:8–18	265
3:25–29	215, 228	2:8–9	299
3:26–29	42, 101, 156	2:9	253
4:1–7	156	2:9b	253
4:4–5	138, 248	2:10	301
4:6	38	2:11–13	101, 302
4:21–31	101	2:14	21, 101, 394
4:22	306	2:14–18	394
4:24–27	314	2:14–21	43
4:29	252	2:14–22	101
5:6	101	2:15	21, 135, 164, 382
5:11	48	2:16	165, 329
5:13	337	2:18, 21	135
5:16–26	346	2:18–20	305
5:18	284	2:18–22	42
5:19–21	55	2:22	343, 344
5:22	344	3:4–6	312
6:10	349	3:6	38, 165
6:11	421	3:10–11	301
6:12	350, 418	3:10–13	390
6:12ff.	418	4:4–6	155
6:14–15	101	4:8	281, 282, 283
6:16	26, 250, 367	4:11–12	338
Ephesians		4:11–13	341
2:11–13	22	4:11–14	339
1:2	24, 42, 135, 358	4:12	337, 343, 388
1:3b	26	4:12, 29	388
1:3–14	226	4:12–13	343
1:4	255	4:17–32	329
1:7	74, 101	4:18	54
1:13–14	22	4:20–24	335
1:13–22	150	4:24	369
1:15–23	43	4:28	349
1:20	135	5:1	23, 330
1:21	358	5:5	62
2:1–10	155	5:8–20	366
2:1–3	47, 160	5:17	330
2:2	358	5:22–25	23
2:2–8	148	5:23	165
2:3	52, 148	5:25	101, 135, 159, 186, 203, 211
2:4–10	162, 163, 279	5:25ff.	159
2:6	128		

Index of Biblical References

5:25–26	155, 156, 334	3:4–6	66, 70, 191
5:25–27	101, 135, 203, 211	3:6	157, 346
5:32	101	3:7–11	48
6:1–9	23	3:18	351, 418
6:10–18	236, 328	3:18ff.	418
6:11	366	3:20	136, 207
6:20	38	3:20–21	136
6:21–22	340, 349	3:21	279
6:22	44	4:2	23, 354
		4:2–3	354
		4:4–7	351

Philippians

1:1	24, 183, 213, 234, 275	4:8	328, 420
1:2	38, 42	4:9	408
1:3–11	43	4:10, 14–16, 18	348
1:9	319	4:10–20	403
1:12–30	213		
1:17	275		

Colossians

1:19–30	234	1:2	24, 42, 218, 351
1:27	38	1:3–14	43
2:1ff.	23	1:3–21	149
2:1–11	388	1:6–8	409
2:1–15	381, 382	1:12–13	96
2:2–4	388	1:12–14	22, 449
2:3, 5	331	1:12–21	143
2:4–11	143	1:13	36, 41, 47, 51, 53, 74, 82, 132, 147, 158, 218, 228, 265, 269, 284, 358
2:5–11	53, 227, 249		
2:5–8	36		
2:5–9	371	1:13–12	53
2:6–10	149	1:13–14	41, 47, 51, 82, 147, 265, 284
2:6–11	372		
2:10–1	336	1:13–15	132
2:14–16a	329	1:13–20	36, 218
2:15	38, 227	1:13–21	228
2:15–16	227	1:14	159
2:17–18	351	1:15	201, 217, 249, 323
2:17b–18	351	1:15–20	249
2:19–24	420	1:18	102
2:25	349, 401, 414	1:20	218
2:25–30	401, 414	1:24	351
3:1–6	48	1:27	209
3:2	136, 207, 279, 297, 365	2:8, 16–18	419
3:2–14	297	2:11	74, 75, 101, 102, 115
3:3	50, 74, 102, 103	2:11–13a	101
3:3–6	102, 103	2:11–23	115

2:13b–15	102	1:5–10	52, 60
2:16	19	**1 Timothy**	
3:1	21, 45, 49, 168, 330, 335, 369	1:11–12	338
3:2ff.	23	1:13	307
3:5–17	329	1:15–16	401
3:8–14	150	2:5	224
3:9–10	243	3:1–7	341
3:9–12	164	3:3	368
3:10	21, 45, 49, 335, 369	3:6	331, 332
3:10–11	49	3:8	342, 362
3:10–14	45	3:8–13	342
3:15	330	3:10, 13	337
4:8	44	4:13	338, 341
4:15	157, 413	4:13–14	338
4:15–17	409	5:10	349
4:17	23	5:17	342
1 Thessalonians		5:22	341
1:1	22, 24, 25, 334, 355	6:16	61
1:3b	347	6:18	349
1:4	255	**2 Timothy**	
1:6–8	213	1:4	351
1:10	355	1:8–14	235
1:12–14	22	1:10	235, 321
2:1–3	341	1:14	208, 210
2:9–16	148	2:8–13	235
2:14–16	60	2:11–13	213
2:16	52	3:14–17	78
2:18	400	4:2	341, 421
3:2, 6	420	4:5	338
4:3–8	171, 226	4:9–13	401
4:9–10	345	4:10	346
4:13–18	341	4:19	412
4:16	24	4:22	421
5:11	341, 343	**Titus**	
5:12–13	342	1:5	339, 341, 400
5:18	330	1:6–9	342
5:23	68	1:7	362
5:26	418	1:7–9	341
2 Thessalonians		1:9	342
1:1	25	2:3	368
1:4	347	2:11–14	61
		3:2	362

Index of Biblical References

3:6	137	13:7, 17	362
		13:16	349
Philemon			
1:2	24	**James**	
1:4–7	43, 340	1:2	136, 192, 213, 348
		1:2–4	136
Hebrews		1:2–8	348
1:1–14	53	1:13–18	79
1:1–4	285	1:23–25	192
1:1–6	149	2:1–7	65
1:8–9	227	2:10	66
2:1–3	148	2:21–23	127
2:5–18	204	2:23	108
2:5–9	228	2:26	41
2:6–13	53	4:5	148
2:17–18	37, 136	5:4–5	362
4:14–16	224		
4:15b	69	**1 Peter**	
5:1–10	231	1:4–5	347
5:1–4	231	1:6–7	136
5:1–5	136	1:6–9	351
5:7	136, 352	1:15–16	176
5:7–10	136	2:4–6	305
7:16	231	2:5	324, 325
7:22	226	2:5, 9	324
9:1–7	170	2:6–8	46
9:7–10	231	2:21–25	388
9:8–28	41	4:9	349
9:9	149	4:12–16	348, 351
9:11–14	136	4:17	148
9:11–15	231	5:5	362
9:13	149	5:14	418
9:22	150		
9:24–27	148	**2 Peter**	
9:24–28	169	2:4–18	60
10:11–18	397	3:2	396
10:29–31	148	3:3–5	60
11:11	122		
11:19	266	**1 John**	
11:24–29	200	1:4	347
12:1–17	136	2:15	328
12:1–3	388, 396	3:16–24	41
12:22	314	3:17	65
12:28	234	4:7–19	344
		4:19	159

4:20–21	344	2:4	262, 346
5:13	396	2:4–6, 14–16, 21–23	262
		2:5	212, 311
3 John		2:15	262
1:3–8	349	2:20–23	175
1:5–8	349	3:1–3	262
1:9–10	353	5:10	216
Revelation		6:16	60
1:3	22	13:8	389
1:4–6	231	18:2–3	55
1:4–8	53	19:7	203, 351
1:5–6	150, 228	19:9	186
1:6	325	21:1–2	314
1:12–18	231	21:5	217, 218
1:18	169	21:22–26	305

Selected Topical Index

Abraham, 8, 18, 20, 26, 27, 35, 46, 50, 66, 69, 94, 100, 101, 102, 103, 104, 110, 111, 112, 113, 114, 115, 116, 117, 119, 120, 121, 122, 123, 124, 125, 126, 127, 128, 129, 130, 131, 132, 133, 134, 135, 137, 138, 140, 159, 164, 182, 187, 208, 216, 221, 225, 228, 238, 243, 250, 251, 256, 257, 260, 261, 262, 263, 265, 267, 268, 274, 277, 278, 281, 310, 311, 315, 317, 318, 319, 320, 321, 323, 326, 327, 328, 329, 331, 332, 334, 342, 359, 410, 414, 443, 447, 450, 458, 472

Adam, 17, 24, 27, 37, 53, 54, 55, 66, 82, 85, 93, 108, 112, 115, 137, 138, 143, 147, 148, 149, 150, 151, 152, 153, 155, 156, 157, 159, 163, 166, 168, 169, 170, 172, 173, 174, 175, 186, 190, 191, 192, 195, 196, 197, 198, 200, 201, 202, 203, 204, 205, 207, 210, 211, 212, 214, 215, 216, 221, 226, 227, 232, 237, 238, 240, 257, 275, 276, 277, 278, 283, 334, 345, 394, 395, 425, 440, 448, 449, 454, 457, 459, 466, 468, 469, 470, 473

adoption, 208, 222, 224, 225, 228, 231, 255, 256, 259

ascension, 16, 290, 293, 294, 295, 394

atonement, 87, 88, 92, 102, 154, 411

Babylon/Babylonian, 12, 35, 39, 40, 48, 51, 74, 85, 86, 90, 92, 100, 108, 109, 137, 138, 141, 144, 172, 211, 221, 230, 238, 242, 246, 252, 256, 258, 276, 279, 286, 288, 289, 297, 302, 303, 309, 317, 331, 335, 351, 362, 385

baptism, 28, 30, 40, 77, 106, 109, 121, 159, 160, 161, 162, 163, 164, 165, 166, 170, 171, 172, 180, 190, 194, 223, 300

Bride/Bridegroom, 10, 106, 141, 142, 163, 167, 177, 182, 190, 193, 194, 200, 205, 211, 212, 213, 214, 220, 224, 229, 240, 243, 299, 305, 306, 340, 341, 343, 350, 368, 442, 464

Christ, 3, 4, 5, 6, 7, 14, 15, 19, 21, 24, 25, 26, 27, 28, 33, 34, 35, 36, 38, 39, 40, 42, 43, 44, 46, 49, 55, 64, 68, 71, 72, 73, 75, 77, 84, 86, 89, 90, 91, 92, 94, 97, 99, 103, 104, 105, 106, 107, 108, 109, 110, 112, 113, 114, 120, 121, 123, 131, 132, 133, 134, 139, 140, 141, 142, 144,

145, 147, 150, 151, 152, 153, 154, 155, 156, 157, 159, 160, 161, 162, 163, 164, 165, 166, 167, 168, 169, 170, 171, 172, 173, 174, 175, 176, 177, 178, 179, 180, 181, 182, 183, 185, 186, 188, 189, 190, 191, 193, 194, 196, 205, 206, 207, 208, 209, 210, 211, 212, 213, 214, 216, 217, 218, 219, 220, 221, 223, 224, 225, 228, 229, 230, 231, 234, 236, 237, 239, 240, 241, 243, 244, 245, 246, 247, 250, 253, 254, 255, 259, 261, 262, 263, 276, 280, 281, 285, 286, 288, 289, 290, 291, 292, 293, 295, 296, 297, 298, 300, 303, 304, 306, 310, 312, 315, 318, 328, 331, 333, 334, 335, 336, 339, 340, 341, 342, 343, 344, 345, 347, 348, 349, 350, 351, 352, 353, 354, 355, 358, 360, 361, 363, 364, 365, 368, 370, 372, 375, 381, 384, 385, 386, 387, 389, 390, 391, 393, 394, 395, 396, 397, 398, 399, 400, 402, 405, 406, 407, 408, 409, 410, 412, 413, 414, 415, 416, 417, 418, 421, 422, 424, 425, 426, 427, 429, 431, 433, 434, 435, 436, 438, 439, 440, 442, 443, 444, 445, 447, 448, 449, 450, 451, 452, 453, 454, 455, 456, 457, 458, 459, 460, 461, 462, 464, 465, 467, 468, 470, 472, 473

circumcision, 6, 12, 19, 20, 26, 27, 42, 69, 71, 74, 75, 76, 77, 79, 93, 97, 98, 99, 103, 104, 105, 106, 109, 116, 119, 120, 121, 122, 123, 124, 126, 127, 128, 166, 173, 223, 249, 261, 262, 265, 282, 311, 319, 320, 328, 367, 370, 410, 416, 439, 443

Death, 176, 447, 451, 454, 457, 462, 465

Egypt, 8, 9, 10, 11, 40, 48, 55, 56, 85, 90, 102, 108, 111, 127, 128, 134, 137, 138, 139, 144, 146, 150, 157, 160, 162, 166, 167, 168, 172, 180, 181, 190, 193, 210, 222, 223, 225, 228, 233, 238, 242, 256, 258, 269, 276, 287, 288, 290, 291, 313, 314, 339

election, 120, 184, 236, 243, 249, 251, 252, 264, 266, 267, 268, 278, 280, 332, 333

Exodus, First, 111, 141, 324

Exodus, New, 13, 14, 16, 27, 32, 39, 41, 51, 87, 110, 131, 134, 137, 138, 142, 167, 188, 213, 220, 221, 232, 250, 252, 253, 255, 293, 294, 296, 297, 309, 313, 336, 340, 350, 384, 387, 415, 447, 452, 459, 463, 467, 468, 470, 473

Exodus, Old, 8

Exodus, Second, 11, 110, 220, 256, 293, 297, 324, 336, 340, 387, 412, 473

firstborn, 9, 89, 91, 130, 134, 137, 146, 209, 220, 226, 227, 228, 229, 236, 237, 262, 264, 265, 271, 331, 337, 339, 340, 345, 415, 433

flesh, 12, 26, 27, 36, 37, 77, 106, 112, 113, 144, 195, 200, 202, 205, 206, 207, 212, 213, 214, 216, 217, 220, 247, 252, 255,

Selected Topical Index

259, 262, 263, 345, 347, 362, 387, 407

Gentiles, 1, 2, 4, 6, 17, 19, 20, 21, 25, 27, 35, 36, 41, 42, 45, 46, 48, 49, 50, 66, 67, 68, 69, 70, 72, 73, 74, 75, 76, 80, 82, 83, 84, 85, 87, 90, 93, 94, 98, 99, 104, 105, 106, 107, 108, 110, 113, 116, 117, 119, 120, 121, 123, 124, 125, 133, 150, 151, 173, 187, 205, 207, 218, 224, 244, 249, 250, 251, 253, 255, 256, 258, 260, 261, 263, 264, 265, 268, 271, 272, 273, 275, 276, 277, 278, 280, 281, 282, 285, 287, 288, 289, 301, 304, 305, 309, 310, 311, 312, 314, 315, 316, 317, 319, 320, 321, 322, 323, 324, 325, 327, 328, 329, 330, 331, 332, 333, 334, 335, 338, 340, 343, 344, 348, 354, 367, 370, 371, 375, 377, 389, 400, 405, 406, 409, 410, 411, 412, 413, 414, 415, 416, 417, 421, 422, 423, 430, 432, 433, 434, 438, 439, 443, 453, 456, 459, 461, 466, 472

Israel, 6, 8, 10, 11, 12, 15, 17, 18, 23, 26, 27, 31, 32, 33, 34, 35, 36, 37, 38, 39, 41, 42, 43, 46, 48, 49, 50, 52, 53, 55, 56, 67, 69, 73, 74, 75, 79, 81, 83, 84, 85, 86, 90, 91, 92, 94, 98, 100, 102, 106, 107, 108, 109, 110, 111, 112, 117, 118, 119, 120, 123, 124, 130, 138, 139, 140, 149, 150, 153, 157, 160, 162, 163, 164, 167, 170, 172, 180, 181, 185, 186, 187, 188, 189, 190, 192, 193, 200, 201, 204, 205, 207, 211, 212, 213, 215, 221, 223, 224, 225, 229, 230,

231, 235, 236, 237, 238, 240, 242, 243, 247, 250, 251, 252, 253, 255, 256, 257, 260, 261, 263, 268, 271, 272, 273, 275, 276, 277, 278, 279, 280, 281, 291, 292, 293, 296, 297, 300, 302, 303, 304, 305, 306, 309, 310, 311, 312, 313, 315, 316, 317, 318, 319, 320, 322, 323, 324, 326, 327, 328, 329, 331, 332, 334, 336, 339, 340, 347, 353, 363, 376, 379, 383, 384, 385, 387, 396, 400, 410, 411, 415, 423, 442, 451, 452, 453, 456, 457, 458, 459, 460, 464, 465, 467, 468, 471, 472, 473

justification, 61, 69, 87, 90, 91, 97, 98, 99, 100, 101, 102, 103, 104, 105, 106, 107, 108, 109, 110, 111, 112, 113, 114, 115, 116, 117, 119, 122, 131, 133, 134, 135, 138, 139, 153, 155, 175, 176, 179, 187, 210, 234, 243, 267, 282, 300

kingdom of darkness, 48, 51, 52, 77, 85, 90, 101, 108, 116, 134, 138, 141, 144, 148, 153, 166, 168, 170, 179, 181, 182, 185, 186, 205, 210, 212, 220, 236, 241, 287, 302, 313, 366, 394

new covenant, 12, 25, 28, 34, 42, 50, 88, 104, 105, 106, 110, 121, 123, 133, 138, 141, 159, 215, 243, 251, 252, 262, 276, 289, 290, 291, 296, 298, 302, 306, 307, 310, 319, 320, 322, 326, 327, 330, 331, 332, 336, 350, 353, 409, 416, 433, 438

new creation, 16, 137, 141, 195, 226, 227, 444

new man, 21, 141, 173, 211, 237, 251, 400, 444

old covenant, 252, 295, 302, 422

old man, 172, 173

Passover, 9, 27, 77, 87, 88, 89, 91, 92, 94, 105, 106, 134, 139, 140, 146, 161, 162, 181, 191, 207, 208, 209, 210, 213, 219, 271, 306, 318, 340, 385, 415, 416, 433, 452, 459, 462, 465

persecution, 9, 222, 235, 241, 242, 244, 361, 364, 366, 441

pilgrim, 26, 137, 142, 161, 167, 215, 225, 238, 239, 242, 243, 278, 286, 303, 351

rebellion, 48, 52, 61, 90, 150, 166, 173, 280, 348, 377, 411

redeemer, 133, 194, 195, 209, 214, 220, 223, 226, 227, 237, 257, 260, 270, 296, 310, 329, 330, 339, 340, 384

regeneration, 160, 161

repent/repentance, 24, 58, 62, 84, 109, 160, 170, 191, 269, 271, 272, 275, 292, 305, 312, 313, 324, 325, 333, 334, 367, 395

resurrection, 16, 38, 39, 40, 41, 42, 47, 48, 50, 80, 97, 120, 133, 134, 138, 140, 141, 145, 166, 171, 172, 178, 208, 219, 229, 230, 231, 245, 258, 286, 289, 294, 295, 296, 317, 324, 331, 368, 394, 407, 444

Satan, 20, 48, 55, 56, 59, 73, 82, 84, 93, 102, 138, 141, 147, 148, 149, 150, 151, 155, 168, 169, 170, 175, 177, 178, 182, 184, 185, 187, 190, 192, 194, 195, 197, 198, 200, 201, 202, 203, 204, 205, 207, 210, 211, 212, 214, 218, 231, 239, 300, 303, 336, 345, 347, 348, 362, 394, 401, 410, 418, 424, 440

saviour, 352

servant(s), 25, 33, 34, 35, 168, 183, 184, 185, 186, 187, 190, 193, 244, 256, 268, 270, 274, 280, 301, 334, 339, 346, 347, 355, 356, 359, 372, 375, 376, 378, 379, 380, 391, 406, 410, 417, 418, 427, 430, 431, 440

sin, 36, 37, 48, 51, 52, 53, 54, 55, 56, 57, 58, 65, 71, 75, 81, 82, 83, 84, 85, 87, 88, 89, 90, 93, 94, 97, 99, 100, 103, 107, 108, 110, 111, 112, 114, 117, 118, 139, 141, 148, 149, 150, 151, 152, 153, 154, 155, 156, 157, 159, 166, 167, 168, 169, 170, 172, 173, 174, 175, 176, 177, 178, 179, 180, 181, 182, 183, 184, 185, 186, 187, 188, 189, 190, 191, 192, 193, 194, 195, 196, 197, 198, 199, 200, 201, 202, 203, 204, 205, 207, 209, 210, 211, 212, 213, 214, 216, 217, 218, 220, 221, 227, 228, 231, 237, 238, 240, 241, 252, 254, 272, 280, 281, 283, 286, 287, 298, 299, 303, 306, 311, 316, 325, 334, 336, 342, 348, 349, 355, 356, 366, 372, 381, 383, 386, 394, 397, 403, 409, 413

solidarity, 138, 152, 168, 173, 174, 190, 195, 210, 252

Son of David, 14, 16, 18, 31, 33, 36, 37, 38, 39, 40, 47, 85, 87,

Selected Topical Index

92, 123, 131, 142, 145, 209, 213, 232, 241, 255, 283, 286, 293, 296, 297, 301, 303, 315, 339, 400, 418

Son of God, 33, 34, 38, 40, 54, 65, 178, 209, 211, 231, 286, 323, 358, 360, 406, 458, 461, 473

Spirit, 11, 15, 16, 26, 28, 38, 39, 41, 51, 76, 80, 104, 105, 109, 121, 137, 141, 143, 159, 160, 161, 162, 164, 165, 166, 167, 170, 171, 189, 190, 191, 196, 207, 208, 209, 211, 212, 213, 214, 215, 216, 217, 218, 219, 220, 221, 222, 223, 224, 225, 228, 229, 230, 231, 232, 233, 234, 236, 239, 248, 253, 254, 258, 263, 286, 290, 293, 295, 296, 300, 320, 342, 343, 344, 347, 352, 353, 357, 360, 361, 363, 369, 394, 400, 406, 408, 412, 413, 414, 415, 417, 425, 431, 434, 454, 455, 464, 472

the Church, iii, 2, 3, 4, 5, 6, 8, 18, 20, 22, 23, 25, 26, 28, 30, 33, 35, 39, 40, 42, 43, 44, 45, 46, 69, 73, 80, 88, 91, 106, 109, 133, 137, 141, 142, 143, 147, 154, 156, 159, 161, 163, 164, 165, 167, 168, 170, 171, 172, 173, 175, 177, 178, 179, 180, 181, 184, 186, 188, 190, 194, 195, 204, 208, 210, 211, 212, 215, 216, 217, 218, 219, 220, 222, 223, 229, 230, 231, 232, 233, 234, 235, 236, 237, 238, 239, 241, 242, 244, 245, 246, 247, 251, 253, 254, 258, 259, 260, 261, 272, 288, 291, 294, 295, 297, 302, 309, 316, 320, 321, 324, 330, 339, 340, 342, 343, 344, 345, 346, 347, 348, 350, 351, 352, 353, 354, 355, 356, 357, 359, 360, 361, 362, 363, 364, 365, 367, 368, 369, 370, 371, 373, 375, 385, 387, 389, 392, 395, 396, 399, 400, 404, 405, 406, 408, 414, 418, 421, 422, 424, 425, 427, 429, 430, 431, 432, 433, 434, 438, 439, 441, 442, 445, 449, 454, 459, 461, 462, 473

the Law, 21, 47, 86, 89, 93, 105, 107, 138, 153, 156, 207, 250, 290, 375, 448, 453, 457, 458, 465, 467, 469

type of Christ, 294

Other books by Tom Holland

- *Contours of Pauline Theology: A Radical New Survey of the Influences on Paul's Biblical Writings,* ISBN978-1857924695

- *Romans: The Divine Marriage: A Biblical and Theological Commentary, Volumes 1 and 2,* ISBN 9781912445202 & 9781912445226

- *Missing Lenses - Recovering Scriptures Radical Focus on Our Common Life in Christ,* ISBN 978-1912445080

- *Tom Wright and the Search for Truth: A Theological Evaluation,* Second Edition Revised and Expanded, ISBN 978-1912445103

- *God and His Children: Learning about prayer through Christians in discus*sion (Volume 1), ISBN 978-1912445059

From www.Apiarypublishing.com

www.ingramcontent.com/pod-product-compliance
Lightning Source LLC
Chambersburg PA
CBHW071552080526
44588CB00010B/883